Swami Ranganathananda Reader

Rajiv Mehrotra, when only ten years old started his spiritual quest at the feet of the late Swami Ranganathananda, who was to later become the president of the Ramakrishna Mission. He has been a personal student of His Holiness The Dalai Lama for more than twenty-five years. It has remained a source of great joy and satisfaction that his first and present teachers were to become good friends and celebrate each other.

For over three decades Rajiv Mehrotra has been a familiar face on public television in India, notably as the anchor of an in-depth, one-on-one talk show. He is currently secretary/trustee of the Foundation for Universal Responsibility of His Holiness The Dalai Lama and Managing Trustee of the Public Service Broadcasting Trust. He is a trustee of the Norbulingka Institute of Tibetan Culture and has served as a judge for the Templeton Prize for Spirituality, on the Governing Councils of the Sri Aurobindo Society and the Film and Television Institute of India. An independent documentary filmmaker, he has won several international and ten national awards from the president of India. He was nominated a Global Leader for Tomorrow by the World Economic Forum at Davos.

His published works include *Thakur – A Biography of Sri Ramakrishna*, (Hay House, 2008) *The Mind of the Guru: Conversations with Spiritual Masters* (Penguin, 2003), *Understanding the Dalai Lama* (Penguin/Viking, 2004) and *The Essential Dalai Lama* (Penguin/Viking, 2005). He is working on a television series on Swami Vivekananda and a spiritual biography of His Holiness The Dalai Lama

Swami Ranganathananda Reader

Edited by
Rajiv Mehrotra

Foreword by
His Holiness The Dalai Lama

Rupa & Co

First Published 2009
Revised Edition 2010

Published by
Rupa Publications India Pvt. Ltd.
7/16, Ansari Road, Daryaganj,
New Delhi 110 002

Sales Centres:

Allahabad Bengaluru Chandigarh Chennai
Hyderabad Jaipur Kathmandu
Kolkata Mumbai

Typeset in Times_Norman by
Mindways Design
1410 Chiranjiv Tower
43 Nehru Place
New Delhi 110 019

Printed in India by
Shree Maitrey Printech Pvt Ltd.
A-84, Sector-2, Noida

This book is dedicated
to the celebrations
marking the birth centenary
of Shankaran Kutty
who was to become
SWAMI RANGANATHANANDA
1908–2005

Contents

Preface

Way back in 1952, the day I met Revered Swami Ranganathanandaji for the first time, I was impressed by his charming personality and simple lifestyle. It gradually grew into deep loving regard. Whenever I visited him, I felt that he always radiated joy and kindled spiritual values. The sterling qualities of his head and heart won him the lasting friendship of people belonging to all walks of life, which led him finally to the topmost echelon of the Ramakrishna Order. Beginning his monastic life in a humble way, he rose to become the thirteenth President of the Order. His inherent talents and capacities, which found their best expression in his speeches and writings, made him a nationally and internationally known spiritual personality. He used to say that he had specially been blessed by Swami Akhandanandaji Maharaj, a direct disciple of Sri Ramakrishna; and he attributed the success he attained in life as an orator to this blessing.

This compilation from his many speeches and writings provides only a glimpse of the great spiritual personality that Swami Ranganathanandaji was, and also a *coup díoeil* of the critical appreciation and understanding of the Swami by Sri Rajiv Mehrotra, the selector and Editor of this book. I believe this selection will be well-received by innumerable admirers of Swami Ranganathanandaji as well as by the general public.

THE DALAI LAMA

Message on the Birth Centenary of Swami Ranganathananda

I first met Swami Ranganathananda in the mid-1980s. At the time I at once shared his deep enthusiasm for dialogue between science and spirituality and between different faiths, which is one of my main commitments.

Subsequently, I learnt through Swamiji how Swami Vivekananda was inspired by the Buddha's vision of the Sangha. He had formed his own comunity of monks and his master, the great mystic Sri Ramakrishna, had engaged in the practices of different faiths to deepen his experience and understanding of the various spiritual traditions of the world, which continues to send out the message and meaning of tolerance. In Swamiji and his fellow monks I sensed a deep commitment to altruism, which is the bedrock of my own aspiration as a Buddhist monk.

This message of mine is a small gesture of celebration for a great and inspiring figure of our times. I am sure that the release of *The Swami Ranganathananda Reader* will go a long way in making his thoughts accessible to even more people and deepen our understanding of the wisdom of a remarkable man.

November 13, 2008

Introduction

Swami Ranganathananda embodied the highest aspirations of scholarship from India's great civilisational heritage. He was a worthy heir to the traditions revitalised by Swami Vivekananda and his master Sri Ramakrishna. He was a man with deep insights into the human condition, an explorer of both the personal and the social predicaments of our time. He wrote as he spoke, with passion and conviction, bred of lived experience and empathy with the suffering of others.

He was born Shankaran Kutty on 15 December 1908 in a tiny hamlet, Trikkur in District Thrissur of Kerala. The portents of his future life as one of the pre-eminent monastics of our times were many. The seeds of his future striving were planted at age fourteen, when he read a borrowed copy of the *Gospel of Sri Ramakrishna*. This was soon followed by reading the works of Swami Vivekanananda. Four years later, he joined the Mysore branch of the Ramakrishna Mission. The young aspirant monk received his final vows from the legendary Swami Shivananda. The first twelve years of monasticism in Mysore and Bangalore were spent largely as a cook and personal attendant to Swami Siddheswarananda. He served with distinction as Secretary and Librarian of the Rangoon Branch of the Ramakrishna Mission from 1939 to 1942, followed by a stint in Karachi. Swami Ranganathananda was the Head of the Mission in Delhi from 1949 to 1962. He was secretary of The Ramakrishna Mission Institute of Culture in Calcutta from 1962 to 1967, where he was also the director of the School of Culture & Humanistic Studies and editor of the monthly magazine. This was followed by a long tenure as head of the Mission in Hyderabad. He was elected vice-president of the order in 1989 and president in 1998. He died seven years later on 25 April 2005. He reached out and touched hundreds of thousands of people in more than fifty countries serving as India's spiritual ambassador.

No accounting of the official positions and offices Swami Ranganathananda held or the honours heaped upon him as he lived and served others with compassion and indefatigable energy or the tributes paid to him when he left his worn out physical form can capture the real spirit of the man—the infectious joy, power and simplicity with which he transmitted profound wisdom to others. The written word is but a poor substitute for the many layers at which a true master communicates.

He declined the Padma Vibhushan conferred on him by the Government of India, unwilling and unable to accept an individual honour, but was persuaded to accept the prestigious international Gandhi Peace Prize and the Indira Gandhi Award for National Integration on behalf of the Ramakrishna Mission.

I was blessed to receive my first lessons in spirituality at his feet in Kolkata in the 1960s when I accompanied my parents to Swamiji's lectures. A slow learner, barely ten years old, I remember listening mesmerised by the magic of his presence and the emotional impact of his oratory. I was touched and drawn then by the warmth and love he radiated, rather than the rich intellectual content that circumscribed his lectures. I was to discover the latter much later, when I returned to explorations of the spirit after long years of youthful abandon. It was a great honour and a seminal moment when I received '*deeksha*' from him.

This selection from Swami Ranganathananda's voluminous and diverse writings is a humble celebration by an unworthy student of his, as he commemorates his teacher's birth centenary. Given the depth and vastness of Swamiji's erudition and intellectual rigour, no selection can do him justice. It can offer no more than a flavour; for a real taste the reader will have to delve into the writings themselves.

Those of us, amongst the hundreds of thousands who flocked to listen to him over some seven decades, mesmerised as we were, touched by his deep insights bred of lived experience and vast knowledge will find a selection even less worthy of him. Yet, despite the hesitation and trepidation with which this volume is offered, I am encouraged by the opportunity this presents for my own learning by going back to thousands of pages of printed text and the hope that in this new age of instant gratification, a distillation of the writings of a great master might serve some small purpose, and if it encourages even a handful of people to turn to the original writings themselves then an important purpose would have been served.

As a Gyan Yogi, Swami Ranganathananda's spiritual and intellectual quest knew no boundaries. While immersed in an exploration of the inner journey to human perfection and self knowledge that liberates, in the highest traditions of the Vedanta, he was equally at home exploring the predicaments of the contemporary householder, the education of children or the qualities of a good manager as he was in the latest discoveries in modern science and the teachings of other religions. He consistently advocated a moving away from our obsessive pursuit of our narrow self interest to a commitment to serving others.

I am deeply grateful for the enormous privilege, blessing and honour working on this book has been. I must thank the Ramakrishna Mission, in particular the General Secretary, Swami Prabhananda for his unwavering support and encouragement to my efforts with this book and my other dreams and projects. He has provided quiet, gentle inspiration and decisive support. I celebrate Swami Sarvabhutananda, Secretary of the Ramakrishna Mission Institute of Culture in Kolkata, Swami Bodhasarananda who administers the Advaita Ashram, the lead publishers for the Ramakrishna Mission, Swami Asimatmananda (Sudarshan Maharaj) who served as an aide to Swami Ranganathananda for many years, Swami Atmashraddhananda, Swami Gautamanandaji and the many monks and fellow devotees who have supported me on the path and kept me from straying too far and less often than I might otherwise have from my not very successful engaging in samsara.

Mr R.K. Mehra, the managing director of Rupa, has always responded with enthusiastic openness to my ideas. He is the rare breed of proprietor publishers who manage and run their businesses with a real feel for books and authors. My thanks to M. Sivaramkrishna, Shyamali Chowdhury, Abhijit Dasgupta, K. Padmanabhan, Ridhima Mehra and Tulika Srivastava. My wife, Meenakshi Gopinath, ever my best friend and fellow traveller makes possible my quest and journey with her care and support.

I dedicate any merit gained from the putting together of this book to the happiness of all sentient beings.

An Introduction to the Study of The Gītā

The Bhagavad Gītā: A Universal Gospel

The *Gītā* is not an original work in the sense in which we usually understand the term, though it is a supremely original statement of what Aldous Huxley calls 'The Perennial Philosophy'. It is a continuation of the ancient philosophy that you find in the Upaniṣads. The *Gītā* summarises the essential teachings of Vedanta and presents them in a popular manner. That is why it has become the scripture of the vast masses in this country. When we study the *Gītā,* we are not merely studying the Upaniṣadic philosophy, but also the ethical implications of that philosophy. We want ethical guidance, and the *Gītā* provides it. A metaphysics which speaks of the highest Reality without reference to everyday life will not be of much use to us. Therefore, the sublime ethical implications of the Vedanta are elaborated in the *Gītā.*

Apart from the ethics of conduct there is another element in the *Gītā* which is *bhakti,* devotion to God. The *bhakti* of the *Gītā* is the expression of the religious mood at its highest and best. It is love of God out of the fullness of one's heart and not out of its emptiness as it is in its early states. It is this that makes the devotee of the *Gītā* an embodiment at once of fearlessness and gentleness. The twelfth chapter is a mighty saga in praise of the perfection of character through this path of spiritual discipline.

From all these considerations the *Gītā* has assumed an importance in our life, and that importance is increasing day by day. In his preface to the English edition of the *Gītā* by Charles Wilkins, Warren Hastings, the first British governor-general of India, declared that 'the writers of the Indian philosophies will survive, when the British dominion in India shall have long ceased to exist and the sources which it yielded of wealth and power are lost to remembrance.' Since these lines were written, the *Gītā* has been establishing an ever-widening empire in the hearts of men and women both in the East and the West. Its appeal to the thinking minds of the modern world, as its appeal to the thinking minds of India in the past, is in sharp contrast to the indifference, and often hostility, displayed by the modern mind to the scriptures and prophets of the world. The source of this power lies in the two important features of its message of its rationality and its universality.

Before going into the *Gītā* proper, it is necessary to say a few words by way of introduction. Most of you must know something of the *Gītā* and its place among the scriptures of the Hindus. When I use the word Hindu, while studying the Vedanta, I use it for want of a better word. Because most of these scriptures and philosophies were elaborated long before there were any other religions in the world—Hindu, Buddhist, Christian, or Muslim. These distinctions did not exist then. The great sages elaborated their concepts of religion with no such distinctions. It is necessary to keep this point in view. Today when we use the word Hindu, it is to demarcate some class of people from others. But when I use this word with reference to the *Gītā,* this demarcation does not exist; only because the sages gave their sublime thoughts not to any particular class of people, Hindus as opposed to all other people, but to all who wanted guidance—without reference to any community or race. Keeping this point in view, we have to approach these ancient books and their teachings. It is the religion of man that is taught there and not of this community or that. Ethics, morality, and metaphysics are propagated for the welfare of humanity and not of any sections thereof. This universality of outlook is thoroughly emphasised in all our ancient works; so much so, the great law-giver Manu develops his Code keeping in view the true welfare not of Hindus only, but of humanity in general. It is the *Mānava Dharma śāstra*—the Ethical Code of Manu for the guidance of his progeny, Man. It is for man in general, in any part of the world he may be inhabiting and to any race he may belong. If man wants to attain happiness and welfare, he has to follow certain ideals and methods, and these are universal and promulgated in this book. Similarly in the Vedas and the Upaniṣads, and later in the *Gītā;* their teachings are not sectional or parochial in their import and appeal. Sects and creeds may use them with profit, but cannot exhaust them; for they deal with human nature; their theme is man's aspirations and struggles after Self-realisation. The division of humanity into various religions and sects is only a later story.

So, when we read through the *Gītā,* we clearly find that its teachings are addressed to all of humanity—men and women who are struggling to realise the higher expressions of their soul. This is what is given by this philosophy and religion. This ideal is also emphasised in the nature of the dialogue which is characteristic of the *Gītā.* This dialogue is between Kṛṣṇa and Arjuna. In our ancient scriptures, Arjuna is considered as the incarnation of Nara, the man, and Kṛṣṇa of Nārāyaṇa—-the supreme Lord. It is not that Kṛṣṇa is imparting his teaching here to any particular sect, but to man, through his disciple Arjuna. In the *Gītā,* therefore, God is face to face with Man—Nārāyaṇa with Nara—and this is what constitutes its solemn and sublime setting.

In our country, for several centuries, the Hindu mind has been directed to narrower and narrower circles of thought; even the universal thought of the *Gītā* has been sought to be limited in these narrow grooves. Even Śṛī Kṛṣṇa has been sought to be imprisoned in a creed, be it Vaisnavism or something else. Śrī Kṛṣṇa was a universal teacher. He made no distinction between Vaiṣṇavism or Śaivism or any other 'ism'. Today we require this rhythm of universality which transcends all creeds and classes and embraces one and all and gives the same kind of inspiration to one and all. Therefore, the *Gītā* is to be viewed in its own setting—as a commentary on the Vedanta given by one who was a universal Being, that is Śrī Kṛṣṇa himself. Universal teachings cannot be given by anybody but a universal man, and they cannot be understood as well by anybody but a universal pupil. If one who is limited by creeds studies the *Gītā,* he will find there only a narrow teaching—an echo of himself—and his conception of Kṛṣṇa will be conditioned by his limited mind. This has been done in the past; but what we now require is an open mind, a universal attitude to life; then alone will the *Gītā* open out its best to us—its spirit of universality and practicality. This accounts for the wide influence that the *Gītā* exercises on the people of this country and outside. The people in this country and outside find in the *Gītā* something which will strengthen their faith and their spiritual endeavour *in their own way.* Whether they be Christians or Muslims or Hindus of various denominations, the *Gītā* intensifies their *śraddhā* in their own faith. Its universality is of a special type. It is not an imposition, but an invitation. The *Gītā* belongs to everyone in his or her own way. Such a universal message we require to mediate between the various religions that prevail at present. Śrī Śaṅkarācārya, in the introduction to his commentary on the *Bhagavad Gītā,* gives us his views as to the nature of the *Gītā* dialogue. There are various views as to how the *Gītā* came to be taught. The very orthodox section holds that all these verses are as they were spoken between Kṛṣṇa and Arjuna. They stick to the letter; but, as the Bible says: 'The letter killeth, but the spirit giveth life'. It is most unreasonable to expect that in a battlefield questions and answers should go on for such a long time, and that too, in verses. Rational people do not accept this view. The great Śaṅkarācārya, who is considered to be the fountain-head of the present orthodoxy, has not accepted this view. He says in his commentary that when Arjuna was confused with difficulties, Śrī Kṛṣṇa gave him some effective advice and this was put by Vyāsa into 700 *ślokas*. This is the view of Śaṅkarācārya, and this seems to be quite reasonable.

We find that a great teaching or ideology always takes its birth under the stress of circumstances and environments. This is true with regard to the birth of any vital idea in any part of the world. The birth of the great Marxist ideology in the nineteenth century—one that is now moving men and women in all parts of the world—is an instance in point. The ideology took birth at a time when society was waiting for it. It is a development out of the accumulated previous conditions. It took shape in the middle decades of the last century. The idea of 'Liberty, Equality, and Fraternity,' which was the war-cry of the French Revolution, took its birth during the stress of the mid-eighteenth century in France. Similarly, when we study the *Gītā* and the conditions that obtained at the time of the *Mahābhārata* and also the circumstances that made for the appearance of the teaching of the *Gītā,* we find there were strong reasons for the promulgation of the ideas of the *Gītā.* In the early days we have the Vedic literature and the ritualistic religion associated with it. So also we have the Upaniṣads and the philosophic religion taught therein. Both these come to us with antagonism. The Vedas promise happiness in this world and in heaven after death. So much so, a person who wants the good things in this life and a place elsewhere after death, tries to attain it by sacrifices to various gods as understood at that time. Later, there was a protest against this heaven-philosophy by the Upaniṣads. When we study the *Kaṭha Upaniṣad* we find that by the first boon Naciketa wants to gain something relating to this world. By the second boon he wants to know how to attain to heaven. But he is not satisfied with these. The protest in the Upaniṣads takes us to a higher purpose and function and that is why the third boon of Naciketa relates to life's problems as viewed by a lofty philosophy and ethics. It is only by an inquiry into the Reality behind life that this problem can be solved. This is the special function of the Upaniṣads. Thus, for the first time, this question is brought to the forefront in the Upaniṣads. At the same time this disparity between this-worldly life and the other-worldly life grew, and there was a great need for a synthesis; and this synthesis the *Bhagavad Gītā* attempts in its teachings. The Vedas teach us *karma,* sacrifices, etc., to secure a fine place in heaven after death. Coming to the Upaniṣads, there is a reaction, and it has nothing to do with *karma,* sacrifices, etc. The ideal is to realise the Reality by meditation; there is no place for action. But in the *Gītā,* we find Śrī Kṛṣṇa's own reconciliation of the demand for action and the demand for thought. No life can be perfect without reconciling these two opposing forces. The man who says 'I shall act without reference to thinking' will not succeed, and the man who merely indulges in thinking without reference to action will not also be perfect. Therefore, the times demanded a synthetic philosophy, and that is what Śrī Kṛṣṇa gave in the *Bhagavad Gītā.* In every chapter of the *Gītā* we come across the terms and concepts which were familiar in the pre-*Gītā* age. Śrī Kṛṣṇa takes them up, but gives them his own meaning and interpretation and presents a constructive philosophy which reconciles the claims of action and thought. This we find specially in his interpretation of action and inaction in the eighteenth chapter.

Secondly, the Upaniṣads speak of a Reality which is the fruit of a sustained metaphysical inquiry, and Śrī Kṛṣṇa wanted to bring out the ethical implications of this philosophy. Man wants a good deal of guidance. If philosophy does not give it, he looks for it elsewhere. We want the guidance of philosophy so that life may be lifted up to a higher level. The aim of the *Gītā* is to lift up life from the ordinary to a high level of ethical and moral values. It placed life under the guidance of a sublime metaphysics.

The second chapter gives us the whole scheme of the philosophy of life as conceived by the *Bhagavad Gītā.* This is how the Upaniṣadic thought developed and evolved till it found a new and original formulation by Śrī Kṛṣṇa in the *Gītā.* As a friend, philosopher, and guide of humanity, Śrī Kṛṣṇa gave his message of a lofty metaphysics and practical ethics which has sustained and will continue to help humanity through the ages.

The Upaniṣads contain the highest and most sublime statement of Indian thought. Max Müller refers to the boldness of the thinkers of ancient India who built up a mighty edifice of philosophic thought led on by their love of truth and reason and undeterred by any fear of blame or lure of fame. When we are in the Upaniṣads, we are face to face with a vast ocean of thought, and the *Gītā* is the attempt made for the first time to put this thought into a systematic form.

The *Gītā* belongs to the *Mahābhārata,* which records events that happened in India in about the fourteenth century BC. This is the conclusion that modern scholars have arrived at. So far as the book itself is concerned, they put it at about 900 BC. Whatever the precise date, there is no doubt that it is very ancient. The chronology of ancient Indian history is uncertain, and it is only from the period of Buddha that some sort of chronology is available; previous to that, everything comes under ancient Indian history. The formulation of the *Gītā* can be considered to be a few centuries before Buddha. There are great ideas in the *Gītā*; but these were not properly understood by the people, and Buddha gave the thought a new form to make people understand the real spirit of the ancient teachings.

The formulation of every great idea has created an epoch in this country, and there has been a mighty personality behind each such epoch. Every national epoch has been the result of the working out of a mighty idea preceded by a great personality who gave it to the race. We had Buddha in the sixth century BC, and later, Śaṅkara in the eighth century AD, and we are still living in the light of these great masters. Coming to modern times, in the nineteenth century, we have had great luminaries amongst us, and today we are guided by them and their ideas. Anybody who studies Indian history is struck by this unique fact that every epoch has been preceded by the formulation of a mighty ideal of thought and life, behind which there has been a great personality as the focal centre of inspiration. There is something unique in this historic phenomenon which has been responsible for the continuity and vitality of our culture. This phenomenon you find nowhere else except in China. Five thousand years of history is behind us; we are the same ancient race, and the same ancient ideals are moving us today. What is it that makes for the permanence of this culture on the world's stage? So many civilisations came on the world's stage and vanished like ripples on water, and in the midst of all these vanishing civilisations there are only two—India and China—which are permanent. This should make us think deeply as to what constitutes the source or sources of our cultural vitality. There was a time when Greece and Rome played with pomp and vigour on the world's stage; much earlier there were Babylonia and Egypt; and today, there is England, already down the road, and there are Russia and America. Those who once played mighty roles have vanished; the countries and their physical features are there, but the continuity of culture is lost, the heritage is broken. Facing ancient Greece and Rome was India, and India is there to greet the newcomers on the world's stage without herself changing, and she will be there to greet others that are to come in future. This is a fact of history, and as students of Indian history it is our duty to inquire into this fact and learn of the lessons that it holds for us. This leads us to an inquiry into the origin and sources of our culture. The thoughts proceeding from the Vedas and the Upaniṣads, reinforced by the ideas of Śrī Kṛṣṇa, Buddha, and Śaṅkara and others have provided the basic inspiration to our cultural values, loyalty to which has been responsible for the continued vitality of our race and our culture. As a race, we had our ups and downs—no progress is continuous—everywhere there have been ups and downs. But the peculiar fact about India is that, whereas others fall and never rise again, we fall and rise again; whereas others live and die and never rise again, India only seems to die and rises again rejuvenated, more glorious than before. The Christian missionaries who came to India in the nineteenth century thought that India was dying, never to rise again. They made this statement on the analogy of the Red Indians, the Mexicans, and the Incas, who had once built up great civilisations in America, but had perished at the touch of the white man. Even we seemed disposed to accept this judgement of the missionaries. But today we, and they, feel differently. Not merely are we not apologetic about our civilisation and culture, but we are facing the world in an aggressive way, 'aggressive' used in the ideal sense. Any culture is said to be living when it overflows. Expansion is life and contraction is death. For the last thousand years we were greeting death; we were building narrow walls around ourselves. But, then, for the last hundred years we have broken through these narrow walls and are facing the world and spreading our ideas in distant parts of the world. It is the same ancient race and the same ancient culture, but rejuvenated and strengthened. This is significant. Whereas other countries make (a) noise and die away, we go to sleep and rise again to face the world with renewed vigour.

Take our history; what do we find there? We find a great man rising about every thousand years. Each one comes to renew the vigour of the same ancient ideals, maybe with a little different emphasis according to the needs of the time. That is why there is an unbroken continuity of our culture. India has survived many a vicissitude. This must make us humble. Let it be constantly kept in view that our culture is preserved because of these great personalities, whom we consider as incarnations of God. Whatever the attitude we take with regard to these great men, whether as *avataras* or otherwise, they come when racial life is at its lowest ebb and their touch breathes a new life into the almost dead bones and muscles of the race. God alone can give life; call them God or men, they breathe life into the dead bones and muscles of the people. One such great man is Śrī Kṛṣṇa. In the whole history of India I do not find another such great personality so supremely dynamic as Śrī Kṛṣṇa. Those who have read the *Mahābhārata* will bear this out. Śrī Kṛṣṇa is loved by one and all. When Kṛṣṇa comes to Indraprastha, you find thousands of people gathering to greet him. Even as we find our people welcoming their great leaders today, you find people crowding on the parapet walls and looking through the windows, showering flowers on him as he passes through the roads of the city. Everyone, from the sage to the ordinary peasant, is full of respect for him. He is the greatest of *Kṣatriyas,* and yet is humble. He goes to make his obeisance to the righteous before undertaking any major task. He is the friend of the lowly and the lost. When he comes to Indraprastha he stays with the poor Vidura, forsaking the splendour of the imperial court of Duryodhana. He is mighty and kings bow down to him, and yet he does not want any kingdom for himself. He is the Gopala loved by the cowherds. He is loved by young and old, men and women, the learned and the ignorant. In the India of his time, everywhere you find the influence of Kṛṣṇa. His presence was felt by every section of the population.

Śrī Kṛṣṇa was a dynamic personality and his teachings are also dynamic; they are a mass of strength-giving ideas. We have to understand this Kṛṣṇa. Up till now, we have had only the Kṛṣṇa who evoked our tears and our softer side. But the Kṛṣṇa of the *Gītā* comes to lift up a people and make them dynamic. There is a Bengali song which invokes Kṛṣṇa with the *sudarśanacakra* to come to the succour of fallen India:

Avanata bhārata cāhe tomāre
Eśo sudarśanadhāri murāri

He is a person who has impressed himself upon the culture of this country in every aspect. Take away Kṛṣṇa, and everything of value in our culture vanishes. His impress is there on our art, literature, music, painting, sculpture, folk dance, etc. Many a foreigner is envious of the rich cultural heritage of India. This culture took its rise as a little stream in the dim antiquity of the Vedas; during its unimpeded course through thousands of years of history, it has received accessions of strength and richness from many a tributary. And today, it is a vast swelling ocean of virtue, purity, and power. Every Hindu can be justly proud of being a participant of this rich cultural heritage. Kṛṣṇa is one such who strengthened and enriched this culture. Long before the separation of humanity into the Hindu, Mussalman, and Christian was dreamt of, he was there. Therefore, Kṛṣṇa belongs to every child of this country, be he Hindu, Mussalman, or anybody else. A time will come when everyone in this country, irrespective of caste, creed, or colour, will recognise Śrī Kṛṣṇa, Buddha, and Śaṅkara as the architects of the nation's mind who handed down a rich cultural heritage to the people of India without any distinction. This culture is the common property of all communities. Just a few days back,[1] Dr. Sukarno of Indonesia, in an article contributed by him to *The Hindu* of Madras (now Chennai), had said that in the blood of every Indonesian the culture of India is there. So, it is not difficult to imagine a time in India when everyone will claim and look to the same ancient culture for inspiration and guidance.

---

[1]Readers should note that this talk was delivered by the author in the year 1946.

When we realise our true condition, we realise the part played by Śrī Kṛṣṇa in the culture of this country. Śrī Kṛṣṇa of the *Mahābhārata* is a mighty philosopher as well as a mighty man of action. Yet he was absolutely detached. He was respected by everybody—the mighty of the land, sages, women, children, and peasants.

The *Gītā* is the teaching of such a mighty and dynamic personality; and he has infused his mightiness and dynamism into his teaching. Such a dynamic teaching can be properly understood only by those who have a little of that mightiness in themselves. When little people take to a great idea they bring it down to their own level, as they cannot rise to its level. For the last thousand years we have produced nothing but soft literature. Swami Vivekananda says that the country preferred softening ideas, with the result that most of the literature of the last thousand years, if squeezed, produces only tears. In the hands of such people the *Gītā* also lost its mightiness. But Kṛṣṇa had no place in his teaching for any sort of weakness or sentimentalism. The very opening verse that he utters to Arjuna is *Kutastvā kaśmalam idam viṣame samupasthitam*—'Whence has this weakness crept into you at this critical juncture?' The Upaniṣads and the *Gītā* speak only of strength. Swami Vivekananda says, 'Strength, strength, is what the Upaniṣads speak to me from every page.' Weak minds can never understand or grasp mighty ideas. In their attempt, they but dilute such ideas with their own littleness. But when we shall develop a little strength and vigour, we shall find in the *Gītā* something that will stand by us in every situation of life. For those who want merely a little soothing of nerves and are afraid to face the hard trials of life, a lot of material will be found in the *Purāṇas.* But those who want stimulation for a higher life through hard struggle will find it in the *Gītā* in ample measure. Only the mighty can understand the value of the *Gītā.* As Swami Vivekananda says, 'Only the elephant knows the strength of the lion and not the mosquito.' The *Gītā* is not meant to soothe us and put us to sleep, but to wake us up from our slumber and lethargy and goad us on to the highest self-realisation and self-expression. The *Gītā* *ślokas* have a power to invigorate us and to make us think in fresh terms; they will not let us move in the old ruts.

ARJUNA'S FIRST LESSONS IN DISCIPLESHIP

Last time we discussed some of the aspects of the *Gītā* in relation to the context in which it was delivered, as also its place among the scriptures of the Hindus. In that connexion, I referred to the special quality of the *Gītā* teaching and the personality of its teacher, Śrī Kṛṣṇa. That was by way of introduction to the study of the *Gītā.* Today we shall enter into the subject itself, but before doing so we shall tarry for some time in the first chapter.

In the first chapter we get the environment in which the *Gītā* was taught. It is a dramatic setting that we get there. In that great battle of Kurukshetra, famous in ancient Indian history, between the Kauravas and the Pāṅdavas, the greatest hero Arjuna, with Śrī Kṛṣṇa as his charioteer, stands between the two arrayed armies and views the warriors on both sides. Suddenly a piquant situation develops: seeing his own kith and kin facing him, Arjuna is overcome with grief. His nerves fail him. He lays down his mighty bow, *gāṅdīva,* with the resolve not to fight against his own people. A sort of revulsion comes to him, and he determines that he will not fight; he thinks that it is better and more ethical to give up the attempt to fight and conquer his enemies, better it is to be defeated and slain by the enemy than to go forward in this line of resistance and war. It is a moving scene that is thus depicted in a telling manner in the first chapter of the *Gītā.* It is a conflict of emotions and ideals, love and duty, all in an environment of conflict and war; war within and war all round.

Whenever such a situation obtains, it becomes fraught with momentous possibilities. A crisis is the precursor of a creation; greater the crisis, better the creation, if the persons involved are of stern stuff. It sees the birth of a creative affirmation or a dynamic idea. This explains the perennial dynamism of the *Gītā* thought.

It is very rare that common people get occasions to experience such intense conflict of emotions. We hardly get an occasion to be violently pulled in opposite directions—'to do or not to do'. But in the case of those who are born to achieve true greatness, there are several occasions when they are placed in such circumstances, when there arises a conflict of loyalties; and it is a hard thing for them to decide as to what is to be accepted and what rejected. This kind of conflict of duty comes with varying intensity to every sincere aspirant of the ethical life. On such occasions, the human mind needs and demands some sort of effective guidance; it is such guidance that Śrī Kṛṣṇa offers us, from the second chapter onwards in the *Gītā.*

When we take the first chapter, it is such a historic presentation of the ethical problem—the question of the nature of duty and the problem of the conflict of duties. This problem and its discussion is there in our ancient thought, and it is there in every type of ethical thought in the world. The *Gītā* discusses this subject in the second chapter in the light of a lofty metaphysics; and it comes in for a more varied treatment in subsequent chapters when it deals with such topics as action and inaction, renunciation and action, *sannyāsa* and *karma-yoga.* The presentation of the subject of duty in the very first chapter of the *Gītā* provides a basis for the building up of a mighty edifice of metaphysics and ethics in the subsequent chapters. We have in the first chapter a dramatic element that furnishes so much of beauty and sublimity to the *Gītā* teaching. It adds an air of reality to the message of the *Gītā;* it imparts a touch of earnestness to the discussion. The discussion is not simply academic, in which case it would have become ineffectual and unrelated to practice. But, being born out of the fire of conflict and struggle, it issued forth in a message of permanent value to man. Here is a sincere seeker in a crisis, face to face with a great teacher. The seeker asks for practical guidance. Naturally, such a situation does not warrant a merely academic solution of the problem. It must take all the facts into consideration and give guidance there and then. It is this that the *Gītā* proceeds to do through the great teacher Śrī Kṛṣṇa. Śrī Kṛṣṇa is in a sense a party and not a mere spectator who has nothing to do with the battle. This realism imparts to the *Gītā* a greater philosophic depth and moral sweep than what partakes of a mere academic discussion of ethical problems. This is its special appeal.

So, in the first chapter, we have this picture of Arjuna facing an army of relations and friends and teachers. He is moved to pity and grief and says: 'What is the use of fighting such a battle? I would rather be a mendicant than engage in this fight.' In moving words Arjuna presents his case and even takes Śrī Kṛṣṇa to task for inducing him to fight: 'Do we not know the misery that is going to be caused? Since we know it, it is better that we desist from such a battle.' Arjuna then declares that he would not fight. There is so much conflict of feeling in Arjuna that he breaks down; his bow and arrow falls from his hands; his voice gets choked and he sinks into his chariot.

This kind of situation comes to us whenever we are faced with conflicting things. In all such situations when we are unable to decide our duty and the circumstances become puzzling, we exhibit a type of behaviour similar to that of Arjuna. Our nerves fail us; but we do not detect it. We bring in arguments to support our behaviour; but they are false arguments which cannot stand the scrutiny of reason and philosophy. Philosophy with most people is, according to Bradley, the finding of bad reasons for opinions which they hold by instinct to be true. This is bad philosophy, the product of rationalisation, but not of reason. This is the case with Arjuna; his nerves and judgement fail him at a critical time owing to an excess of attachment, delusion, and grief; it is rationalisation that is seen at work when he invokes the aid of 'nonviolence', 'non-resistance', and 'humanity' for withdrawing from the battle. The great virtues of nonviolence and non-resistance are brought in to help the tired nerves of Arjuna when he says that it is better to withdraw or die than to fight and kill. He appeals to Kṛṣṇa for support in his arguments. But, strangely enough, he does not get that support. Philosophy cannot support rationalisation, for it is based on reason which takes all the circumstances and conditions of a problem into account before offering a solution. So, when Arjuna says 'I don't want to fight' and seeks the support of Śrī Kṛṣṇa for his act, he is startled to find that he does not get it. Here philosophy is typified by Śrī Kṛṣṇa, and the moral conflicts and the confusion resulting therefrom are typified by Arjuna. The one is calm and collected, whereas the other is all confusion, shaken in his resolve to fight, and nerve-broken. Thus ends the first chapter entitled, in the very telling words of Vyasa, *Arjuna-viṣāda-yoga*—'The Grief of Arjuna'. The calm reason of philosophy is face to face with the confused unreason of dynamic life. The product of this encounter is the philosophy of life contained in the seventeen subsequent chapters of the *Gītā.*

When we come to the second chapter, we are at the very dawn of true philosophy. The very first task for philosophy is to bring steadiness and confidence into the mind of the student. That is what Śrī Kṛṣṇa does to Arjuna. This is the significance of verses 2 and 3 of the second chapter:

> *Kutastvā kaśmalam idam viṣame samupasthitam;*
> *Anāryajuṣṭam asvargyam akīrtikaram Arjuna*

'In such a crisis, whence comes upon thee, O Arjuna, this dejection, un-*Ārya*-like, disgraceful, and contrary to the attainment of heaven?'

> *Klaibyam mā sma gamaḥ pārtha naitattvayyupapadyate;*
> *Kṣudram hṛdayadaurbalyam tyaktvottiṣṭha parantapa*

'Yield not to unmanliness, O son of Pṛthā! Ill doth it become thee. Cast off this mean faint-heartedness and arise, O scorcher of thine enemies!'

In these two verses we have the application of a mental tonic by Śrī Kṛṣṇa to Arjuna; and that tonic is necessary before any teaching could be fruitful. When a person is grief-stricken and his nerves are shattered, no amount of teaching or advice whatever can bear fruit; and much less philosophy. Intense calmness is necessary, a calmness that is dynamic and not merely passive. The spirit of the whole teaching of the *Gītā* we can derive from the latter of these two verses. Says Swami Vivekananda, in his 'Thoughts on the Gītā' *(Complete Works,* Vol. IV, Eighth Edition, p. 110): 'If one reads this one *śloka—"Klaibyam...parantapa"*—one gets all the merit of reading the entire *Gītā;* for in this one *śloka* lies embedded the whole message of the *Gītā.'* It is not merely for Arjuna, but for every person who is at his wit's end this teaching comes to rouse him up. We require to be roused up again and again, for the mind has always a tendency to sink and slumber but there is also the other capacity to rouse up the mind and apply it to the battle of life, which capacity is practically dormant in the majority of people. But this capacity is to be developed. If we cannot do it ourselves, we shall require somebody else to do it for us; that is what a great teacher, a scripture or an ideal does for us. Śrī Kṛṣṇa played this part in the case of Arjuna. We require some great man to do it for us. The Vedanta says that infinite resources are there in every individual; man is divine, but he has to tap the resources; and a great teacher has the power to bring out this potential capacity from out of himself as well as from others. By the mere touch of a great teacher we begin to manifest great energy and power of which we were not even conscious before. Śrī Kṛṣṇa gave that magic touch to Arjuna by the words *naitattvayyupapadyate*—'Ill doth it become thee.'

In the sentiment contained in that famous short sentence we have the appeal through psychology to every individual to rise higher and higher, and to find new sources of strength within himself. The educational value of this appeal is supreme. How to help another person, how to make him stand on his own feet, is a great educational problem. How to undertake the task of making that person rise higher and find ways and means to develop his own life and power? In this larger context, this consideration becomes relevant; because Śrī Kṛṣṇa's appeal is a general appeal. It has a positive content. The earliest method of inducing behaviour in another was through fear. This appeal to fear was to one's social and religious emotion. But the appeal to fear is fraught with danger; it entails much that is bad along with a bit that is good. In all religions you find this appeal to fear in the theories of hell and judgement, etc., designed to induce good behaviour in the individual. This is a primitive conception in religion: that through the hope of heaven or the fear of hell men do good or abstain from evil. Coming to the social sphere, we find people desisting from evil for fear of police and social boycott. This is what happens either in primitive society or religion or even in civilised society. But these appeals do not serve to bring out the best in the individual, for it is only a negative way. Corresponding to the appeal to hope and fear is the appeal to vanity. These have played their part in the evolution of humanity. Probably, at some stage humanity has need of their services. This is the utmost that we can say of them. But the least that we can say of them is that they are not the best means available for inducing correct behaviour. We may not be able to give them up for the reason that humanity is at varying stages of evolution. Behaviour based on fear is all that most people are capable of understanding as also the kind based on the prospect of enjoyment. But when you come to educational psychology, when you come to the question as to what is really beneficial to the individual, the best is what Śrī Kṛṣṇa does when he appeals to the sense of self-respect of the individual. In all cultured families, influencing the behaviour of children is done through this appeal to their self-respect and not to their sense of fear. In uncultured societies parents resort to the fear-appeal either through ghosts or darkness, which are sources of fear. But in all such cases, what we seek is not the education or development of the individual, but merely the temporary influencing of his outward behaviour through methods that tend to leave permanent scars on the inner man. That proves their worthlessness as educational appeals.

If we want to institute an appeal which is constructive and positive, which will help one to develop his or her capacities, that must be based upon the notion of the self-respect of the individual. When we tell a child, 'This conduct of yours is not fit for you; I expect you to be better; this is not up to the mark', we are appealing to a positive element in the child. It is positive and constructive, and not negative and destructive. Modern psychology throws much light on this problem.

Modern psychology recognises self-regard or self-respect as the foundation of character-building. According to McDougall, it is the master sentiment and character is the product of the organisation of sentiments and emotions round this master sentiment of self-regard. No character can be built without self-regard as the basis—take away whatever self-regard a man has, and you can never make him a man or help him to develop his character. The difference between a man and a brute is this self-regard or self-respect. Men have been reduced to the level of brutes as a result of the taking away from them this precious quality of self-regard by social tyranny and social neglect. Take a slave; there is little of self-regard left in him; for society, by continued oppression, has all but destroyed this quality in him. The instilling of this fundamental virtue in such a person is a difficult process. It will have to be done by those who are themselves free. That we can rekindle in him this virtue is because in becoming a slave he has only forgotten, but not forfeited, his real nature. A slave must therefore first develop self-regard as the very first step in self-development. The greatest harm that one can do to another is to touch his self-respect. Whatever you do, do not destroy another's self-regard, for by that we pave the way for his ruin. This maxim is a sure and wise guide in all social relationships. Unfortunately, this is observed more in its breach than in its observance, for we are not capable of informing action with thought. We see the masters treating their servants as if they are lifeless property. The servant works for the master, but he has not sold his soul to him. The master, through his thoughtlessness, injures the servant's self-regard. That is why sensitive servants complain to the master: 'You may beat me, but please don't abuse me,' for abuse touches the very sensitive part of an individual—his self-respect. If we want to educate a man and do real good to him, we must preserve and develop this priceless quality in him. Modern theories of education are based upon this supreme psychological fact.

Psychology teaches the great value of this master sentiment in the formation of character. Teachers and parents who destroy the self-respect of their wards through their thoughtless dealings are enemies of society. The modern theory says that we are not dealing with pots and pans when we are dealing with children. We are dealing with delicate, vibrant, living personalities. We are dealing with unformed minds, and whatever we do sticks on; hence the need for expert care.

In this lies all the essence of the Vedanta. Swami Vivekananda puts it in his own memorable words: 'Each soul is potentially divine. The goal is to manifest this divine within, by controlling nature, external and internal. Do this either by work, or worship, or psychic control, or philosophy, by one, or more, or all of these—and be free. This is the whole of religion. Doctrines, or dogmas, or rituals, or books, or temples, or forms, are but secondary details.' In our dealings with an individual, we are dealing with a vast reservoir of power which at present is lying dormant. But given a proper training, it can develop into an immense flood. One who is rightly trained is a powerful personality, and one who is badly trained is a truncated personality.

This great psychological truth is embodied in the appeal contained in Kṛṣṇa's exhortation to Arjuna: *Naitat tvayyupa-padyate*—'This does not befit you.' The world knew who Arjuna was one who had fought many a battle victoriously. Should he be subject to fear and despair? Should he not rather try to pit his inborn heroism against the challenge of a trying environment, bringing out more and more of his inborn power and perfection in the process? This is true education in the hard school of life. And Śrī Kṛṣṇa is the guide of Arjuna in that profound educational process. It is education based on a profound philosophy. Vedanta and modern educational theory are in full accord here.

We shall come to the ethical implications of this Vedantic teaching in the course of our discussion of the verses of the second chapter. Vedanta holds that if we express our real nature, we can never be criminal or wicked men. In committing sin or wicked acts we are not expressing our real nature, which is pure and perfect, but only our apparent nature which is centered round the ego. Ethical conduct, according to the Vedanta, is the expression of one's own real nature. Man lives the true life when he expresses the divinity within him. Selfishness is not our real nature; it is only on the surface.

When you express the surface nature, you are not expressing your real nature. Only then am I perfect when I am living the true life, that is, when I am expressing my true self. That is highest ethics according to Vedanta.

Arjuna's action has to be viewed from the context of the ethics of duty, and the ethics of duty from the context of the metaphysics of the Real. Ethics leads us to the problem of Reality; that is metaphysics. The *Gītā* has tried to place ethics under the guidance of metaphysics. In modern times, many thinkers ask us not to bring into ethics the question of Reality. That is what certain sections of positivists tell us. But in this country, we discussed it long back and found that no problem could be discussed in thoroughness without bringing ultimate questions. About any action, if you ask, 'Why should I do it?' you enter into wider spheres of thought and discussion. The *Gītā* places ethics under the guidance of a metaphysics which deals with life in its totality. The second chapter of the *Gītā* deals with the subject of the true nature of the individual and of the supreme Reality and studies the nature of conduct and action in the light of this knowledge and wisdom. It weaves round the immediate problem of Arjuna a philosophy and ethics of action which, in turn, becomes a guide to other men in all situations of life. This applicability to one and all is the fruit of philosophy. If philosophy was not at the back of the advice to Arjuna, that advice could not have become applicable to others. The *Gītā's* advice, therefore, was not meant for Arjuna only. Its scope is universal; that is why, even after these four thousand years, it appeals to us. If it was a mere matter-of-fact advice and guidance, it would not have appealed to one and all. It might at best retain a literary appeal, but not a philosophical appeal. But when you put the literary in the context of the philosophical, it becomes universal. That is what Śrī Kṛṣṇa has done in the case of the *Gītā*.

The *Gītā* lights the lamp of wisdom in the hearts of men and leaves them to solve their own problems. In a later chapter, Śrī Kṛṣṇa would say that what he does to every individual is to light a little lamp of wisdom in his heart by which he would see truth and avoid error. He does not give the final decision for us. Philosophy does not decide things for us; it only offers to guide us. The *Smṛtis* do prescribe what we should do every minute of a twenty-four hour day. It becomes soul-killing. It makes us serfs and slaves.

Philosophy releases mankind from these bondages. It gives only stimulation; it places a light in our hands by which to find our way. Anything more would take away from our initiative. But man is weak; he says, 'I want all help; I want someone to come and take me by the hand.' Then come the *Smṛtis*. Here is no true ethics, but only routine ethics. It is a kind of complacency of mind which requires something to hang on. True philosophy does not burden us with a huge number of books or a rigorous set of rules. It is like the light of a lamp. It just imparts wisdom. Philosophical guidance is the simplest guidance. Philosophy does not require us to elbow out other contents from life. We can understand philosophy without the aid of many books. Some people say: 'Action and thought cannot be done at the same time. If I have to think of philosophy, I have to stop work. But you ask me to combine philosophy and action. This is impossible.' Śrī Kṛṣṇa wants us to combine both philosophy and life, for it is life that needs the guidance of philosophy. When there is no life there is no guidance required. How shall we solve the problem? Some say: 'Cease from acting; congeal life to a point; that is the best solution of the problem. Take away the world, for it is the cause of all problem.' But if there is no problem, what is the use of the solution? A solution is no solution in the absence of the problem itself. Another comes and says: 'There is no solution; so don't worry about the problem at all, but just go on acting and living with whatever faith you can muster.' It is here that Vedanta comes to our help. In all boldness it dares to face the problem and give us a solution. Unfortunately, even our people have not understood this aspect of Vedanta. What we understand is the Vedanta of books, the Vedanta of leisure. But this is only academic Vedanta. Śrī Kṛṣṇa did not teach this Vedanta. He taught the Vedanta of, and for, a battlefield. It is not a pursuit of leisure hours. It is a pursuit of excellence in the midst of difficult situations and struggles of daily life. This aspect of Vedanta has been mostly neglected in the later developments of religious ideas in our country. We have now to bring out this aspect of the *Gītā* in all its practical bearing.

The *Gītā* has a simplicity which we very often miss. We are accustomed to complicate things. We cannot appreciate simple things. The human mind wants, in the name of philosophy and religion, something striking in the form of books, dress, rituals, etc. Simple character or simple ethical beauty is not much appreciated. Simple beauty is not understood by ordinary men. Truth which is simple is clothed in a variety of ways, and we get not the naked truth but a clothed truth. When you come to the *Gītā,* we have the presentation of this simple truth which helps to take us across life's problems. It frees us from all attachments to joys and sorrows and good and bad. It gives us absolute calm, and a freedom from all conditions—external and internal. We want this independence and freedom of the individual to be maintained at all costs. This is what philosophy seeks to confer on life. If we have this, what else do we require? One who attains this remains fresh in spite of life's aging and retains the freshness of a new-born babe even unto death. He has philosophy to guide him. This is the true test of philosophy—a philosophy which helps us to pass through life's struggles without getting scorched, which helps us to remain as fresh at the end of the journey as at the beginning.

At the very beginning of the second chapter, Śrī Kṛṣṇa has given out these life-giving ideas. Those who have the requisite courage and strength of mind can understand the true teaching of the *Gītā.* A mind which is grief-stricken and attached cannot understand these mighty ideas. A tired mind cannot understand truth; it has to be made calm and strong before the advice can take root. Grief-stricken Arjuna is first calmed and steadied and then is taught the wisdom of Truth. In a grief-stricken state we see things in a narrow perspective; when we are calm, we see things in their true perspective.

That is why Arjuna says: 'My mind is confused as to what is really to my welfare; therefore, tell me clearly what is to my welfare, teach me now that I have taken refuge at your feet.'

In the eighteenth chapter (verses 72-73), after all the teaching was over, Kṛṣṇa asks Arjuna, 'Are you satisfied; is your mind calm and doubt cleared?'

Kaccid etat śrutam pārtha tvayaikāgreṇa cetasā;
Kaccid ajñānasammohaḥ praṇaṣṭaste dhanañjaya

'Has this been heard by thee, O Pṛtha, with an attentive mind? Has the delusion of thy ignorance been destroyed, O Dhananjaya?'

Arjuna replies:

Naṣṭo mohaḥ smṛtirlabdhā tvatprasādāt mayācyuta;
Sthito'smi gatasandehaḥ kariṣye vacanam tava

'Destroyed is my delusion, and I have gained my memory through Thy grace, O Acyuta. I am firm; my doubts are gone. I will do Thy word.'

The *Gītā* brings light and removes the umbra of confusion. The *Gītā* removed Arjuna's confusion; that is its originality and power. In the case of all of us also, it will have fulfilled its purpose only when it will have removed our confusions and doubts and enabled us to see life steadily and see it whole.

Śrī Kṛṣṇa: The Ideal Teacher

Striking a note of robust optimism, Śrī Kṛṣṇa asked Arjuna to shake off his weakness and to steady himself. It was the intention of Śrī Kṛṣṇa to make Arjuna's mind steady before he could give him any kind of wisdom, for a grief-stricken mind is not at all a fit receptacle for wisdom. Unless we get out of the depressed state and become calmer, we shall not be able to assimilate any lofty advice. This is seen in our everyday experience. Therefore, the first thing necessary was to pacify the mind of Arjuna and then only could he listen to reason and advice. So Kṛṣṇa exhorts Arjuna in powerful accents *(Gītā,* II. 3):

'Yield not to this kind of unmanliness, O Arjuna, for it does not befit you; give up this faint-heartedness and rise up and do your duty.'

The result of this kind of rebuke was wholesome; it steadied the mind of Arjuna. For, as we proceed on, we find that Arjuna becomes calm and there is some sort of reason in his talk with Śrī Kṛṣṇa. Now he begins to put forth his doubts in a more cogent language and without much sorrow and emotion. He says *(ibid,* II. 4):

'How shall I fight against Bhīsma and Droṇa with these sharp arrows? They are fit to be worshipped by me; they are my elders and are respected by one and all.'

Again *(ibid,* II. 5):

'Instead of killing these great ones, who are our *gurus,* respected and honoured persons, instead of that, I would rather live a mendicant's life. If I kill them because they have joined the enemies' party, who are running after wealth and power, even if I get all this wealth and power it will be blood-smeared. I shall secure the enjoyment of wealth and power, but it will be smeared with the blood of innocent people and our own relatives.'

Arjuna then surrenders himself to his teacher *(ibid,* II. 7):

Kārpaṇyadoṣopahatasvabhāvaḥ
pṛcchāmī tvām dharmasammūḍhacetāḥ;
Yacchreyaḥ syāt niścitam brūhi tanme
*śiṣyasteham śādhi mām tvām prapanna*m—

'With my nature overpowered by weak commiseration, with a mind in confusion about duty, I supplicate Thee. Say decidedly what is good for me. I am Thy disciple; instruct me who have taken refuge in Thee.'

Arjuna, in these words, places his problem before Śrī Kṛṣṇa and seeks his guidance. In the midst of destruction and confusion the mind bows down to some higher power. Arjuna was fortunate in that he had Kṛṣṇa to show him the way. 'I am in confusion as to what is right and what is wrong. I am in the midst of a piquant situation; therefore I fall at your feet. My nature has been smitten by narrow-mindedness. Therefore I ask you this question. I am unable to decide what is *dharma* and what is *adharma;* what is my present duty in reference to my true welfare? I want your answer taking into full consideration the circumstances of my case.' In all critical situations we shall have to seek a way leading to our true welfare and not merely what is pleasing to us. We want what is *śreyas* and not what is merely *preyas.* This we see in the *Kaṭha Upaniṣad* (I. ii. 1) where Yama tells Naciketas:

Anyat śreyo anyat utaiva preyaḥ
te ubhe nānā arthe puruṣam sinītaḥ;
Tayoḥ śreya ādadānasya sādhu
bhavati hīyate arthāt ya u preyo vṛṇīte

'One thing is the good and (quite) different indeed is the pleasant; having been of different requisitions, they both bind the Puruṣa. Good befalls him who follows the good, but loses he the goal who chooses the pleasant.'

A fool takes what is pleasant and comes to grief in the end. He misses the true end of life. That is how Yama discusses a most important problem of ethics in the second chapter of the *Kaṭha Upaniṣad.* Here Arjuna asks this question:

'What is the most excellent thing for me to do? Of the two, pleasant and beneficent, please tell me what is beneficent and I shall do as you tell me. Decide for yourself what is to my welfare, for I am in confusion and do not know what is to my good; I am your disciple and I accept your decision. I accept you as my friend, philosopher, and guide.'

Thus the beautiful seventh *śloka* of the second chapter opens the way for the imparting of the wisdom of the *Gītā.* For here, troubled and confused, Arjuna surrenders to, and seeks the guidance of Śrī Kṛṣṇa—the confused mind surrenders to calm philosophy. It is not that we should surrender to every A, B, or C who comes to lord over us, and destroy what little wisdom we possess. The *Kaṭha Upaniṣad* (I. ii. 5) warns us of this danger:

Avidyayām antare vartamānāḥ
svayam dhīrāḥ paṇḍitam manya mānāḥ;
Dandramyamāṇāḥ pariyanti mūḍhā
andhenaiva nīyamānā yathāndhāḥ

'Fools, dwelling in the very midst of ignorance yet vainly fancying themselves to be wise and learned, go round and round staggering like blind men led by the blind.'

From what we have seen of Śrī Kṛṣṇa, we realise that he was a man of wisdom and the world around him looked up to him for guidance. It is no wonder, therefore, that Arjuna asked him for guidance. As I have often pointed out, Kṛṣṇa was always detached, deep in the midst of things yet keeping his mind above the things. Emerson, when discussing the ideal life, paraphrases a famous *śloka* of the *Gītā* and says that it is easy to lose oneself in the crowd or to be calm when alone, but the ideal man is one who, remaining and functioning in society, keeps his head in solitude. If, when the world orders we weep, and if, when the world orders we smile, it is but a very ordinary thing, but perfection comes only when even in a market-place the mind is kept calm. Otherwise, it is one sided development only.

While Arjuna is in confusion, Kṛṣṇa is calm and speaks with a smile, knowing fully well that he could remove it. So, to surrender to such a person is to ensure our progress. Here the disciple is a great soul and the teacher too; and when a great disciple is facing a great teacher, we expect the statement of a life-giving thought as the issue of that contact. The *Kaṭha Upaniṣad* (I. ii. 7) refers to this in these words: *āścaryo vaktā kuśalo'sya labdhā, āścaryo jñātā kuśalānuśiṣṭaḥ*—'When a wonderful disciple and a wonderful teacher come together, there is born great wisdom.' Arjuna accepts, therefore, Śrī Kṛṣṇa as his guide. If, after examining the credentials of a person in all aspects and finding him worthy, we surrender ourselves to him, we are safe in his hands. On the contrary, if we give away our independence into the hands of any and every person without discrimination, there is every chance of our ruining ourselves. In this country we have to take notice of this. Where there are many *gurus* and a few disciples, you do not know to whom to surrender. There is a beautiful verse which makes a caustic remark about this state of things:

Guravo bahavaḥ santi śiṣya-vittāpahāriṇaḥ;
Tam ekam śaṅkaram vande śiṣya-santāpahāriṇam—

'There are thousands of *gurus* who remove the wealth of the disciple; but different from all such *gurus,* I bow down to the one *guru,* Śaṅkara, who removes the miseries of the disciple.'

Once we get such a teacher, there is no harm in surrendering ourselves to him, for we are not surrendering to any particular person, but to the wisdom incarnated in him. On the contrary, if we surrender to any and every person, it will be harmful both to the teacher and the disciple. As Śrī Ramakrishna used to say: 'Once a water-snake caught a frog, but it could not swallow it. The frog was croaking in pain as the snake could neither swallow it nor leave it out. The snake also was put to great hardship. But if a cobra had caught the frog, it would have been silenced with one or two croakings.' If the *guru* is not a man of wisdom, both the *guru* and the disciple will suffer. The *guru* must have great power to digest his own as well as the students' miseries. He must be able to lift him up and save him.

In the *Vivekacūdāmaṇi* (verse 33) Śrī Śaṅkarācārya gives the qualifications of a true *guru:*

Śrotriyo'vrjino'kāmahato yo brahmavittamah;
Brahmaṇyuparataḥ śānto nirindhana ivānalaḥ;
Ahetukadayāsindhuḥ bandhurānamatām satām--

'Who is well versed in the Vedas, sinless, unsmitten by desire, and a knower of Brahman *par excellence,* who has withdrawn himself into Brahman, is calm, like the fire that has consumed its fuel, who is a boundless reservoir of mercy that knows no reason, and a friend of all good people who prostrate themselves before him.'

Every word in this verse is full of meaning and significance. *Śrotriyo,* 'a true *guru* must know the spirit of the *śrutis;* not the mere letter, but the spirit of the *śāstras;* he must have lived the life which the *śāstras* teach.' *Āvṛjino,* 'free from sinfulness,' only a sinless man can possess the saving powers. And this belongs to one who has achieved perfection in morality and ethics. *Akāmahataḥ,* 'he should not be smitten by any desire, he must be absolutely free from the promptings of selfish desires; his sole desire must be to do good to others.' *Brahmavittamaḥ,* 'he who is the best among the knowers of Brahman,' one who is merged in God, so that any point you touch you get only God out of him. *Śāntaḥ,* 'absolutely tranquil;' you cannot bring tranquillity to another without yourself being tranquil. He need not teach; but wherever he is he becomes a living temple, a living church, or a living mosque, because he has touched the feet of God. How does he attain it? *Nirindhana ivānalaḥ,* 'like a flaming fire which has burnt itself out;' the human mind is compared to a flaming fire; for desires are there like a burning fire and the objects of desires are like the fuel. The true *guru* must be a person in whom all fire of desire has burnt itself out. When the fire ceases to be fed by fuel, it is put out, and it is all calm and quiet. That is the mind which has destroyed all desire, which has become *āptakāma, ātmakāma,* and *akāma,* 'the mind which has fulfilled all desires, which has *ātman* for its content of desire, which is desireless in every other sense.' We have various desires, and we want to satisfy them. But his heart is full. How does he become full? Because his desires pertain to the Atman. *Ātmakāmatve ca āptakāmata, 'ātmakāmata* connotes the fullness of heart;' it is also the catalytic agent which destroys all other desires.

Desire in the heart of an individual is, from the modern psychological point of view, in the nature of a craving for fulfilment. Everyone of our desires is prompted by a vacuum in our heart which craves for fulfilment. All desire, therefore, signifies a vacuum in our heart. It requires an action outside to satisfy it. There are thus two stages preceding every action. First, there is the feeling of a want within, an urge which seeks satisfaction. This urge takes the form of a desire for a corresponding object which is capable of conferring this satisfaction. And lastly, there is the action for the satisfaction of the urge. Psychology lists about fourteen primary urges of man like hunger, sex, etc. Taking the most familiar one of hunger, for instance, we find its three stages in: i) the urge within; ii) the desire for an external object; and iii) the act of appropriating that object. The last stage, act, ends in the fulfilment of the urge. When the stomach is full, there is no hunger, there is no desire for food, and there is no corresponding activity to satisfy that urge. Activity, therefore, is conditioned by the urge within and the desire for the corresponding object without. In the absence of the urge, there will be no desire and no activity. Life is a round of activity because the heart is a volcano of urges and desires. If you can conceive of a hypothetical state of existence where these urges and desires are not there, you get a state free from all desire-ridden activities as well. The Vedanta speaks of a state of perfection free from craving, desire, and desire-prompted activity. This desirelessness—*akāmata*—comes from *ātmakāmata,* the desire for the *ātman.* Lest we mistake this state for emptiness of heart and death, the Vedanta adds a third important characteristic feature of this state which connotes the fullness of being—*āptakāmata.* The tranquil mind without any desire is compared to a beautiful calm lake without a single ripple on it. The tranquillity of the lake is disturbed by the throwing of a stone into it; the desires that arise in our mind cause waves in it. In ordinary life the mind is never calm except in deep sleep. Through meditation and self-control, we have to capture this calmness as a feature of our waking state. Even a bit of this tranquillity is a great asset in our daily lives. What to speak of the value and power of the fullness of tranquillity attained by a perfected soul! He is a teacher, *par excellence,* an ocean of compassion—*ahetukadayāsindhu*—his compassion flows in a steady stream to tranquilise the world; there is no self-interest to check it. It just overflows its bounds and seeks to tranquilise the minds of others around. It wants to impart its tone to others around it, to those who are confounded and confused. He works without any motive. The flow of his love does not depend upon anything on our part. There is no artificial attempt, it simply overflows. That mercy knows no kind of contractual relationship. *Bandhurānamatām satām*—he is a friend of all who resort to him. Such a guru will be our unfailing friend, because whatever he does will be for our good only.

Śaṇkara exhorts us to take shelter under such a person, if we can get one. Such a teacher can really do something to lift us up. But, unfortunately, such teachers are few and far-between; surrendering to anyone less than such is fraught with danger. And therefore, it is good for us to learn to depend upon ourselves till we secure the shelter of such a guide. But, then, we can get help from lesser guides also. We can take lessons from any and everybody, provided we have a dynamic mind. A dynamic mind takes lessons from everything in nature. Everything in nature is a source of wisdom to such a person. For him every river and brook is a *guru.* It is best, therefore, to learn to depend upon one's own clear undertṣtanding. To surrender one's independence to lesser *gurus* is absolutely foolish. The Vedanta does not permit it. But in the case of Arjuna, it was his good fortune that he was able to get a universal teacher like Śrī Kṛṣṇa.

So Arjuna takes refuge in him. In our case Śrī Kṛṣṇa may not come in flesh and blood and whisper to us in audible language; but his teachings come to us in clear accents. Short of his presence in flesh and blood, we can have recourse to his teachings and have every other advantage.

Again, humility is an essential condition for the acquisition of wisdom. It may not be so much necessary for worldly wisdom, but even there it is necessary to a certain extent. But when you come to spiritual knowledge, it is absolutely necessary. Arjuna's humility was born of strength, and so his humility is true humility. Such occasions do come to all when he or she feels the stress and strain of circumstances and the whole personality bows down and asks, in a mood of supplication, for wisdom. Arjuna is in such a mood when he is asking Śrī Kṛṣṇa in all humility to guide him. Arjuna is in the right mood for the seed of advice to sprout and bear fruit. In the absence of this humility and earnestness, ethical and spiritual quests lose their fruit-bearing power. All idle quests are sterile. A man while passing by the road flings an idle question: 'Is there God?' and does not even wait for an answer; he is indifferent. For him the question has no meaning. In the case of most people, questions regarding God and the spiritual life belong to this category. Without the backing of earnestness, questions and their answers lose their vitality and fruit-bearing power. The value of a teaching is heightened by the interest you take in the subject. In the case of Arjuna it was a burning question with him. Arjuna's question is born out of the crucible of the moral struggle. This vitality of the question makes for the tenfold vitality of the answer.

Thus begins the teaching of the *Bhagavad Gītā.* The problem that is presented is a problem of confusion resulting from the conflict of moral duties. The wisdom that is imparted in the answer is meant to remove that confusion. Did Śrī Kṛṣṇa's teaching remove the confusion in Arjuna's mind? Only if it did does it deserve our reverential acceptance. In the case of Arjuna, we can very well say that the imparting of wisdom on the part of Śrī Kṛṣṇa did remove the confusion in his mind. In the eighteenth chapter Śrī Kṛṣṇa asks Arjuna *(Gītā* XVIII. 72):

Kaccid etat śrutam pārtita tvayaikāgreṇa cetasā;
Kaccit ajñānasammohaḥ praṇaṣṭaste dhanañjaya

'Has this been heard by thee, O Pārtha, with an attentive mind? Has the delusion of thy ignorance been destroyed, O Dhanañjaya?'

And Arjuna answers *(ibid,* XVIII. 73):

Naṣṭo mohaḥ smṛtirlabdhā tvatprasādāt mayācyuta;
Sthito'smi gatasandehaḥ kariṣye vacanam tava

'Destroyed is my delusion, and I have gained my memory through thy grace, O Acyuta. I am firm; my doubts are gone. I will do thy word.'

How can doubts go without right knowledge? Doubt which is creative is the mother of all knowledge; and with the rising of knowledge, all doubts are destroyed. This is the function of philosophy in relation to life. Life raises problems at every step; the mind is assailed by doubts and confusion; we turn to the wisdom of philosophy, as to a lamp, for guidance. Every individual is the possessor of a little wisdom which helps him to negotiate life's placid waters. But this little wisdom and light fails us when storms and stresses set in. It is then that the human mind seeks for a steadier light and asks the question: 'Is there a better light, a light which will not flicker and which will be of use in every circumstance?' We want a steadier wisdom which will stand us in all circumstances of life. Philosophy is the pursuit of that wisdom which is itself steady and which helps to steady our feet in the midst of life's slippery path. We want the guidance of a steady wisdom to steer the bark of life through the tempests of circumstances. The Vedanta has the capacity to provide us with this wisdom which will help us to keep our feet steady and head firm. Śrī Kṛṣṇa seeks to give us this wisdom; he seeks to impart right knowledge to bring order out of doubt and confusion. As a result of the teaching we find Arjuna saying that his doubts are gone and that he is prepared to do whatever he was asked to do. But Śrī Kṛṣṇa does not direct him to do this or that. He says: 'Thus have I taught you wisdom which is subtler than the subtlest; having examined it well, act as you think best.' The best teachers are those who help the disciples to solve their own problems, never imposing set solutions of their own on them. They never ask their disciples to surrender their independence of judgement. The mention of a great name should not result in the surrendering of our independence of judgement. That is what Śrī Kṛṣṇa would say, and also the great Buddha. In fact, every right type of teacher would say the same. Turn whatever they say upside down and examine it well. Or as Yama said in the *Kaṭha Upaniṣad:* 'Go round and round and examine it well from all sides and from all points of view.' First examine the teacher and the teaching, and then accept it. Sri Ramakrishna used to say, 'Test me as a money-changer would test his coins.' That is what he said to Swami Vivekananda. How few are the teachers that can stand this test! We have to see how many of them have the true ring. A true teacher would say: 'I am here to place the lamp in your hand, and you go on your own way.' Philosophy is a lamp which you can take in your hand for a guide through the jungle of ignorance. In the tenth chapter Śrī Kṛṣṇa again says: 'I put a little wisdom in the hearts of the seekers by which they find their own way. My function is just to light the lamp.' That is the little help we get from outside, but that is more than enough if we can utilise it properly. The true teacher demands independence for himself as well as for the disciple. After all, we create a disciple out of our own mould. If the teacher is a small mould, the disciple who is cast in it will also be of the same type, even though he may have larger capacities. A teacher who is himself subject to confusion creates more confusion in the disciple. So there must be independent judgement.

In the *Gītā,* in all the eighteen chapters, we are face to face with a philosophy which seeks to impart redeeming wisdom by which men may work out their own salvation. This is its dynamic feature. On our own endeavours depends the taking hold of this wisdom and making something out of it. Philosophy, understood in the Vedantic sense, should not be mere academic study and discussion, but should be closely related to life and its problems, sustained by life and helping to sustain life in turn. That is the philosophy which is going to be revealed in the succeeding verses of the *Gītā.*

How to be an Ideal Householder*

In the *Gospel of Sri Ramakrishna,* there are several chapters entitled 'Advice to Householders' etc. Sri Ramakrishna's advice to householders is a great subject. When we say 'householder,' it means that it concerns 99.9 percent of the population. That means the people at large. How they will live their life is a very great question. There is one sentence in Swami Vivekananda's lecture where he says, 'I don't call anyone a Hindu who is not spiritual.' What a beautiful idea it is! They must be spiritual, not merely religious; to be religious is very easy: put on a sandal mark or ashes on your forehead, you become a Hindu; put on a cross, you become a Christian; and put on a moon crescent on the cap, you become a Muslim. Thus it is easy to become religious. But what is wanted is that we should be spiritual, and not merely being religious. And this concept of spirituality comes to us from the Upanishads, because the Upanishads describe that the human nature is essentially spiritual. Behind the body-mind-complex is the Atman, of the nature of *cit* and *sat*—'consciousness' and 'reality.' Infinity is our true nature. This is the discovery; we call it a scientific truth

---

*A talk by Swami Ranganathanandaji delivered on 17 May 1998 at the Ramakrishna Mission, New Delhi.

about the human being. By examining the human beings in depth, our sages of the Upanishads discovered this great truth. In the *Kathopanisad,* we read this beautiful sentence. During the course of his teaching, Yama said to Naciketa (3.12):

Eṣa sarveṣu bhuteṣu gūdho ātmā na prakāśyate;
Dṛśyate tvagrayā buddhyā sukśmayā sukśma darśibhiḥ

'This Atman is present in all beings but hidden and so not manifest; but it can be realised by a sharply one-pointed subtle mind, by those who are trained in dealing with subtle and still more subtle realities.'

This profound truth of the Atman, the divine pure consciousness, ever pure, ever free and immortal, is present in every human being. Only it is hidden, not manifested. Does it always remain hidden? No. It has been realised by the great sages; and it can be realised by one and all. Human beings have the organic capacity for it. How? When the mind is trained to discover subtle truths, the subtlest minds can discover this subtlest of truths, the Atman.

Today's nuclear science proves this to you. A subtle mind can see the subtle nature of matter. That matter consists of energy is the discovery of the subtle mind of the modern scientists. It was not there at Newton's time. He had a subtle mind up to that; more subtle it became in the twentieth century. Similarly, in dealing with the truth of the human being, there are two dimensions: ordinary mind and subtle mind. We need a very subtle mind. How do we get it? *Sukśma darśibhiḥ*— those who practice dealing with subtle truths and still more subtle truths, will develop the subtlest minds which can penetrate into the subtlest truth of the Atman hidden within. This is a statement from the third chapter of *Kathopanisad* where you have another great utterance, like a marching order (1.3.14):

Uttiṣṭhata jāgrata prāpya varān nibodhata

'Arise, awake, and stop not till the goal is reached.' This is Swami Vivekananda's free translation of the text which literally means Arise, awake, and enlighten yourself by approaching the great ones.' What a wonderful message!

Becoming householders, we are passing through one phase of our life. According to the Vedic conception of human life, one hundred years is the limit of human life. Śankarācārya writes: *Tāvad hi puruṣasya paramāyuṭḥ nibodhitam*—'That much is the length of human life.' So, we divide this human life into four portions: First as a student, *brahmacārin,* to study and develop knowledge. There is so much knowledge to acquire. A human child needs about twenty to twenty-five years to acquire knowledge and get educated. The animal child does not take so much time. When a calf is born, within one hour, it learns how to jump about. It goes out here and there and its education is over. But a human child, for about twenty-five years, is in the process of being educated. This is the *brahmacarya* period. This kind of life-analysis you will find in no other literature. Then, after you become about twenty-five, the next is the life which is called *gṛhastha,* householder. It means marriage, living as wife and husband; two people join together, creating a family with one or two children. Nature wants it, nature dictates to the human being, saying, 'Yes, you produce one or two children.' Today's biology tells you that nature is not interested in any species which does not reproduce itself. If there is no reproduction, nature cannot continue, evolution cannot proceed. Therefore, in the human being, we have this function in life where you become an instrument of nature to continue the evolution of the human race with one or two children.

Formerly there used to be hundred children to a human being when there was no population problem in the world. Today, however, it is strictly one or two. Nothing more we need. This is one phase. But, in the course of doing nature's work, you are also to develop your spiritual life. Even as a *brahmacārin,* the human being starts realising his or her divine nature that is within. If you manifest the divine, you learn how to love people, how to serve people, how to live together in peace in society. What can I do for you? How can I help you?—this capacity comes to you. It is a wonderful idea—'I am not alone in this world, so many other people are also there. How can I negotiate with all these people in a friendly way?' What a beautiful concept! We are not in a crowd, but in an integrated society. That integration comes from the capacity to love people, to serve people. Then you are able to lead a happy life by mutual help, mutual development. The *Gitā* says (3.11):

Parasparam bhāvayantaḥ śreyaḥ paramavāpsyath

'By loving and serving each other, all can attain the highest.' To achieve great welfare, we need the capacity to help each other, interact with each other in a positive way. This is the ideal householder's life. In this way, the householder will have mental peace and fine children who will continue and further enrich the human culture and civilisation.

Here, modern biology tells you one profound truth—human uniqueness—the distinction between pre-human species of animals and the human species. One distinction is, they have only one inheritance, the genetic. We also have genetic inheritance—father and mother gave us our body. In this way, genetic inheritance goes on. But a human being has another inheritance also; they call it cultural inheritance. Today biology tells you that culture is cumulative knowledge, cumulative experience. In the Vedic times they had some experience. That did not get lost with their death; they put it in writing, and it became the Vedas. It becomes the property of the next generations. Thus literature, art, science, religion, and philosophy get richer and richer and become the inheritance of the human generations. That is called 'cumulative culture.' It goes on expanding and expanding. No animal has cultural inheritance. The human child inherits not only the hereditary system from the parents and grandparents, but also the culture coming from olden times. So, a double inheritance we have as human beings and we have to develop that culture, expand that culture, giving to the next generation something richer, something better, from our own experience. That is the householder's responsibility.

This is what we in India had forgotten since some centuries till now; we became a stagnant culture—no change, no development, nothing but absolute stagnation for the last several centuries. In the earlier period, great developments were there in various fields; but somehow, for a thousand years, we were down and down. It was a cultural stagnation. We did not communicate with people of other countries. We kept people away by discovering the word and concept of *mleccha.* All other nations are *mleccha.* Don't touch a *mleccha;* don't cross the borders of our own country. Swami Vivekananda noted it and he has said in one sentence:

'The fate of India was sealed when she discovered the word *mleccha* and stopped communication with the world outside.'

We suffered much from it. In not communicating with others, we became stagnant like the Bourbon dynasty in France about which historians say that the Bourbons learned nothing new and forgot nothing old, and so the violent French Revolution came. And the same statement comes to you from the great Arab traveller, Al Beruni, who came to India in the tenth century AD along with Muhammad Ghazni. Al Beruni knew Sanskrit and much of Indian philosophy. Ghazni came to loot the material wealth of India and Al Beruni came to take India's philosophical wealth. His observations on India are contained in his book *Al Beruni's India.* He says: 'What happened to the people of India? Their ancestors were not narrow-minded like *this;* they don't mix with anybody, they don't give their knowledge to anybody, they won't take knowledge from anybody. Their ancestors were not like this.'

That is the language we find there. What Swami Vivekananda said is what Al Beruni had said earlier, about a thousand years ago. That India is no more the same now. We have become open. Now we can exchange ideas with people, receive and give ideas, and thus develop a universal concept of humanity as one. Today's biology describes humanity as a single species. Even one insect has hundreds of species. But the human being is a single species, interbreeding and inter-thinking. What a beautiful concept! We are all one physically speaking; but the Vedanta adds that spiritually also we are one. The Upanishads discovered that one infinite Atman is in you, in me, in all. Spiritually we are all one. We must know this truth. Physically also we are one. So, we framed our life in India from that point of view. Later on, narrow-mindedness came, we did not go out and learn new developments; and the result was that we lost our political freedom to foreign invaders. They used guns, we used only arrows and bows. And so we lost every time, because we did not know what developtments had taken place elsewhere. Today we have learnt that lesson. Our mind is open to receive and give. Swami Vivekananda particularly emphasised this point again and again.

But today's householder is a unique type of person. He can give to others, and he can take from others; this is the way to develop a human consciousness, a human culture. The world is developing in that direction, and India will contribute to that. Today's householder, therefore, cannot be narrow, cannot be exclusive. That is why we are breaking down all caste exclusiveness and all narrow social attitudes. During the British period, caste awareness was very strong. When the governor or the viceroy would meet a prince of an Indian royal family, he had to receive them, talk with them, and even shake hands with them. After their guests had gone away, the prince used to take a bath secretly to remove the pollution! That was the narrowness we had at that time. Today that is all gone. Most of our people are open now. This time is the best to build up our life in the correct manner as given in our Vedanta—the profound, comprehensive, and humanistic philosophy and spirituality of the Upanishads and the *Gitā*. Much of it is found in the Puranas also. But these two are the main source. They contain universal, spiritual, philosophical teachings, not for Hindus only, but for every human being. They always kept in view humanity as a whole.

Śṛṇvantu viśve amṛtasya putrāḥ

'Listen to me, O children of immortality, of the whole world.'

See the language of the *Śvetāśvatara Upaniśad,* addressing all human beings, the verse which Swami Vivekananda quoted and expounded in the Chicago Parliament of Religions in 1893, which had a telling effect on the vast audience. 'Listen to me, O children of immortality everywhere! You are not children of sin. It is a sin to call a man so, it is a standing libel on human nature.' This is the language Swamiji used in the Chicago Parliament. So, the human being is a child of immortality. That is what the Upanishads had pro-claimed a few thousand years ago; whether it is in India or outside is just the same—Hindu, Muslim, Christian, atheist, agnostic—all are children of immorṭtality. We are essentially the immortal Atman. That is our true nature. *Tat tvam asi*—You are That, you are all that divine immortal Atman. That is the language of the *Chāndogya Upaniśad,* 6th chapter. This kind of profound message of the Upanishads and the *Gitā* is there to guide us. No other guidance can be taken as primary, but this is primary. This will produce a Vedantic India. If that is taken up earnestly, a new type of householder's life will develop in India—full of vigour, full of strength, full of humanistic impulse.

A *gṛhastha,* wife or husband, is one who lives in a *gṛha* or home. Is he or she to be confined to the home and to the care of his genetic family members? If so, the home becomes a prison. No, he or she is to be concerned with the welfare of the society of which he or she is a member. In India we neglected this idea in recent centuries. But a new situation has arisen in the modern period. India is a vast, free democratic country today; it has no princes, kings, or emperors. Its sovereignty rests in the millions of its democratic citizens. That freedom of citizenship is the status of all our *gṛhasthis* today—of both men and women. On their shoulders rests our democratic state. That freedom must be enriched by a sense of national responsibility by every householder today. Such free and responsible citizens alone can energise our various political institutions, from *grām pañcāyats* through state legislatures up to the Union Parliament, as well as our cooperative and other societies.

Among his or her national responsibilities today is controlling of our population growth which has been uncontrolled since our Independence in 1947. All our poverty alleviation and mass education programmes become nullified by this one factor. We have to achieve zero population growth as soon as possible. We have remained an underdeveloped country even after years of freedom because of this galloping population. All our people must discharge their citizenship responsiṭbility to their nation by actively helping the Union and State governments' efforts in this direction by adopting the small family norm themselves and influencing others also to do so by taking all help from spiritual and medical resources.

Till now, our householders had certain weaknesses. Firstly, they harbour a lot of superstitions. Any superstition can get into the mind of a householder. A sadhu going about in a village can tell this and that, and they all believe what they hear. In this way, you will find the experience of fear, the product of superstition. That is the constant feeling of householders in India and that fear can receive stimulus from small, untoward happenings also. In this way, you will find all over India many superstitions cultivated by the minds of householders whose ideas of religion are more magical and not spiritual. Somebody came to the house, and the next day the child fell ill. 'Oh, that man's visit has brought this illness of my child'—the parents come to this unscientific conclusion. There is nothing of science or even common sense in it; it is all anti-science, superstition. It is based only on the scientific method of agreement. Two things happening together is interpreted as one being the cause of the other. To get a scientific conclusion, you must apply a second method also—the method of difference. Withdraw one factor, and if the result is the same, then that cause and effect conclusion of the method of agreement becomes falsified. In a book on logic and scientific method, an example is given about the insufficiency and fault of depending on the method of agreement alone. A man used to come out of the post office every day at 7 o'clock. The sun used to rise at that time. And some people concluded that the man's coming out is the cause of the sun rising! It is an absolutely foolish conclusion; it must be corrected by asking the man not to come out at 7 o'clock, and watching whether the sun rises or not. This is the method of difference. Then there is the method of concomitant variation and the method of residues. All these scientific methods are there to establish correct cause and effect relations. But in family life, people rely only on the weakest method of agreement. Education will correct this to some extent. 'Knowledge destroys fear' is a famous statement. Hindu and Indian society will be different when some kind of scientific thinking comes to our people. Then only can our people understand Vedanta and benefit from it. Vedanta is very, very scientific. What is the meaning of 'scientific?' It means that which deals with truth as it is. That is called scientific. You only discover that truth, you don't create it, you don't alter it, you don't abolish it, you just recognise it. Ādi Śankarācārya calls it *vastu tantra jñāna; kartum, akartum, anyathā kartum na śakyate, vastu tantratvāt eva,* in his *Brahma Sūtra* commentary, and adds: *brahmajñānam vastu tantra jñānam—*'

knowledge of Brahman is based on the existing truth of Brahman.' 'Fire is hot' is a truth, not an opinion. Most people have only opinions, they don't know the truth of things. In his *Brahma Sutra Bhāṣya,* Śankarācārya writes in the Introduction, as said already: *brahmajñānam vastu tantra jñānam.* Vedanta presents this to you as the truth, not as an opinion. The word used is *vastu tantra jñānam.* See the technical term! *Vastu* means existing reality; *tantra* means based on; and, *jñānam* means knowledge—'knowledge based on existing reality'. What a beautiful concept! So he says: *Brahmajñānam vastu tantra jñānam.*

Kartum, akartum, anyathā kartum na śakyate, vastu tantratvādeva—'Knowledge of Brahman is based on the existing Reality of Brahman. You cannot create it, cannot abolish it, or alter it, because it is an existing Reality.'

That is called scientific truth. The other is called *puruṣa tantra jñānam.* 'I shall fast on a Monday.' It is up to you. There is no objective or universal truth about it. You may as well say, 'I shall fast on a Saturday.' It is up to you. It is called *puruṣa tantra jñānam*—'knowledge based on the person concerned'. In this way, Śankarācārya, towards the end of that section, says:

'*Ātmaikatva vidyā pratipattaye sarve vedānta ārabhyante*'—All the Upanishads are intended to convey to you the knowledge of the unity of the Atman.

There is only one Atman, of the nature of pure Consciousness. Consciousness has no plural, it is always a singular. It is a wonderful statement in the Upanishads.

And today what the nuclear scientist, Schroedinger, says adds strength to it: 'Consciousness is a singular of which the plural is unknown.' It is just like space which has no plural. Space is one—inside the room or outside the room—all one space only. You seem to divide it, but you cannot divide it. So also the Atman, as pure Consciousness, is only one, in you, in me, in all. That is the great Vedāntic teaching which the Upanishads convey to all people all over the world. What a profound philosophy! What possibilities will be realised when this philosophy is applied to life, individual and collective! Physical unification is taking place through technology. Today you can travel quickly. The East India Company people used to take one and a half years to reach India from England. But today, within five or ten hours one can reach here. Similarly, communication of ideas also—telegrams, and now fax. In one or two minutes, your information reaches a far-off destination. But, the minds and hearts of people must also be close to each other. That is not yet possible. It can be possible only through this unifying message of Vedānta, the product of a science of man in depth. Take it up, verify it for yourself. This is what the *Śvetaśvatara Upaniṣad* says:

Vedāhametam puruṣam mahāntam

'I have realised this Infinite Man behind the finite man,' and

Tameva viditvā atimṛtyumeti,
nānyaḥ panthā vidyate ayanāya—

'By knowing Him alone one can overcome death and delusion; there is no other way to freedom and fulfilment.'

You can transcend death and delusion. You realise this truth yourself. Somebody else's realising will not make you achieve this thing. In *Vivekacūdāmaṇi,* Śankarācārya says: 'You have to eat yourself if you are hungry. If someone else eats on your behalf, it will not benefit you.' You have to realise the Truth for yourself. Therefore, in our whole life we have these beautiful ideas given to us. We have never touched even a bit of them all these one thousand years. Some superstition, some mythology; especially, we are fond of mythology, and India has produced the largest quantity of mytholṭogy in the world. Vivekananda said that we can fill the world's libraries with books of Indian mythology. Let some mythology remain; some mythology has sometimes a scientific background. Science itself becomes mythical at a higher level, especially in astronomy. Today's India must realise this truth that scientific thinking and scientific temper must develop in our people, making them to ask this question, 'What can I do with this wonderful life? I have got a packet of energy within me. How shall I handle it?' You will get guidance from the Upanishads and the *Gitā*. Our scriptures say that there are three types of energy in every human being. First is called *bāhubalam,* muscular energy. *Balam* is a word for strength or energy. This is very ordinary. Today we have multiplied this energy million-fold, through our rockets. 'The horse power' we also call it. These powerful rockets could send a man to the moon. One Voyager has already gone outside the solar system. That is called muscular power, immensely multiplied through technology. The second is *buddhibalam,* intellectual energy. You go to the university, study books, science, and everything, acquire intellectual strength, *buddhibalam.* But is it all? Today's understanding is only that much—*bāhubalam* and *buddhibalam.* But our scriptures say: No, there is also *Ātmabalam,* spiritual energy. That is tremendous; there is nothing to compare with it.

How do you know about this *Ātmabalam?* That is the main subject that modern humanity must ask and find an answer. Up to that, we have come very well. Beyond the physical or sense organ level, we do not know anything. Today, science has nothing to say on this subject. But the most important energy is there waiting to be acquired—*Ātmabalam.* All kinds of temptations are coming to people everyday and man has no energy to withstand them. *Buddhibalam* has not that power. But *Ātmabalam* can do it. A little *Ātmabalam* can say *no* to all temptations. Every day our society is suffering from big and small people falling to temptations. Women are suffering, girls are suffering, boys are suffering. Everywhere you find this kind of weakening of moral resistance to antisocial temptations. Because of that we are facing increasing social problems. So, we need to develop a little of *Ātmabalam* to be able to control our minds and sense organs. These senses are very troublesome if they are not properly restrained.

Our ancient teachers gave us a beautiful idea. They said that there are six enemies of every human being—*ṣaḍripu*. *Ṣaḍ* means *ṣaṣṭha,* six; *ripu* means enemy. They are not outside, but within us. What are they? *Kāma, krodha, lobha, moha, mada, mātsarya*—unrestrained lust, anger, greed, delusion, pride, and violence. These are the six enemies in every human being—this is a profound analysis of the human psyche. These are the enemies that create all the trouble. Today whatever trouble you find in the world spoiling inter-human relations is the product of these enemies—one or two or three in most cases—*kāma, krodha* and *lobha.* We have to check them. Who has to check them? The mind has to check them; the mind is meant for that. But if the mind is weak, it follows them, not checks them. Then we fall down before all temptations. This is what is happening to many people. For, neurology tells us today that the higher brain system is meant to control the entire sensory system. It is the special gift of evolution to humanity. But if this higher brain becomes the servant of all the sensory systems—it is unfortunately so for many people—then all moral values become eroded. Then instead of the head of the dog wagging the tail, the tail starts wagging the head of the dog. That is happening to increasing numbers of human beings today. That is why all these social problems and sufferings are multiplying every day. So, this cerebral system must become independent, must be able to control all the sensory systems. Then these enemies will not arise and trouble the individual and society. These enemies can be controlled by the human being. In the third chapter of the *Gitā,* in the last seven verses, Arjuna asks a question on this subject, and Śrī Kṛṣṇa gives a profound answer. This is the question (3.36):

Atha kena prayukto'yam pāpam carati pūruṣaḥ;
Anicchannapi vārṣneya balādiva niyojitaḥ

'O Kṛṣṇa, by what impulsion does a human being commit a crime, against one's own willingness and as if compelled by a force?' He does not want to do it; but he is compelled to do it by some force; what is that force?—that is the language. Every human being has this problem. And the answer comes from Śrī Kṛṣṇa:

'*Kāma* and *krodha*—lust and anger are the two enemies. They overcome you and then make you do this and that; you must control them, you have that power.' Where from that power comes? He is giving you the answer towards the last few ones up to the 7th verse—*Indriyāṇi parāṇyāhuḥ.* 'Sense organs are very sensitive and very helpful.' You can understand the world around you through them. Then, there is the mind above the sense organs—*Indriyebhyaḥ param manaṭḥ.* Then, *Manasastu parā buddhiḥ*—'beyond and higher than the *manas* is the *buddhi,* discriminatory faculty.' Is this right or wrong—that knowledge comes at the *buddhi* level. And beyond *buddhi* is the Atman—*Yo buddheḥ paratastu saḥ.* Therefore, *Evam buddheḥ param buddhva*—'realising the one that is beyond *buddhi,'* namely, the ever pure, ever free, and ever illumined Ātman; realise that truth. Then you will be able to control other lower levels that are troubling you. No more enemies you will have within yourself.

Evam buddheḥ param buddhva saṁstabhyātmānam ātmana;
Jahi śatrum mahābāho kāmarṃūpam durāsadam

'Realising the one higher than the *buddhi,* and controlling the lower self by the higher self or Ātman, conquer the enemy, O mighty armed, of the nature of *kāma,* unrestrained lust, which is difficult to satisfy.' 'Conquer the enemy,' just like a general telling the army to capture a fort. That is the language Kṛṣṇa is using there, a warrior addressing another warrior!

So, today's householders will develop into fine citizens, working together with others, if this kind of training goes on within oneself. This is not understood in today's Western thinking, because they stop at the sensory level. Even mind is treated only as a tail of the sensory system. Take any book on the brain. It will say there is no separate mind as such, only the brain is there. But many neurologists are differing from it; they want to accept the Indian idea that the mind is higher than the brain which is only a physical instrument. But the mind is higher. And, higher than the mind is *buddhi,* the discriminative faculty, behind which is the supreme reality of the Ātman, ever pure and immortal. This truth is slowly penetrating the western thinking today. Men like Sir Charles Sherrington, the famous neurologist, says in his book, *Integrated Action of the Nervous System* (it is a famous book, every medical student has to study that book): 'One factor alone is not enough. Two factors are needed—brain and mind, not brain alone.' Some others also say so. I have quoted them in my small book *Neurology and What Lies Beyond.* So, here Vedānta has the knowledge of the depth dimension of the human personality which the West has yet to develop by studying the human being in depth. They have never studied it. They know anatomy, physiology, and neurology; beyond that, they do not know. Even psychology they are trying to understand more and more. One such psychologist has given us a beautiful idea. That was Carl Jung of Zurich, at the beginning of the century. He wrote the famous book *Modern Man in Search of a Soul.* I have got a body; very fine, but where is my soul? It has been lost in the debris of civilisation. That is why he wrote the book *Modern Man in Search of a Soul.*

There is a fine passage in that book I would like to share that with you. This life of a householder must be divided into two parts. In the first part, we engage ourselves in education, getting a job, marriage, raising a family, getting a good name and fame in society. He calls it achievement. Then, the second part of life which begins after middle age, calls for a change. Don't carry this philosophy of achievement to the second part. The second part must be devoted to personality development or culture, he says. Mere achievement should not be continued after middle age. If you go on continuing 'achievement,' you will suffer from diminution of personality. Develop your inner life; that should be the purpose of the second part. You have neglected it in the midst of the struggle for achievement. Now you have time to concentrate on that.

This is exactly what Indian thought has long upheld—a householder becoming a *vānaprasthi* at a particular age. This *vānaprastha* or forest life requires today a re-consideration. When these ideas were developed in ancient India, there were plenty of forests close to any city, town, or village. But today, due to enormous population growth, forests have become very limited and exist far away from habitations. Our forest tribes also are getting educated and going for jobs outside the forests, slowly and steadily. Under these circumstances, our *gṛhasthas* must learn the spirit of the *vānaprastha* ideal and convert the home itself into a *tapovana,* or forest retreat, as mentioned in *Hitopadeśa* (Sandhi 89):

Vanepi doṣā prabhavanti rāgiṇām
gṛheṣu sarvendriya nigrahaḥ tapaḥ
Akutsite karmaṇi yaḥ pravartate
nivṛtta rāgasya gṛham tapovanam

'A person with worldly attachments will experience troubles even in the forest; living at home with all the senses under control is tapas or spiritual austerity. For one who is engaged in unblemished actions, and free from attachment, the very home becomes a *tapovanam.'*

In the *Manusmrti,* there is a very interesting verse. When shall I give up my worldly pursuits and concentrate on my spiritual life? This question is asked. And Manu says (6.2):

Gṛhasthastu yadā paśyet valīpalitamātmanaḥ;
Āpatyasyaiva cāpatyam tadāraṇyam samaśrayet

'When a grhastha sees his own hair turning grey and the face of his offspring's offspring (grandchild), then he should resort to the forest.'

What beautiful language! When you find your hair turning grey, that means old age is coming on you, and seeing the grandchild's face means you have done your duty to nature. Time is running out. You have neglected a beautiful thing—your own inner development. You were busy only with achievement, name, fame, and all that. That won't do. Reduce stress on them and concentrate on enriching your inner life. Then Jung warns: 'He or she who carries over "achievement" to the second half of life will suffer from diminution of personality.' Strength and stability, a sense of inner enrichment, come from the knowledge of the Atman. 'Even a little understanding of one's spiritual nature is the destroyer of fear,' says the *Gitā,* in the second chapter. In the pursuit of life also you may get spiritual strength to some extent. But now you can concentrate on it much more. This is what we also understood as *vānaprastha* as well as *sannyāsa.* What a novel idea—two sectors of human life! If a householder wants to live a happy life, he or she must be spiritual; that makes one expand the self to take in other selves also. Without this *ātmavikāsa,* one becomes confined to one's body or genetic system. Why is it so? Because, there will be constant conflict between husband and wife for not having the capacity to dig affections in each other. Conflict is bound to be if there is no spiritual growth in the individual. We have many religious men and women who come into conflict with each other. The mother-in-law is often very religious but unspiritual and hence oppresses her daughter-in-law. A little spiritual growth will change all this.

So Sri Ramakrishna comes with a beautiful statement: This 'I,' when it is unripe—*kācā āmi*—will collide with other unripe 'I's in society. Agnostic thinker, late Bertrand Russell, said that some human beings are like billiard balls always colliding with other human beings. A billiard ball does not know how to live with or enter into other billiard balls. So, Sri Ramakrishna said that this little 'I' must become expanded, must become *pākā āmi,* to be able to deal happily with other 'I's in society.

Today there are too many 'billiard balls' in our society, full of conflict, whether it is in politics, administration, household, or anywhere else. Even family life is suffering because of too many contracted selves. But if a little spiritual development takes place, spiritual expansion, *ātmavikāsa,* then everything will be smooth and peaceful, and life will become happy and fulfilled. Sir Julian Huxley referred to this expansion of 'I' in the language of modern biology. The unripe 'I' is called individuality, and the ripe 'I' is called personality. Individuality must grow into personality.

What is meant by the word 'person'? Huxley defines it in his Foreword to Teilhard de Chardin's book *The Phenomenon of Man:* 'Persons are individuals who transcend their organic individuality in conscious social participation.' A person has the capacity to live happily with other persons in society. Individuals cannot; they only collide. If the husband and wife are individualities, they will often indulge in conflicts. If both are personalities, absolute peace will reign in the family. This is the teaching. All these can be achieved by everyone. Apart from college education, this is the real education. You grow—the word is growth. If a child grows spiritually, you can say to him or her, that he or she will be very happy. Children are fond of the word 'growth.' You must grow, don't quarrel with other children. Make friends with them. In this way, when you tell children, their *kācā āmi* slowly becomes *pākā āmi.* This education parents must give to their children. Today they don't give it. They give them just the opposite. 'Strengthen your *kācā āmi* again and again, try to be selfish, don't care for anybody'—that is the teaching we generally give to our children. And so this wonderful idea of spiritual growth as *kācā āmi* becoming *pākā āmi* must be kept in view to have a happy family life. *Śāntimaya, sukhamaya gṛhastha jivan* is possible if there is a little *ātmavikāsa.* That is the householder's life; he or she need not try to become a sadhu or a mystic. Spiritual life need not be mystically showy. Pure spiritual development finds expression in character development, capacity to work together in a team, and love and service. Individuals always try to pull down each other; but persons will never do so. They know how to work together. Today we are lacking in the power of teamwork because of this too much of individuality. So, Vedānta contains this profound philosophy of the depth dimension of the human personality centred in the Ātman. A little of its manifestation is enough to make life rich and beautiful. As Śrī Kṛṣṇa said in the *Gitā* (2.40):

Svalpamapyasya dharmasya trāyate mahato bhayāt

'Even a little of this teaching will save one from great fear,' says Swami Vivekananda in his lecture on 'Vedānta in its Application to Indian Life' (*Complete Works,* Vol. 3, p. 237):

'Strength, strength is what the Upanishads speak to me from every page. This is the one great thing to remember, it has been the one great lesson I have been taught in my life; strength, it says, strength, O man, be not weak. Are there no human weaknesses? says man. There are, say the Upanishads, but will more weakness heal them, would you try to wash dirt with dirt? Will sin cure sin, weakness cure weakness? Strength, O man, strength, say the Upanishads. Stand up and be strong. Aye, it is the only literature in the world where you find the word *Abhih,* "fearless," used again and again; in no other scripture in the world is this adjective applied either to God or to man.'

Spiritual energy within manifests itself as values in human life—love, compassion, spirit of service. 'What can I do for you? How can I help you?' What a change will come in our society if people develop this spiritual growth within! Till now we never had it except in some persons. Most people, however, are usually religious; they go to the temple, put on marks on the forehead, do some ritual, but remain always what they are—full of conflict with others at home or in society. To settle mutual quarrels, they go to the courts. That is why our courts are full of cases; thousands and thousands of cases are waiting in many of our courts. India has the largest number of litigations anywhere in the world, because we do not know how to settle matters by talking to each other. Human relations became very poor for the last thousand years.

All that will change in the modern period. That is the message of practical Vedanta, message of Sri Ramakrishna and Swami Vivekananda. The Ramakrishna-Vivekananda literature contains profound ideas about how to develop happy human relations with other people. That is how a new India will develop. Our householders will be fine citizens of India and citizens of the world, possessed of *ātma śraddhā,* faith in oneself, and faith in others. Self-respect is very important which is lacking today. Many of our householders will be telling: 'I am a householder, what can I do? I am a *saṁsāri,* what can I do?' That feeling must go. Sri Ramakrishna said to his householder devotees: 'You are not a *saṁsāri,* you live in *saṁsāra,* but *saṁsāra* should not be in you.' Then only can you establish happy relations with family members and society. So, let us not allow *saṁsāra* to live in us. We must have the feeling that we are citizens of democratic India, or that we are the devotees of God. Sri Ramakrishna gave this example: A boat may be on the water, but water should not be in the boat; then the boat will become stagnant and unfit for the purpose for which it is meant.

History tells us that we in India used to quarrel, individuals with individuals, groups with groups, and foreign invaders made use of this trait to establish their long rule over our country. Even today we are quarrelling with each other, in political and social life and weakening our democracy thereby. We must learn to cooperate with each other when national interest is involved. Maharashtra and Karnataka, Tamil Nadu and Karnataka, engage themselves in unending conflicts, as if they are two separate foreign states. That old characteristic is still lingering. So, this kind of human development will take place in India when Vivekananda's literature inspires a good section of our people. It is human development in a fundamental way, not merely getting a degree and getting a good salary; that is not enough. Have I become truly developed as a human being? Have I become a source of strength to our democratic state? That is the question we have to ask and get a positive answer. That is why if our householders—and as I said earlier, 99.9 percent of people are householders only—follow the teachings of Swami Vivekananda and the *Gitā's* practical Vedānta, they will become healthy and strong, and endowed with the humanistic attitude, that will make the whole country strong and gentle.

In this connection, it will be instructive to acqaint oneself with the famous story of Dharmavyādha in the *Vana Parva* of the *Mahābhārata,* narrated by sage Mārkaṇḍeya to Yudhiṣṭhira, during the Pāṇdavās *vanavāsa.* The story is of a brāhmaṇa ascetic, Kauśika, receiving spiritual lessons, first from a housewife and then from a meat-seller. The story emphasises the spiritual value of serving one's aged parents and the greatness of householders *(Araṇya Parva,* 197, 1-21):

A Brāhmaṇa ascetic by the name Kauśika was doing austerities under a tree. A bird, balākā, sitting on the tree, passed stool which fell on the ascetic. He looked up and saw the bird on the tree; his angry look made the bird fall down dead in front of him. The ascetic was grieved at the scene and said to himself that anger made him do an evil act.

Soon after, he went to the village nearby and approached a home of a householder for alms. The wife of the householder received him and requested him to wait a little; just at the time her husband came back home. Requesting the ascetic to wait a little, which he did not like, she took time to serve her husband with love and devotion.

The ascetic was angry that he is being neglected by her in order to serve her husband. He told her that an angry brāhmaṇa can burn up things. She replied: 'I am not insulting you; please excuse my neglect of you; among all the gods, I consider the service and care of my husband as most important. Brāhmaṇa, I know that you have burnt, a little ago, the balāka bird by your uncontrolled anger. Anger is the enemy of human beings. One who renounces anger and delusion is a true brāhmaṇa, so say the gods. In the country of Mithilā (now Bihar), there is a dharmavyādha, meat seller; he will teach you about dharma or ethics and morals; please go to him. Please excuse me if I have been impertinent in advising you.'

The ascetic understood her greatness and reached Mithilā passing through many forests, towns, and cities, and went to the shop of the dharmavyādha. He received the ascetic and said to him: 'You are welcome. I know your burning of the balāka bird and the advice given to you by that chaste housewife and why you have come to me here. This place (meat shop) is not a fit place to converse; we shall both go to my home.'

There also the ascetic had to wait till the Vyādha or hunter had served his aged parents. Then comes a long discourse on dharma by the hunter-meat-seller, to the Brāhmaṇa ascetic, of which the last 17 to 21 verses I give below:

Indriyāṇyeva tat sarvam yat svarganarakāvubhau;
Nigṛhīta visṛṣṭāni svargāya narkāya ca

'What are called heaven and hell, both are nothing but the sense organs; when they are controlled and disciplined, it is heaven; when they are let loose, it is hell.'

Eṣa yoga vidhiḥ kṛtsno yāvadindriya dhāraṇam;
Etat mūlam hi tapasaḥ kṛtsnasya narakasya ca

'The discipline of the senses is the sum total of the means of (man's) attaining all spiritual advancement; its presence or absence is at the root of man's every experience of spiritual enrichment (which is heaven) and all hell (which is spiritual impoverishment).'

Indriyāṇām prasaṅgena doṣamṛcchatyasaṁśayam;
Sanniyamyatu tānyeva tataḥ siddhim samāpnuyāt

'By indulging in them (men and women) undoubtedly contracts all vices; when, on the other hand, they are controlled and regulated, (men and women) attain spiritual freedom and fulfilment.'

Ṣaṇṇām ātmani nityānām aiśvaryam yo'dhigacchati;
Na sa pāpaiḥ kuto'narthaiḥ yujyate vijitendriyaḥ

'The self-controlled person who has acquired mastery over the six senses (five sense organs and the sense-bound mind) within himself, or herself, is tainted neither by sin nor by other evils.'

Rathaḥ śarīram puruṣasya dṛṣṭam
ātmā niyantā indriyāṇyāhuḥ aśvān;
Tairapramattaḥ kuśalī sadaśvaiḥ
dāntaiḥ sukham yāti rathi iva dhīraḥ

'The visible human physical body is said to be like a chariot, his or her soul, the controlling charioteer, and his or her senses, the horses; the wise and efficient person, with reason, calm and unperturbed, rides in happiness (and peace) like a capable and uninebriated driver controlling his or her disciplined horses.'

I went to Bihar to give a Hindi lecture at Chapra, four or five years ago, on *Gṛhastha Dharma* (that has been published as a booklet in many languages). There I saw a weak society, full of crime, full of poverty, feudal in attitude; because too many Buddhist monks were there, thousands of them, who, in a period of decay, became lazy, and householders imitated them. A firm development of household life, with divine virtues and graces, is needed today in a big way, not only in Bihar, but all over India. The gṛhastha is highly praised by our *Manusmṛti.* I want to convey to you that verse conveying a sense of self-respect, steadiness, and energy, which our *gṛhasthas* have lost for the last many centuries (3.78):

> *Yasmāt trayopyāśramiṇo jñānenānnena cānvaham;*
> *Gṛhasthenaiva dhāryante tasmāt jyeṣṭhāsramī gṛhī*

The greatness of the *gṛhastha* is mentioned in these words: *tasmāt jyeṣṭhāsramī gṛhī*—'Therefore the *gṛhastha ashrama* is the pre-eminent ashrama.' Because *trayopyāśramiṇo jñānenānnena cānvaham gṛhasthenaiva dhāryante*—'because the other three ashramas *(brahmacarya, vānaprastha and sannyāsa)* are nourished constantly with education and food by the *gṛhastha* only.' A *brahmacāri* does not earn; a *vānaprasthi* does not earn; so also a *sannyāsi.* Only a householder works and earns. By that one group, all the other three groups are educated and fed; that is its greatness. What a beautiful and true conception! Our *gṛhasthas* had forgotten it. They have to recapture it once again. That will be a new chapter of householder's life. They can work together and achieve great things together. Our parliament, assemblies, municipalities, and *pancayats* will be revolutionised. That kind of togetherness must be achieved. As it is, our *gṛhasthas* will more often trouble their neighbour. If I sweep my house, I put the dirt in front of my neighbour's house; I don't put it in front of my house. Everywhere in India this is a common practice. All good things for me and bad for others! Forsaking this petty attitude, our people must learn to work together.

There is more than one chapter on 'Advice to Householders' in the *Gospel of Sri Ramakrishna. A* householder asked Sri

Ramakrishna, 'Can we realise God?' 'Why not?', Sri Ramakrishna said, 'God is your own self, the Self of your self. You can realise Him. Only necessary changes you must adopt in your life. Then it will be possible.' In this way, 'spiritual growth' will become the key words of human development hereafter. Along with physical and intellectual growth, there must be stress on spiritual growth. 'Have I grown spiritually?' every one must ask this question. Go to a temple and worship; return and ask yourself, 'Have I grown spiritually?' Going to a temple and all other religious practices have got their purposes fulfilled only if this is done. You eat food; and if you don't grow physically, what is the use of eating? Similarly, in spiritual life, there is such a thing as *adhyātmika vikāsa*—spiritual growth. Keep that principle in view. Then *gṛhasthashrama* will be a beautiful experience. The salvation of India will come through such a *gṛhasthasramas.*

I convey to you all the blessings of Sri Ramakrishna for this achievement of being true gṛhasthas. It is the sense in which Vedanta and the *Gitā* and Sri Ramakrishna express it.

Way to Attain Bliss in Old Age

In many countries, old age is a botheration, absolutely dull, without any interest; and they want to make it interesting by extraneous means, generally by alcoholism. Nowadays even drugs are used. Mostly smoking is also there. I went to some old age homes in America, but I saw that there the people felt no joy in life; they wanted to kill their boredom by all sorts of extraneous means which are not at all good. This should not happen in India because of our wonderful spiritual tradition and our interest in this tradition.

More and more people are taking interest in the spiritual heritage of India so that even though we are old and weak, our mind is joyous because of a profound philosophy of human development given to us through our Upanishads and other books. 'Vedanta' is the word we use, a beautiful system of philosophy, for total human development and perfectness. We have it in the form of Upanishads, the *Gita*, Buddha's teachings, Shankaracharya's commentaries, and today in the message of Sri Ramakrishna, Swami Vivekananda and other teachers like Ramana Maharshi.

The one difference between the Western approach to philosophy and ours is, our philosophy you can question, you can investigate, but in the West whatever philosophy is there, nobody can question. So, the rational mind is not satisfied. Whereas in India, even the most rational minds are satisfied by questioning, and getting adequate answers to their questions. Take for example, Shankaracharya's *Vivekachudamani.* It is a wonderful book wherein a student puts questions to the teacher about the nature of human life, our real destiny, and so on. And in answer, the teacher takes the student step by step towards moral development. Then a little spiritual hunger is aroused, followed by a search for what steps we will have to take. Finally they lead him to spiritual realisation.

In *Vivekachudamani* there are 580 verses in beautiful Sanskrit with an English translation giving a wonderful exposition of man's spiritual life. I have covered these in twelve classes, which is now available in the form of cassettes. When you hear these cassettes, you can see the text being followed, word by word. So, in this way, by thinking on such higher ideas, our life becomes more meaningful, more joyous. Any kind of attempt to drown our boredom by external means is weakening. It brings no sense of joy, but when we are related to our own infinite Atman which is our real nature, which is of the nature of bliss, then we find inner joy coming from within, without any external stimulus which is generally a costly affair. That is why drug takers are generally thieves. They steal from their own fathers; they will also steal from neighbours. So, here is a teaching which can save us from this problem. But we have to implement it. Till now we did not need it, as we lived in a feudal society. But now we need it, everybody needs it. That is the importance of this type of meeting in the evening once in a while, carrying on some sort of spiritual practice in day-to-day life, some meditation, some bhajans—these are all very enriching experiences. Our bhajan-culture particularly is conquering—the western world now. They all want bhajans. In the motor cars they play the bhajan cassettes. When they take me in the car they put on our bhajans. This was a common thing: in every household I found our bhajan cassettes.

Bhajan is a tremendous experience; if you cannot achieve the knowledge of Brahman, at least you can enjoy the Brahman through singing bhajans. That is why bhajan is a spiritual experience, meditation also is a spiritual experience. Just going to the temple, taking a coconut, ringing a bell, etc., produces no spiritual experience. But in bhajan, there is a spiritual experience and the whole world is seeking that spiritual experience.

Sri Ramakrishna in one of his sayings has told us that there are three joys available to every human being (*The Gospel of Sri Ramakrishna* p.478). The word for joy is *ananda.* Those three *anandas* are available to every being. The first is called *vishayananda. Vishaya* means sense objects, sensory experiences like eating and other pleasures. This is called *vishayananda*—*ananda* coming from external objects. We don't look down on *vishayananda* in Vedanta. A baby wants only *vishayananda,* he does not know anything else. Everyone can have *vishayananda,* but we should know that there are also higher levels of *ananda.* That is what Vedanta says. A baby is fond of *vishayananda* but it must get other *anandas*—going to school, getting knowledge, and so on. Let it proceed with this *ananda* at that physical level—the *vishayananda.* The second is called *bhajanananda*—a wonderful *ananda* that comes from within, not from without. A part of this experience comes from bhajan, or meditation and study of various spiritual books, even scientific research. All this joy comes from within. This is called *bhajanananda.* Essentially it means singing God's name. All our saints have sung bhajans—Guru Nanak has done it, so also all the other Sikh gurus. Then there is Sankara Deva in Assam, Mirabai, and Surdas in North, and so many saints in South India. Their songs constitute a tremendous source of spiritual education and strength for our nation. They have spread throughout India and influenced everybody. That is why Kenneth Galbraith, the American Ambassador in Delhi, once came to the Planning Commission and told the Planning Commission Members, 'Well, I have seen poverty everywhere in the world, dismal poverty, and I have seen poverty in India, but Indian poverty has uniqueness because there is a gleam in the eyes of the poor people here which I did not find anywhere else, and the poverty does not make for crime in India whereas in all other countries poverty means drunkenness, crime and a sense of newer frustration.'

Dominique Lapierre has written a book about a slum in Kolkata, *The City of Joy*. By chance somebody gave it to me. While travelling I just went through it. It is a very interesting book. In a Kolkata slum everything is dismal from every point of view. But people are happy, just joyous, smiling children, though, there is dirt everywhere. The whole book is on that subject. That section of Kolkata is called Anand Nagar'. I am telling this only to point out that with our poor people, though their pocket is poor, their heart is not poor. They help mutually, if you go to them also, they help. The writer has given many instances to prove how generous they are. What else is required except this—generosity, kindness and hospitality? That is the sign of culture. So, our people have to cultivate this culture coming from this *bhajanananda,* given by the great saints of both North and South India. We have to retain that *bhajanananda.* That comes from within. When we are boys and girls, we do experience *bhajanananda* in some measure. But we can really enjoy it when we finish with all responsibilities, and are retired from day-to-day pressures. Now, why should we stick to *bhajanananda* all the more? Because the third level of *ananda* is very high. They call it *brahmananda.* When you actually realise God, immense joy will be your share. But *bhajanananda* is available to us, *brahmananda* is too high, *vishayananda* is too ordinary. That is why *bhajanananda* is most important for all of us. Just when the day's work is over, responsibilities are over, we sing bhajans or listen to bhajans. It is very good, it is a great experience. Gandhiji sang *Ram dhun* even during India's political struggle. Sometimes, there were one lakh people present, and how much they were influenced by Gandhiji's *Ram dhun*!

Bhajanananda is open to all. We all can have a little joy from within. We get refreshed thereby. This is how we develop our spiritual life through applying appropriate techniques. *Vishayananda* is all right when we are young. Youth is beautiful. But when the afternoon of life comes, then we must try to find joy from within, not from without. Otherwise there is big trouble. Carl Jung in his book, *Modern Man in Search of a Soul* specially mentions it: 'Forenoon of life has one objective. Afternoon of life has another objective. Don't carry the forenoon into the afternoon.' By the word 'Forenoon' is meant how to get established in the world, earn money, raise a family, enjoy the delights of life and get a good name in society. That is called 'forenoon'. Now don't carry this into the afternoon (old age), otherwise there will be a great diminution of personality and want of inner qualitative enrichment. When our work is over in the world, our objective must be to find out what will brighten our old age, brighten the age after sixty. Old age is not dismal at all, you can brighten it. Sri Ramakrishna puts it in a beautiful saying:—When you have work to do, hold the feet of God with one hand and do the work with the other hand. When the work is over, hold the feet of God with both the hands (*The Gospel of Sri Ramakrishna* p.325). That is the way of putting it, that is all.

In this way *bhajanananda* becomes a tremendous source of spiritual strength and inspiration and that moodiness, that kind of frustration that affects many old people will not be there. You will always be cheerful, thinking: 'Though the body is weak, there is something in me which makes me full of cheer.' *Payo ji mai ne, Ram Rattan mai payo*—one of the great bhajans we sing in Hindi meaning thereby, 'I have obtained the gem of Rama in my heart,

I don't miss anything.' We must be able to say this to ourselves: 'Yes, some profound truth has come, this life is really wonderful. When we have nothing else to do, we have got something very big to do which I had to neglect during my hard days. Now I am free.' That is how the whole of post-retirement life becomes a life of joy of a different type—purer and nobler life, with the blessings of everybody in the house. You can smilingly bless all of them. Don't expect anything from anybody, for we are finding joy from within ourselves, and that joy we communicate to others. Normally that is not there. If there is no spiritual background in life we don't communicate the joy at all. We communicate only our worries and troubles. Here, note that we have digested all our troubles. After all, physical pain will always be there. All right, as you say, the old buggy motor car (our physical body) becomes older, but the mind is different. I have just trained that mind.' In this way, we can bring a spiritual quality to our life.

Many western countries are taking this inspiration from India into their own life. That is why older people today sit in meditation, they enjoy these prayer sessions, except for those who are intensely worldly, who have no higher ambition. But many people are turning in this direction to make their life richer and purer. This is India's gift to the world. But let us use it ourselves, right in our life. That is why it is intensely practical to think that though the body has become old and weak, it has to become so, something in us never becomes old and weak. When Bhagwan Buddha was here 2500 years ago, he was about eighty years old when he died. On the eightieth year he told his assistant Ananda: 'Ananda, look at my body—how many hills it has climbed, how many miles it has walked. Now it cannot stand on its own. This is like an old bullock cart which has to be tied with strings to make it move. That has been the case with this body, at one time how much work it has done. Now look at the body.' 'I am not the body which is just like a bullock cart'—this is an Indian attitude. We have to see something deeper than the body. There is something within the body, that is our true Self.

Our body is an external covering—that knowledge is imprinted upon us in our culture. That is why in our language, we say about death: 'I cast away my body', that is how we call 'death'. 'I cast away my body—*maine sharir chod diya'*—that is the way we put it. In the West it is different. 'I cast away my soul'—that is the language in the West. 'I am the body and I cast away my soul'. That is why they preserve the body. They preserve the body, we don't preserve it; we burn it off, for its work is over. That is a wonderful idea of cremation, a tremendous idea from the Vedic times. When the body has finished its work, we just cremate it, it has nothing more to do. We also have a subtle body, the *sukshtna sharira,* and that may take a new gross body. All these ideas are attracting millions of people in the West. This idea was not treated as valid recently. The church tried to destroy this theory. The reincarnation theory was in vogue throughout the Christian world till the sixth century AD. Then an assembly of priests by a majority vote banished this truth from Christianity. Now it is entering through the back door. People are taking this idea because that is the truth. There is something profound within man, he is not just this body. It is an external covering and we call it *sthula sharira*—the gross body. The soul that wears this, remains. So, Krishna says in the *Gita*: When the soul enters into a physical configuration at birth, and when the soul leaves that configuration out, what happens? The sages know that this blind eye, what is called the 'gross eye' cannot see that truth. *Vimudah na'nupasyanti, pasyanti jnana caksusah*—those who have *jnana caksu* (divine or wisdom eye) they are able to see, that what is going away is only the body, the soul is immortal, birthless, deathless, that is the Self. This idea is so impressed upon the minds of the people of India. Say, somebody asks you, 'Do you believe in incarnation?' You will say, 'It is not a question of belief, it is in my blood, it is natural to us.' We go through various aspects of human experiences from childhood onwards—luxuries, comforts, then challenges, sufferings, and so on. By the time we retire from active life, a certain maturity comes, a maturity by which we can feel compassion for the world. If that attitude comes, 'I have done very well with my past, previous years of life, all the struggles, defeats—all have chastened me.' That 'chastening' is a wonderful word. In the youth's mind it is not that quiet, but by the time we become old, it is chastened. What happens then? We can feel compassion for the world—old people feeling compassion for the young people who are struggling, and with a smile we try to help them, bless them because our heart is full. This fulness is real; it leaves no sense of emptiness. That is where spirituality comes in. No mere ritualistic thing can give this to us. It is experience in religion alone that can give us this inner enrichment. That is why a little meditation every day will take that mind away from this external world and slowly make it inward. Somewhere in the depths of consciousṭness God is hidden; let us find it, let us go closer and closer, just as, when some gold is discovered in some jungle, people rush there to take that gold, even facing death on the way. If that is so with gold, why will this not be true with this also? It is a profound truth—the Atman hidden in all of us. I could not attend to it till now, I was busy with the world outside. Now I have some time for this great purpose.' This is how old age becomes an object of envy for the younger people. Young people are active. Nowadays some old people are also active. They compete with young people, naturally they are defeated because the younger people are better than them in running and jumping around; the old people can't do that. But this feeling of inner joy and peace comes to the old people. The young cannot compete with the older persons in that. That is why they become envious, that is good.

The younger generation becomes envious of the older generation because 'the older people have got an opportunity to seek a treasure which the younger generation never had.' When they become old, they should seek that treasure. They become an example for the people of the next generation. This is what is written in our scriptures. In the *Isha Upanishad*, one finds a devotee with a noble mind, struggling to achieve spiritual life throughout his career. Now his life is ending, how is he going to face death? That is a wonderful thing—facing death in a grand manner. He is lying down, and he is thinking, 'Yes, the body is dissolving, it is only a chemistry laboratory, that has been brought together, now the time has come to disband this laboratory. That is the nature of the body.' Then he says, 'O mind! Think of the highest. This body is about to go and fire will reduce it to ashes, its work is over; but O mind, think of the good deeds you have done, the good life you have lived, and think of higher and higher things'—that is how a grand manner of dying is described there—full of positive thinking at the time of death. That is the test of a man's life and how he stayed in this world. So many examples I am getting of people who have displayed wonderful courage at the time of death, with strength of peace coming to them.

In Delhi we had one devotee, who was the Home secretary, Mr. Behl, ICS. His wife, Mrs. Usha Behl, was a very good devotee. Everybody remembers Usha; her grandfather was famous Punjab leader Mahatma Hansraj. Then one day she was diagnosed with cancer. She had been doing wonderful work for our Mission. She was treated for cancer in Switzerland and in Bombay. But there was no hope; it was only spreading. Then one day many people—her husband, relatives and others—went to see her in Bombay and there they talked to her in the room. After some time she said, 'Please bring that picture of Sri Ramakrishna from the wall, I want you to put it in my hand.' They gave it to her. Then she said, 'Would you please go to the next room for a few minutes? I want to be alone for a little while.' And they went to the next room leaving the picture in her hand. When they opened the door after a few minutes, she had gone—she was no more. Her husband felt that to be in that room was like being in a shrine. What a wonderful kind of death! Many others also have experiences like this.

My host in Jalandhar was Mr. Jagannath Tandon, whose wife was Maya Devi. Mr. B.R. Tandon, ICS, who was in the Government of India, was his brother. His son was Subhash Tandon, who was commissioner of Delhi Police for some time. That family was from Karachi. Maya Devi (wife of Jagannath Tandon) was very much devoted and I stayed with them in Jalandhar. What happened in Bombay just three years ago? Both wife and husband got up at 4 am and then they sat singing bhajans for one hour. Then she said to her husband, 'Go to the room and take a little rest. You are tired now, you go.' And then she slept. When he got up, he found Maya Devi was no more. What a courageous manner of giving up the body! She was always a cheerful type of lady, an ex-student of Kanya Maha Vidyalaya of Jalandhar. In Karachi, she used to speak about that college to me. I had spoken there two or three times.

So, in all these things you will see how we shape our life. We don't allow to be carried away by external forces. We know how to be shaped and have full control of the whole system. That is where spirituality comes in. It is a palpable experience; to be spiritual is the aim of religion, not to be just religious. To be religious is very easy. If you put some *tulsi* in the ear or smear some *vibhuti* or *namam,* you are religious. But spirituality is something more.

The younger generation has mostly neglected it till now. Let them not neglect it anymore. That is how even when one is young, one can be spiritual; and when one is old, he becomes intensely spiritual because there are no other things to interfere; then life becomes a joy. The body will get weaker and weaker. There is no doubt that it is the nature of the body to become old. We have got a wonderful intellectual formulation of the subject. Anything that is a combination of parts cannot be eternal. It must separate and go away, that is the idea. What is the body, but a combination of parts? It has got a growth, a development, a decay and finally a departure. Even the sun will one day disappear. The sun has no permanent life, it is a combination of so many elements and these elements separate and they go away. This is the profound truth of six-fold waves of change as given in *Vivekachudamani.* Shankaracharya describes it and says that the Atman is free from the six-fold waves of change. *Shat-bhir-urmibhi*—'Urmi' means wave, 'Shat' means six. *Shatbhirurmibhi*—the Atman is untouched by the six-fold waves of change. What are they? *Jayate-it* is born, then *asti-it* gets the quality of existence; then *vardhate-it* grows; *viparinamate-it* transforms; *apakshiyate-it* declines; *vinashyate-it* dies. But everything in this world is subject to the six-fold waves of change. Only the Atman is free from all this. 'And I am That'—that is the knowledge we are taught in Vedanta. As a child of God, as the Atman, we are That, we are not this tiny body. That is my servant, that is my instrument, that is the house in which I live. That is how the body is valued. When this knowledge is strengthened, though we grow in age, in mind we become younger. It is absolutely possible. I may be physically grown up, but mentally I can be immature. Many people are physically mature, but mentally immature. That is why in our country today this is the quality of human life—physically mature, but mentally immature. On the other hand, in old age, the body becomes weak, but the mind can remain vigorous, and strong. How? Through this spiritual touch. Just behind every man is God, is the Atman. But the mind does not know it. We must learn to look beyond and see. This is the nature of spiritual life.

Children are afraid when they are alone and they cry. When they see that the mother is there, the crying stops. So, the presence of God in man is exactly like the mother behind the child. The child has no fear when he is conscious that his mother is there. He just looks back and says, 'Yes, Mother is behind me.' Otherwise he becomes full of fear. One of the Bengali songs which Sri Ramakrishna used to sing says this: '*Ma aachen aar ami achi bhavna ki ache aamar*'

Mother, i.e., the Divine Mother, is with me. Where is the need for me to worry then? She is always with me; she feeds me and takes care of me. Hence, I have nothing to worry or fear. When I am in darkness, I feel afraid: 'What has happened? What will happen?' Then comes Her gentle hand, giving me consolation that She is holding me; I have nothing to fear.

That is how Sri Ramakrishna has put this idea in the form of a bhajan.

Something behind this body—eternal, infinite—that is God himself. We generally do not take God like this. Instead, we feel that He is far away in the sky or something in the temple, in an image. We forget that He is our inner Self, he is the *antaryamin* like a thread that runs through the entire garland. God is described in the Gita: 'I am the thread that runs through all the pearls.' Through the practice of meditation and spiritual life, we try to realise the nature of the thread—that pure consciousness, one and non-dual, running through all the different things of the universe. That is the Divine and we can approach Him through this inwardness, and that inwardness will give us the experience of the Divine in our normal day-to-day life. Whenever we repeat God's name in the midst of work, we get a new strength. Vivekananda says that when you are working, say, sweeping the floor, doing this work or that work, once in a while you repeat 'Shiva, Shiva'. Remind yourself of your Shiva nature. That is spiritual practice, uttering 'Shiva, Shiva, Shiva'. When you get angry, for example, simply repeat 'Shiva, Shiva', all that anger will go away. That is called a little spiritual infusion coming into the mind at a critical situation. All these constitute spiritual practice. Spiritual practice does not mean that we should go to Rishikesh. At home you can do plenty of spiritual practice in your day-to-day life also. So, this kind of inwardness is necessary. When I am waiting for a bus it takes ten minutes. Why should I become restless? By restlessness the bus will not come early. So, I become calm, a little inwardness comes in, just as much as we can get at that time. In this way, being inward, little by little, throughout the whole day, makes a lot of spiritual practice. This is how we have to shape our life.

Once I addressed an old age home in Cleveland, America. The two girls who were running it said to me, 'Swamiji, please visit the old age home.' So, from the airport I straightway went to the old age home. That was my first experience, and I found high-profile people living there—but absolutely dry life, no joy. There were some eighty chairs and eighteen wheel chairs in their assembly hall. The organisers were not sure many would come that day. But fortunately almost all came that day. Otherwise it is very difficult to persuade them even to leave their rooms and come. But they all came. When I was sitting there, they introduced me. Then I spoke for forty minutes on how to make old age joyous. It is a challenge before them. Vedanta gives you ways to face that challenge. And what those two girls—one black and one white, said later on? They said, 'Swamiji, we have never seen this in our institution till now, that so many of them sat for forty minutes. Normally they sit for one or two minutes and quietly go away. They do not want to continue. But now they have received something worthwhile, and understood something. Then I told them, 'The government can do anything for you to make you happy. But unless you have the *will* to be happy, you cannot be happy. That is where Vedanta comes in. There is a divine spark in all of us, you must know the truth. Then this life will be full of joy.' They have all the facilities, but no will of being joyous or being fulfilled. Therefore, they are in a dry condition of human life. This experience was very revealing to me. In fact, some of our Vedanta devotees wanted to start an old age home near New York. I told the devotees, 'If you do it, you will be contributing something wonderful to America, a sense of joy.' So, my love and good wishes to all of you.

Our Spiritual Heritage

This evening I come before you in a capacity differing somewhat from that of previous occasions when I have lectured at this Institute of Culture. On those occasions I was a guest, but now I am a host, and I am extremely happy to be here in Calcutta, after nearly thirteen years in New Delhi, to work as secretary in this important branch of the Ramakrishna Mission.

The subject of my talk to you this evening, and this talk will be the first of a series of studies of the great spiritual literature of India comprised in the *Upaniṣads* and the *Bhagavad-Gītā*, is one which is in the very spirit of this Institute—'Our Spiritual Heritage'. This Institute seeks to assimilate the spiritual legacy of humanity of both East and West. And part of that legacy of humanity is the eternal legacy of India which is spiritual through and through. The visions which have been embodied in the immortal literature of this country, particularly in the *Upaniṣads* and the *Bhagavad-Gītā,* have something eternal about them. They are the visions of the seers, sages, and thinkers of ancient India. These visions were embodied in a cultural experiment which involved a seventh of the human race. The continuity down the ages, right down to our own time, of this vision of the sages is one of the most impressive features of world history. Other things in world history may come and go, but the visions of the sages of the *Upaniṣads* remain for ever.

So we find that this theme, India's spiritual heritage, is one that is dear to the hearts of men and women in both East and West. In my travels in various countries, the thing that impressed me the most was—this response of the human mind everywhere to India's spiritual heritage. Going beyond all other considerations, whether of geography, history, or political and economic systems, is the appeal of this Indian message to the human heart. There is one India which, like other nations, has its political, social, economic, and other limitations; there is, however, another India, unlimited in range and scope, which has borne witness to the reality of the highest in man and nature, which has bequeathed to the world visions of human glory and greatness. It is these visions which can well form the sheet anchor of man's collective and individual existence in the modern world.

The tremendous response which Swami Vivekananda's utterances aroused in the West was not an isolated or freakish event in history. The modern world has been in search of universal values for *some* centuries. There are today the world over, including the communist countries, as I myself experienced, an increasing number of people, including young people, who respond to the philosophical and spiritual heritage of India when they get a chance to hear or know about it. This message of India has nothing credal, nothing dogmatic or sectarian about it, for it speaks in terms of man's development, his progress, his achievement of the highest excellence. It is just this that the world is waiting for. In Czechoslovakia, people told me that their inherited idea of religion and philosophy had been quite different, and that they had felt greatly impressed with the way the Vedanta expressed the idea of man's development of total excellence. This idea has nothing parochial about it; it is not tied down to any particular credal or social or political expression, but is universal and human. They were very much impressed with these ideas, and their response was immediate.

It is my sad experience that the world knows very little of this aspect of Indian thought. In fact, even in India itself, people do not yet realise what treasures there are in their own heritage. Yet we do not speak of our spiritual heritage merely as a national heritage, as a matter of national glory. When we speak of these things it is the glory of man as man that becomes the theme. Man in India has achieved certain greatnesses, he has scaled great heights of experience, and he has left these as a legacy for the rest of humanity. We do not claim a copyright for them, for the great achievements of man in one place are the achievements of man everywhere. Today we hear much about man climbing Mount Everest and other high peaks. India has climbed the heights of experience and of greatness, and this is her legacy to the whole world, a legacy which has nothing parochial or narrow about it, but which speaks of the highest attainments of the human mind, of human thought, of man's total excellence.

The Challenge of Human Experience

The long line of evolution through which life has passed has revealed to man great visions of beauty, of strength, of power, of greatness. India carried these forward to their highest levels of expression. India asked, ages ago, 'What is the highest excellence of man?' This question was tackled by her with a thoroughness which is very impressive. Man, endowed with a body, with the senses, with various capacities, has yet to rise to the point of his highest excellence, which he has in a small measure even in his very childhood. The achievement of this highest excellence is the product of a converging life endeavour; it is education and religion in one. India tackled this fundamental problem very early in her cultural history through a creative minority of sages and thinkers.

The results of their investigations into this problem have come down to us in that immortal literature, the *Upaniṣads*. This literature is immortal because its theme is immortal. Man's supreme excellence, say the *Upaniṣads,* consists in transcending his limitations of the senses. We have transcended many things. Our animal ancestry we have transcended to some extent in this human psycho-physical organism, but this is not the last, nor the highest, achievement. Even man's technical achievements to date do not touch a fringe of his total possibilities; in spite of these intellectual developments, he has still about him and in him much of the primeval evolutionary, slime; he has to shed much of his animal ancestry. He represents a great advance in evolution, but evolution has still greater heights to scale in him and through him. The present state is only a passing phase; man is not yet; he has to surpass himself and achieve still higher levels of expression.

The *Upaniṣads* took up this challenge, the challenge of human evolution, of deeper levels of human experience, and they forged ahead to scale the peaks of thought and experience. They gave us visions of man's true excellence as consisting in the realisation of his immortal divine nature. This is the theme of the *Upaniṣads,* and this theme they have imparted to a whole cultural experiment, for it became the theme of Indian culture as well. In our time, this theme found glorious expression in Sri Ramakrishna. There is a continuity from the *Upaniṣads* to Sri Ramakrishna, and that continuity is one of the most impressive aspects of world history. No culture can be continuous in historical expression unless it has kept alive within itself the vision of the eternal and the imperishable. Only when a culture raises its edifice on the rock bottom of experience, when it has seen and touched the fundamentals of life, only then does it succeed in ensuring its unity and continuity; then it becomes a beacon light, inspiring human life age after age.

This is how we view the history of India; India tackled life from various angles. Many people have a wrong notion that Indian thought tackled only the idea of man as a religious aspirant, searching for the secret of other-worldly or transcendental values. But that is not correct. We find that the Indian nation experimented with and developed all aspects of life, individual and collective: social organisation, political systems, positive sciences, arts and literature, and various forms of happy, joyous living. The history of India reveals that there was no lack of emphasis on a life of joy; the life of the citizen is to be a happy one from every point of view.

But along with this, another development of thought took place which, starting as a critique of all relativistic views of man and the universe, reached its development in the vision of the One *behind* the many, and its consummation in the vision of the One in the many, the One *as* the many. Having achieved a modicum of security and welfare in the social field, the creative minds of the community began to forge ahead, asking more and more fundamental questions. Is this psycho-social individual, the psyches' physical being, the last stage in evolution? Or can it evolve into something higher still? Of course, these questions were the product of the creative thinking of a few people only, those who had the capacity, the flair, for this type of adventure. It is only a few gifted minds who, in any given society, participate in the quest for fundamental truth; and these may belong to any strata of society. As we turn the pages of the *Upaniṣads,* we come across, 'among its creative thinkers, men, women, and children, intellectuals, kings, and common men. What impresses us is the persistence with which these thinkers ask this one question: What is perfection? What is the highest level of human existence? Endowed with clarity of mind and purity of living, these thinkers achieved the answer to this question through a life of self-discipline and meditation; and in beautiful expositions, impressive dialogues, and fine snatches of poetry they bequeathed it to posterity. This is what has made this literature immortal.

The True Nature of Man

Romain Rolland, in his book, *The Life of Ramakrishna,* writes (Sixth Edition, p.13):

'The man whose image I here evoke was the consummation of two thousand years spiritual life of three hundred million people.'

That a man like Sri Ramakrishna (AD 1836-86) could appear in our time and live such a glorious life is entirely due to the fact of this continuity of India's spiritual tradition. It is a perennial river, flowing down the ages. Many of us, perhaps, do not know it. Many of us, perhaps, have not been able to take advantage of it. For some it is too lofty a theme. But all who hear about it look up to it in wonder and in admiration. There is a verse in the *Bhagavad-Gītā* (II. 29) which says:

Āścaryavat paśyati kaścidenam
āścaryavat vadati tathaiva cānyaḥ;
Āścaryavat cainam anyaḥ śṛṇoti
śrutvāpyenaṁ veda na caiva kaścit

'Some look upon this Ātman as a wonder, some speak of it as a wonder, some hear of it as a wonder, but, in spite of all this, few truly know this Truth, the eternal glory of man!'

What, then, is this 'eternal glory of man'? It is his inborn divine nature, birthless, deathless, pure, and holy. He is not the body, nor the senses; these are but the instruments of his manifestation and action in the spatio-temporal world. He is the limitless One expressing itself through the little finite forms of body and mind. This is the true nature of man. This is not a mere philosophical concept, but a realised fact. All sensitive minds are inspired by these ideas. They inspired people at the time when the Upaniṣads were composed; they inspired people a thousand years later; and today, after three or four thousand years, they still inspire us. Neither the phenomenal progress of science and technology, nor the wealth and power of the modern world, has been able to reduce the relevancy of these ideas of the *Upaniṣads;* they have only increased it. The world is seeking for precisely this spiritual growth for man; it is the only means of breaking through the stagnation which has come upon the human mind. The human mind has lost its bearings in the delusion of wealth and power', *pramādyantaṁ vittamohena mūḍham (Kaṭha Upaniṣad,* II. 6). Continued stagnation means death. So the Upaniṣads give us their gospel of hope for man through their grand theme: Man shall have wealth; man shall have power; man shall have all this; but he shall not get lost in any one of these. These are the means, not the end; he shall break through the crust of experience, and realise the Ātman, his divine Self, which is Sat-Cit-Ānanda, Existence-Knowledge-Bliss. Thus do the *Upaniṣads* show us the way to creative living and life fulfilment.

Creative living is a beautiful term, but what is 'creative'? Merely doing the same things over and over again does not indicate creativity. The body, the senses, the nervous system, their recurring excitements and titillations, do not make for creative living. Some time or other we have to break through the prison wall of body and mind. Then we reach true creativity, and it is this type of creativity that the Upaniṣads represent. That is why the Upaniṣads are inspiring to the modern man and woman.

Those who are modern fall into two categories. First, there are those who are modern simply because they use modern amenities. That is the ordinary meaning of the word 'modern'. But there is another meaning, a more profound meaning, to this word. In this second meaning the modern man is he who is nourished on the spirit of science, who is alert of mind and on the track of truth, who has the capacity to question, 'to seek, ask, and knock' as Jesus expresses it. That man is modern who is inquisitive, who has a passion for truth and the power of rational investigation, who never takes things for granted but always strives to get at the heart of things; his heart constantly asks, 'What next? What next?' Such a modern mind is the mind that is closest to the spirit of the *Upaniṣads*. For in the *Upaniṣads* too there is this atmosphere of alertness, this mood of constant seeking, a deep passion for truth, a constant desire to forge ahead and not take things for granted in a complacent spirit. It is here that you find the close kinship between the Upaniṣads and the modern spirit.

So we find today that scientific thinkers, those who continually seek for deeper vistas of truth, those who strive to take life to higher levels of expression, when they become acquainted with the literature of the *Upaniṣads,* they become charmed, fascinated. Swami Vivekananda (AD 1863-1902), referring to the *Upaniṣads*, said (Complete *Works,* Vol. HI, Eighth Edition, p. 110):

'If there is one word in the English language to express the effect which the literature of India produces upon mankind, it is this one word fascination.'

The reason for that fascination is precisely that they draw the mind up to something higher, purer, loftier. The *Upaniṣads* send out a clarion call to lead us ever upward and onward. In the

Kaṭha Upaniṣad (III. 14) we read: *Uttiṣṭhata! Jāgrata! Prāpya varān nibodhata!* 'Arise! Awake! And enlighten yourself by approaching the great ones!'

The Moving Power of the Spirit

This is the clarion call which the modern man needs to carry him forward out of the present stagnation. This fact of stagnation is a recurring phenomenon in world history. Civilisations sometimes get stuck up in the mud of finite values, and become stagnant; and history tells us that there is only one way by which to overcome the deadlock. No political methods, nor social, economic, or financial manipulations can help to redeem man from such crises; these can be temporary palliatives at best; but they cannot raise a culture or a civilisation from its stagnation and impart to it creative dynamism. The malady is a spiritual malady; its remedy also lies in the spiritual sphere. There is only one method of effecting a remedy, and that is to bring the power of, the indwelling spirit to bear upon the psycho-physical organism, as, also upon the psycho-social organism, the machine of our collective life.

This is what India did again and again. Repeatedly in Indian history we get evidence of the expressions of this power of the spirit to move a static world and make it dynamic. In the *Bhagavad-Gītā* (IV. 8), for example, Śrī Kṛṣṇa says: *Dharmasamsthāpanārthāya saṁbhavāmi yuge yuge*—'I come age after age to establish righteousness in the world.' When life becomes static, and moves in the narrowest circle possible, then God, the indwelling Spirit in man and nature, comes once again and imparts a new dynamism to the social process which then develops a new assimilative power and manifests fresh energy of movement.

Another illustration of the power of the spirit to make the world dynamic may be seen in the example and words of Buddha (563-483 BC), who appeared about a thousand years after Śrī Kṛṣṇa. At Sarnath, in his first discourse after his enlightenment, Buddha spoke of his mission as the 'setting in motion of the wheel of *dharma*'. The very title of the discourse is significant: *Dharmacakrapravartana Sutra*—'Discourse on the setting in motion of the wheel of *dharma*'. *Dharma* is conceived as a wheel, and human life, collective as well as individual, is conceived as a cart on wheels. A wheel gets stuck in a muddy road and will not move until a strong shoulder comes and pushes it. So a society or an individual may get stuck in the little things and trivial enjoyments of the body and the senses. History tells us that the Roman society decayed and fell for just this reason, and we find similar periods in our own history also. Lost in enjoyment and pleasure, and losing sight of the higher values of life, society stagnates and dies. So Buddha, in his discourse at Sarnath, said: 'Come, let us put our shoulders to the wheel, and make it move.' The very concept of the wheel implies something in motion. Buddha said: 'I have come to set the wheel of *dharma* in motion.' Śrī Kṛṣṇa said: 'I have come to set in motion the power of *dharma.*' And it is just this that has happened again and again in Indian history. What did Sri Ramakrishna do in our time? Apparently he did nothing; he lived a quiet life, outside the political and social movements of his time. But the energies that he created and released from his inner life powerfully influenced men and movements around him, and bid fair, at the not too distant future, to transform the modern world itself. He lived the life of the spirit in all its intensity and extensity, and showed the authenticity of man's spiritual life. He demonstrated the true purpose and function of religion, and the harmony between the different religions, and showed that there is no need to quarrel and fight in the name of religion. Quarreling and fighting make of religion a sham. But religion is not a sham. It invites man to the highest adventure in life, the realisation of his true freedom, which is the freedom of the spirit.

Physically and socially, man is not free; he is conditioned by external and internal factors. Freedom is in our spiritual nature. That is our true nature, immortal and divine, and we must realise it in life. This alone is true progress, development; this alone is true religion. This great idea Sri Ramakrishna lived, and, in so living, imparted such a power to it that, when other people received this idea, they received that power as well. They became convinced of the authenticity of this idea because Sri Ramakrishna had actually lived it.

This is the way by which a static society becomes dynamic and is made to move again. As blood flows through a healthy body, so through the body politic must flow the blood of spiritual life. A great teacher comes, and with him comes great power, a new influx of energy. We start moving once again, and the stagnation begins to vanish. Once more man begins to seek the higher values of life. In the wake of the great teacher come creative individuals who ask deep questions, and strive to discover the answers for themselves: What is the true nature of man? How can man realise it? What is his destiny and how can he achieve it? Is spirituality the prerogative of only a few, select, gifted individuals? Or is it the prerogative of everyone?

The *Upaniṣads* boldly proclaim that spirituality is the prerogative of every individual. This Ātman, the divine, the immortal, is the Self of every man and woman and child. It is the true nature of man It is also the true nature of all animals, but animals cannot realise it. It is only man with his unique psycho-physical system, aided by the psycho-social environment created by himself in the course of his evolution, that has the capacity to realise this truth. *Man is specially fitted for this great adventure.* He has certain advantages, and when he starts using these advantages he is able to rise to the highest level of spiritual life. The *Upaniṣads* tell us that wealth and power are not the highest glory of man. The *Upaniṣads* do not condemn man's pursuit of worldly wealth and power; they never condemn any values pursued by man. Only they say, 'There is something better and higher than these'. The *Upaniṣads* ever urge us to go on to the realisation of this something better within us. Sri Ramakrishna, in one of his parables, tells the story of a woodcutter who, going into the forest to cut wood, was told by a holy man to go forward. Following this advice, in due course the woodcutter came across, first, a sandalwood forest, then, a silver mine, then, a gold mine, and, going deeper still into the forest, he found at last a diamond mine, and became exceedingly rich. Telling this story, Sri Ramakrishna said, 'Therefore I say that, in whatever stage of life you may be, you will realise better and purer things if only you go deeper and deeper *into* yourself'.

The Need for Broad-based Education

If Indian culture is strong today, even in this highly advanced age of science and technology, it is because India has not forgotten this teaching. The way forward for India today is the assimilation into her own ancient culture of the best that is in modern western culture. But India can do this only if she is conscious of her own heritage, if she has become inspired and strengthened by that heritage. The source of this heritage, so far as literature goes, is the *Upaniṣads,* and a study of the *Upaniṣads* is one of the most rewarding studies for man today, in both East and West.

As far as India is concerned, this study will bring to her children an acquaintance with those basic values which have shaped their history and which are sustaining them even today. We, perhaps, are inclined to take those values for granted, just like the air we breathe. But culture is not like that. It requires education; it requires assimilation. It is this education in, and assimilation of, their own cultural values that will give to Indian men and women of this age the power to handle the forces of the modern world, to tame and harness them in the service of human happiness and welfare within India and outside. And so the need for every educated citizen of this country is to understand and assimilate the *Upaniṣads* and the *Bhagavad-Gītā;* not merely to study them as literature, or even as philosophy, but to enter into their spirit and to breathe in unison with their breath.

When we become strong in our own inheritance, we shall feel the strength to take in also the legacy which the West, from the time of the Greeks to the modern age, has left for us. For today, legacies are not parochial. Today, every cultural legacy is a human legacy for the whole world. The world has become so small that all provincial barriers are anachronisms today. Every achievement in any part of the world becomes a legacy for the whole world. So the whole human heritage has to become the subject of education for every individual today. A boy or girl going to school and college in India today studies the western heritage through science, sociology, and various other subjects; thus our boys and girls become the recipients of the best thought of the western world. In the same way, the education of the western boy or girl must be broadened to include the rich cultural heritage of India. It is broad-based education of this kind that will solve the problems of the modern world. Provincialism, which has done so much harm to the world in the past, will thus be completely eliminated, and the world turned in the direction of global unity.

As far as India is concerned, we have been fortunate to have had thinkers, and some of the greatest of them appeared in this modern age, who have placed before us this broad objective. From Raja Rammohun Roy (AD 1774-1833) to Swami Vivekananda, each one of these modern thinkers has been proud of India's heritage and yet has told us, in all humility, to sit at the feet of other nations of the modern world and learn the legacy which is theirs to give.

These great leaders of modern India will not permit us to be parochial. They did not ask us to be proud only of our own heritage; they asked us to open our minds to receive the best that the world has to give. They also told us that *the capacity to assimilate modern western culture is directly proportionate to our prior assimilation of our own* culture. Without a proper understanding of our own culture, we shall never be able to enter the soul of another culture, nor profit from it. This is, unfortunately, what we see happening today. Our capacity to assimilate the best of western culture is very little, because most of us, through our faulty education, did not get the opportunity to understand our own culture, to be acquainted with the great thoughts behind our own culture. Our education is largely cut off from the currents of our own cultural inheritance. The nation is trying to remedy this; but it is a fact that an educated citizen of India today is mostly ignorant of the fundamentals of his own culture, of his own traditions. I found this to be true of large numbers of Indian students I came across in foreign countries, and I have heard from several western friends, and I have also read in newspaper articles written by western well-wishers of India, that Indian students and Indian diplomatic personnel in countries abroad are most inadequately equipped in their knowledge of India and her culture. In the absence of the strength which comes from an assimilation of one's cultural inheritance, when we try to take in western culture, what is taken in proves to be only the cheaper side of that culture, and not the strength that is behind that culture. That *strength we can touch only on the basis of our own strength.*

This defect in our education must be remedied. As far as our schools and colleges are concerned, it will take some time for us to remedy it. But the general citizen can remedy this defect for himself by opening his mind and heart to the rich legacy which is his in his own literary and artistic inheritance. If the Upaniṣads had not been written, if the sages had simply thought these thoughts and passed away, it is probable that the atmosphere of India would still have contained those thoughts, but most of us would not have been able to come into touch with them. A gifted soul like Sri Ramakrishna is able to open his mind to the wonderful vibrations of thought which the seers have left behind, but ordinary people cannot do that. Fortunately for us, and for all humanity, the mighty thoughts of these sages were written down, enabling you and me to receive this communication from them. The inheritance of culture comes through communication, through the language of symbols, literary and artistic. Man can communicate his experience to coming generations, and this is how he acquires culture, the cummulative effect of inherited tradition. Through communication and transmission, a culture goes on growing and developing, getting richer and richer in the process. Today we have the opportunity to live in the atmosphere in which the sages lived by studying the great literature which they have left as a legacy to us. Reading the *Upaniṣads* today, we also may have an experience of 'sitting close to those teachers', which is the literal meaning of the term *upanisad.*

A Message of Fearlessness

The *Upaniṣads* stand in a class by themselves. They are immortal literature, and so we call them the *Śrutis*, the truths realised in transcendental experience beyond the reach of the senses and the sense-bound mind, but realisable by the pure mind. These truths are universal and perennial and will always inspire humanity. Today, the opportunity has come through modern means of communication, modern methods of transmitting ideas, to effect the widest diffusion of this immense fund of inspiration. Before Swami Vivekananda's time, very few people knew about the Vedānta, about the philosophy of the *Upaniṣads*. He took it upon himself to proclaim these truths from the housetops, both in the East and in the West (Complete Works, Vol. III, *ibid.,* p. 238):

'Let me tell you that we want strength, strength, and every time strength. And the *Upaniṣads* are the great mine of strength. Therein lies strength enough *to* invigorate the whole world; the whole world can be vivified, made strong, energised through them. They will call with trumpet voice upon the weak, the miserable, and the downtrodden of all races, all creeds, and all sects, to stand on their own feet and be free. Freedom, physical freedom, mental freedom, and spiritual freedom are the watchwords of the Upaniṣads.'

Śaṅkarācārya (AD 788-820) was the first teacher in historic times to make the *Upaniṣads* popular in this country. Before that, only a few select people, largely of the monastic community, knew the glory of the *Upaniṣads*. But Śaṅkarācārya opened up these treasures to householders and to all citizens. It will do them good, he said. But still the *Upaniṣads* reached only a small minority.

Today, however, thanks largely to the work of Swami Vivekananda, they are the property of one and all. They are there, in almost every Indian language, as also in English and several other foreign languages, for all who care to take them and be nourished by them. Proclaims Vivekananda *(ibid.,* p.225):

'The truths of the Upaniṣads are before you. Take them up, live up to them, and the salvation of India will be at hand.'

The *Upaniṣads,* however, require close study. A newspaper is also a kind of literature; but it is read in the morning and thrown away in the evening, and thus stands at the lowest level of the literary spectrum. The *Upaniṣads* are not like that; they stand at the highest end of that spectrum. They must be read again and again; every step in growth of mental maturity and clearness brings us closer and closer to the heart of this great literature. The more we read them, the more we get out of them, because their words come from the depths of the heart, 'Where words come out from the depth of truth,' says Tagore in his *Gītāñjali.* The words of the *Upaniṣads* come out from the depth of truth. The sages experienced Truth; they *saw* something profound in man and nature, and they tried to capture and communicate this vision in snatches of poetry. The sublime poetry of the *Upaniṣads* has moved the hearts of thinkers and poets from ancient times to the present. Take this verse from the *Muṇḍaka Upaniṣad* (II. ii. 7):

Yaḥ sarvajñaḥ sarvavid yasyaiṣa mahimā bhuvi

'He, the all-knowing One, the all-seeing One, whose glory is this universe.'

But is His glory confined only to nature outside, nature spread out in space and time? No, says the *Upaniṣad;* His glory is specially manifest in man himself, in the profound depths of his being:

Divye brahmapure hyeṣa vyomnyātmā pratiṣṭhitaḥ

'This Ātman, the Self of man, is established in the luminous city of Brahman, which is the heart of man.'

His presence is felt through speech and mind and thought: *Manomayaḥ prāṇaśarīranetā pratīṣṭhito'nne hrdayaṁ sannidhāya*—'He manifests as mind and thought; the psychic and vital energy in the human system functions in and through Him; and, present in the heart, He animates the physical body of man'.

Then the verse concludes with a beautiful, joyous note:

Tadvijñānena paripaśyanti dhīrā
ānandarūpam amṛtaṁ yadvibhāti

'The wise ones realise. Him everywhere, inside as well as outside, Him whose form is bliss and immortality and whose glory overflows as the visible universe.'

The word *dhīrā* in the text means 'the wise one' and indicates a combination of intelligence and courage. The *Upaniṣads* speak of man's greatness in two forms: first, his intelligence by which he understands the facts of the outer and inner worlds; second, his courage, heroism, by which he not merely knows but also achieves truth and excellence. Mere intelligence is not enough; courage is also necessary. Their combination makes for the highest character where the power of knowledge becomes transmuted into the energy of vision.

The capacity to scale the Everest of experience, to scale the highest peak of truth, comes to intelligence only when it blazes forth as courage. He is the *dhīrā,* the wise one; he alone is entitled to realise the Ātman. What is the form of that realisation? *Pariṭpaśyanti,* 'he realises Him everywhere', inside as well as outside, in man as well as in nature. The whole of nature becomes ablaze with divinity to his purified vision. He realises Him as *ānandarūpam amṛtaṁ yadvibhāti,* 'of the form of bliss and immortality which has overflown as nature, as the visible universe'. The universe becomes transformed into waves and waves of bliss;

into waves of bliss, *ānandalaharī,* and waves of beauty, *saundaryalaharī,* as expressed by Śaṅkarācārya. The Ātman shines in man and nature, in the sun and moon and stars, in every particle of dust. Now here is a vision captured in a snatch of poetry. This is just a sample; there are scores of such in the *Upaniṣads*.

This beautiful poetry of the *Upaniṣads* is the vehicle of the most profound thought. That thought cannot be penetrated easily. A superficial reading will not suffice; constant study and constant probing are required. In this study we are not studying a bit of nature outside of ourselves, like physics or chemistry. We are studying nature as expressed in our personality, and searching for the very core of that personality; our study relates to something very closely connected with ourselves, our development, fulfilment, our total realisation. Every sentence in the *Upaniṣads* has something corresponding to the deep-felt urges in ourselves. Śaṅkarācārya tells us in his *Brahma-Sūtra bhāṣya* that Brahman, the Absolute, which is the theme of the *Upaniṣads* and the starting point of the *Brahma-Sūtras,* is not an abstract truth remote from us and from our daily lives, but is a given datum of experience as the inner Self of all.

So there is great need for us to study this legacy, to understand it. The whole country will become galvanised with a new energy, a new resolve, a new discipline, even if only a little of the wisdom of the *Upaniṣads* can come into our lives. We read in the *Bhagavad-Gītā* (II. 40): *Svalpamapyasya dharmasya trāyate mahato bhayāt*—'Even a little of this *dharma* will save us from great fear.' Here is the message of fearlessness, of strength, of growth, development, and realisation. Man must rise higher and higher and reach out towards perfection which is the unity of all-encompassing love and knowledge. This is the message, the clarion call, of the Upaniṣads—a call to dynamic action in the pursuit of Truth and total excellence, a call to carry forward evolution to the level of total life fulfilment through spiritual realisation. What a hopeful message it is!

Universal Man

The *Upaniṣads* summon man to a constant struggle to gain the highest, the struggle to achieve the eternal, the permanent, the immortal imbedded in life and experience. Other races and other cultures have spoken of man as a dominator of external nature, as a creator of values in the context of man's collective life. In Greek thought, for example, we have the concept of the Promethean spirit, the power of the human spirit to overcome external obstacles and establish man's supremacy over the forces of nature and, if necessary, over the forces of other human beings as well. The great defect in this line of thought, when pursued by itself, is that it does not carry all humanity together. It is based on the concept of man dominating everything external to himself; it does not stress the need to chasten and overcome the ego which results from such domination of his external environment. Man dominating his environment is a valid concept; it is a form of human excellence. The West has carried it to the highest level of expression; and we in India stand in great need of education in this excellence on a nation-wide scale. But this *is* not the highest that man is capable of; Indian thought will not accord it the highest point in the scale of human excellence. That point involves the transcendence of the ego and the emergence of the universal within man. When man achieves supreme self-transcendence he finds that there is nobody to dominate. He finds that he is one with all, for he has realised the Self in all.

In other words, he discovers himself as the Universal Man, integrated within and without, and himself pulsating in the heart of man and nature. The liberation of this Universal Man out of the common men and women that we are is the aim of the *Upaniṣads*. It is this that makes the *Upaniṣads* of such contemporary interest and importance today. Universal Man is the theme of all progressive thinking today, and so the Upaniṣads stand in the forefront of all progressive thought in the modern world. Man, who has been completely submerged in nationalistic, racial, sectarian, or various other forms of limiting milieus, needs to be redeemed. Swami Vivekananda shared with modern man the glory of this Vedantic message and showed what blessings it could confer on modern society. He also taught how to make this philosophy practical in workaday life. So a study of this profound literature, the *Upaniṣads* and the *Bhagavad-Gītā,* an intelligent study of the philosophy imbedded in it—the Vedanta—in relation to contemporary thought and needs, will prove a rewarding experience for men and women everywhere.

The Spiritual Life of The Indian People*

Introduction

I have been asked to speak on *The Spiritual Life of the Indian People*. That you have chosen this subject is indicative of your keen desire to have a closer insight into the life and thought of the people of a country, from which you of Japan have derived a large part of your own spiritual life. And no better subject could have been chosen for this purpose; for religion has formed and still forms the keynote of the music of Indian national life; and no understanding of India will be adequate or proper which does not impart an insight into the spiritual life of her people.

India: Its Immensity and Variety

Two things I would request you to bear in mind constantly: one, the vastness of India in size and population; two, its long history

---

*Lecture delivered at Tokyo University, Japan, on 30 September 1958, and at the Naprastek Museum Hall, Prague, Czechoslovakia, on 23 June 1961.

running into over five thousand years. These two facts have imparted an amazing diversity to Indian culture and life. From the snowy peaks of the Himalayas in the north, to the land's end, the Cape Comorin or Kanyākumāri, on the Indian Ocean in the far south, a length of about 2,000 miles, from the jungles of Assam on the border of Burma (now Myanmar) in the east to the deserts of Rajasthan and the beautiful valley of Kashmir on the border of Pakistan in the west, a distance of over 1,800 miles, India contains a wide variety of climate, flora, and fauna, of culture, language, and human types. This vast land and its people have the pressure or the stimulus of over five thousand years of history and tradition behind them, a long history, during which the national mind has had the opportunity to experience life from various angles and various levels—prosperity and adversity, victory and defeat, freedom and subjection, knowledge and ignorance, illumination and darkness. The people had been taught one great lesson by their earliest leaders and thinkers, namely, that the object of life is not pleasure or pain, but knowledge, through a dispassionate study of both.

The Philosophic Temper of the Indian People

The people of India have more or less accepted this outlook on life, the thinking people more and the ordinary people less, for which the land became known abroad as a land of philosophers; for that attitude is the characteristic of a scientific and philosophic mind. Equipped with such a mind and temper, an individual achieves a greater and deeper measure of maturity of knowledge and outlook, the longer his life and the more varied his experience. Without this temper of reflection, long life means only long existence, nothing more; it just means a repetition of the first round of experience, not capable of producing maturity of outlook and chastening of mind and heart.

The English poet Wordsworth referred to this chastening process when he sang (*Lines above Tintern Abbey*):

For I have learned
To look on Nature, not as in the hour
Of thoughtless youth; but hearing oftentimes
The still sad music of humanity,
Nor harsh nor grating, though of ample power
To chasten and subdue.

This is true not only of individuals, but also of nations and cultures. Cultures, with violence imbedded in their hearts, represent the failure to capture this maturity of philosophic temper. Fortunately for India, her teachers and leaders, from the great sages of the *Upaniṣads* and Rāma and Kṛṣṇa of the prehistoric past, through Buddha and Śaṅkara of the historic period, to Ramakrishna and Vivekananda of our own times, have helped her people to capture this mood and temper, which accounts for the compassion and humanism in her culture and her spirit of tolerance and peace.

The Upaniṣads, and the Science of Religion

It was the great sages of the *Upaniṣads* who first expounded the science and philosophy of man's spiritual life; this was about five hundred to a thousand years before Buddha. Religious acts of worship and ritual, and religious beliefs of myth and legend, obtained even before the *Upaniṣads*, in the early Vedic and the pre-Vedic or Mohenjodāro periods. In fact, such expressions of religion are co-extensive with human existence itself; they characterise the life of all men from the primitive to the advanced. *But questioning these religious acts and beliefs, bringing a meaning out of them through comparison and contrast, and grading them into stages according to their spiritual content—in short, the development of a science of religion, of a full psychology and philosophy of religion—these were achieved first in the* Upaniṣads *or Vedanta, and later in various other limited formulations.*

The practice of meditation, sitting with eyes closed and mind indrawn, was prevalent in India five thousand years ago, during the Mohenjodāro period, which has yielded, through excavations, the statue of a god sitting in *yoga* pose, with eyes closed and mind indrawn and surrounded by tame and wild animals, much like the image of Śiva of the later ages. The *Ṛg-Veda* largely depicts a religion of worship and prayer and praise of the various gods of its pantheon, in the context of a close kinship of nature, gods, and men. It is a religion of this-worldliness aiming at health, wealth, and welfare of man in society. The worshipper keeps his eyes open and directs them to the gods of wind, rain, and sunshine in the sky. It was marked by simplicity and spontaneity. These two forms of religion became accepted by Vedānta as two valid expressions of the religious impulse All the higher religions of the world contain these two phases, often living apart and unreconciled, with the claims of this world standing in sharp contrast with those of the world beyond. Judaism, Christianity, Islam, Zoroastrianism, Buddhism, and Hinduism have these two elements in them, the social, and the trans-social or mystical, in varying proportions, with a rule-of-thumb method of adjustment between them. According to the preponderance of these two elements, the world religions can be broadly classified as mystical or non-mystical. Hinduism, Buddhism, and Christianity belong to the mystical type, while Judaism, Islam, and Zoroastrianism belong to the non-mystical. In the same country, there may be both types of religions present, like Shintoism and Buddhism in Japan and Confucianism and Taoism in China, with mutual adjustment based on social expediency rather than philosophic necessity.

The Innate Divinity of Man

The *Upaniṣads* carried the development of the mystical religion to its highest point, where they discovered the real Self in man behind his apparent self, the former immortal, ever pure, and ever free, while the latter finite, mortal, and bound. And they declared the great truth that *Man is Divine,* which was echoed centuries later in the declaration of Buddha that *nirvana* is the *birthright of every being,* and still later in that of the New Testament: 'The Kingdom of Heaven is within you.' If Divinity is the inmost core of man, the path to it lies through the withdrawal of the senses and the mind from the world of sensate experience and turning their energies inward in a supreme effort of concentration. By such inward penetration, man achieves realisation of his true nature, the non-dual, immortal, changeless, and pure Ātman, behind his apparent self of changeful individuality. This is the well-known *yoga* technique and achievement as expounded in Vedānta, of which one of the most glorious examples was Buddha.

The Spiritual Unity of the 'Within' and the 'Without' of Nature

But the *Upaniṣads* did not stop there; they asked the important question as to the true nature of the world outside as well. Their knowledge of the Divine within helped them to penetrate into the nature of the world without, for, as Arthur Eddington tells us, at the farthest limits of our knowledge of the external world, we realise that 'consciousness is the first and most direct thing in experience; all else is remote inference'; or, as Jeans tells us, 'in the last resort, those waves which we describe as light-waves, and those other waves which we interpret as the waves of an electron and proton, also consist of knowledge, knowledge about photons, electrons, and protons respectively.' The answer the *Upaniṣads* received to that question raised the thought of Vedānta to supreme philosophic heights. They discovered Divinity at the core of the world as well, as they had earlier discovered it at the core of the human soul. The universe, to their purified vision, revealed itself as spiritual through and through. Nature was Divine and man was Divine. Thus God became the unity of man and nature; their duality was relegated to partial, limited knowledge, revealed through the prism of the senses and the sense-bound mind. When viewed without these human limitations, the world is Divine. This conclusion the *Upaniṣads* couched in some of the most pithy and majestic utterances: *Sarvaṁ khalu idaṁ brahma,* 'All this is verily Brahman (the spiritual Absolute)'; *Ekam eva advitīyam*—'One only, without a second'; *Neha nānāsti kiñcana*—'There is not the least duality here'; *Ayam ātmā brahma*—'This Self is Brahman'; *Satyaṁ jñ ānam anantaṁ brahma*—'Brahman is Truth, Knowledge, and Infinity'; and *Brahmaivedam amṛtam*—'All this universe is Brahman, the Immortal.'

Yoga as the Science and Art of the Spiritual Life

Thus the *Upaniṣads* bridged the gulf between man and nature by proclaiming the solidarity and oneness of all existence. This one great idea precluded the maintenance of the whole host of those sharp distinctions between this world and the next, the non-mystical and the mystical, reason and faith, life and religion, as also between religion and religion and faith and faith. It was left to Śrī Kṛṣṇa, a few centuries later, to gather up these apparently diverse spiritual elements in a sweeping synthesis of a comprehensive spirituality in the *Bhagavad Gītā.* The *Gītā* achieves the synthesis of the mystical and non-mystical religious elements, of the 'Shintoistic' and 'Buddhistic' elements of all religions, in a comprehensive spirituality based on the metaphysics of the *Upaniṣads*. This is the *yoga* of the *Gītā,* as different from the Pātañjala and other *yogas. Yoga* in the *Gītā* is the science and art of the spiritual life. In the light of this total vision, the *Gītā* discovered two different manifestations of the spiritual life; one in the form of social ethics, which the *Gītā* broadly designates as *dharma;* the other, in the form of trans-social spiritual striving, which it designates as *amṛta.* In the first, man learns to chasten his emotions and thoughts, through the discharging of his family and social responsibilities, and experiences the delights thereof. This spiritual education gives him an experience of self-transcendence within the context of his social life itself, a rising from the limited, truncated ego to the largeness and fullness of a social personality. The only austerity he is called upon to undertake at this stage is the austerity of expansion of his interests and affections; it is the austerity involved in love and service; and it is always sought in the context of delight and joy. He is required to cultivate active virtues; for manliness is the end sought to be achieved in this sphere.

When his social personality has become fully developed, when he has achieved manliness, he is called upon to enter the next stage of spiritual education through a direct confrontation with the divinity within. This harder path becomes easy to tread after the achievement of manliness in the earlier stage. There is a change in forms and techniques here, consequent on the change in the field of action. Calm endurance of external circumstances with a view to fitting the mind to penetrate the internal core of his being becomes the virtue to be developed. The emphasis shifts from active to passive virtues, from action to contemplation, from love of society to love of solitude, without, however, involving any hatred of society as such. This training imparts a depth to the human personality, a stability and strength to man's character, and a tranquillity and poise to his bearing; for he is reaching out to the centre of all power and energy within him, his true Self. Every step gained in this direction makes him more peaceful, more joyful, more compassionate, and more efficient. When, at last, he gains the vision of the Self, he becomes illumined, with all bondages of the heart destroyed and all finiteness transcended. He realises an infinite individuality, the culmination of the process which had started with education through social ethics. Herein is the achievement of the full meaning of the Delphic exhortation: 'Man, know thyself.' 'The man of spiritual vision perceives equality everywhere, realising the Self in all beings and all beings in the Self', says the (VI. 29). 'One who perceives all beings in the Self and Self in all beings will not, in virtue of that realisation, hate anyone or practise dissimulation. When, to that knowing sage, who has realised supreme unity, all beings have become the Self, what delusion, what grief, can afflict him?, says the *Īśā Upaniṣad* (6-7).

Unity of Action and Contemplation

Thus has the *Gītā* gathered up the two-fold Vedic *dharma,* which is representative of the two-fold forms of all religions, the social, and the trans-social or mystical, *dharma* and *amṛta,* in a comprehensive statement of human spiritual life. Vedānta very aptly designates these two forms of all world religions as *pravṛtti dharma* and *nivṛtti dharma*—religion of social action and religion of inward contemplation.

Vedānta holds that every man and woman has to pass through the discipline of these two *dharmas* in order to achieve spiritual fulfilment. Both social ethics and mystical spirituality become the earlier and later phases of one continuous spiritual education of the human soul; there is not, and never can be, in the view of Vedānta, any conflict between them. Conflict arises only when one takes a limited view of the scope of human life, or when one refuses to move to higher levels of life expression; in short, conflict arises from stagnation at any particular level.

The *Upaniṣads* described life as a dynamic movement, and used the symbol of the chariot with its horses and driver to illustrate its dynamic nature. They discovered a goal to all this movement, physical, social, and spiritual, and called that goal the achievement of freedom and fullness, Self-realisation, or God-realisation.

Ācārya Śaṅkara (AD 788-820), the greatest philosopher of India, refers to this two-fold form of religion in the Introduction to his commentary on the *Bhagavad-Gītā:*

'The Vedic *dharma* is verily twofold, characterised by *pravṛtti* (social action) and *nivṛtti* (inward contemplation), designed to promote order in the world; this twofold *dharma* has in view the true social welfare and spiritual emancipation of all beings.'

The Four Yogas

The classification of religion into *pravṛtti* and *nivṛtti* was based on the felt interests and longings in the heart of man. Vedānta also makes another classification of religion based on temperament and inclination. This is the wellknown classification into the four *yogas of jñāna* (philosophy), *bhakti* (devotion), *rāja* (concentration and psychic control), and *karma* (dedicated action). Buddhism in its Theravāda form and certain aspects of Vedānta belong to the *jñāna* type; Christianity, popular Hinduism, Islam, Judaism, Zoroastrianism, and Mahāyāna Buddhism belong to the *bhakti* type; *rāja-yoga* and *karma-yoga* enter into the above two expressions in a general way, though they are not absent in their specific forms among a certain type of seekers both in ancient and in modern times. The active type of men and women, of an extra-religious or extra-philosophical temperament, have always resorted to the pure form of *karma-yoga;* similarly, the contemplative type of men and women, who are extra-religious and extra-philosophical, have always been drawn to the *rāja-yoga* for its experimental attractions.

Vedānta holds that this classification is not exclusive, but it rests on the predominance of a particular temperament and inclination. In a further reduction, Vedānta and the *Gītā* speak only of two *yogas:* the *yoga* of *jñāna* and the *yoga of bhakti,* to the latter of which is joined *karma* and *rāja yogas.*

The Pre-eminence of Bhakti

The *Gītā* expounds the latter of the two as the royal spiritual path for the majority of men and women, giving them a scheme of practical spirituality leading to breadth of outlook, strength of character, and efficiency of actiony. The guidance of *jñāna* or philosophy, however, is always to be there as its background. The devotee here is moved by love of God, God who dwells as the inner Self of all beings and in all nature; to that God of love he dedicates his life and actions; with Him he seeks to commune in prayer, song, and meditation; and Him he seeks to serve in all His creatures.

This is the characteristic religious attitude and temper of the majority of the Indian people, as it is also the characteristic attitude and temper of the majority of the religious people of the world.

Unity in Diversity

It is against this ideological background that we have to view the spiritual life of the Indian people. The first thing that strikes us is the vast diversity of its expressions. India did not believe in uniformity of type either in religion or in culture. It believed in a variety of expressions held together by a central thread of unity.

This idea derives from its philosophy, which holds that *unity in variety* is the plan of the universe and not a dull, dead *uniformity.* India speaks of the search for God as the search for the One in the many, the One that gives meaning and significance to the many, like the figure 1 behind a zero or zeros. And so, in religion, she consistently upheld the idea that the goal was one, but the paths were many.

The Spirit of Active Toleration

To the people of India, therefore, toleration of different forms of faith and culture, of belief and practice, becomes a natural corollary of their outlook and philosophy. Śrī Kṛṣṇa's proclamation in the *Gītā:* 'Through whatever paths men approach Me, I receive them through those very paths; all paths, O Arjuna, ultimately lead unto Me only,' has gone into the bone and marrow of the Indian people, and made the spirit of positive toleration or universal acceptance pervasive of the entire range of their long history.

India defines religion as realisation *(anubhava,* in Sanskrit), and not as a matter of forms, ceremonies, and dogmas. The latter are valid as means, but not as ends. Secondly, India does not equate religious scholarship with spirituality. Knowledge of religious tenets is not the same as religion. Such knowledge is also valuable, but only as means and not as end; it must reach out to experience. As *The Imitation of Christ* expresses it: 'I would rather feel compunction than know the definition thereof.' Thirdly, atheism is not such a bugbear to India as to Semitic religions; for these are merely academic affirmations and negations; in the absence of an earnest endeavour to *realise* God, India does not find much difference between the affirmation of the theist and the negation of the atheist.

Moreover, *India holds that consistent atheism is an impossibility, because the God it preaches is not an extra-cosmic God, but the Divine Self in the heart of all—in the theist and the atheist, in the wise and the ignorant.* No one can deny such a God without first denying oneself; no one, on the other hand, can affirm such a God without first afforming oneself.

As a fruit of this view, there has been very little heresy-hunting in Indian history; India's toleration extended not only to different groups of the faithful, but also to different groups of the faithless who could not arrive at any faith in God.

Sanātana Dharma

The majority of the people of India belong to one or other of the various branches of the ancient religion of the country, Vedānta. It has another significant name *Sanātana Dharma* or Eternal Religion. This was the name that the people of India gave to their religion. It is based on the eternal impersonal principles discovered by different sages at diffṭerent times and collected together in the *Upaniṣads*. As such, *Sanātana Dharma* is not derived from the authority of any single personal founder.

The sages of the *Upaniṣads* discovered the truths of religion, and these sages are honoured as such; but the truths themselves are eternal, and can be discovered by any person in any age. In fact, *Sanātana Dharma* holds that it is precisely this effort to discover the truth by oneself and its final realisation that constitute religion, and not the effort to believe in a creed or dogma about God or soul.

This impersonal foundation of the Indian religions stands in sharp contrast to the personal authority of a founder of all the other world religions. Early Buddhism was an impersonal religion; Buddha discovered the Truth and showed the way to Truth to others. He described himself as the Tathagata, the path-finder, and declared that Buddhahood was a state, not a person, and that it was attainable by all.

In this, he was a teacher of *Sanātana Dharma,* and his teaching was close to the spirit of the *Upaniṣads*. Later, when he was transformed into a personal founder of a particular religion, a spirit of exclusiveness developed; and from being, like Vedānta, an Eternal Religion, *Sanātana Dharma,* it was changed into a religion with history, so much so that, without the authority of the personal founder,' the religion so interpreted cannot stand.

This limitation of its scope was one of the important reasons for its later disappearance, in name and form though certainly not in substance, from India, a phenomenon in Indian history not confined to this one instance only.

Vedānta or *Sanātana Dharma* is not the same thing as Hinduism. The words 'Hindu' and 'Hinduism' were not coined by the people of India to refer to themselves or to their religion. As was said earlier, they themselves designated their religion as *Sanātana Dharma,* Eternal Religion. 'Hindu' was a term coined by foreigners, especially the ancient Persians, to designate the people of India in a territorial sense; it only meant the people living on the east of the river Sindhu (modern Indus), and they pronounced 'S' as 'H'. Thus the 'Sindhu' of Sanskrit became 'Hindu', and their land, Hindusthan. The Greeks avoided both 'H' and 'S' and pronounced it 'Indos' from which was derived 'India'. Thus the word 'Hinduism' originally meant the religion of the people of Hindusthan. In actual fact, however, it is not one religion that exists in India, but many religions. Apart from the religions that came to India from outside in the course of her long history, namely, Judaism, Christianity, Zoroastrianism, and Islam, all of which are based on a personal founder or founders, there are several indigenous religions, each complete in itself, and all loosely called by the single name of Hinduism.

The Impact of Vedānta on India's Popular Religions

Among these indigenous religions, three are particularly important, both as to philosophy, tenets and long history, and as to the number of the adherents involved. These are Vaiṣṇavism, adoring Visnu or his incarnations, Rāma or Kṛṣṇa, as the Deity; Śaivism, adoring Śiva as the Deity; and Śāktism, adoring Śakti, the Divine Mother as the primal divine Energy, as the Deity.

Among these, Śaivism and Śāktism are practically one, as both the deities are objects of worship in each of them. These deities and incarnations have been the objects of worship for millions and millions of the people of India during these two to five thousand years. These religions have not remained the same during all these millennia of history. They have undergone changes—even profound changes—in their every aspect, in theological structure as much as in their mythology and ritual.

Their contact with the rational philosophy of the Upaniṣads gave rise to the changes in their theology, while this orientation, in turn, produced relevant changes in their mythology and ritual. *This story of the peaceful evolution of the Indian religions under the stimulus of a lofty philosophic thought, and in response to changing cultural situations, is one of the most impressive chapters in the history of religion.* Through this process, primitive forms of religion were allowed to grow and develop into highly spiritual religions, without getting smothered by more advanced ones.

The Evolution of the Śākta Religion

The history of the Śākta religion is significant in this connexion. Originating as the worship of the Mother-Goddess patronised by the primitive groups in all parts of India, in the hills and in the plains, this religion slowly evolved under the stimulus of Vedānta and became, centuries ago, a complete religion of deep philosophy, profound mysticism, and appealing ritual.

Some of the greatest personalities of Indian history, including the great philosopher Śaṅkara, were followers of this religion. Conceived as the Divine Mother of the universe, and called by different names, such as Devi, Durgā, Bhagavatī, Kālī, Bhavānī, Annapūrṇā, or Mīnākṣī, this Deity centralised within Herself the entire range of the Mother-Goddess cults of the vast continent of India. Some of the sublime poetry and mysticism of India is centred in Her worship; while its philosophy has become almost identical with that of Vedānta itself.

In modern times, this religion became associated with the name of Sri Ramakrishna, who worshipped this deity as Kālī in the Dakshineswar temple, near Calcutta. The Brahman and *Māyā* of Vedānta are conceived as a unity, the quiescent and dynamic aspects of Reality. Śākti or Kālī represents this dynamic aspect, which brings about the birth and evolution of the universe out of itself and finally withdraws it into itself. And Brahman represents that quiescent state.

Worship of Divine Incarnations

Though *Sanātana Dharma* is based on impersonal principles, it provides plenty of scope for the play of personality as well—personalities come into the religion as illustrations of the principles. So, immediately after the age of the Upaniṣads, India saw the emergence of two towering personalities, Rāma and Kṛṣṇa, whose influence on the totality of Indian culture, religion, poetry, art, and life has been the deepest and the most pervasive. Their influence has been not only on India, but also on the countries of South-East Asia, where Indian culture had penetrated during the first ten centuries of the Christian era, to result in the beautiful flowering of native cultures. *Sanātana Dharma* looks upon them as incarnations of God, who came to establish righteousness on earth. Buddha's status in *Sanātana Dharma* is also the same.

The worship of these *avatāras* or incarnations of God has been long recognised in India as effective spiritual help, and it forms an essential part of India's religion of *bhakti* or love. In fact, the worship of Rāma and Kṛṣṇa forms the major part of the religious life of India. The largest number of temples in the country are dedicated to their worship. This worship consists of a series of rituals and services rendered to the image in the temple, exactly in the spirit of service to a living personality. Devotees join this worship, especially the evening services, when lights are waved and songs sung before the image, often in chorus. This chorus singing is a prominent part of India's spiritual life; the chorus song composition in Sanskrit in praise of Rama known as *Rāma-nāma* or 'Name of Rāma,' is especially very popular throughout India. Mahatma Gandhi was very fond of this chorus, and used to have it sung in his prayer meetings. It is very pleasing to the ear and elevating to the heart.

Songs relating to Kṛṣṇa will fill several volumes. He is worshipped as the personification of the God of Love; but there is also the worship of him as the Child Kṛṣṇa, a worship enriched by relevant poetry, song, and mysticism, which is unsurpassed in its lyric of tenderness and pure spirituality. The birthdays of these two incarnations of God—of Rāma, in March-April, and of Kṛṣṇa, in August-September—are big events in the religious calendar of India.

Śiva and Buddha

The worship of Śiva seems to have been the most ancient of the worships in India, with the exception of Śākti or the Mother-Goddess. Śiva is conceived as the god of the *yogins,* men of contemplation. He is the ascetic god with the snowy Himalayas for his natural abode. He represents the state of *bodhi,* the state of illumination attained by Buddha, the soul, enjoying the beautitude of its own divine nature. But Śiva is also compassionate; the word 'Śiva' in Sanskrit means auspiciousness, goodness; and he comes down from his state of divine absorption to bless a seeking aspirant or redeem a soul in distress. Śiva is thus a state as well as a deity, the latter as the symbol of the former; he is also the special god of Indian monasticism.

The close kinship of this concept of Śiva to Buddha and his religion made for the blending of the two in several respects in the later evolution of Buddhism.

Śiva and Śakti

The worship of Śiva is marked by a spirit of seriousness and austerity. This worship is closely allied to the worship of Śakti or the Divine Mother, known also as Kālī, Durgā, etc. In the symbolic language of popular Hinduism, Śakti is the wife of Śiva, and both are looked upon as the parents of the whole universe. This idea of Śiva and Śakti as the father and mother of the universe has inspired poets and philosophers, artists and mystics, saints and devotees, in India, for hundreds of years. The great national poet Kālidāsa sang in praise of them in the opening verse of his epic poem *Raghuvaṁśam:*

'Inseparable as 'Word' and its 'Meaning' are Śiva, the supreme Lord, and Pārvatī, the Divine Mother, Whose grace I seek for culturing the soul of language.'

Pārvatī literally means the daughter of the mountain, the Himalayas; her other two names, Durgā and Gaurī, also derive from her association with the mountain.

The marriage of Śiva with Pārvatī or Śakti is the symbol of the union of the immobile Absolute and the mobile Creative Energy—the potential and kinetic states of the total energy, physical and spiritual, of the universe. The two are ever inseparable.

This marriage is the theme of another long epic poem of Kālidāsa, known as *Kumārasaṁbhavam* (The Birth of the Heroic Child). Śakti stands for the unity of the energies of Mother Nature in all her aspects—physical, biological, mental, and spiritual, and represents a generalisation of the energies of Nature far beyond what physical science gives today. Śakti is the unity of the physical and non-physical energies of Nature. It is termed *cit-śakti,* the Energy of Consciousness, out of which the whole world of conscious and unconscious entities proceeds. It is viewed in the feminine, and conceived not as 'creating' the world from outside, but as 'giving birth' to the world from within itself. So it is the

Divine Mother of all, as Śiva is the Divine Father of all; both form an inseparable unity, two aspects of the same Reality, the unity of Becoming and Being. Buddha experiencing the immobile state of *bodhi* or *nirvāṇa* represents the Śiva aspect, and Buddha engaged in active public ministration represents the Śakti aspect.

Spiritual Life: Three Stages

India discerns three stages in the expression of man's spiritual life. In the first stage, man's religious impulse seeks to find expression in outward acts of worship and adoration; his God is outside. He resorts to temples and churches, images and symbols, hymns and songs, fasting and pilgrimages. This is the first stage of every religion, the effort to capture an intimation of the Eternal through the concrete and the gross. The discipline of this stage must lead the devotee on to the second stage—that of inward contemplation. He has now learnt to feel the presence of God within, close. In this, there is very little of the external expression, there is very little of the noise and show associated with the first phase. In fact, true religion begins only at this stage; the first one is treated as just the kindergarten of religion. When the heart becomes purer and purer, it is able to *experience* the pull of the Divine within; and religion then becomes a joyous communion of the soul with God. The practice of meditation beṭcomes a delight. Continued practice of this stage draws down the grace of the Divine and the soul enters the third stage, in which it achieves the fullness of realisation. The seeker sees God within, in contemplation, and also without, in the field of action. India considers this as the aim of all spiritual striving; every devotee in India places this as his or her final spiritual objective; but he or she knows that it is difficult to achieve in a single life, but it will surely be achieved some day. Śrī Kṛṣṇa says in the *Gītā* (VII. 3):

'Out of thousands of people, only a few strive for perfection; and out of thousands that so strive, only a few realise the truth of My true being.'

Again *(ibid.,* VII. 19):

'Striving through several births, the wise one realises Me as existing in every being; such a *mahātman* (great soul) is rare to come across.'

Japa and *Dhyāna*

With the knowledge of the above stages in view, the worshipper in India not only engages in external ritual worship, but also practises *dhyāna* inward meditation, aided by *japa* or repetition of the divine name. This repetition of the divine name is a universal practice in the *bhakti* religions of India; it is also prevalent in some form in all the religions of the world.

This *japa* and *dhyāna* are the central core of the spiritual practices of the Indian people. A devotee chooses a particular form of God or Incarnation as his 'favourite object of adoration'—his *iṣṭa-devatā.* India allows perfect freedom of choice in this matter, as the people are taught by Vedānta that the supreme Truth is One, though called by various names and conceived under various forms, for the facility of comprehension and approach. In modern times, through the benign influence of Śrī Ramakrishna, who had realised God through both Hindu and non-Hindu forms of adoration, this choice of 'object of adoration,' which was till now confined to the various deities and incarnations of the specifically Hindu religions, is being extended to Christ and Buddha as well, who also are viewed as incarnations of God, just like Rama and Kṛṣṇa.

Pilgrimages

Pilgrimages occupy an important place in the spiritual life of India. India's important holy places are scattered over its length and breadth; some of the holiest are in the interior of the Himalayas, including the holy mountain Kailāsa, the abode of Śiva, in Tibet, holy to Hindus and Tibetan Buddhists alike. At the southern extremity of India are the temples of Rāmeśvaram and Kanyākumārī. Two other important centres are Dvārakā and Purī, on the western and eastern seaboards of India respectively.

The Sacredness of Gaṅgā

A special object of reverence in India is the river Gaṅgā, whose water is treated as the symbol of God Himself. No river in the world is treated with such reverence as the Gaṅgā in India, and this from pre-Buddhistic times. Millions of Hindus bathe in it every year and carry its water in brass pots and jars to their homes, even to foreign countries, to sip a few drops every day or on special occasions. A few drops of the sacred water of the Gaṅgā are put into the mouth of dying persons by their relatives. On its banks, thousands of people practise meditation and austerity, getting the stimulation of its holy atmosphere. The Gaṅgā, with its sacredness, has been carried to Ceylon and South-East Asia in the wake of Indian culture. In some of these countries, every river is known as Gaṅgā.

It is conceived as the river of heaven brought down to earth by a great emperor of ancient India, Bhagīratha. This historic-mythical episode has formed the theme of much literature and art. The river fell from heaven on the matted hair on the head of Śiva, who was then absorbed in contemplation on the snowy peaks of the Himalayas, and then flowed down in winding streams through the tortuous mountain valleys, eventually to enter the plains at Hardwar (an ancient holy pilgrim centre about 120 miles north of Delhi), to become the great river of material and spiritual prosperity for India. Bhagiratha had to undergo infinite troubles and austerities before he had the satisfaction to see the river flow into the plains. And the name of Bhagīratha in Indian culture now stands for all energetic and holy endeavour for the good of man, just like Prometheus in Greek culture.

Indian Monasticism

Before I close, I would like to say a few words about Indian monastic life, which is such a significant expression of the Indian spiritual life. An institution with hoary antiquity and prestige, it was ancient and well established even at the time of Buddha,who became one of its greatest representatives. The *sannyāsin* or monk, in virtue of his total renunciation and emancipation from personal and social bonds, is given divine veneration in India. And the best representatives of this Holy Order fully deserve this national reverence. Buddha, Śaṅkara, Caitanya, Ramakrishna, and Vivekananda belong to an unbroken line of monastic tradition, which goes back to Śuka, Yājñavalkya, and Sanatkumāra in prehistoric ages. In several monastic Orders, the monastic initiation is preceded by a *homa (goma,* in Japanese), fire ceremony, in which the candidate, who is a celibate from birth or has become celibate after a spell of the married state, pours into the lighted fire, which is the symbol of the Absolute, in the form of material oblations, his desires, senses, mind, and the ego and realises himself as pure Spirit without the touch of worldliness. He is then given a new name and a new apparel (coloured with a special kind of earth) to signify his death in the flesh and birth in the Spirit. Homeless and without possessions, he starts a new life of practical direct religion, the 'march of the alone to the Alone', and love and service of all beings without distinction.

Conclusion

India does not believe in a rigidly controlled central church to regulate religion or monasticism. When the new social order evolves a welfare state in India, the monastic Order will become a constructive force for human happiness, and welfare in India and abroad; for the same clarion call of *bahujana hitāya, bahujana sukhāya* (for the welfare of the many, for the happiness of the many), which Buddha had sounded to inspire his Order, has been sounded in this age by Swami Vivekananda to inspire the monastic life of modern India, before which he has placed the great ideals of 'Renunciation and Service'. The teachings of Swami Vivekananda and of his great Master, Sri Ramakrishna, are the most dynamic spiritual forces in modern India, helping her people, both lay and monastic, to evolve a new form of spiritual life adequate to the aspirations and purposes of the modern world.

Science And Religion*

A Need to Foster the Scientific Spirit

Modern environmental and ecological problems may be making for the unpopularity of technology, or rather of over-technology, especially in advanced countries; but *pure science, with its passion for truth and human welfare, will always remain as one of the noblest pursuits of man;* and our country, which has nurtured this love and pursuit of truth in the fields of physical sciences, religion, and philosophy in the past, must continue to nurture it in all fields in the modern age. Religion and philosophy in India, as given to us in our Upaniṣadic tradition, is but the continuation of the scientific search for truth at the sense-data level to the higher aesthetic, ethical, and spiritual levels of experience, as I hope to show in the course of this address. I appreciate this pioneer effort of the Bangalore University to inculcate the scientific spirit among its students and staff and the general citizens. I wish, however,

*The first lecture, under the auspices of Bangalore University, on 5 August 1976, in its seventeen-themes lecture series on *Science, Society, and the Scientific Attitude;* a revised version of the original lecture.

that the training of our people in the scientific attitude and outlook begins from the stage of primary education itself. That is the only way to purify and strengthen the rational and spiritual heritage of our country by draining away its impure, weakening, and centuries-old contaminations of magic and superstition.

Relationship of Science and Religion: A New Approach

The subjects of science and religion are getting more and more important to man in the modern age. They are two great disciplines which, in the light of Indian wisdom, reveal that, when relied on separately, can be counter-productive in the long run, but, when combined harmoniously, can bring about an all-round expression of human genius and total fulfilment. But, unfortunately, for the last few centuries, the relationship between the two in the Western context, and everywhere else also due to the worldwide impact of Western culture, has not been quite happy. In the twentieth century, however, a new approach is becoming evident, and the representative thinkers among scientists and religious people are beginning to discern a close interrelation between them. They are slowly veering round to the point of view that science and religion can heartily embrace each other, without detriment to the cause for which each stands, and work for the good of humanity. It is being realised more and more by both that there are elements in science that religion can adopt in order to fortify itself, and elements in religion that can deepen and strengthen science. I shall here touch upon some of the sources of the discord between the two and the significance of the points of contract between them, and discuss the methods and results of both the disciplines, against the background, and in the light, of the unity and totality of all human knowledge and the synthetic and synoptic approach and vision of the Indian philosophical and spiritual tradition.

The Scientific Discipline

The civilisation in which we live today is the product of the discipline of the human mind known as modern science. When we study science from close quarters, in the way the great scientists have applied themselves to this pursuit, we find two aspects to this discipline. The first is *pure science,* science which tries earnestly to understand the truth of nature through a dispassionate inquiry; and the second is *applied science,* in which the truth discovered by pure science flows as technical inventions for the enhancement and enrichment of human life. These two, science as *lucifera* and science as *fructifera,* science as *light* and science as *fruit,* are intimately related. Knowledge leads to power and power leads to control and manipulation of the forces of nature, enabling man to condition his life and environment with deliberation. Every new discovery in pure science, at some stage or the other becomes converted into applied science, into control and manipulation of the forces of nature. And the result, as revealed in recent history, is the great saga of modern scientific discovery and invention resulting in the worldwide technological civilisation of today. It is a most fascinating study how the human mind, disciplined in this pursuit of science, develops the capacity to wrest from nature truth after truth, hidden and jealously guarded by her, leading to our extraordinary modern age of nuclear science and space travel.

What is the nature of that movement of thought which has produced these remarkable results? What do we mean by the term 'modern' as applied to thought, and what is the special feature of modern scientific thought which has rendered thought so explosive and revolutionary? An answer to these questions will help us to reassess the role, of the other great human disciplines, such as religion, ethics, art, politics, and economics in the modern age.

The architect of the modern world is science, and by modern thought is meant, scientific thought. The aim of science is to study nature and human experience objectively. To quote Karl Pearson *(Grammar of Science,* 1900, p.6):

> The classification of facts, the recognition of their sequence and relative significance, is the function of science, and the habit of forming a judgement upon these facts unbiased by personal feeling is characteristic of what may be termed the scientific frame of mind.

This quality of the scientific mind, and the mood and temper of its approach, have enabled science to wrest from nature its secrets, first from one field, then from another, and transform nature's forces into agencies for the service of man. The sum total of achievements in the theoretical and practical fields in the various departments of scientific inquiry in physics and chemistry, mathematics and astronomy, biology and psychology, as also in their various subsidiary branches, constitute an impressive record of human development, by the side of which long ages of past achievements in the same fields pale into insignificance. That is modern science in its methods and results.

Science Versus Departments of Science

Science so understood is not tied up with any particular body of facts. In the words of one of the great biologists, J. Arthur Thomson *(Introduction to Science,* Home University Library edition, p.58):

> *Science is not wrapped up with any particular body of facts; it is characterised as an intellectual attitude. It is not tied down to any particular methods of inquiry; it is simple sincere critical thought, which admits conclusions only when these are based on evidence.* We may get a good lesson in scientific method from a businessman

> meeting some new practical problem, from a lawyer sifting evidence, or from a statesman framing a constructive bill. *(italics not by the author).*

Objectivity and precision, both as to thought and its verbal formulation, are two important characteristics of the scientific method. Any study possessing these characteristics will be science, whatever be the field of that study. Science as such is, therefore, not tied down to any particular order of facts, though the various departments of science, like physics or chemistry, biology or sociology, are tied down to particular orders of facts. These departments have limited scope, but science itself is unlimited in scope; and these various departments, starting with the study of separate fields tend, in their advanced stages, to overstep their particular boundaries and merge into one converging scientific search, the search for the meaning of total experience. In this expansive context, the idea of a science of religion, the science of the facts of the inner world of man, as upheld in ancient Indian thought, and as expounded in the modern age by Swami Vivekananda, becomes also a scientific study of far-reaching significance.

The Spirit of Inquiry

The driving force behind this unique modern achievement is the spirit of free inquiry characteristic of modern science. The mind that questions, and questions with a serious intent and purpose, and tests and verifies the answers it gets, has a dynamic quality about it, which enables it to forge ahead in the world of thought and things. In so forging ahead, it disturbs the wayside calm of untested dogmas and comfortable beliefs, and the magic and miracle and superstition wrongly associated with religion and leading to the vulgarisation of this great discipline. Science is verified knowledge. The explosive character of modern scientific thought is the product of the impact of a rapid succession of verified knowledge against an intractable fund of untested dogmas, assumptions, beliefs, magic, miracle, and superstitions. The organised opposition of the latter in the West sought to stifle scientific inquiry, first, at its birth and, later, at every stage of its progress. But the walls of the *bastille* of ignorance and prejudice fell one by one before the onrushing waves of inquiry and illumination, illustrating the great saying of the Upaniṣads *(Muṇḍaka Upaniṣad,* HI, 1.6):

> '*Satyameva jayate, nānṛtom*—Truth alone triumphs, not untruth.'

The history of science in recent centuries is thus the history of the triumph of the spirit of free inquiry over mere opinion, untested belief, prejudice and dogma. It is a remarkable adventure of the human spirit which has borne abundant fruits, not only mental but also material; for science as *lucifera* has flowed into science as *fructifera,* giving a bumper crop of discoveries and inventions which has transformed beyond recognition the world in which we live.

Eclipse of Dogma-bound Religion

The success of science has meant the defeat of its opponent. It is one of the unfortunate episodes of history, especially of modern European history, that the organisation of the forces of prejudice and blind belief against science and its spirit of inquiry came from the side of religion; and that, reason, which is the life-breath of science, was viewed as the death-knell of religion. By the end of the last century, science had acquired high prestige and authority, while religion had been discredited, first, as a dangerous error, and later, as a harmless illusion.

The end of the nineteenth century thus saw the eclipse of religion in the West. But there was an uneasy feeling in the hearts of many thinkers that something of deep value to man and his civilisation had been overthrown; and they attempted a reassessment of the meaning and scope of religion with a view to making it accord with the spirit and temper of science. To this great task of reconstructing the mental life of modern man by bridging the gulf between faith and reason, on the basis of a unified view of man and a truer conception of the spiritual life, the contribution of Indian thought is unique and lasting.

Vivekananda on Reason and Religion

Tracing the recurring conflicts of science and religion in the West to the absence of a broad rational and experiential approach, Vivekananda said (*Complete Works,* Vol. II, ninth edition, p. 433):

> We all know the theories of the cosmos according to the modern astronomers and physicists, and at the same time we all know how woefully they undermine the theology of Europe; how these scientific discoveries that are made act as a bomb thrown at its stronghold; and we know how theologians have in all times attempted to put down these researches.

When religion refuses to take the help of reason, it weakens itself. Alluding to this in the course of a lecture on 'Reason and Religion', delivered in England in 1896, Swami Vivekananda said *(ibid.,* Vol. 1, eleventh edition, p.367):

> The foundations have been all undermined, and the modern man, whatever he may say in public, knows in the privacy of his heart that he can no more 'believe'. Believing certain things because an organised body of priests tells him to believe, believing because it is written in certain

> books, believing because his people like him to believe, the modern man knows to be impossible for him. There are, of course, a number of people who seem to acquiesce in the so-called popular faith, but we also know for certain that they do not think. Their idea of belief may be better translated as 'not-thinking-carelessness'.

And pleading for the application of reason in the field of religion, he continued *(ibid.):*

> Is religion to justify itself by the discoveries of reason through which every other science justifies itself? Are the same methods of investigation, which we apply to science and knowledge outside, to be applied to the science of religion? In my opinion, this must be so; and I am also of the opinion that the sooner it is done the better. If a religion is destroyed by such investigations, it was then all the time useless, unworthy, superstition; and the sooner it goes the better. I am thoroughly convinced that its destruction would be the best thing that could happen. All that is dross will be taken off, no doubt, but the essential parts of religion will emerge triumphant out of this investigation. Not only will it be made scientific—as scientific, at least, as any of the conclusions of physics or chemistry—but it will have greater strength, because physics or chemistry has no internal mandate to vouch for its truth which religion has.

A study of the *Upaniṣads* reveals that the subject of religion was approached in ancient India in an objective dispassionate manner; and the aim of the study was to get at truth, and not to hug pleasing fancies and illusions or to idolise tribal passions and prejudices.

In several of his lectures and discourses, Swami Vivekananda has expounded this scientific approach as upheld in Indian thought.

In his lecture on 'Religion and Science', he says *(ibid.,* Vol. VI sixth edition, p.81):

> Experience is the only source of knowledge. In the world, religion is the only science where there is no surety, because it is not taught as a science of experience. This should not be. There is always, however, a small group of men who teach religion from experience. They are called mystics, and these mystics in every religion speak the same tongue and teach the same truth. This is the real science of religion. As mathematics in every part of the world does not differ, so the mystics do not differ. They are all similarly constituted and similarly situated. Their experience is the same; and this becomes law. ...
>
> Religion deals with the truths of the metaphysical world, just as chemistry and the other natural sciences deal with the truths of the physical world. The book one must read to learn chemistry is the book of nature. The book from which to learn religion is your own mind and heart. The sage is often ignorant of physical science, because he reads the wrong book—the book within; and the scientist is too often ignorant of religion, because he, too, reads the wrong book—the book without.

Indian thinkers discovered by their investigations that there are two fields in which man lives and functions; one, the external world; the other, the internal. These are two different orders of phenomena. The study of the one alone does not exhaust the whole range of experience. Also, the study of the one from the standpoint of the other will not lead to satisfactory results. But the study of the one *in the light of the conclusions from the study of the other* is helpful and relevant.

Referring to this approach in the course of a lecture on 'Cosmology,' Swami Vivekananda said *(ibid.,* Vol. II, ninth edition, p.432):

> There are two worlds, the microcosm and the macrocosm, the internal and the external. We get truth from both of these by means of experience. The truth gathered from internal experience is psychology, metaphysics, and religion; from external-experience, the physical sciences. Now, a perfect truth should be in harmony with experiences in both these worlds. The microcosm must bear testimony to the macrocosm, and the macrocosm to the microcosm; physical truth must have its counterpart in the internal world, and the internal world must have its verification outside.

Thus the sages and thinkers of ancient India said: Here is the physical life of man, and here is the physical universe that environs him. Let us study both in a scientific spirit. But let us also study him in his depths, his nature as revealed by his consciousness, his thoughts, his emotions, his ego, and his sense of selfhood. These latter also constitute a vast group of phenomena that need to be investigated. Every advance in this field is bound to advance man's knowledge about the truth of the mystery of the external world. For, to quote mathematician-astronomer, the late Sir Arthur Eddington *(Philosophy of Physical Science,* p.5):

> We have discovered that it is actually an aid in the search for knowledge to understand the nature of the knowledge which we seek.

The Upaniṣads and the Spirit of Critical Inquiry in India

Ever since the time of the *Upaniṣads*, India has tenaciously held to a view of religion which makes it a high adventure of the spirit, a converging life-endeavour to realise and grasp the hidden meaning of existence. Faith, in India, did not mean a cosy belief to rest by, but a torch to set the soul on fire with a longing for spiritual realisation. In the absence of this longing and struggle, the belief of the faithful does not differ from the unbelief of the faithless. Belief with most people is simply another name for mental laziness. Religious earnestness with people of this class means, especially when organised under a militant church or a theocratic state, either the pursuit of aggressive religious proselytism or of *jehads* and crusades. They cannot understand the meaning of that earnestness which proceeds from an inner spiritual hunger. No dogma or creed or frenzied acts can satisfy this hunger of a religious heart. Its only bread is spiritual realisation. Religion is a matter of inner experience, a coming in touch with spiritual facts, and not a matter of belief or dogma or conformity.

Strengthened by the spirit of the *Upaniṣads,* no all-powerful church, therefore, rose in India to organise the faithful on the basis of dogma and creed, and claiming divine authority for its opinions and judgements. No such authority could thrive where religion was expounded as a quest and not a conformity. A spiritual view of religion, as different from a creedal or dogmatic view, makes religion not only cultivate a spirit of toleration, questioning, and inquiry in its own sphere, but also foster it in every other department of life. The *Bhagavad-Gītā* (VI. 44) declares that a spirit of inquiry into the meaning of religion takes an aspirant beyond the authority of the words of scripture and mandate of tradition. He becomes an experimenter himself, instead of remaining a mere believer. Indian religious thought emphasises *sādhanā,* experiment, as the dynamics of religion; it has recourse to *jijñāsā,* or inquiry, for the formulation of its views, be it *Brahma-jijñāsā,* inquiry into the nature of Brahman, i.e. God as the one Self of all, or *dharma-jijñāsā,* inquiry into *dharma,* i.e., social ethics and personal morality.

This sublime attitude to religion and thought is the fruit of the unified view of the mental life of man which India learned from her *Upaniṣads,* and which she assimilated into her mind and mood by a universal acceptance of all forms of faith and by showing due regard to all knowledge, whether sacred or secular.

'*Vidyā Dadāti Vinayam*—Knowledge Bestows Humility'

Science in the modern age has lengthened man's intellectual tether, but this has only helped to bring into sharper focus the mystery of the unknown and the significance of the *parā vidyā* (higher knowledge or wisdom) of which the *Upaniṣads* speak. In the words of J. Arthur Thomson *(Introduction to Science,* Home University Library edition, 1934, p. 205):

> *At the end of his intellectual tether, man has never ceased to become religious.*

It is no wonder, therefore, that several scientists during the last few decades, have been forced to overstep the limits of their sciences and tackle the problem of the unknown at closer quarters in a mood of humility and reverence, illustrating the dictum of Indian wisdom: '*Vidyā dadāti vinayam*—knowledge bestows humility', and the saying of Coleridge quoted by J. Arthur Thomson *(ibid.,* p.208):

> All knowledge begins and ends with wonder; but the first wonder is the child of ignorance; the second wonder is the parent of adoration.

Dogmatism and cock-sureness which stifle the spirit of free inquiry are as much enemies of true science as of true religion. There are not wanting scientists today who would, taking a narrow view of the scope and function of science, prefer to go the dogmatic way and cry halt to advancing knowledge and unified experience. That way spells danger to science now, as it has spelt danger to religion before. *A greater devotion to the spirit of free inquiry and a broader conception of the aim and temper of science is our only safeguard against such a pitfall.*

If the nineteenth century was the century of conflict and division, the twentieth century bids fair to become the century of reconciliation and union, as a result of a sincere effort on the part of both science and religion to reassess itself and to understand the other. The humility of twentieth-century physical science presents a sharp and welcome contrast to the cock-sureness of its nineteenth century counterpart. It has realised that the spirit of free inquiry, on which it has thrived, may find expression in fields beyond its own narrow departments, and that it is this spirit, unbiased by personal attachments and aversions, that makes a study scientific, and not the mere subject-matter of that study. This wider view of science as a discipline and a temper enables us to class as scientific, the study of the facts of the inner world which religion has set to itself for inquiry.

And this has been the Indian approach to religion. It was the absence of this approach that made religion in the West less and less equipped to meet the challenge of advancing knowledge.

Limitations of Physical Science

When we go deeper into the nature and scope of physical science, its limitations become apparent. To illustrate: Two branches of science, namely, physics, including astronomy, and biology, including behaviouristic psychology, have given us a vast body of knowledge regarding the nature of the universe and man. Up to the end of the nineteenth century, physics was warped in its final judgements. It saw materialism and mechanism reigning supreme in the universe. There was then a cock-sureness in its pronouncements; but, in the twentieth century, an element of humility is discernible in the attitude of the great physicists of the age. In the nineteenth century, knowledge of the physical world was not deep enough, and scientists looked only at the surface of things. But, along with the discovery of such facts as radioactivity and insight into the nucleus of the atom, the realisation has come that there is a severe limitation placed on our knowledge regarding the truth of the external world. Science owns today that it deals only with *the appearances of things* and not with *the reality behind these appearances.* Some of the greatest of modern physicists tell us that what science has revealed of the world around us is only the outer aspect of things. Behind this *observable* universe, there is an *unobservable* universe, as well as the *observer* himself. This is a great confession of the limitations of science and its methods. Science is dealing with phenomena revealed by the senses or by apparatuses helpful to the senses. But these senses reveal so little, and what they reveal only tells us that there are realities behind the sense world determining it and controlling it. Physical science restricts itself to the understanding of the observable part of the universe and to controlling its energies for the use of man.

A similar situation obtains in the science of biology. In the last century, it was cock-sure about its pronouncements. By a study of the different aspects of the phenomena of life, it arrived at the great theory of evolution, from which it drew certain conclusions influenced by the mechanistic materialism of contemporary physics, which directly led to a form of materialism, that equated man with the animal, and both to a machine. Today, scientists tell us that they were not happy titles that Darwin chose for his famous books: *The Origin of Species* and *The Descent of Man.* Sir Julian Huxley suggests that these could have been more appropriately titled: *The Evolution of Organisms* and *The Ascent of Man (Evolution after Darwin,* Vol. I, The University of Chicago Press, p.17). But, then, these books appeared at a time when a fierce controversy was going on between emerging science and the entrenched Christian dogma of supernaturalism upholding man as a special creation of an extra-cosmic God, and this had its impact even on the choosing of the titles of great scientific books. The science of physics with its thorough-going materialism and mechanistic determinism, and the science of biology with its newly discovered evolutionary theory and its domination by the general materialistic outlook of science and scientists of the age, helped to shatter nineteenth century man's faith in that view of religion and spiritual values which was presented to the West as supernatural and antiscience.

The limitations of physical science, admitted by many modern scientists themselves, proceed from the adjective *physical,* but science itself is not limited similarly. Reality may be studied, but not exhausted, by the physical sciences, whose limitations proceed from their dependence entirely on sense-data. This limitation has been pointed out by the mathematician-astronomer, the late Sir Arthur Eddington *(The Philosophy of Physical Science,* p.16):

> Let us suppose that an ichthyologist is exploring the life of the ocean. He casts a net into the water and brings up a fishy assortment. Surveying his catch, he proceeds, in the usual manner of a scientist, to systematise what it reveals. He arrives at two generalisations:
>
> 1. No sea-creature is less than two inches long
> 2. All sea-creatures have gills.
>
> These are both true of his catch, and he assumes: tentatively that they will remain true however often he repeats it. ... His generalisation is perfectly true of the class of creatures he is talking about—a selected class perhaps, but he would not be interested in making generalisations about any other class.

Earlier, Eddington, had said in his Preface to the above book *ibid.*, p.ix):

> I am not among those who think that, in the search for truth, all aspects of human experience are to be ignored,

save those which are followed up in physical science. But I find no disharmony between a philosophy which embraces the wider significance of human experience and the specialised philosophy of physical science, even though the latter relates to a system of thought of recent growth whose stability is yet to be tested.

'Materialism—an Intruder'

When physical science or scientists forget or ignore this limitation implied in the adjective 'physical', and pronounce judgements on life or reality as a whole, it or they become dogmatic, and forsake truth-seeking; one such dogma that is stifling the spirit of modern physical science is *materialism,* against which distinguished scientists have protested and warned. After terming materialism *an intruder* earlier in his book *Methods and Results* (Volume I, p. 161), Thomas Huxley, the collaborator of Darwin, repudiates materialism as a philosophy of life (*ibid.,* pp.164-65):

> *If we find that the ascertainment of the order of nature is facilitated by using one terminology or one set of symbols, rather than another, it is our clear duty to use the former; and no harm can accrue, so long as we bear in mind that we are dealing merely with terms and symbols. ...*
>
> *But the man of science who, forgetting the limits of philosophical inquiry, slides from these formulae and symbols into what is commonly understood by materialism, seems to me to place himself on a level with the mathematician who should mistake the x's and y's with which he works the problems for real entities— and with this further disadvantage, as compared with the mathematician, that the blunders of the latter are of no*

> *practical consequence,* while the errors of systematic materialism may paralyse the energies and destroy the beauty of a life.' *(italics not by the author).*

Physical Science and the Mystery of the Universe

The universe was a mystery to man in the primitive stage; it has not ceased to be so for civilised man even in this twentieth century. We find scientists like the late Sir James Jeans writing books on the scientific view of the universe with such titles as *The Mysterious Universe.* If, after all these marvellous scientific discoveries and inventions, the scientist still treats nature as profoundly mysterious, if, in spite of all the vast knowledge that he has gained, the scientist feels that he has only scratched the surface of nature, that he is yet far far away from the heart of the problem of the universe, we have to pause and ask the question as framed by Śaṅkarācārya: *tataḥ kiṁ tataḥ kim*—'What else? What next?' Says Sir James Jeans in his *The New Background of Science* (p.68):

> Physical science set out to study a world of matter and radiation, and finds that it cannot describe or picture the nature of either, even to itself. Photons, electrons, and protons have become about as meaningless to the physicist as x, y, z are to a child on its first day of learning algebra. The most we hope for at the moment is to discover ways of manipulating x, y, z without knowing what they are, with the result that the advance of knowledge is at present reduced to what Einstein has described as extracting one incomprehensible from another incomprehensible.

Physical Science and the Mystery of Man

Even while confronted by, and engaged in, tackling the mystery of the external universe, modern science has become impressed with a deeper mystery, the mystery of man himself, the challenge of the inner world of man. His physical dimension poses no challenge to a science which has achieved revolutionary advances in its branches of anatomy and physiology, neurology and microbiology, medicine and behaviouristic psychology. But these point out to a mysterious depth in him which reveals a new dimension to nature herself, namely, her *within,* over and above her *without.*

Man reveals dimensions that cannot be reduced to the merely physical, the merely material. These latter are his 'not-self aspects which enter into the constitution of his body, which obviously is just a speck of dust in that vast world of the notself, but there is in him also something transcendental, which cannot be so reduced. He is the self; that is his primary inalienable aspect. And if science is to progress further, it has to choose for investigation this field of the mystery of man which towers over its erstwhile study, namely, the mystery of the external universe. This is a vast field of study—the field of man's self-awareness, the field of his consciousness, his ego, his being the *subject* and not the object. Science will find here a vaster and more fascinating and rewarding field of study than in external nature. Already scientists in the West are slowly turning their attention to this great mystery, that of *Man the Unknown,* in the words of the American scientist the late Alexis Carrel, apart from that of *Man the Known,* which is the subject of the positive sciences like physics, chemistry, biology and behaviouristic psychology.

Physics and the Mystery of Man

Man is the creator of science and technology, culture and civilisation; he is also today the only possible destroyer of his civilisation. Everything about him is a mystery. As Lincoln Barnett says in his study of Einstein's contribution to modern scientific thought *(The Universe and Dr. Einstein,* Mentor edition, pp.126-27):

> *In the evolution of scientific thought, one fact has become impressively clear; there is no mystery of the physical world which does not point to a mystery beyond itself. All highroads of the intellect, all byways of theory and conjecture, lead ultimately to an abyss that human ingenuity can never span. For man is enchained by the very condition of his being, his finiteness and involvement in nature. The further he extends his horizons, the more vividly he recognises the fact that, aś the physicist Niels Bohr puts it, 'We are both spectators and actors in the great drama of existence'.* Man is thus his own greatest mystery. *He does not understand the vast veiled universe into which he has been cast for the reason that he does not understand himself. He comprehends but little of his organic processes and even less of his unique capacity to perceive the world around him, to reason and to dream.* Least of all does he understand his noblest and most mysterious faculty: the ability to transcend himself and perceive himself in the act of perception. *(italics not by the author).*

Or, as expressed by the mathematician-mystic Pascal:

> In space, the universe engulfs me and reduces me to a pin-point. But through thought, I understand that universe.

Biology and the Mystery of Man

Pleading for the viewing of man in his depths on the part of modern science, the eminent paleontologist, the late Pere Teilhard de Chardin says (*The Phenomenon of Man,* Collins, London, 1959, pp.35-36):

> *When studied narrowly in himself by anthropologists or jurists, man is a tiny, even a shrinking, creature. His over-pronounced individuality conceals from our eyes the whole*

> *to which he belongs; as we look at him, our minds incline to break nature up into pieces and to forget both its deep inter-relations and its measureless horizons. We incline to all that is bad in anthropocentrism. And it is this that leads scientists to refuse to consider man as an object of scientific scrutiny except through his body.*
>
> *The time has come to realise that an interpretation of the universe—even a positivist one—remains unsatisfying unless it covers the interior as well as the exterior of things; mind as well as matter.* The true physics is that which will, one day, achieve the inclusion of man in his wholeness in a coherent picture of the world. *(italics not by the author).*

The *Upaniṣads* of India discovered the finite man as but the outer crust or layer of the infinite and immortal man within. In his finiteness, he enters, and is entered into by, the finite world of myriad changes around him. In this, he is a *speck* of dust in the vast immensity of space in which 'the universe engulfs me and reduces me to pin-point', in the profound words of Pascal quoted above. But in his infinite dimension as the imperishable Self, he *understands* the universe and also *transcends* it. The dimensions of this inner aspect of man and, through him, of his environing universe, are slowly dawing on modern scientific thought.

Asking the significant question: 'Up to now has science ever troubled to look at the world other than from without?' (*ibid.*, p.52), Chardin proceeds to say *(ibid.,* p.55):

> In the eyes of the physicist, nothing exists legitimately, at least up to now, except the without of things. The same intellectual attitude is still permissible in the bacteriologist, whose cultures (apart from substantial difficulties) are treated as laboratory reagents. But it is still more difficult in the realm of plants. It tends to become a gamble in the

> case of a biologist studying the behaviour of insects or coelenterates. It seems merely futile with regard to the vertebrates. Finally, it breaks down completely with man, in whom the existence of a within can no longer be evaded, because it is the object of a direct intuition and the substance of all knowledge.

The world outside, as much as most people in India itself, do not yet know that it was the higher part of, what Julian Huxley terms, *a science of human possibilities,* that India developed ages ago in her *Upaniṣads* and the *Gītā,* and has continued to foster, up to our own times, as Vedānta and Yoga, as the *adhyātma-vidyā,* the *vidyā,* or science, of man in depth, the science and technique of a comprehensive spirituality encompassing action as well as contemplation. *Indian philosophy sees no conflict between physical sciences and this science of spirituality, between 'man, the known' and 'man, the unknown', between the physical man and the spiritual man.* And Chardin concludes (*ibid.,* p.56):

> It is impossible to deny that, deep within ourselves, an 'Interior' appears at the heart of beings, as it were seen through a rent. This is enough to ensure that, in one degree or another, this 'interior' should obtrude itself as existing everywhere in nature from all time. Since the stuff of the universe has an inner aspect at one point of itself, there is necessarily a double aspect to its structure, that is to say, in every region of space and time—in the same way, for instance, as it is granular: coextensive with their without, there is a within to things.

It is high time that our people today, particularly our teachers and students, turn their critical attention, interest, and inquiry, and direct their searchlight of research, into this fascinating and rewarding constituent of their hoary national tradition, into the mystery of this inner dimension of nature revealed in nature's unique product, namely, man. If man does not acquire this strength of spirituality from within, he will have to depend more and more on external sources for stabilising himself. Such external dependence, for clinical purposes occasionally, is understandable. But to make it the normal pattern of human life *is to drain human life of all spiritual values and to surrender human destiny to social engineering techniques such as of molecular biology, and convert human society to an animal farm.* That such dismal possibilities are there before man, due to a wholesale dependence on physical sciences and technology, is revealed in recent books with grim titles like *The Biological Time Bomb* by G. Ratray Taylor. *The science that will do so will cease to be science and become ne-science!*

As we advance into this inquiry and research into our tradition, we shall get an increasing grip on the human situation in our country, through the reformulation and implementation of educational goals and processes in the light of our own philosophy of man, whereby a happy synthesis of physical sciences with the science of spirituality will be achieved, resulting in total human enrichment, internal as well as external, qualitative as well as quantitative.

Says the great neurologist, Sir Charles Sherrington *(Man on His Nature,* Pelican edition, p.38):

> Today, Nature looms larger than ever and includes more fully than ever ourselves. It is, if you will, a machine, but it is a partly mentalised machine and in virtue of including ourselves, it is a machine with human qualities of mind. It is a running stream of energy—mental and physical—and unlike man-made machines, it is actuated by emotions, fears, and hopes, dislikes and love.

Evolution: Organic Versus Psycho-social

In a lecture on 'The Evolutionary Vision', delivered in 1959 at the closing session of the Chicago University symposium on 'Evolution after Darwin,' held to commemorate the centenary of the publication of Darwin's *Origin of Species,* the noted biologist, the late Sir Julian Huxley, gave a spiritual orientation to the evolutionary process *(Evolution after Darwin,* Vol. III, pp. 251-52):

> Man's evolution is not biological but psycho-social; it operates by the mechanism of cultural tradition, which involves the cumulative self-reproduction and self-variation of mental activities and their products. Accordingly, major steps in the human phase of evolution are achieved by breakthroughs to new dominant patterns of mental organisation of knowledge, ideas and beliefs—ideological instead of physiological or biological organisation. ...
>
> All dominant thought organisations are concerned with the ultimate, as well as with the immediate, problems of existence or, I should rather say, with the most ultimate problems that the thought of the time is capable of formulating or even envisaging. They are all concerned with giving some interpretation of man, of the world which he is to live in, and of his place and role in that world—in other words, some comprehensive picture of human destiny and significance.

Further, Huxley reveals the trend of evolution, at the human stage, towards *quality* (*ibid.,* Vol. Ill, pp.261-62):

> It (evolutionary vision) shows us mind enthroned above matter, quantity subordinate to quality.

In his essay on 'Emergence of Darwinism', Huxley sums up the goal of the evolutionary process at the human level as *fulfilment* (*ibid.,* Vol. I, p.20):

> In the light of our present knowledge, man's most comprehensive aim is seen not as mere survival, not as numerical increase, not as increased complexity of organisation or increased control over his environment, but as greater fulfilment—the fuller realisation of more possibilities by the human species collectively and more of its component members individually.

And pleading for the development of a *science of human possibilities,* Huxley further says *(ibid.,* Vol. I, p.21):

> Once greater fulfilment is recognised as man's ultimate or dominant aim, we shall need a science of human possibilities to help guide the long course of psycho-social evolution that lies ahead.

Psycho-social Evolution

What is meant by psycho-social evolution? From the living cell up to man, biological evolution was motivated by organic satisfactions, numerical increase, and organic survival. But with the appearance of man, these become, says modern biology, secondary and not primary; the primary motivation becomes *fulfilment:* and evolution itself becomes, at the stage of man, conscious and deliberate and goal-oriented, unlike the blind processes at the pre-human stages. This revolutionary change is the result of the fully developed cerebral system in man, in virtue of which the evolutionary process itself undergoes a revolutionary change; *what was organic evolution becomes psycho-social evolution.* Organic evolution has no primary significance in the case of man endowed by nature with the versatile cerebral organ, with the aid of which he can invent any organs he may need more efficiently and quickly than what nature can do for him through her slow and wasteful evolutionary processes. Accordingly, evolution has risen from its organic to the psycho-social level in man, says biology.

In a self-centred man, as in all pre-human species, the psyche or mind or soul is limited and confined to the physical organism. In a moral or ethical man, it expands, goes beyond the limitations of his physical organism and enters, and is entered into by, other psyches of the social milieu. This is the fruit of psycho-social evolution. What biology calls psycho-social evolution is what the science of religion calls ethical awareness and social feeling, the by-product of the early phases of the *spiritual growth* of man.

With the onset of this psycho-social evolution, men develop the capacity to dig affections into each other *as a matter of conscious choice,* thus revealing a higher dimension to the human individuality than what is revealed by his physical individuality with its organic appetities and choices. All ethical theories presuppose a distinction between a lower self and a higher self in man; and the liberation of the higher self is what man achieves through psycho-social evolution or spiritual growth; it is renunciation of the lower self and manifestation of the higher self.

The subject of the spiritual growth of man, of evolution as psycho-social, is a pregnant theme to man in the modern age. It points out to him the way to rescue himself from the tyranny of the sensate and the quantitative, and from the prevailing stagnation of worldliness, and helps him to continue his evolutionary march to *qualitative* richness and fulfilment, individually and collectively.

The initial focus of self in man is the ego, which appears on the evolutionary scene only with the appearance of man; and even at the stage of man, it appears only after the human infant is about two or two-and-a-half years old. And it is significant to note that, till its appearance, the human infant is as helpless and dependent on the environment like all pre-human species and that, with its appearance, the infant begins to dominate the environment. A human child of four or five years of age can control and manage animals like horses or other cattle immensely larger physically than itself. Modern neurology attributes this unique phenomenon to the emergence of a new datum in the human child, with new capacities and energies as its fruit; that datum is the self as the ego and those capacities are imagination, reason, judgement, will, etc. Referring to this, neurologist Grey Walter says *(The Living Brain,* p.2):

> Thus the mechanisms of the brain reveal a deep physiological division between man and ape. . . . If the title of soul be given to the higher functions in question, it must be admitted that the other animals have only a glimmer of the light that so shines before men. . . . The nearest creature to us, the chimpanzee, cannot retain an image long enough to reflect on it, however clever it may be in learning tricks or getting food that is placed beyond its natural reach. Unable to rehearse the possible consequences of different responses to a stimulus, without any faculty of planning, the apes and other animals cannot learn to control their feelings, the first step towards independence of environment and eventual control of it. The activity of the animal brain is not checked to allow time for the choice of one among several possible responses, but only for the one reflex or conditioned response to emerge. The monkey's brain is in thrall to its senses. Sentio ergo sum (I sense, therefore I exist) might be the first reflection of a slightly inebriated ape, as it is often the last of alcoholic man; so near and yet so far apart, even then, are they.

The brain of lion, tiger, rhinoceros, and other powerful animals also lack the mechanism of imagination, or we

> should not be here to discuss the matter. They cannot envisage changes in their environment, so they have never sought to alter it in all their efforts to retain lordship of their habitat.

Man alone achieved this power of *imaging* ideas; and this power was not an isolated phenomenon in him. Within the increased area of the cortex of the ancestral organ, nature evolved for man capacities for a series of new processes: observation, memory, comparison, evaluation, selection, judgement, and deliberate action. And in achieving these, he achieved two things:

Firstly, discovery of the path leading to the processing of raw experience into knowledge, of knowledge into power, and power into control and manipulation of the environment constituted of the not-self aspect of experience.

Secondly, a faint awareness of the reality of himself as the subject, as the self, behind the fleeting images in his mind, and the discovery of the road leading inward to the total comprehension of this new dimension of reality, resulting in the increasing liberation of moral, aesthetic, and spiritual values in his life, action, and behaviour.

Man's steady advance on these two fronts constitutes the story of culture and civilisation; it constitutes also the march of evolution at the post-human stage. With the emergence, on the evolutionary scene, of the mind of man against the background of self-awareness, and disciplined in the seeking and finding of knowledge of the self and the not-self in varying degrees, nature yields, in increasing measure, to one of her own products, the control and manipulation of the evolutionary process.

Rising from Knowledge to Wisdom

In spite of his rudimentary self-knowledge which gave him a measure of control of the animal and natural world, the earliest man largely remained an animal in appetites and behaviour. A little more of this self-knowledge, gained through reflection in the context of social experience, helped to increase his control over himself and to humanise him. This process, ever in operation in human cultures and civilisations and socio-political organisations, has led up to the man of the modern age, with his almost total control over the not-self environment through an efficient technology, with his global sweep in socio-cultural interests and contacts, and with his yearning for the universal and human.

Yet, the disparity between his knowledge of his self and control over his inner nature, on the one hand, and his knowledge of, and control over, the external nature, on the other, between, in short, his moral efficiency and his technical efficiency, confronts him with the most serious problem that his evolution has so far seriously posed. This is thwarting his urges and efforts to achieve fulfilment. Neglected and unsolved, this problem may as well make him the only possible destroyer of his civilisation, of the fruits of evolution, and of his species as well. In the meantime, he is destined to move from one tension to another, from one sorrow and unfulfilment to another.

The only solution lies in the deepening and strengthening of his moral and spiritual awareness. Biological evolution achieved a measure of this in the life of earliest man in his rudimentary knowledge of his own self. Social evolution, guided by human intelligence, advanced this still further, by which a physical and organic self, separated from all other selves, gave place to a social self, morally related to an increasing number of other human beings. The dynamism of human evolution demands that this education of man must contnnue till he rises from ego-centredness to ego-transcendence, and jrom knowledge to wisdom. Referring to this urgent need to rise from knowledge to wisdom, the late Bertrand Russell says *(The Impact of Science on Society* pp.120-21):

> *We are in the middle of a race between human skill as to means and human folly as to ends. Given sufficient folly as to ends, every increase in the skill required to achieve them is to the bad. The human race has survived hitherto owing to ignorance and incompetence; but, given knowledge and competence combined with folly, there can be no certainty of survival. Knowledge is power, but it is power for evil just as much as for good. It follows that,* unless men increase in wisdom as in knowledge, increase of knowledge will be increase of sorrow. *(italics not by the author).*

Biology speaks of the principle of homeostasis, or homeorhesis, as clarified by biologist Waddington, by which nature effected an automatic stabilisation of internal conditions in the organism of the higher mammals. This helped in the slow evolution of the brain until, in man, she perfected the higher brain. The organism's need for physical survival and organic satisfactions, and her own need for numerical increase—all these have been relegated by nature to the care of man's lower brain, thus releasing his higher brain, 'for functions surpassing the wonders of homeostasis itself', according to modern neurology *(The Living Brain,* p.16), or to function as the most wonderful instrument for carrying evolution to its specifically human fields, namely, the psychosocial, or the moral and the spiritual, according to Vedānta.

Psycho-social Evolution as Spiritual Growth

The capacity and fitness of the higher brain to undertake and fulfil this high function is directly proportional to its freedom from thraldom to his lower brain, from slavery to his sensory apparatus and its appetites, from the pressures and pulls of his lower nature. It is obvious that his higher brain, with its powers of imagination and reason, may stultify itself by functioning as the *tail-end* of the sensory apparatus and of the lower brain. It may, on the other hand, redeem itself, and also become true to itself, by becoming truly higher. It is ethical discipline, what Vedānta calls *śarna* and *dama,* discipline of the mind and discipline of the senses, that helps the higher brain to thus redeem itself, and become the agent also of man's redemption. *This is human reason and will in its true form,* what Vedānta calls *buddhi,* the supreme instrument which lifts life from knowledge to wisdom and from bondage to freedom. Referring to the significance, through homeostasis, of this development of the higher brain, Grey Walter claims (*ibid.,* p.18):

> 'For mammals all, homeostasis meant survival; but for man, emancipation.'

Thus the spiritual growth of man is a fact. And the more we know the science and technique of this growth, the better for us and for our society. Growth, both the concept and the word, is of protean significance. We know and recognise two types of human growth, namely, physical and mental, the second less palpably than the first. A baby at birth is about seven pounds in body weight; and every day it increases in weight. It drinks its mother's milk, to be followed by other types of food and drink; and it grows steadily until it becomes a full-frown healthy man or woman of seventy or eighty kilos weight. This is the palpable physical growth of man; and we ensure it by appropriate physical nourishment accompanied with exercise. Equally important, though less obvious, is his mental growth. Through education, a human child grows in alertness, self-confidence, and a sense of individual worth and dignity; this growth continues till he becomes an intellectual giant or a giant of will. This is the mental growth of man which we ensure through appropriate mental nourishment—through education, institutional and non-institutional.

These two types of growth are necessary, but not sufficient. There is a third type of growth, most vital and significant, but least recognised, without which the other two will prove his undoing, individually and collectively, without which his craving and search for fulfilment will only result in unfulfilment and defeat. This is his spiritual growth, or growth in his spiritual dimension, which finds expression in ethical awareness and social feeling to begin with, and finds, according to Vedānta, its consummation in the experience, by him, of the infinite, universal, and divine dimension of his individuality, the Atman.

Status of the Ego in Evolution

The ego that made man dominate nature is not his true self, but only an initial datum, a promise of greater things to come. It is like the tip of a rock seen above the water level, with the immense rock mass itself lying unseen, and waiting to be revealed, below the water level. The real Self of man, says India's *adhyātma-vidyā,* science of man as the Ātman, is inaccessible to the sense organs and to the sense-bound mind, but accessible to the *buddhi,* or reason, when it becomes subtle and pure—*buddhi-grāhyam, atīndriyam,* as the *Gītā* expresses it. That the ego is unreal, that man's individuality or selfhood does not consist in the ego, is the central truth also of Buddhism; and this is affirmed by modern biology also. In the words of *The Science of Life,* a voluminous digest of modern biological knowledge by H.G. Wells, G.P. Wells, and Julian Huxley, in its section dealing with the philosophical implications of biology (pp.878-79):

> Alone, in the silence of the night, and on a score of thoughtful occasions, we have demanded: can this self, so vividly central to my universe, so greedily possessive of the world, ever cease to be? Without it, surely, there is no world at all! And yet, this conscious self dies nightly when we sleep, and we cannot trace the stages by which in its stages it crept to an awareness of its own existence.

> Personality (centred in the ego) may be only one of nature's methods, a convenient provisional delusion of considerable strategic value. ...
>
> The more intelligent and comprehensive man's picture of the universe has become, the more intolerable has become his concentration on the individual life with its inevitable final rejection. ...
>
> He escapes from his ego by this merger (identification with and participation in a greater being), and acquires an impersonal immortality in the association, his identity dissolving into the greater identity. This is the essence of much religious mysticism, and it is remarkable how closely the biological analysis of individuality brings us to the mystics. ...
>
> The Western mystic and the Eastern sage find a strong effect of endorsement in modern science and the everyday teaching of practical morality; both teach that self must be subordinated, that self is a method and not an end.

The science and technique of spiritual growth, from the 'convenient provisional delusion' of the ego to the true self, is the special contribution of ethics, aesthetics, and religion. It provides spiritual nourishment to man both when he is at work and when he is at worship, when he is in society and when he is alone. Work done in a spirit of service and dedication, reinforced by an inward penetration through worship and meditation, through *bhakti* and *bhajan,* forms the twin technique of spiritual growth, according to Śrī Kṛṣṇa's teaching in the *Gītā* (VIII. 7):

> *Tasmāt sarveṣu kāleṣu*
> *māmanusmara, yuddhya ca*

'Therefore, at all times, meditate upon Me, and engage yourself in the battle (of life)'; and, again, in verse 55 of chapter XI, introducing which Śaṅkarācārya says:

Adhunā sarvasya gītā-śāstrasya
sāra-bhūto artho niḥśreyasārtho
anuṣṭheyatvena samuccitya ucyate

'Now is proclaimed the practical implications of the essence of the meaning of the entire science of the *Gītā* designed to lead one to spiritual freedom:'

Matkarmakṛt, mat-paramo,
mat bhaktaḥ saṅga-varjitaḥ;
Nirvairaḥ sarvabhūteṣu
yaḥ sa māmeti Pāṇḍava

'Perform work (in a spirit of dedication) to Me; make Me the supreme goal (of your life); be My devotee, free from attachment and enmity to all beings; such (a seeker) attains to Me alone, O Arjuna.'

The laboratory for this science of spiritual growth is life itself, with its twin arenas of work outside and meditation within. The temple or church or mosque outside, or the worship room within the house, properly used, also provides another laboratory. More important than these two is the laboratory of a trained and pure mind. Worship and rituals and other religious practices form useful aids, if they are not done as items of a static piety, not done as ends in themselves, but as means to spiritual growth, as instruments of a dynamic spirituality, as a depth education for character.

Kinship between Ancient Vedānta and Modern Science

Swami Vivekananda has shown that religion, as developed in India in her Vedānta, and modern science, are close to each other in spirit and temper and objectives. Both are spiritual disciplines. Even in the cosmology of the physical universe, in the theory of the unity of cause and effect, in the unity and conservation of matter and energy, and in the concept of evolution, cosmic and organic, the two reveal many points of contract. Unlike as in the super-naturalistic theologies of the West, the fundamental position in the cosmology of both Vedānta and modern science is, what Swami Vivekananda calls, 'the postulate (of the ultimate reality), of a self-evolving cause'. Vedānta calls it Brahman, which is a universal spiritual principle. The *Taittirīya Upaniṣad* (III. 1) defines Brahman in a majestic utterance, which will be welcomed by every scientific thinker:

Yato vā imāni bhūtāni jāyante,
yena jātani jīvanti;

yat prayantyabhisaṁviśanti;
tadvijijñāsasva; tad brahmeti

'Wherefrom all these entities are born, by which, being born, they abide; into which, at the time of dissolution, they enter—seek to know That; That is Brahman.'

To the modern scientist, that self-evolving cause is a material reality, the *background material* or *cosmic dust,* as astrophysicist Fred Hoyle terms it; whereas, to Vedānta, *which views it also in the light of the consciousness revealed in its evolutionary product, namely, man,* it is a universal spiritual principle, the *cit ākāśa.*

Referring to this spiritual kinship between modern science and ancient Vedānta, Swami Vivekananda said in his speech at the Parliament of Religions held at Chicago in 1893 (*Complete Works,* Vol. I, eleventh edition, p.15):

> Manifestation, and not creation, is the word of science today, and the Hindu is only glad that what he has been

> cherishing in his bosom for ages is going to be taught in more forcible language, and with further light, from the latest conclusions of science.

Although modern scientific thought does not yet have, like Vedānta, a recognised place for any spiritual reality or principle, several scientists of the twentieth century, including biologists like Teilhard de Chardin and Julian Huxley, as pointed out earlier, have endeavoured to soften the materialism of physical science and to find a place for spiritual experience in the scientific world picture. Even Thomas Huxley, as quoted earlier, had termed materialism *an intruder.* In this century, this protest has come from great physicists also. Sir James Jeans found that the final picture of the universe emerging from twentieth-century physical science was one in which the notion of matter was completely eliminated, 'mind reigning supreme and alone' (*The New Background of Science,* p.307). Astrophysicist R.A. Millikan considered materialism 'a philosophy of unintelligence' (*An Autobiography,* last chapter).

Philosophy: Synthesis of Science and Religion

If twentieth-century physics is thus turning its face away from thoroughgoing materialism, twentieth-century biology is not behind it in this orientation. The whole of modern scientific thought is in the throes of a silent spiritual revolution with the emergence, on the horizon of scientific thought, of the challenge of mind and consciousness, and the consequent need to develop, what Jeans terms, *a new background of science* in the light of what he says further (*The New Background of Science,* pp.2-6):

> The old philosophy ceased to work at the end of the nineteenth century, and the twentieth-century physicist is hammering out a new philosophy for himself. Its essence is that he no longer sees nature as something entirely

> distinct from himself. Sometimes it is what he himself creates or selects or abstracts; sometimes it is what he destroys.
>
> Thus the history of physical science in the twentieth-century is one of a progressive emancipation from the purely human angle of vision.

Julian Huxley and Chardin find the spiritual character of the world-stuff successively revealed in the course of organic evolution. Biology, in its theory of evolution, they hold, reveals what Chardin calls a *within* to nature, over and above and different from the *without* of nature revealed by physics and astronomy. Vedānta terms the 'within' as the *pratyak rūpa* and the 'without' as the *parāk rūpa* of one and the same nature.

When the significance of this *within* of things is recognised in modern science, the scientific 'background material' will undergo a spiritual orientation and thus come closer to Brahman, the 'background reality' of Vedānta. *The synthesis of the knowledge of the within and the without is philosophy;* and this was what India achieved in her Vedānta ages ago as *saṁyak-jñāna,* comprehensive or perfect knowledge of total Reality. Reality itself does not know any distinction between a within and a without. These distinctions are made only by the human mind for the convenience of study and research and daily life.

As the different branches of the physical sciences are but different approaches to the study of one and the same reality, namely, physical nature, and as all such branches of study, when pursued far enough, tend to mingle and merge into a grand science of the physical universe, *into a unified science of the 'without' of nature,* so the science of the 'within' and the science of the 'without' mingle and merge in a science of Brahman, the total Reality. This is how Vedānta viewed its *Brahmavidyā,* science of Brahman, the term Brahman standing for the totality of Reality, physical and non-physical. The *Muṇḍaka Upaniṣad* (I. i. 1) defines

Brahmavidyaā as *sarva-vidyā pratiṣṭhā,* the *pratiṣṭhā,* or basis, of every *vidyā,* or science. Says Śrī Kṛṣṇa in the *Gītā* (XIII. 2):

> *Kṣetra-kṣetrajñayor jñānaṁ*
> *yat tat jñānaṁ mataṁ mama*

'The knowledge of *kṣetra,* the not-self (the 'without' of things), and of *kṣetrajña* the knower of the *kṣetra* (the 'within' of things), is true knowledge, according to Me.'

Dealing with the all-inclusiveness of this Vedāntic thought as expounded by Swami Vivekananda, Romain Rolland says *(The Life of Vivekananda,* p.289):

> But it is a matter of indifference to the calm pride of him who deems himself the stronger whether science accepts free Religion, in Vivekananda's sense of the term, or not; for his Religion accepts Science. It is vast enough to find a place at its table for all loyal seekers after truth.

In his lecture on 'The Absolute and Manifestation' delivered in London in 1896, Swami Vivekananda said *(Complete Works,* Vol. II, ninth edition, p.140):

> Do you not see whither science is tending? The Hindu nation proceeded through the study of the mind, through metaphysics and logic. The European nations start from external nature, and now they, too, are coming to the same results. We find that, searching through the mind, we at last come to that Oneness, that universal One, the internal Soul of everything, the essence and reality of everything.... Through material science, we come to the same Oneness.

Śrī Kṛṣṇa's Synthesis of Science and Religion

The *Śrīmad Bhāgavatam* refers to this complementary character of physical science and the science of religion, with respect to human knowledge and fulfilment, in a profound utterance of Śrī Kṛṣṇa (XI. vii. 19-21):

Prāyeṇa manujā loke
loka-tattva-vicakṣaṇāḥ;
Samuddharanti hyātmānam
ātmanaivā-śubhāśayāt

'Generally, in the world, men who are efficient in the investigation of the truth of the external world or nature, uplift themselves by themselves from all sources of evil.

Ātmano gururātmaiva
puruṣasya viśeṣataḥ;
Yat pratyakṣānumānābhyāṁ
śreyo'sau anuvindate

'For a human being, particularly, his *guru* (teacher) is his own self; because he achieves his welfare through (inquiring into) direct sense experience and (inductive-deductive) inference based on the same.'

Puruṣatve ca māṁ dhīrāḥ
sāṁkhya-yoga-viśāradāḥ;
Āvistarāṁ prapaśyanti
sarva-śakty-upabṛṁhitam

'In this very human personality also, wise men, who have mastered the science and art of spirituality, clearly realise Me (God, as the one universal Self of all) as the infinite reservoir of all energies.'

Vedāntic Vision of Evolution

Vedānta views the entire evolutionary process as progressive evolution of structure and form, and as greater and greater manifestation of the infinite Self within. It is evolution of matter and manifestation of spirit. Twentieth-century biology recognises, in the first appearance of living organisms, the emergence, in a rudimentary form, of the unique datum of *experience,* through the unique datum of awareness. The living cell, described by biology as self-duplicating matter, discloses the emergence of *experience* as a new value which the immense cosmos never revealed in its billions of years of history.

This spiritual value of awareness 'grows' as it were, in richness and variety, as we move up the evolutionary ladder, defining and enlarging progressively the datum of experience with its two poles of the experiencer and the experienced. The evolution of the nervous system discloses progressive development of awareness in depth and range, and consequent increase in the grip of the organism on its environment.

This awareness achieves a new and significant breakthrough with the appearance of man on the evolutionary scene. 'Man is unique in more ways than one', says Julian Huxley. The field of awareness of all other organisms is, largely, the exterṭnal environment and, to a small extent, also the interior of their bodies—the 'without' of nature. Man alone has awareness of the self, as the *subject* of experience, along with awareness of the not-self, as the *object* of experience, of both the *within* and the *without* of nature.

That is the uniqueness of man, according to both twentieth-century biology and ancient Vedānta. Self-awareness, which neurology considers as the source of the dominance of man over all nature, and which nature achieved through the evolution of the human cerebral system, and which remains a minor and hazy pole of experience in the early stages of human evoluṭtion, is a new dimension of awareness containing tremendous implications, says Indian philosophy, for man's further evolutionary destiny as much as for his philosophy of man and nature.

The Vedāntic view of evolution and of man's uniqueness finds a unique statement in the *Śrīmad Bhāgavatam* (XI. 9. 28):

Sṛṣṭvā purāṇi vividhā-
nyajayātmaśaktyā
vṛkṣān sarī-sṛpa-paśūn
khaga-daṁśa-matsyān;
Taistaiḥ atuṣṭa-hṛdayaḥ
puruṣaṁ vidhāya
brahmāvaloka-dhiṣaṇaṁ
mudam āpa devaḥ

'The divine One, having projected (evolved), with His own inherent power, various forms such as trees, reptiles, cattle, birds, insects and fish, was not satisfied at heart with forms such as these; He then projected the human form endowed with the capacity to realise Brahman (the universal divine Self of all), and became exṭtremely pleased.'

India's Religious Urge: Realisation and Not Speculation

Evolution has revealed that the mystery of the universe stirs in man as the mystery of the self. The mystery of the universe will ever remain a mystery until this mystery of the self is cleared. Till then, all our conclusions about the truth of the universe, proceeding from science or philosophy, theology or logic, will be speculative ventures yielding mere postulates and conjectures. The Indian mind was not content to remain at the stage of mere speculation or conjecture in so important a field as the knowledge of the ultimate truth about man and nature. Her thinkers boldly penetrated into the world within, taking the facts of awareness and the ego as the clue, as the *footprints,* in the words of the *Bṛhadāraṇyaka Upaniṣad* (I. 4. 7). And when they penetrated to the depth, they discovered the one infinite and eternal reality behind the finite and the time-bound, and designated that reality as *anubhava svarūpa,* 'of the nature of (infinite) *Experience', cit svarūpa,* 'of the nature of *Pure Consciousness',* of which the infinite varieties of objects and subjects in the world are but passing configurations. The *Bṛhadāraṇyaka* registers this approach, and the object of its search, in another significant passage (HI. 4. 1):

Yat sākṣāt aparokṣāt brahma,
ya ātmā sarvāntaraḥ

'The Brahman that is immediate and direct, the Ātman that is the innermost Self of all.'

'That thou art' (*Tat tvam asi),* proclaims the *Chāndogya Upaniṣad* (VI. viii. 7), aligning mortal man with the immortal divine. Again and again, the Upaniṣads reiterate this great truth. If man as scientist has such a profound dimension that he can comprehend the vast universe in a formula given by his thought, what must be the dimension of man as the Ātman, as Pure Consciousness, as the unchangeable infinite Self? The Reality that 'remains undivided in the divided things and processes of the world', as the *Gītā* puts it (XIII. 16). The mystery of the universe was finally resolved through the solution of the mystery disclosed within man himself. The sages of the Upaniṣads discovered the centre of the universe in the centre of man. Through that discovery, man was revealed in his infinite dimension; and the universe was also revealed in all its spiritual glory. Realisation of this truth is the only way to life-fulfilment, say the Upaniṣads. Says the *Śvetāśvatara Upaniṣad* (II. 15):

Yadātma-tattvena tu brahma-tattvam
dīpopameneha yuktaḥ prapaśyet;
Ajaṁ dhruvaṁ sarvatattvaiḥ viśuddham
jñātvā devaṁ mucyate sarva-pāpaiḥ

'When the self-controlled spiritual aspirant realises in this very body the truth of Brahman (the infinite Self of all) through the truth of the Ātman (the Self), self-luminous as light, then, knowing the Divinity which is unborn, eternal, and untouched by the modifications of nature, he is freed from all evil.'

This and similar other verses from the Upaniṣads communicate a profound joyous discovery, as can be seen even from the language in which it is couched in that immortal literature. In reaching the ultimate Truth of the Ātman, they had reached also the ultimate of being and knowledge, peace and joy, the unifying *Field of Infinite Experience* itself. Hence they communicated their discovery as the discovery of the inexhaustible mine of *satyam* (truth), *jñānam* (knowledge) and *anantam* (infinitude), or of *sat* (existence), *cit* (knowledge) and *ānanda* (bliss). In the struggle to realise this truth and the life-fulfilment it involves, they saw the true meaning of the entire course of cosmic and organic evolution, especially of human evolution.

The organism seeks fulfilment; that is the end and aim of all its activities and processes, says modern biology. In the Upaniṣads, we have the beautiful concepts of *mukti,* freedom, and *pūrṇatā,* fullness. We are bound now; we are fragmented now. We want to become free; we want to become integral, and experience fullness. Jesus Christ calls it 'perfection': 'Be ye therefore perfect, even as your Father which is in heaven is perfect' (Matthew, V. 48). To experience the delight of freedom, to enlarge the bounds of man's awareness, to get *bodhi,* complete enlightenment, as the Buddha expressed it, is the great aim of human evolution. Education, science, culture, socio-political processes, and religion are meant to increase and enlarge the bounds of human awareness and the range and depth of human fulfilment, by increasing man's knowledge of, and control over, not only the outside world, but also the deep recesses within himself. Knowledge is power, in the positive sciences; it is still more so in the science of religion, the science of the inner nature of man, where the power that is gained is not only greater in human terms of quantity, *but also higher in terms of quality.*

Dharma as Social Ethics

Man cannot advance on the long road of his spiritual growth, or psycho-social evolution, without *disciplining* his urges for organic satisfactions; he has to bring a certain measure of stabilisation in his inner life through such discipline, by his own knowledge and efforts; this is the second homeostasis to be achieved by him, over and above the first homeostasis achieved by nature for him, and to be dealt with in more detail later. It is this second homeostasis that is emphasised by the *Gītā,* namely *samatvam yoga ucyate*—'*Yoga* is called *samatvam,* equanimity;' this is the spiritual equivalent of the dictum of the great French physiologist Claude Bernard to be dealt with later: *A fixed interior milieu is the condition for the free life.*

It is this discpline that is indicated in the Indian concept of *dharma,* or ethical sense, which is inseparable from any ordered human society. Bereft of it, man becomes reduced to a beast, says Indian wisdom: *dharmeṇa hīnāḥ paśubhih samānāḥ.* Dharma, as the principle of integration between man and man in society, does not mean religion in the sense of creed, doctrine or ritual, nor any scheme of an other-worldly salvation. A mere accumulation of bricks does not constitute a building; it needs cement to unite brick to brick to make for its integrated structure. Similarly, a mere aggregation of individuals does not constitute a society; there is an integrating principle that makes for the evolution of a dynamic and expansive *personality* out of a static *individuality,* and that helps to hold its members together; and that principle is *dharma*; it stresses the idea of mutuality, inter-dependence. Man needs the context of other human beings for his very humanisation. This is how Śrī Kṛṣṇa expounds *dharma* in the *Mahābhārata: Dhāraṇāt dharma ityāhuḥ, dharmo dhārayate prajāḥ.*

The *Puruṣārthas* in the Context of Psycho-social Evolution

Indian spiritual tradition does not frown, or look down upon *kāma,* organic satisfaction or *artha,* wealth, which is the means to *kāma,* but treats them as valid pursuits, or *puruṣārthas.* But it considers, *lobha,* or greed, and *moha,* or delusion, arising from unchecked organic cravings, as unethical, because they are anti-social. And to restrain these two pursuits from becoming antisocial, it presents a third vital human pursuit, or *puruṣārtha,* namely, *dharma,* ethical sense. It is this third *puruṣārtha,* namely, *dharma,* that helps all people, not just a few powerful and clever ones only, to experience the first two *puruṣārthas,* namely, *kāma* and *artha.* The validity and creative role of *kāma* is presented in the *Gītā* by Śrī Kṛṣṇa, the human manifestation of the one divine Self in all, in his statement (VII. 11):

Dharmā-viruddho bhūteṣu
kāmo'smi bharatarṣabha

'I am that *kāma,* sensual desire, in all beings, which is unopposed to *dharma.'*

Indian spiritual tradition refers to *dharma, artha,* and *kāma,* as the *trivarga,* the inseparable group of three, treats them as the universal warp and weft of all ordered human society, theistic, atheistic, or agnostic, and presents *mokṣa,* absolute freedom of the spirit, as the fourth *puruṣārtha,* which is an optional trans-social pursuit meant for those few who desire, and who dare, to go deeper into the spiritual dimensions of reality and realise one's true nature in all its glory. For all the rest, this *moksa* experience comes,- within the limitations of the social context, as *dharma. Dharma, thus, is the confluence of the secular and the spiritual, of the social and the trans-social;* and every sacred and secular literature of India sings its glory. Indian culture is rooted in, and inspired by, this great value of *dharma.* The mystical heights of Indian, and of all world, religions are the expressions of the trans-social *mokṣa* ideal and value.

It is an echo of this great value of *dharma* that we get in the concept of *psycho-social evolution* of twentieth-century biology and in its corollary concepts of *quality* and *fulfilment* as the criteria of evolution at the human stage. And in the emphasis on detachment from the ego, and from the organic system and its cravings centred in it, modern psycho-social evolution echoes the ancient *anāskti-yoga* of the *Gītā.*

Religion: Ethnical Versus Spiritual

A scientific study of religion reveals two dimensions to every religion, especially to every one of the highly developed world religions, namely, religion as a socio-political expression and religion as a path to the experience of God, or any value equivalent to it. The first consists of the do's and don'ts of religion and the rules and regulations about food, dress, marriage, and other social disciplines, besides myths and legends and cosmological theories. These constitute the sociopolitical constituents of religion, which find a place for it in the census registers and which demarcate it from other religions. It cannot constitute the science of religion but only a historically conditioned socio-political expression of religion. A science of religion will classify religions in terms such as of their *bhakti-yoga, jñāna-yoga, rāja-yoga* and *karma-yoga* contents. This second dimension consists of the truly spiritual part, with its emphasis on personal morality, worship and adoration, and the disciplines designed to ensure the spiritual growth of man. These constitute the essential and the invariable and the universal core of religion, while the former form its variable non-essential part, which is also relevant, but only when it does not choke the spirit of the latter.

Indian tradition calls the former the *smṛti,* and the latter the *śruti,* constituent of a religion, and considers the *śruti* as eternal and universal in validity and the *smṛti* as local, parochial and temporary in application. Accordingly, the *śruti* represents the *sanātana dharma,* eternal religion, which remains, while the *smṛti* represents the *yuga dharma,* the religion for a particular *yuga,* or age, which changes. India, therefore, considers the *yuga dharma* constituent of a religion not only not applicable for all people universally, but even irrelevant to its own people of a later age, due to changes in conditions of life of the people concerned. So Indian tradition provides for appropriate changes in the *smṛtis* and the *yuga dharma,* to make them relevant for the changed social circumstances which render them obsolete, and often harmful. Sri Ramakrishna expresses this Indian wisdom in a brief and meaningful utterance: The Moghul coins have no *currency* under the East India Company's rule. Human and social distortions are the product of the dominance of these obsolete elements of a socio-religious tradition; they sustain the rigidities of social customs, anti-human practices, inter-religious and intra-religious frictions, disharmonies, and persecutions, and the stagnation and immobility of human attitudes.

The fundamental message of all religions, however, derives from their central core of essential spiritual truths, which constitute their *śruti* element. These spiritual truths are *apauruṣeya,* impersonal, and therefore, universal; they were discovered by the scientists of religion, the mystics. The authenticity of these truths lies in their being experienced by spiritual experimenters *and in their being capable of re-verification by others.* Explaining this authenticity with respect to the Vedas of the Hindu tradition, Swami Vivekananda said in the course of his address at the Chicago Parliament of Religions in 1893 *(Complete Works,* Vol. I, pp.6-7):

> By the Vedas no books are meant; they mean the accumulated treasury of spiritual laws discovered by

> different persons in different times. Just as the law of gravitation existed before its discovery, and would exist if all humanity forgot it, so is it with the laws that govern the spiritual world. The moral, ethical, and spiritual relations between soul and soul, and between individual spirits and the Father of all spirits, were there before their discovery, and would remain even if we forgot them.
>
> The discoverers of these laws are called ṛṣis (sages), and we honour them as perfected beings. I am glad to tell this audience that some of the very greatest of them were women.

The above description can be relevant only with respect to the *śruti* constituent of Hinduism, and of every other world religion. The only difference lies in this, that it is only in the Hindu tradition that this distinction between the universality of the *śruti* and the limited relevance of the *smṛti* is fully recognised and applied; and that social innovators and religious prophets are not only not persecuted and killed, but are honoured and followed. And this blessing Hinduism owes to its immortal literature of the Upaniṣads, which is all *śruti* and with no touch of *smṛti.* They are the only sacred books, both within Hinduism and outside of it, which addressed themselves *exclusively* to the discovery of spiritual truths and to leading man, irrespective of caste, creed, and race, to their realisation in human life, and to the creation in India of a dynamic and healthy climate of active toleration and harmony as the inalienable characteristic of Indian culture and life.

In the light of this *śruti-smṛti* concept, we see the kinship of science only with that aspect of religion as a spiritual path to God, the *śruti* constituent, and very little kinship with its sociopolitical expression, the *smṛti* constituent. The term *ethnical religion* emphasises the dominance of this *smṛti* element, with its group exclusiveness and tribal loyalties. And it is this ethnical religion that stagnates in course of time, resists social change, and collides against physical science and all creative social endeavour. In all religions, the ethnic element, in course of time, becomes increasingly centred in the priest and the feudal power, and the universal spiritual element is centred in the Prophet and the divine incarnation. The ethnical aspect of religion will continue to remain; but it must be subordinated, says the Hindu tradition, to the spiritual aspect, if it is to aid man in his spiritual growth.

India and the Scientific Approach to Religion

The methods of investigation in the field of religion are largely the same as in the positive sciences: Collection of facts, their classification, a dispassionate study of these so as to reveal the law or laws underlying them, such knowledge leading to the control over the phenomena concerned, and, finally, the application of such knowledge for the technique of man's spiritual growth, for the alleviation of human suffering, and for the enrichment and fulfilment of human life. This kind of study of religion, as a thorough scientific study of the facts of the inner life, was undertaken by the great sages of ancient India; the insights which they gained were re-tested and amplified by a galaxy of subsequent sages, leaving to posterity the invaluable legacy of a rich and dynamic scientific tradition in the field of religion.

It is because of this adamantine, rational, and experiential base that Indian spirituality, and the culture deriving nourishment from it, have stood the test of time. That also explains its hospitality to modern physical science, and its pride in the remarkable achievements of this sister discipline developed by the modern West.

Says Romain Rolland about this quality of Indian philosophical thought *(The Life of Vivekananda,* p.196):

> The true Vedāntic spirit does not start out with a system of preconceived ideas. It possesses absolute liberty and

> unrivalled courage among religions with regard to the facts to be observed and the diverse hypotheses it has laid down for their coordination. Never having been hampered by a priestly order, each man has been entirely free to search wherever he pleased for the spiritual explanation of the spectacle of the universe.

After a thorough investigation into the real nature of man, the sages of the Upaniṣads made a fundamental discovery; man, in his essential nature, is divine; behind the finite man is the Ātman, ever free, ever pure, and ever luminous.

The body, the mind, and the ego are merely the externals of the real man who is immortal and divine. This discovery led to the further discovery that the same divinity is the ground of the world as well. This they termed Brahman, the totality of the Self and the not-Self, which they characterised as *satyaṁ jñānam anantam*—'Truth, Consciousness (or knowledge) and Infinity.'

Parā Vidyā and Aparā Vidyā

In the *Muṇḍaka Upaniṣad,* we find this question put by an earnest student to a great teacher (I. I. 3):

> *Kasmin nu bhagavo vijnāte sarvam idaṁ vijñātaṁ bhavati*

'What is that reality, O blessed One, by knowing which we can know all that there is in this manifested universe?'

Is there such a unique reality by knowing which we can understand all the manifestations of nature, internal as well as external? Is there a unity behind this diversity, a one behind the many? To this question, the teacher gave a very significant reply (*ibid.,* I. 1.4):

> *Dve vidye veditavye, iti ha sma yad brahmavido vadanti,*
> *parā caiva aparā ca*

'Two are the *vidyās,* or sciences, to be acquired by man; so say the knowers of Brahman. One is called *parā vidyā,* higher science or knowledge, the other is called *aparā vidya,* ordinary science or knowledge.'

Both these must be investigated. Of these, the *aparā* or ordinary knowledge, says the teacher of the *Upaniṣad,* consists of the sacred Vedas, phonetics, the code of rituals, grammar, etymology, prosody, and astronomy. In fact, it includes, what we would today call, the entire gamut of positivistic knowledge, including the *second-hand* knowledge of the experience of religion, contained in the sacred books of all religions.

Here, we have a scientific mind of the highest order—impersonal, objective, and detached. There is no desire to put forth a pet opinion; truth alone is the motive power, even if that truth goes against one's pet attachments and aversions. The teacher says that even the Vedas, the sacred books of the whole people, belong to the category of ordinary knowledge. Who would dare to say that his own sacred books are ordinary, except he who is of a detached and scientific frame of mind, and is in search of truth and not a dogma—he who has no truth to hide, no opinion to uphold, no prejudice to defend, who just wants to know the truth and is prepared to sacrifice everything else into the bargain? No religion except that derived from the *Upaniṣadic* tradition has practised this bold detachment. The follower of every other religion, if asked what is ordinary knowledge, would unhesitatingly reply: All the sacred books of all the religions except my own. But this teacher of the *Upaniṣads* has the detachment and boldness, proceeding from love of truth, to say that even the Vedas, held in such veneration by himself and by his people, were secondary; all the sacred books and all the positive sciences and the arts are but lower knowledge—*aparā, vidyā.*

Sri Ramakrishna, in our time, re-emphasised this spirit when he said: The Vedas and all other sacred books do not contain God, they contain only *information about* God. They are like the Hindu almanac which contains forecast of the rainfall of the year. But, added Sri Ramakrishna, by squeezing the almanac you won't get a drop of water! Similarly, by squeezing the sacred scriptures, none can get God; but by squeezing one's own experience, all can realise God; for He is the one Self of all.

What, then, is left to be included in the category of *parā vidyā,* higher knowledge? The teacher proceeds to indicate this elusive theme. There is a tremendous field of knowledge, area of experience, still left, he thinks; but it belongs to a different order. So he says (*ibid.,* I. 1.5):

Atha parā, yayā tad akṣaram adhigamyate

'That is *parā, vidyā,* or higher science, by which the imperishable (Reality) is realised.'

Physical science and all the rest deal only with things that change, that are perishable. As Sir Arthur Eddington has put it, science gives us 'knowledge of structural form and not knowledge of content'. The sacred books give us, in the words of Sri Ramakrishna referred to above, only *information about* God, and not God Himself. And yet we feel that, in the words of Eddington, 'all through the physical universe runs that unknown content'. What is that content? And how can we get at it? If the positive sciences cannot get at it, there must be another discipline, another line of inquiry, which must be able to give us that truth.

If the sacred books contain only information about God, there must be a discipline which gives us God and not merely information about Him. It is this inquiry that pervades the Upaniṣads and that has made them immortal even as literature. And the nature and scope of that inquiry, and the way *it* was conducted, and the truths gained therefrom, have something superb about them. There is no effort to uphold a mere opinion, however dear; no struggle to pronounce a dogma and cling to it, and thrust it upon others; there is no trace of tiredness, or laziness of mind, seeking a resting place on the way. Truth, and nothing but truth, is the watchword. Suffused with the spirit of truth, they declared *(ibid.,* III. 1.6):

Satyameva jayate nānṛtam,
Satyena panthā vitato devayānaḥ

'Truth alone triumphs, not untruth; the path to the luminous Reality is spread out with truth only.'

And this path to the luminous Reality is strewn with the debris of discarded opinions, pleasing dogmas, broken hypotheses, and even dethroned gods! Thought was not allowed to rest on any of them for long; it forged ahead on the two wings of *critical discrimination* and *inner detachment, viveka* and *vairāgya,* and wafted by the current of a single-minded passion for truth. One sage puts forth his conclusion about the data of the internal world gathered by him; another shows it as inadequate; this stimulates further inquiry, leading to a deeper pronouncement.

There was this unwearied and joyous search, and graceful conflict of thought between the most gifted minds, through which thought forged ahead. There was no national dogma or authoritarian church to suppress or arrest it. The whole process reached its consummation in the profound discovery of the imperishable Self of man, the Ātman, and its spiritual unity with the Self of the universe, the Brahman. The entire process was a joyous voyage of discovery; looking back, they saw that the steps left behind were also valid, and that man travels not from error to truth, but from truth to truth, from lower truth to higher truth.

India's Spiritual Vision of Unity in Diversity

It is in this context, against this background, that the Indian approach to religion becomes significant. From the time of the Upaniṣads to our own times, India has sought in religion, not a finished dogma to believe in, but a method and a means to pierce the veil that hides the ever-present truth behind man and nature. The Upaniṣads glowingly register this passion of the Indian mind to seek and find truth through a penetrating study of experience. In the appreciative words of the American missionary Robert Ernest Hume *(The Thirteen Principal Upaniṣads,* p.30, footnote):

> The earnestness of the search for truth is one of the delightful and commendable features of the Upaniṣads.

The sages of the Upaniṣads, after a critical and penetrating search into the depth of man—'by means of the subtle *buddhi,* or reason, that had been trained by the sages in the search and discovery of subtle truths', as one of the Upaniṣads puts it—*agryayā buddhyā sūkṣmayā sūkṣmadarśibhiḥ (Kaṭha Upaniṣad,* III. 12)—had discovered that imperishable reality as the one and non-dual Self, the Ātman. The opening verse of the *Īśā Upaniṣad* proclaims this sublime truth in a verse which has inspired the philosophy of the *Gītā* and innumerable spiritual seekers thereafter: *Īśāvāsyam idam sarvaṁ yat kiñca jagatyāṁ jagat*—'All this universe, in all its changing forms, is enveloped by the Lord.' The second verse of chapter five of the *Kaṭha Upaniṣad,* which Śaṅkarācārya introduces in his commentary in the words: 'The Ātman is not a dweller in the "city" of one (the human) body only; what else? He is the dweller in all bodies', says:

> *Haṁsaḥ śuciṣat vasu-rantarikṣasat*
> *hotā vediṣat atithir-duroṇasat;*
> *Nṛṣat varasat ṛtasat vyomasat*
> *abjā gojā ṛtajā adrijā ṛtaṁ bṛhat*

'He is the swan dwelling in the heaven (in the form of the sun), the air filling the atmosphere, the fire dwelling on the altar, the holy guest in the house; (He is) in man, in gods, in the sacrifice, in the immensity of space; (He is) born in water (as the aquatic creatures), on the earth (as insects, reptiles and mammals); (He is) born as (the fruit of) sacrifice, born of the mountains (as rivers flowing from the mountains to the ocean); (He is) the True, the Infinite.'

This great verse, conveying a profound spiritual vision, occurs also in the *Ṛg-Veda* (VI. 40. 5), with the last word omitted. This is the vision that determined the Indian attitude to nature, to the physical, botanical, zoological, and human environments, not as an enemy to be conquered, as in the West, but as a friend to be understood and respected and wisely used. As an enemy, man plunders and ravages nature; that attitude inevitably passes on to other human beings also, resulting in wars and colonial exploitations and slave trade; it also produces serious ecological imbalances, until violated nature begins to violate and mutilate the perpetrator himself. This is the tragedy that is being experienced by modern man, and that is posing a serious challenge to human wisdom today.

Divine Gall—An Interview with Swami Ranganathanandaji

'Monastic life was open to all those who felt the (Divine) call and had the necessary inner strength and that caste, creed and sex was no bar to it.'

–Swami Ranganathananda

Swami Ranganathananda, fondly called 'Shankaran', was born in a wealthy agricultural family of Sri Neelakantha Shastri and Smt. Lakshmi Kutty at Trikkur village in Kerala.

Swamiji's childhood was full of different activities like games, gardening, swimming and at the same time he had a great interest in Vivekananda literature. As a young boy, he had a vivid dream that bright light came out of the Shiva temple near his house and engulfed him. The *Gospel of Sri Ramakrishna* enhanced his spiritual vision influencing him to join the Ramakrishna Mission. It is this 'divine call' that transformed a village boy into a great saint.

When were you born, Sir?

Swami Ranganathananda: 15 December 1908, in a little village called Thrissur, six miles from the town of Trichur, in Kerala.

Can you tell us some details about your childhood, adolescence, and youth, Swamiji?

Swamiji: I used us to feel full of energy as a child. In my boyhood, I took great interest in gardening and swimming. Even today, I am a very swift swimmer. Then, of course, games. Not much of study, except at the age of fourteen, when I took interest in Vivekananda literature.

Did you mix with other children and play?

Swamiji: Plenty, plenty. I was very good at gathering children for play—and even for work. In that far-away-period, 1917-18, there was a road in the village which had become slushy due to heavy rain. I gathered boys of my age and set about making the road better. Such kind of group activities I used to love and organise. And I was very fond of play.

What kind of games?

Swamiji: Mostly village games. What you call 'hadu dudu' or 'kabaddi' was my favourite. Then came marbles—if I sat down to play at noon, I would get up only at seven in the evening. I was an expert in marbles. In fact, whatever I used to do, I used to do with such zest, that I would forget the whole world at that time.

As a boy of twelve years, I had an experience, while going to school, I threw a stone at a youth, not expecting that it would go that far; but it did hurt him. His parents complained to my mother; she was naturally upset. When I returned from the school in the evening, I found my mother sullen and grave, 'You have to receive ten canings', she said. I said, 'Yes, I shall, for I have harmed that youth.' Then the elder brother, in mother's presence, gave me ten canings on my palms. I received it and came and sat peacefully by my mother's side and soon forgot all about it. No trauma!

At the age of about twelve or thirteen, in my mother's presence, I used some foul words against a person. My mother immediately reprimanded me lovingly thus: 'My boy, your tongue is the abode of *Vani* or *Sarasvati,* the Goddess of knowledge and wisdom. Don't soil it by using foul language against others.' That advice went straight to my head and heart and has influenced me all these seven or eight decades.

When my mother fell ill, the family had to get medicine from an ayurvedic doctor living a mile up the river on the bank of which were our paddy field and home. Our cook agreed to go to meet the doctor in a boat up the current, if one of the elder sons of my mother agreed to help to row and punt the boat. No elder brother agreed to go. When I was asked, I readily agreed due to two factors, namely, love for the mother and love of adventure. We met the doctor and brought the medicine. It was a play and fun for me to row the boat up and rowing it back. This love of adventure and dislike for easy life, and the German philosopher Nietzsche's dictum, live dangerously, has been with me ever since.

When I was a school student, our headmaster one day said, 'Children, you must learn one thing—plain living and high thinking.' That went into my head. I pondered over this statement: Plain living and high thinking! What a wonderful idea! Two or three years later I studied the *Gospel of Sri Ramakrishna*. There I found an excellent model of plain living and high thinking. When I read later the life of Holy Mother Sarada Devi, there too I found the same model. Here was a simple village woman externally, but internally there was the shining soul of infinite motherhood, the pulse of the infinite mother-heart. The life of many of our people today is just the other way around. Their external life is striking, but inwardly it is just empty; it is high living and plain or nil thinking!

In English there is a saying, 'Procrastination is the thief of time'. I remember an incident; when I was studying in class VII, my teacher came to the classroom. There was no regular class that day. So, he said this: 'Boys, procrastination is the thief of time.' 'What is that, Sir?' we asked. We could not make out the meaning. He was a fine type of person. He went to the board and drew a picture of a doll head with four pieces of hair sticking from the back of the head. Then he said, 'Boys, this head is time. It is rolling all the time. It is never quiet.' 'How do you catch this head? How to catch time? When those four pieces of hair come towards you, catch them. If you miss them, then you will have to wait for its next round. Just catch that hair when it comes towards you.' 'Take time by the forelock' is the English saying. He was illustrating this on the board. So, the students were happy and they laughed tremendously at the humour of the teacher. Then, he said, 'Boys, you are having irrepressible laughter.' 'What is the meaning of the word "irrepressible", Sir?' someone asked. He went to the board and wrote the word 'irrepressible' in a quick way, and the board fell down. There was still more laughter. That was an interesting incident in our school life. So, in that lesson we learnt that procrastination is the thief of time. So, we have to take time by the forelock. Then we can achieve many things in life. I often tell people, 'don't say I do not have time for is and for that'. A trained mind will achieve much in twenty-four hours, which an untrained mind will not achieve. Winston Churchill, you, and I have twenty-four hours a day, But Churchill did so much in twenty-four hours, and we do so little. We don't know how to train the mind. That is the one lesson to learn, Never complain about time. Complain, rather, about your own mind which doesn't know how to squeeze time and get the best out of it. So, procrastination is a *tamasik* quality.

At that time you were fourteen?

Swamiji: Fourteen and a half. Up to seventeen and a half, this continued—this kind of study. From this long study, two great ideas emerged strong in my mind. One, love of God who is the centre of our spiritual tradition; another, love of Man—love for the common people.

At such a tender age?

Swamiji: There was absolute surety and clarity about these two goals—there was no need for worry or hesitation. The idea was driven home in my mind—that this life is to be dedicated to God and Man, God in Man. Swami Vivekananda emphasises it again and again. 'Look at these—the poor, the illtreated, the exploited—they are your God. Worship them, serve them.'

It appears that your family influence must have come in this. A spiritual atmosphere was prevailing in your home, you said.

Swamiji: No, they were religious—but I will not call them spiritual. Because, this kind of religion is associated with a feudal social set up, with all those do's and don'ts. But they were generally human, generally good-hearted, within the limits of the feudal system. When I became slightly older, that feudal system did not suit me. Untouchability somehow repulsed me from the very beginning. I used to break all these rules even in the village. I used to go to school and come back without bathing. I would touch everybody after touching untouchables!

What was your idea behind it?

Swamiji: Because I felt it was absolutely wrong! Why should you treat human beings in any other way? Nobody came to tell me all these things, but it came on its own. So I used to befriend the untouchables and even eat with them—all against opposition from the people at home. But I didn't care. That's why the untouchables used to adore me. In fact, when I left, for *Sannyas,* they shed tears. What feelings they had! And this became philosophically strengthened after reading the Vivekananda literature.

What did your parents think of the career you were going for?

Swamiji: They wanted me to be with them, and they knew that I had an extra dose of public spirit. I never cared for myself, whether at home or outside. So they had great love for me, and expected that I will help them in their family affairs, improve their financial condition, and so on—as parents everywhere expect.

When they found me taking interest in this sort of literature, at first they did not object. But when they found me getting deep into it, they became afraid. So, once they tried to stop me and even compel me a little. But I stood firmly and said, 'This is my personal matter. Whatever I think worthwhile, I will do.'

That was at the age of fifteen. And thereafter they didn't trouble me at all, because I was so obedient and disciplined in everything else in the house. But, in this matter, I stood firm.

My house in Trikkur is situated on the bank of the river Manali, and to the east of my house is an ancient rock cave temple of Siva on a hill: about half a kilometre away I was studying in the eighth class at that time in the high school at Ollur, five kilometres from Trikkur on the road to Thrissur. A classmate brought a book from the library of the Vivekodayam High School in Thrissur. 'Would you like to read this book?', he asked me. 'Yes, I would like to read it', I replied, not knowing what it was. It was the *Gospel of Sri Ramakrishna*, by 'M' published by the Madras Math. He gave it to me. I started reading it. It gripped my attention, and I could not stop till I had finished one hundred pages continuously; later I read the whole book. Then other books on Thakurand Swamiji came from that Thrissur library.

That was in 1924, I was only fifteen and a half years old then, and was waiting for an opportunity to join the Ramakrishna Order, In 1926, after finishing my school final examination, I joined a typewriting institute in Thrissur to learn shorthand and typewriting. Some fees had to be paid. I took three rupees from my house and came to Thrissur. From there I wrote to the Madras Math that I wanted to join the Ramakrishna Mission. One Brahmachari replied, 'Here there is not enough room, There is a new centre in Mysore; it is in need of a Brahmachari. So, please write to the swami-in-charge, Swami Siddheshwaranandaji'.

So, I wrote to Swami Siddheshwaranandaji at Mysore. By that time, however, Siddheshwaranandaji himself came to Thrissur to meet his parents; his father was the Second Prince of the Cochin state. I met Maharaj. He said, 'Yes, you can come. Have you got enough money to go to Mysore via Ooty?' I said, 'I have just three rupees, nothing more.' But I had my ear-rings; even boys used to wear them in Kerala. I could sell them in the market; but it was Sunday, no shop was open. But one person gave me two rupees, and Siddheshwaranandaji gave me two rupees. So, I had now seven rupees in my pocket. But that was not enough for the journey to Mysore via Ooty. How was I to go with Siddheshwaranandaji to Ooty by train at 8.30 pm. that day? I was greatly disturbed in my mind. I was not fully committed to go, but I also wanted very much to go. Such was my mental struggle. And I was very young then, only seventeen and a half years old. I went to the Sri Ramakrishna Shrine in the Thrissur Vivekodayam High School to pray for Thakur's grace. I often used to bring flowers from my house for worship in that shrine. With tears in my eyes, I prayed to Thakur to arrange for my renunciation and departure to Mysore with Siddheshwaranandaji. Even now, after seventy years, the memory of that event in that shrine stirs me.

Then, at the last minute, I went to Siddheshwaranandaji's house. He was ready to start for the railway station. He said, 'All right, come with me tonight by the 8.30 train to Ooty.' I did not know anything about initiation. I wanted to join the Mission, and I had read some books about Thakur and Swamiji, and had memorised the *Prakritim Paramam* hymn on the Holy Mother. That was enough to inspire me to dedicate my life to the Mission. So, at 8.30 pm, we got into the train and it reached Ooty next morning. Ooty is about six thousand feet above sea level. Siddheshwaranandaji, familiarly known as Gopal Maharaj, myself, and three students were in the party, Mahapurush Maharaj was then living in a rented house at Ooty, which he loved very much. The present Ooty Ashram was being built on a site nearby, and was to be opened in 1927, I was allowed to stay in Mahapurush Maharaj's house and have breakfast, but was to eat outside in a hotel. There was no arrangement in the Ashram then for feeding so many people. So, with the money I had, I would eat outside. By the time I finished one week in Ooty, the money I had was exhausted. It was on 25 June 1926, that I left Thrissur for Ooty, and on 30 June my initiation by Mahapurushji took place.

I entered the room in which Mahapurush Maharaj was sitting for the ceremony. To his left was my seat. I sat down and looked at the whole scene. A dream I had three or four years earlier came to my mind then. I used to worship regularly Śiva in the village rock cave temple. In that dream, I was lifted high up in the sky;

then I reached a beautiful place. An old venerable looking person was sitting there; and my mind recognised him as Siva. He asked me to sit to his left and gave me some spiritual instructions. That much was the dream, and I found an exact reproduction of that dream in that particular situation in Ooty. Mahapurush Maharaj asked me, 'Do you worship Sri Ramakrishna?' I said, 'No, I don't actually worship, but I keep a picture of his, and salute it regularly.' And he said, 'That is all right.' He then gave me the mantra and asked me, 'Have you brought any guru dakshina?' 'Nothing,' I said. Only one shirt, one dhoti, and one towel—that was all I had brought from my house. He took two or three mangoes from his right side and gave them to me and said, 'Now give them back to me as guru dakshina.' I offered them back to him, made pranams to him and came out of the room.

After two days, on July 2, we had to take leave of Mahapurush Maharaj to go to Mysore. Swami Siddheshwarananda and I went to his room to take leave of him. It was about 5.30 am. He was sitting there on a chair counting some currency notes. 'Gopal, do you want some money? I can give you,' he said. Gopal Maharaj said, 'Not necessary, Maharaj' though Mysore Ashrama was very poor at that time. I made pranams to my guru. 'Yes, you go to Mysore. Serve Gopal,' Mahapurushji said to me. That was the only message he gave me then—'Serve Gopal.'

Seeker

> 'At His door everything is available—enjoyment, liberation and even the knowledge of Brahman. But, my child, you will have to seek, you will have to ask longingly. This seeking is what is called spiritual practice. If one sincerely longs for the vision of Him, He is sure to bless him. When once out of compassion He opens the gate and awakens

the *kundalini*—the latent spiritual power—you realise that everything is within. But nothing can be achieved without the awakening of the *kundalini* through His grace.'

Swami Shivananda

As a young monk of tireless energy, Swami Ranganathananda Maharaj, a genuine seeker spent the first twelve years of his monastic life in hardwork, study and meditation. He aspired to be instrumental in inspiring young people with Swamiji's ideas. Swamiji strengthened his spiritual insight while walking in the footsteps of Swami Vivekananda and by interacting with students, teachers, and instructors in various walks of life. Amidst the busy routine Swamiji found time to memorise *Gita* and *Vivekachudamani* with deep understanding. Swamiji was very keen for spiritual guidance; and was fortunate enough to get pearls of wisdom from many direct disciples of Sri Ramakrishna Paramahamsa.

My service of Gopal Maharaj continued for nine years in Mysore and three years in Bangalore. He was holy and kind and loving. We parted only when he went to open the Paris Vedanta Centre in 1938, So, we took leave of Mahapurush Maharaj and left by bus at 7.00 am, and reached the Mysore Ashram at 9.00 pm. Later, I saw an entry of Rs. 7 spent by the Mysore Ashram towards my Ooty-Mysore journey.

For the first time I saw a big town with electric lights and all that. As a village boy, I did not know about town life. I did not know even how to post a letter, how to cash a cheque, etc. That night, at 9 o'clock, for the first time in my life, I got a glass of milk and two pieces of bread for my supper from a boy who was living in the Ashram. I still remember the taste of that first meal in the Ashram, of bread and milk, that took place seventy years ago. That was on 2 July 1926. On 3 July, my long hair was cut and my earrings were removed,

Then, on 4 July, I entered the Ashram's kitchen. There was no paid cook, since the Ashram's income was very little. Siddheshwaranandaji's health was poor due to bad food. I was a good cook with two years' experience of cooking in my house for the whole family even from the age of twelve to fourteen. So, everybody in Mysore Ashram began to get good food from that time. For the next six years, I was a cook, dish-washer, and house-keeper in the Mysore Ashram. Collection of monthly subscription, garden work and some other things also were added later on. Whenever I requested people for subscription, I spoke about Swami Vivekananda. They were happy and used to give me tea and tiffin, and sometimes somethings also for taking to the Ashram. So, in this way, my life went on, with plenty of study also in between work. In spite of heavy work, I never complained of want of time for study or *japa-dhyana.* I was always happy and cheerful, and enjoyed doing any and every type of work as Thakur's service. I never experienced any tiredness. I wrestled with students in the Ashram's *akhada* (wrestling arena/ground) and later on played volleyball.

In 1929, time came for my *brahmacharya* initiation. So, in March 1929,1 came to Belur Math. My *brahmacharya* was on Buddha's birthday, 23 May. For about four months I stayed in Belur Math at that time. On the day of *brahmacharya diksha,* Mahapurush Maharaj came to the room behind the old shrine, and sat with a smiling face in the verandah, facing the ceremony going on in the room and various *mantras* were chanted, and homa was performed. These *mantras* are wonderful. The essence of these *mantras* are, 'I dedicate this life, with all its talents, for the service of God and Man.'

As soon as the ceremony was over, we were given a new set of clothes, along with a new name. Parents gave the name Shankaran. Now it became Yati Chaitanya. The word Chaitanya means spiritual consciousness.

The most memorable experiences during my stay at the Math were the daily morning sessions in Mahapurush Maharaj's room after breakfast, lasting sometimes for over an hour. Monks and probationers would come in batches and prostrate before him and stand aside. He would be sitting on his bed or in his chair, indrawn, often with the *hookah* (hubble-bubble) in front, from which he would draw a puff now and then, mostly absent-mindedly, and would occasionally exchange courtesies with the monks and novices present. When the indrawn mood would relax, he conversed on various topics with those present, interspersing it with humour and laughter, an endearing trait especially characteristic of Sri Ramakrishna and his disciples. Sometimes the talk would turn to deep spiritual themes, and those present would hang on to every word that then fell from his lips. In between all these, one heard him utter, in a tone suffused with deep devotion, such spiritual phrases as: *Sat-chit-ananda Shivam, Jai Guru Maharaj, Jai Ma,* etc.

One of my daily duties in Belur Math then was sweeping the spacious front courtyard. Sometimes, as I swept, the wind would carry the dirt back, so I had to sweep again. But it did not bother me; it was a play for me. Washing Thakur's puja vessels was another work. Serving tea to members in the tea-stall which was situated to the left of the present temple site was yet another duty. Some other duties like bringing water on my head for Mahapurush Maharaj's bath from Lilua tube-well, a small quantity of curd from the Belur market for his dog, and serving in the dining hall were also there. I was ready for everything. I was very young then, and full of tireless energy. There was also a *kusti akhada* (wrestling arena/ground) situated near where the dining hall is now. Swami Apurvananda, Mahapurushji's sevak, was a good wrestler. I had wrestled with him and with two or three others also in that *akhada.* Many people used to gather to see our wrestling. One cook from Varanasi Sevashrama had come, He was also a good wrestler. When he gripped my hand, it became powerless; such strength he had, though he appeared ordinary. Then there was Jnan Maharaj's parallel bar, fixed where at present the platform is erected during the celebrations. There I used to do a little bit of bar exercise. I had time for everything.

I was very hungry all the time except after lunch and dinner. Morning breakfast was tea and a thin slice of bread, as thin as the knife blade, with a little butter on it. As for tea, there was only one glass of milk for all the inmates together with plenty of water and sugar. Revered Suddhanandaji, the then general secretary, and Revered Swami Virajanandaji, and other senior swamijis also would be present, and I used to serve them. To satisfy my hunger, I used to take *muri* (puffed rice), in my shirt end, kept in a big tin on the Math verandah, and eat a lot of it. Food was very poor due to financial stringency; dal was watery, but *'chachari'* and *'alu dam'* were tasteful.

When I was in Belur Math as a brahmachari, Khoka Maharaj, Swami Subodhanandaji, was living in the room north of Swamiji's bedroom. I used to spend some time with him. He would be lying on the *verandah* facing Ganges, enjoying his hookah like a child. I would sit by his side. I was very free with him, massaging his belly with my hand very freely while he would talk to me about various things.

When I first read the *Gospel of Sri Ramakrishna* at the age of fifteen, I developed a great love and respect for its author 'M' or Mahendranath Gupta. So, while at Belur Math for *brahmacharya* in 1929, I was happy to get the opportunity to meet him and to pay my loving respects to him, One day, I went to pay my respects to 'M' in Calcutta, along with two other sadhus. We went upstairs in the evening and met him and spent nearly three hours, listening to his talk on Sri Ramakrishna. He spoke about Sri Ramakrishna only nothing but Sri Ramakrishna. While taking leave of him, he gave us a basket of fruits and sweets. As I was taking it, I asked him, Is it for offering to Thakur?' 'No, no,' he said, 'it is for sadhus, sadhus; that is enough. Thakur has told me to serve the sadhus.' That is the language he used. So I brought it and gave it to the Math *bhandar* (kitchen store) for distribution to sadhus.

So far as Mahapurush Maharaj is concerned, his guidance has been a tremendous source of spiritual strength to me. In reply to my letters, he used to write to me, addressing me 'My dear Yati Chaitanya' or 'My dear Shankaran.' These letters bear the handwriting of his secretary, late Swami Gangeshananda or Dvijen Maharaj, whom once I asked whether these letters contain any lines by him. He replied. 'Never. It was all his (Mahapurushiji's); I only wrote what he dictated.' From 1927 to 1931, I had written some eight letters to Mahapurush Maharaj, seeking spiritual guidance; and I used to get suitable replies. To my earnest request to be allowed to stay with him and serve him for long periods, he pointed out the futility and impracticability of seeking to be physically near one's Guru, and exhorted me to serve the Guru through devoted service to the Order in the various fields of its activities. I have given these letters to the Belur Math Ramakrishna Museum.

In 1933, I came to Belur Math again, this time for *sanyasa.* It was Swami Vivekananda's birthday, 23 January 1933. It was a beautiful occasion, but Mahapurush Maharaj was rather weak at that time and could not come to the ceremony held in the room behind the old shrine. He was in his room. After the *sanyasa havan,* we, nine of us, including the late Swami Hitananda and Swami Krishnatmananda, went to his room and received *sanyasa mantras* from him.

Then, finally, a new set of clothes, all of *gerua* colour, were given, along with a new name, ending with the word *ananda,* bliss. The name is chosen by the Guru. Swami Ranganathananda—finally this name came—that's my monastic name. That's what Swami Shivananda did, so far as I am concerned.

It is interesting to mention that with Mahapurush Maharaj's permission, I had been wearing *gerua* cloth since my fourth or fifth month in the Order, from 1927. I did not know much about *sannyasa* at that time.

I continued to stay at the Belur Math for about four months. During that time, a desire arose in my mind to go to Sargachi and meet Swami Akhandanandaji Maharaj. When I was reading Swamiji's works, I had found Swamiji praising Swami Akhandandaji very much. He was the first to implement Swamiji's message of service to the poor and the downtrodden. 'You are my man, you are my man!'—Swamiji had praised him. So, I had nursed a secret desire to meet Swami Akhandanandaji in Sargachi. I took Mahapurush Maharaj's permission to go to Sargachi to meet him. In those days, we had weekend return tickets; it was very cheap then—Friday you go and Sunday you return. So, with Mahapurushji's blessings, I went to Sargachi. I had a wonderful weekend there. I met Akhandanandaji, made pranams and explained my heart's desire. I was a newcomer from faraway Mysore *Ashrama,* and I was quite young, hardly twenty-four or twenty-five. But Swami Akhandanandaji treated me like a VIP guest—special cup, special saucer, special kettle—everything special for me. And he would ask the hostel boys, 'Go and make *pranams* to the Swami.' I protested that it should not be done in his presence. I said, 'Maharaj, what are you saying? Should they do it in your presence?' But he would say, 'Hey, you have come from Mysore' and turning to the boys would repeat, 'Make *pranams.'* All the boys would come and make *pranams* then.

Then the time came for me to take leave and go to the railway station. One can see the station just a little away from the Ashram. I went to his room, made *pranams,* and said, 'Maharaj, I want your blessings, I am working with the people, especially young people. Bless me that I become an instrument of Swamiji for inspiring our young people with Swamiji's ideas. With your blessing, I am sure,

I will get that capacity. I have not seen Swamiji, but I have met you, and he loved you very much. Your blessing is for me Swamiji's blessing.' As soon as I said it, all that light-heartedness went away from him. He became very grave and put both his hands on my head and said, 'I bless you, I bless you!' I felt a tremendous feeling of elevation within, some sort of strength arising within. Then I made *pranams* and silently came to the verandah, and started going towards the railway station. And looking back, I saw him standing there in the verandah, looking towards me, till I disappeared into the station.

After reaching Calcutta, first I went to *Advaita Ashrama* and then reached Belur Math. When I reached the Math, I found Swami Akhandanandaji had already reached there since he had come directly, and I, through *Advaita Ashrama.* He had received a telegram about Mahapurushji's cerebral stroke. Seeing me, he said, 'Shankar, *dekho* (see), Tarakda's condition. Is it for this you asked me to come to Belur Math? See what has happened.' For the first one month, Mahapurush Maharaj was unconscious and his condition was very serious. But slowly consciousness returned. Though he was unable to speak, he could smile and move his hands. Careful nursing had been done. Many packets of ice were kept on the head all the time, and that made for improvement in his condition.

I then took leave of Mahapurursh Maharaj. He just lifted his hand to bless and indicated by signs to his dear *sevak*, Shankar Maharaj (Swami Apurvananadaji). 'Give something to him for Chamundi temple and for Ashrama Thakur offering.' Shankar Maharaj understood what he meant. He got some money and gave it to me, and I made my *pranams* to him and to Akhandanandaji, and left for Mysore. I did the puja in the Chamundi temple, which Mahapurus*hji* had visited earlier, and in our Ashrama also, and sent the prasad to him to Belur Math and oil to Akhandanandaji. Next year, in February 1934, Mahapurush Maharaj passed away and Akhandanandaji became the president. This was my association with the president of the Sangha, Mahapurush Maharaj, and the vice-president, Swami Akhandananda Maharaj.

My next visit to the Math was during Sri Ramakrishna centenary celebrations in 1937 when Swami Vijnananandaji Maharaj had become the president. He was in far away Allahabad. From Belur Math, I went to Benaras. I said to myself, Allahabad is nearby, let me go to Allahabad and visit Vijnananandaji Maharaj, the present president of our Sangha.' So, I went to Allahabad from Benaras. I went to the Ashrama, and made *pranams* to Vijnananandaji Maharaj on 1 April 1937.

I had the occasion to meet Swami Abhedanandaji Maharaj in his Calcutta Ashrama. He talked about his lectures. I had read his lectures before. I attended his lecture in the Town Hall of Calcutta during Sri Ramakrishna centenary in 1937. It was a very interesting lecture. I had also heard Rabindranath Tagore's lecture in the University Institute.

Swamiji, what were your first impressions on joining the Ramakrishna Mission?

Swamiji: My home—I felt I belonged to it all through, in spite of pull from my home. I had loving parents, loving brothers and sisters, and a very beautiful country atmosphere in Kerala.

How far was it from the Ashrama?

Swamiji: Oh, nearly 300 miles away. So, to leave all that, I felt a little sorry. But the chance of living a great life in an ashrama enabled me to overcome those feelings. It was a poor ashrama, not much to eat and hardly any convenience. But what did it matter? This life is given to us by Sri Ramakrishna—it belongs to him. Now I am only to work out his great Mission. That thought sustained me and I started working very hard for the first six years.

What type of routine did you lead there?

Swamiji: The ashram in Mysore had no money, it had no servants, it had no cooks. So I had to do all the cooking, washing, cleaning and everything. For six years I was the cook, dish-washer, house keeper, gardener. And I did it with immense joy. Even when I look at it now—what a joy it was!

When you took on the robes, did you experience any feelings of anguish or doubt?

Swamiji: There are some very beautiful villages in Kerala and I loved our home, the people and my family there. But what I sought I loved more! So there was no anguish or regret. I went from something lower to something higher and the higher includes the lower and the lesser.

How did you get motivated to join the Ramakrishna Mission, of all places?

Swamiji: Well, Swami Vivekananda writes and speaks to you all through—'Why not sacrifice one life for the good of the common people?' He repeats this again and again. 'What is the use of this life for the sake of self-advertisement, when millions have been starving for ages? This is the time to do great work.' These ideas there are a plenty in Vivekananda's lectures and letters. And when I used to read them, tears used to come from the eyes—what a noble life it is! So that idea grew in the mind and, within three years, it became thoroughly fixed—this would be my goal in life.

Once (in 1937) I was addressing a public meeting in a place called Madanapalli in Andhra Pradesh. I didn't know who the audience were. They asked me this question. 'What induced you to become a monk?' I replied: 'When I read Vivekananda's lectures, this particular sentence gave me tremendous inspiration: There are greater things to be done in this country than aspiring to become lawyers and picking up quarrels!'

There was such a burst of laughter from the audience, because most of them were pleaders! This kind of literature is not just a book—it is a message, there is a special power in it. Every word is a source of power. This is my experience, and of thousands of others, including Romain Rolland, the great French biographer of Ramakrishna and Vivekananda, and the man who received the Nobel Prize for Literature. In his book on Vivekananda, he says:

'His words are great music stirring rhythms like the march of Handel choruses. I cannot touch these sayings of his, scattered as they are through the pages of books at thirty years' distance—without receiving a thrill through my body like an electric shock. And what shocks and transports must have been produced when, in burning words, they issued from the lips of the hero?'

When I first read it, I said, 'How true!' Along with me, there are thousands who have received that shock. A tremendous shock!

And even today, there are hundreds who are experiencing that shock. That humdrum life becomes shocked. You get a real aim in life—worthwhile, noble. That is a great stimulus.

'About Mahapurush Maharaj I consider myself thrice blessed for getting shelter under a teacher of his spiritual eminence, for being offered by him at the feet of Sri Ramakrishna, and for receiving his ample blessings in as much measure as I could spiritually digest and assimilate.'

Philosophy of Service

The True Basis of Human Dignity

Every one of us, therefore, in whatever fields of action we may be engaged in, is essentially a citizen of India; and, as citizen, the only form of inter-human relationship that we can have is that of service. Whether we are administrators, doctors, lawyers, engineers, ministers, legislators, teachers, housewives, industrialists, or labourers, we must always remember that our primary personality is our citizenship of free India and that these are the functions which we perform in discharge of that civic responsibility. Earning a living thus becomes an integral part of the discharge of national responsibility, and subordinate to it. This attitude at once converts all action into service, or, in the language of Vedanta, all work into worship, the worship of God in man, the worship of the *Virāṭ*. The simple shoemaker on the roadside and the mighty administrator in the Secretariat, both are engaged in the service of society. Only, each has to be made conscious of this truth; that is possible only when each realises his or her true dignity and worth. No work is high or low in itself; but our motivations make it high or low. Without the spirit of devotion behind it, the work of a temple-priest becomes low work; with the spirit of national service behind it, the work of the farmer or industrial labourer becomes high work; if motivated only by the three 'p's,' namely, pay, prospect, and promotion, the work of the administrator becomes low work, static and humdrum. But when illumined by the spirit of national dedication and service, it becomes high and noble. The spirit of service, therefore, raises all work, high or low in worldly estimation, into high work in the ethical and spiritual estimation, precisely because that spirit raises the worker behind all work to the high level of spirituality, to that level where man achieves a qualitative improvement in his life. The spirit of service, therefore, becomes a universal milieu in which all human life and action are spiritualised. *This is the transformation that life and work undergo in the light of philosophy.* We need to be inspired by this philosophy in India today. This is what will strengthen India, make for national integration and all-round national efficiency. This philosophy will impart to India a vision of high human excellence and the urge to actualise it in life and character. The real source of strength for a nation lies in this type of men, men endowed with *prajñā* or creative intelligence, and not in its treasury, in its defence organisation, or in its foreign alliances. Says Vidura in the *Mahābhārata* (Bhandarkay Critical Edition, 5. 37. 51): *Yat balānām balam srestham tat prajñā balam ucyate.**

The Ethics of National Integration

National integration is the result of ethical awareness. Mere aggregation of individuals does not constitute a nation, just as mere accumulation of bricks does not make a building. It is cement that joins brick to brick to make for the integrated structure

---

*Of all strengths, that which is superior strength is called the strength of *prajñā*—creative intelligence.

of the building. The cement that joins man to man to result in the integrated structure of a nation is ethical sense, or what the *Mahābhārata* terms Dharma, as defined by Krishna in the *Karṇa Parva* (Bhandarkar Critical Edition, 8. 49. 50): *Dhāraṇāt dharma ityāhuḥ dharmo dhārayati prajāḥ.*

The five hundred and fifty million people thrown together in this blessed land of ours do not automatically constitute a nation; we need an integrating principle or value that will unite man to man. That principle is ethical sense, which we have to manufacture from within, each one of us; for it is spiritual value that liberates man and advances his spiritual growth. Ethical sense cannot be manufactured outside man; it cannot be produced by payment of material and other inducements, or by the injection of a serum. So long as man is content to live in the stagnation of *samsāra* or worldliness, he cannot manufacture this value even if offered all material and other inducements. For this value is the product of man's spiritual growth, and that growth takes him beyond the tyranny of the physical and the sensate, beyond the tyranny of the delusion of worldliness which is 'I and mine.' When this value is liberated in the hearts of increasing sections of our vast population, we shall witness a tremendous phenomenon of human integration in about a seventh of the human race. It will convert India into a national grid of awakened humanity, just as we are taking all steps to achieve a national electrical grid for the industrial unification and development of our country. *This is enduring nation-building through man-making.* And the clarion call that can inspire us today is what Vivekananda has given to us from the *Kaṭha Upaniṣad:* 'Arise, Awake, and stop not till the goal is reached.'

The Capacity for Impersonal Loyalty

This glowing picture of what India can be tomorrow is marred by our knowledge of what she is today. The present is undoubtedly unpropitious; but it is the product of a long tradition of political unwisdom and moral stagnation of our people. Every citizen should be aware of this national weakness and consciously work to end it. We had established in India many political states in the past; a study of why and how they failed and why we failed to establish an enduring national state will contain many salutary lessons for us today. Our states of the past were ruler-centred. The heart of the state was the person of the king or the emperor. As at the top, so at all the lower levels also, it was the person in authority that counted, whether it be the commander-in-chief, the viceroy in the province, and such other functionaries lower down. The people's loyalty was to the person of the ruler or of the other functionaries below. Our big country failed to develop either at the provincial or at the central level *an impersonal political loyalty* to an Indian state. Our loyalties became shaken with the death or removal of the person of the ruler, or the death or removal of the person of the commander-in-chief. Foreign invaders seem to have known this weakness of our people and of our state or states. It is not an isolated experience in Indian history of our national armies, fighting bravely against an invader, melting away when the king or the emperor or the commander-in-chief was killed during the battle. And foreign invaders would often aim their arrow or their shot at the king or the emperor or the commander- in-chief seated on the howdah. Such melting away of our armies has taken place even by the spread of false news to the same effect by the invaders. Not only the army and the people in general, but also the officers and the feudal lords failed to develop an impersonal awareness of, and an impersonal loyalty to, an Indian national state. Their loyalty was primarily to themselves and to their self-interests, and secondarily to the person of the ruler as a means to the former.

The lessons of the failures of our past efforts to build an enduring political state in India should be burnt into the minds and hearts of our people today. We must assimilate the truth that a strong and enduring political state cannot be built on the basis of mere personal loyalties. We need to develop an impersonal loyalty to our new free national state and to the high principles embodied in its Constitution. We need to develop a respect for our Constitution and an impersonal capacity to respond to the rule of law. This addiction to principle only and not cheap sentiments, which we have inherited in abundance, becomes an additional source of strength for national integration. We are slowly and painfully learning this lesson of impersonal loyalty to our infant democratic state. Whatever strength it has shown during the last twenty years of its existence, whatever stress and strain it has faced and stood, is derived from this source. Whatever weaknesses have shown themselves up, similarly, reveal only the long distance the nation has yet to travel to acquire this basic virtue, which we need not only to strengthen our political state, but also to strengthen, purify, develop, and ensure the continuity of all collective and institutional activities within the state. It is not a rare thing in India to hear people say: 'I used to take keen interest in such and such an institution when so and so was its head, but now that he or she is gone, I have no further interest.' An institution represents a certain social vision and the effort at its realisation. If our loyalty is to that vision, we would continue to bear witness to that vision by continuing to serve the cause of the institution even if circumstances have necessitated change in the person at the head, involving, however, no departure in the ideals and programmes of the institution.

The Capacity for Imaginative Sympathy

The cultivation of this impersonal loyalty, however, involves a spiritual growth within man from the psycho physical self to the psychosocial self. This proclaims the intimate relationship between ethics and all true politics.

By such impersonal growth, man becomes a richer personality, says ethics. It is this impersonal-personal attitude that constitutes the ethical content of a citizenship, without which citizenship merely means that one has only to stand in the queue and wait until he or she attains the age of twenty-one. Unfortunately, this latter view of citizenship is what most people in India have understood and acted upon, and it has contributed not a little to the prevailing national weakness and despair. Nepotism, bribery, business-malpractices, and other evils which are afflicting free India, have their sources in the preponderance of blind *māyā* over lucid *dayā,* and in the absence of that detachment from the worldly personality, in the absence of that spiritual growth into the impersonal which alone endows one with mental clarity and moral strength to follow the path of justice when called upon to adjudge the claims between less qualified personal kith and kin and better qualified other persons. Attachment to oneself and to one's relatives is *māyā,* and love for all is *dayā,* says Sri Ramakrishna.

This spiritual growth of the citizen will not only enhance the spirit of justice in society—and justice is one of the most stabilising and integrating social forces which alone can make individuals and groups accept gracefully the shortages and privations of a developing economy—but it will also enhance greatly the citizen's capacity for sympathy and fellow-feeling. During the past centuries, our character had for its ingredients a bundle of negative virtues instead of positive ones. Our traditional outlook for sympathy was as much limited and prejudiced by this and by personal factor referred to earlier, as was our traditional loyalty to the state. Our religious and social codes did teach us to be kind and sympathetic; but our response to human suffering was neither imaginative nor sustained. As a people, we did not fail to respond to suffering and distress in front; but this response took the form of tossing a coin or two to the sufferer and then passing on; it looked as if we did this more to be relieved of the sight of suffering than out of a moral concern to see that the sufferer's suffering is relieved. We did not care to follow it up to see that social maladies are traced to their very roots and eradicated. Better if this so-called sympathy could have come out of its prevailing static, piety-fringed worldliness and self-centred sociopolitical attitudes.

When we substitute a dynamic spirituality for that piety-fringed worldliness, and a deep social concern in place of our bundle of negative virtues and self-centred socio-political attitudes, we develop a capacity for *impersonal service,* a sympathy of a wide-ranging and sustained quality. This is *imaginative sympathy.* It is not tied down to a concrete suffering in front, nor does it end up by the tossing of a coin to the sufferer. Imaginative sympathy proceeds from a deeper source in the human personality; it proceeds from its spiritual dimension from which dynamic ethical and social values proceed.

This is the personality of the citizen. Such citizens alone are the guarantee of social health and social progress. And when administrators are recruited from a social *milieu* which consists of a general body of such citizens, the administration becomes responsive to social urges and needs. The difference between a police state and a state aiming to be a welfare state lies in this social responsibility of the latter. And this is the product of that spiritual growth of the members of the administration yielding the precious capacity for impersonal sympathy, for imaginative sympathy. The secretariat and other institutions or offices of the state are far away from the actual scenes of human life with its urges and privations. Yet the administrator, through his imaginative sympathy, recognises, and responds to, that far away social situation. With his imaginative sympathy, he sees the file in front of him stirring into life and whispering many human urges and dissatisfactions. Every citizen needs to develop this rare capacity, but the administrator and the politician need it more. Without it, they both, singly or in combination, can turn a nation into a mess of problems; with it, they can lift a nation from utter suffering to a sun-lit height of cheer and hope.

Dynamic Spirituality

It is this transformation of man in India that will fill our politics and administration with a sense of urgency, with a sense of purpose and direction. With this imaginative sympathy, things will move faster and faster in the administration, and the nation will march faster and faster towards its destined goal of general welfare. It is the greatest asset for the administration of a state such as ours where the most glaring fact is its centuries-long arrested development, and mounting urge, since independence, for the minimum of human happiness and welfare gushing out of the hearts of millions and millions of its people, who have been, in the pungent words of Vivekananda, 'living the life of next door neighbours to brutes'. The grasping of this fact and an adequate response to it by an administrator provides the finest and the only scope for the development of his character and efficiency, and for the retention of his youthful zest and joy in his life and work.

This is the type of glory and greatness that should descend upon men and women in India in general, and the members of the administrative services of the centre and the states, in particular. It will make for liberation of the spirit of service as a pervasive principle, lighting up the dark and dismal horizon of our nation today, and raising the spiritual quality of the life of its citizens. To go here and there to be spiritual is like going here and there to breathe. It is all *here* and *now.* We have to realise that spirituality is not magic or cheap mysticism, that it is not to be sought merely in caves and forests, but that it is birthright of one and all, and is to be cultivated in the fields of one's life and work, in the midst of its ups and downs.

Our people need to be inspired by this practical and realisable ideal which Vivekananda has put before us in the modern age. He exhorts us that it is far better to live for an ideal for an instant than to lead for years the life of jellyfish existence. The words uttered by Queen Vidula in the *Mahābhārata* for the benefit for her son, king Sanjaya, breathes a heroic message for all our youths *(Udyoga Parva,* 120,15):

> *Muhūrtam jvalitam śreyo na tu dhūmāyitam ciram*—'It is better to flame forth for an instant than to smoke away for an age.'

Some of the great men of India like Śaṅkara and Vivekananda lived short but intense lives. Theirs was an intense dedication to God and man, to God *in* man; and it changed the course of human history. It is better to live intensely for an ideal and vision than to vegetate for long years in a humdrum existence. *This is a powerful sentiment that can drive away the clouds of cynicism and frustration from the sky of India.* Every educated citizen has to teach himself or herself that he or she not only is *in* India but is also *of* India, and is responsible for the nation's well-being. We have to inspire ourselves with the conviction that we have been called upon to be an instrument of our nation's purposes. What can be a greater glory for man in India today than this, that he is living in the most creative period of his nation's history and that he is privileged to contribute to it, big or small. When cynicism and frustration lay their cold hand of death on a person, he or she is unable to respond to any higher value, and becomes suspicious of all values except his own self-interest. Bernard Shaw refers to this type in a famous passage:

> 'This is the joy in life, to be used for a purpose which you consider mighty; to be a force of nature, and not a clod of ailments and grievances ever complaining that the world does not devote itself to making *you* happy.'

These are the two alternatives before us in India today. Here is the great current of Indian national life; I am a part of it, shaping its course and being shaped by its current, losing my smallness and meanness in that great national participation. But if I cut myself away from that current, I become a stagnant pool, swampy and malarious, a clod of ailments and grievances, ever complaining that the nation has not done this or that good to me. 'All expansion is life, all contraction is death', says Vivekananda. More people have taken the path of spiritual contraction, bringing the nation to the verge of despair and disintegration. From now on, let more and more people take the path of expansion, expansion of social awareness and sympathy, and the capacity for calm, silent, hard work inspired by team-spirit, and we shall arrest this downward trend and turn the nation to progress and prosperity, unity and strength.

Bhartṛhari's Social Classification

We can better understand the anatomy of our society today by listening to what poet-king Bhartrhari says about the human types in a society. Bhartṛhari hailed from the Malwa region of Madhya Pradesh and lived over a thousand years ago. Says he in his *Nītiśataka* (Verse 74):

> *Ete satpuruṣāḥ parārthaghaṭakāḥ svārthān parityajya ye,*
> *sāmānyāstu parārthamudyamabhṛtaḥ svārthāvirodhena ye;*
> *Te'mī mānavarākṣasāḥ parahitam svārthāya nighnanti ye,*
> *ye tu ghnanti nirarthakam parahitam te ke na jānīmahe*

'There are some *satpurusas,* good people, who engage themselves in the good of others sacrificing their own self-interest; the *sāmānyās,* the generality of people, on the other hand, are those who engage themselves in the good of others so long as it does not involve the sacrifice of their own self-interest. There are those others, the *manavarākṣasās,* devilish men, who sacrifice the good of others to gain their own selfish ends; but alas, what am I to say of those who sacrifice the good of others without gaining thereby any good to themselves or to any one else!'

The first category is that of the *satpuruṣa,* the good man. What does his goodness consist in? It is an overflowing goodness uncontaminated by any selfish motive. Such people always work to ensure the welfare of other people without caring for their own self-interest. This is the most glorious type in any society; they form its spiritual elite; they are, as the *New Testament* puts it, the salt of the earth.

Apart from those whom the world looks upon as divine incarnations, the *satpuruṣa* category includes men like Gandhiji. He might have remained a barrister and could have led a comfortable life. But he discovered himself in others and, dying to himself, lived for others. He dedicated himself to the work of rescuing from slavery and fear millions of his fellowmen, and making them realise the dignity and worth of their manhood and womanhood.

The poet then speaks of the second category—the *sāmānyās,* the generality of people—the majority in every society. What is their mental make-up? They serve the interest of other people so long as it does not collide with their own self-interest. That is what British ethical and political philosophy calls 'enlightened self-interest'. And the majority in any society will be of this type. And what India needs today is an intelligent appreciation and application of this philosophy on the part, especially, of her industrialists and businessmen.

They have to realise that it is in their own self-interest to see that the nation prospers and grows. Industry and business have to realise that a flourishing economy demands the widest diffusion of purchasing power among the people. Foolish ways of getting wealth by which the rich become richer and the poor poorer are destructive of the process of wealth-getting itself in a *laissez-faire* state. The difference lies precisely in this that, in the latter, the motivation is *mere* self-interest, in the former, it is *enlightened* self-interest.

Ethics does not demand of this category of people that they sacrifice their self-interest to do good to others. It permits them to seek their self-interest; but it tells them to widen their concept of self by fully grasping the truth of the interdependence of men and groups in society. If I keep my premises scrupulously clean, but do not care to see that the town or village in which I live is also kept clean, I cannot escape the consequences of an epidemic breaking out from that insanitation in my environment. It is therefore in my own interest to see that my environment is sanitary. As societies become larger in territories and population, the concept of self in man's view of his self-interest needs to be correspondingly broadened. A narrow idea of self-interest is based on utter ignorance of the social mechanism, with its subtle interdepending processes. Hence, it is *unenlightened* self-interest. This becomes more glaring as a society becomes more complex with not only national but also international interconnections. Hence the need for raising self-interest to the level of the *enlightened* variety. This philosophy of enlightened self-interest is today inspiring international relations in such fields as the sharing of economic prosperity and technical know-how through trade and aid extended by advanced countries to developing countries. But it needs to be implemented much more within the national societies themselves, where all self-interest needs to be purified by the touch of *enlightenment.*

The poet then goes on to describe a third category which he characterises as *mānava-rākṣasās,* devilish men. What is devilish about them? They destroy other people's welfare to gain more profit and pleasure for themselves. This is the *rākṣasa* type; and I am sorry to say that, since independence, we have been manufacturing this type in large numbers in our country. Every conceivable form of food and drug adulteration and corruption afflicts our nation today. What is the source of this affliction? Men and women are out to gain profit and pleasure for themselves at the cost of misery and unhappiness to millions. Why do they do so? Because they have failed to grow beyond their physical, biological selves. They have sharpened their intelligence and will by education, but failed to give a moral orientation to them. By putting these great powers in the service of their lower selves, they have become efficient instruments of social evil and suffering; and this is what *mānava-rākṣasa* means. At this end, one of these people adulterates drugs to gain extra profit to himself; at the other end, the drug is administered to hundreds of children with no effect; the children suffer and die. But what does he care about the social consequences of his action! He cares only for the profit from his business, and is callous about its consequences to his fellowmen.

This is the *rākṣasa* type, a low type of humanity; but many of them are capable of being corrected by social and state action, and transformed into the second type, the enlightened self-interest category.

The poet can understand the ways and motivations of these three types of people; but he is at a loss to deal with the next, or the fourth, category, and exclaims: *te ke na jānīmahe,* 'I am not able to understand them'! Why? Because they believe in wanton destruction; they destroy other people's welfare even though they do not gain any benefit to themselves thereby. Every society contains a few such morally demented people. Our nation has a more than healthy share of this type today.

Conclusion

This is the picture of human society everywhere. These four types are there in Russia, America, Japan, China and in all the countries of the world, as we have them here in India. The only difference is in the ratio of the four types. And this difference in ratio makes the difference between society and society.

As for the first type, the *satpuruṣa,* every society does have a small minority of this group—unselfish, compassionate, morally alert, and spiritually sensitive. Every society must zealously create and nourish this small minority. Every society will have a majority of its population belonging to the second type—the *sāmānyās,* motivated by self-interest, but of the enlightened variety. But every society should take steps—educational and preventive—to see that the ranks of the third category are thinned, if not entirely eliminated. And the fourth should be completely eliminated; it should never be allowed to rise again. As to the second category, there is great need for vigilance so that it does not slide down to swell the ranks of the third category by too much preoccupation with self-interest and too little with enlightenment. This group has to be specially alert to see that its self-interest is illumined by its being subjected to the larger interest of society. The moral health of the nation entirely depends upon this immense group steadying itself by drawing inspiration from the small minority of the *satpuruṣa* group above it.

I do hope that, as remarked by me earlier, the self-criticism which is evident in our nation today, and which is a sure sign of the basic health of our society, will slowly generate the necessary moral forces to cure the nation of its present ailments. The ailment is a moral ailment and the remedy has to be a moral remedy. We all desire that our nation should be healthy, physically as well as mentally. We have achieved some notable successes in tackling our physical diseases. We have practically conquered malaria which was such a scourge even two decades ago. We are on the way to conquer the scourge of tuberculosis, with leprosy next on the list. As a result of these measures, we have considerably raised the nation's life expectancy from about twenty-nine to about fifty years since our independence, besides improving the general health of the nation. *But the greatest challenge to the nation today is the malady that afflicts its mind and heart. Cynicism, self-centredness, and utter unconcern for others are more deadly than the most deadly physical diseases and the viruses that cause them; for they corrode the nation's resolve to stay free, to be united, and to march onward to progress.* We cannot be blind to the fact that this disease has already invaded our body-politic, including our youths. We have to take energetic measures to arrest the further progress of this disease and to eliminate it from the body-politic. And the nation has to be alert thereafter to see that these deadly mental viruses do not invade our society again. This is the responsibility of every patriotic citizen. We have no king or emperor ruling over us today as in the medieval and other periods. We live under a democratic set-up which derives its strength from its free, disciplined, responsible, and responsive citizens to whom service of the nation is politics and religion in one, and in whom the nation has its guarantee of unity, strength, and continued progress.

The subject of the philosophy of service, therefore, is not meant for academic discussion in the dull philosophy courses of our universities; it should stir the minds and hearts of every section of the population. It is thus that the nation will get the necessary strength to meet the recurring challenges this age of revolutionary transition will throw at it. If India succeeds in responding to these challenges adequately, she will become a beacon of hope not only to herself but also to the whole of humanity. We have responded successfully to many a challenge to our national existence and integrity in our long history. And we shall face and overcome this challenge as well. With this faith in ourselves and in our national destiny, let us, from this day onwards, enter our respective fields of life and activity with hope and courage.

India's Educational Vision*

Our Emerging Nation

What is the society that is waiting to receive an Indian youth who has completed his university education today? In a national system of education, this is a vital question to be asked and answered by every student. If there is one characteristic that distinguishes modern India from all her past epochs, it is the quality of youthful dynamism. What we witness all around us today is the rapid modernisation of an ancient society; sensitive minds can catch the sounds of crumbling social edifices all round and the coming up of new ones.

It is already evident that the modern transition in India is not going to be a mere patchwork affair. The nation is dead set to create a new future for itself and not a mere repetition of any of its past epochs, however glorious they may have been. The revolutionary aim of the modern renaissance in India was termed *root and branch reform* by Swami Vivekananda, one of its most authentic leaders and spokesmen. Conveying Vivekananda's vision of the India of the future, Sister Nivedita says in her famous book *The Master As I Saw Him* (pp.201-202):

---

*Address delivered at the Calcutta University Convocation on 15 February 1966.

'I had asked him, in the morning, to tell me, in broad outline, what he felt to be the points of difference between his own schemes for the good of India and those preached by others. It was impossible to draw him out on this subject. On the contrary, he expressed appreciation of certain personal characteristics and lines of conduct adopted by some of the leaders of other schools, and I regarded the question as dismissed. Suddenly, in the evening, he returned to the subject on his own accord.

'I disagree with all those,' he said 'who are giving their superstitions back to my people. Like the Egyptologist's interest in Egypt, it is easy to feel an interest in India that is purely selfish. One may desire to see again the India of one's books, one's studies, one's dreams. My hope is to see again the strong points of that India, reinforced by the strong points of this age, only in a natural way. The new state of things must be *growth from within*.'

New India: A Growth from Within

What is the meaning and significance of the national hope voiced by Vivekananda in the above passage? Let us view the three constituent elements in this hope: First, he refers to the strong points in the old Indian tradition; second, he speaks of the strong points of the modern age, meaning thereby the tested and universal elements of the modern Western tradition; and third, he envisages the forging of new India as a *growth from within,* by the assimilation by her people of the strong points of the modern age with the strong points of their own age-old national tradition.

The strong points of any cultural tradition lie primarily in its concept of human excellence and in the measure of its achievement. Among the many cultural legacies that the modern age has inherited, we can discern two types, one represented by the Greco-Roman and the other by the Indian. In each of these two legacies, we can discern a distinctive view of man and his highest excellence. The initial material bases of culture were generally common in almost all developed cultures of the past; these are a certain measure of socio-economic security through settled agriculture and simple arts and crafts, and some measure of effective socio-political organization. Once this is achieved, cultures begin to diverge from each other; the sole determinant of the divergence of each culture from the rest, at this stage, is the direction of its mental life, the questions it asks, and the answers it receives, from experience. These stirrings in the mind of man signify the onset of a conscious and deliberate control and guidance of life's forces. In man, biological evolution, at this level, becomes self-conscious and purposive. It advances from the organic or physical to the higher fields of mind and thought. Twentieth-century biology recognises this as the special Geld of human evolution where, in the words of Sir Julian Huxley, quality replaces quantity as the central criterion of progress. Endowed with the unique capacities for speech communication and transmission of accumulated experience, man becomes endowed with a highly resilient cultural inheritance over and above his largely fixed and static genetic inheritance. With the aid of these, the mental component of culture advances from generation to generation, limited only by the prevailing level of technological efficiency.

Concepts of Human Excellence: Greek and Indian

It was this advance of evolution into the higher fields of mind and thought, into what Julian Huxley terms 'the science of human possibilities,' that took place in two distinct areas of the ancient world, namely, India and Greece. The fruits of that advance have an universal and undying quality about them. They have nourished

India, and through her, the Asian countries, on the one side, and the Greco-Roman world, and through it, the modern Western world, on the other.

The concept of man and his excellence in modem Western culture is derived from the ancient Greek concept of man as essentially a member of a community. The concept of human excellence in ancient Chinese culture is closely akin to this Greek type. This is what one may call the *political* view of man, in which even religion is viewed from the political point of view, tending to make it this-worldly and communal. Out of this view, however, has arisen all political, economic, and social struggles to improve the lot of man, on the one hand, and aggressive wars and colonial exploitations, on the other.

The finest fruit of this view is humanism. It tends to concentrate the energies of a culture in the field of the amelioration of the lot of man in *this* world. With its stress on social ethics, it helps man to achieve character, by educating him in social virtues and graces. By upholding the dignity of man, it enhances individual freedom and responsibility, and the sense of equality between man and man. On the intellectual plane, it directs the mental life of man to the adventure of knowledge, to the inquiry into the phenomena of nature and man. Through the knowledge so gained, man achieves increasing control over nature's forces and the forces of collective human life. The first constitutes scientific, and the second sociopolitical, technology. Armed with these two disciplines, man achieves increasing hegemony over his external environment, and steady enhancement of his own welfare, individual and collective.

The Greek Concept of Man: Its Strength and Weakness

This was the concept of human excellence upheld in Greco-Roman culture. It gives us a picture of disciplined energy and resource, physical, emotional, and intellectual; it conveys the idea of man fired with the Promethean spark, unafraid of nature, unthwarted by obstacles, and inspired by the heroic maxim of 'dare, ever dare, and always dare,' as voiced by Danton of the French Revolution. This concept of man was the priceless legacy left by the Greco-Roman culture to the modern Western culture. The Greco-Romans did not contribute much to the sciences of nature; they were largely averse to experimental science. Their special field was the science of man, of man in society, of man, frankly, this-worldly, creating and enjoying the delights of culture and civilized existence. To quote from E.M. Forster's preface to Lowes Dickinson's *The Greek View of Life:*

> Greece hadn't science, it is true, and she had no global commitments, but she encomtpassed within the tiny circuit of her city states much that affects and afflicts the modern man in his relationship to society. And because her writers were intelligent and because they were sensitive, she has been able to send us news on these urgent matters which is still fresh, although it is over two thousand years.

India and the Challenge of the Modern West

Into this Greco-Roman humanist legacy, the modern West has infused a new energy, namely, the energy of science and technology. The combined energy of the ancient and the modern in the Western tradition has burst all regional bounds and become pervasive of the whole world, throwing a challenge to every cultural legacy in the modern world. It is this challenge with its strong and weak points mixed up together, that India has been facing since the nineteenth century. Few cultures in the modern world have been able to stand up to this powerful challenge. In the passage from Nivedita quoted earlier, we have seen Vivekananda referring to the strong points of the Indian cultural tradition. What are these strong points in our culture which can stand up to the modern challenge, meet it on an equal footing, and contribute something substantial to its enrichment, even while enriching itself with its contributions?

I have earlier said that India has been experiencing the crumbling down of many of her old social edifices in the wake of her contact with the West. Old social edifices crumble when the values which sustain them become outworn and obsolete, just like old buildings falling apart when the cement between their bricks becomes weak and loses the power to bind. It can be expected therefore that nothing that is weak in the Indian cultural tradition, nothing that is outworn and obsolete, nothing that is out of tune with the demands of the modern age, will be able to stand the onrush of the modern transition. It is worthy of mention that all the leaders of the modern renaissance in India, who had insight into the inherent strong points of the Indian tradition, welcomed the impact of the modern Western culture on India and the opportunity it provided to build a stronger and purer India.

Vivekananda and the Indian Renaissance

This positive approach is most evident in Vivekananda who, in the sweep of this thought and the loftiness of his vision, may be ranked as the foremost architect, not only of his own country's future, but, what may eventually turn out to be, one of the architects of a more healthy future world order as well. Speaking about him to Romain Rolland, Rabindranath Tagore said:

> 'If you want to know India, study Vivekananda. In him, everything is positive and nothing negative.'

In his book, *Discovery of India,* Jawaharlal Nehru says about him (p.400):

> Rooted in the past and full of pride in India's heritage, Vivekananda was yet modern in his approach to life's problems; he was a kind of bridge between the past of India and her present.

If Vivekananda envisaged a 'root and branch reform' and welcomed the impact of modern world forces in India, he also had intimate communion with, and faith in, the strong and undying elements in his country's heritage. He had seen in the glorious life of his own master, Sri Ramakrishna, the re-authentication of these strong and undying elements, and also experienced them in his own life. This strong and undying element is initially the contribution of the *Upaniṣads,* in their vision of a new dimension of human excellence distinct from the one bequeathed by the Greeks. As the Greeks and others specialised in the subject of man in society, man in space and time, India through the *Upaniṣads* specialised in the subject of man in depth, man above and beyond his political and social dimensions. This yielded the *spiritual* view of man as distinct from, as was stated earlier, the *political* view of the Greeks. Ancient Greece studied the *without* of nature as revealed by the senses, and ancient India inquired into the *within* of nature as revealed in one of nature's unique products, namely, man, as revealed in the depths of his consciousness and ego sense.

The Upaniṣads and Indian Culture

It was an inquiry which challenged not only life but also death, and did not stop till it had revealed the immortal and divine Self of man, the Atman, of which, as the Vedas express it, life and death are but shadows—*yasya chāyā amartaṁ yasya mṛtyuḥ.*

No culture can achieve depth without its sponsoring philosophy tackling the problem of death. This was one of the major drawbacks of Greek culture, which failed to assimilate to itself the deeper legacy left by Socrates and the Mystery Religions. This may also be said of the modern Western culture which has failed to *assimilate* to itself the deep spirituality of the Christian religion. Says Lowes Dickinson in his *This Greek View of Life* (p.68):

> The more completely the Greek felt himself to be at home in the world, the more happily and freely he abandoned himself to the exercise of his powers, the more intensely and, vividly he lived in action and in passion, the more alien, bitter, and incomprehensible did he find the phenomena of age and death. On this problem, so far as we can judge, he received from his religion but little light and still less consolation. The music of his brief life closed with a discord unresolved and even before reason had brought her criticism to bear upon his creed, its deficiency was forced upon him by his feeling.

What the ancient Greeks neglected became the ruling passion of the ancient Indians. Starting as a trickle in the earlier period, this intimation of something profound and significant within man became a flood in the epoch of the *Upaniṣads,* issuing in a systematic, detached, and scientific pursuit of the truths of the inner world, of the depths of experience. The Upaniṣads convey to us an impression of the tremendous fascination that this new field of inquiry held for the contemporary Indian mind. And that fascination has continued to hold India's mind in thrall down to our own times. This new field is today beginning to attract the serious attention of advanced thinkers in the modern age.

The Indian Concept of Man: Its Strength and Weakness

By their emphasis on inner penetration, by their whole-hearted advocacy of what the ancient Greeks centuries later formulated in the dictum: 'Man, know thyself, but at which they themselves had stopped half way, the *Upaniṣads* gave a permanent orientation to the Indian cultural experiment, and initiated a scientific and non-dogmatic tradition in the field of religion. To adapt E.M. Forster's remark about the legacy of Greece, quoted earlier, 'much that *affects* us and *afflicts* us' in India, and in the countries influenced by Indian culture, is the fruit of this *Upaniṣadic* orientation. The stress on inward depth had, however, one special consequence for Indian culture, in that all its expansive outward movements throughout history have been non-aggressive; every word of its message for man 'has been spoken with a blessing behind it and peace before it... and therefore we live', as remarked by Vivekananda *(Complete Works,* Vol. III, Eighth Edition, p.106).

The supreme fruit of this inward penetration was, as was said earlier, the discovery of the Atman, the immortal divine Self of man and the universe, infinite and therefore non-dual. Referring to the significance of this concept of human excellence in his address at the Chicago Parliament of Religions, Vivekananda says:

> 'Is man a tiny boat in a tempest, raised one moment on the foamy crest of a billow and dashed down into a yawning chasm the next, rolling to and fro at the mercy of good and bad actions—a powerless, helpness wreck in an ever-raging, ever-rushing, uncompromising current of cause and effect.. The heart sinks at the idea, yet this is the law of nature. Is there no hope? Is there no escape?—was the cry that went up from the bottom of the heart of despair.'

The answer to this cry of the human heart came to the purified heart of an *Upaniṣadic* sage who proclaimed his realisation in trumpet voice to all humanity, addressing them as *amrtasya putrāḥ,* children of immortality (*Svetāśvatara Upaṇisad,* 2.5 and 3.8):

Śṛṇvantu viśve amrtasya putṛāḥ
ā ye dhāmāni divyāni tasthuḥ;
Vedāhametaṁ puruṣ aṁ māhāntam
ādityavarnaṁ tamasah parastāt
Tameva viditvā atimṛtyumeti,
nāyaḥ panthā vidyate ayanāya

'Hear, ye children of immortality! Even ye that reside in the higher spheres! I have *realised* the infinite Self of man, luminous as the sun and beyond all darkness (of ignorance and delusion). Realising Him alone can man transcend death; there in no other way to the goal.'

Īśāvāsyamidaṁ sarvaṁ yat kiñca jagatyāṁ jagat—'All this that is changeful in this ephemeral world must be enveloped by the Lord,' sings the opening verse of the *Iśā Upaniṣad.*

The *Upaniṣads* exhort man to realise this truth for himself. In the trail blazed by this spiritual discovery marched India, first one part, then another, until the intital spiritual leaven had leavened the whole country. It is an arresting procession of spiritual seekers, among whom the most epoch-making luminaries were Buddha, Śaṇkara, and Caitanya in the historic past, and Ramakrishna and Vivekananda in the present.

Universality, non-aggressiveness, and humanism are three of the essential values which Indian culture derived from the spirituality of her *Upaniṣads*. Its concern is with man as such and not with man cut up into caste, creed, sect, or race. The achievement by man of his highest glory and excellence is what it seeks and advocates. The *Upaniṣads* taught India to see that excellence in spirituality.

The distinctiveness of a culture is revealed in the type of man in whom that culture finds its own highest excellence embodied. A culture is worldly, if wordly success is what its most admired hero represents; it is spiritual or unworldly, if renunciation and spirituality are what its most admired hero embodies. Such admiration acts as a silent leaven in the rest of the body-politic. If there is any truth in calling Indian culture spiritual, it is not because all or most of the Indians are more spiritual than other people; but it derives from the fact that the most admired hero of the Indian people has been, and is, the man of God; and that the deep-felt aspiration of the Indian people is to be spiritual themselves. To quote Dr. Radhakrishnan from his book *Eastern Religions and Western Thought* (pp.381-2):

> The ideal man of India is not the magnanimous man of Greece or the valiant knight of medieval Europe, but the free man of the spirit, who has attained insight into the universe by rigid discipline and practice of distinterested virtues; who has freed himself from the prejudices of his time and place. It is India's pride that she has clumg fast to this ideal and produced in every generation and in every part of the country, from the time of the *rsis* of the *Upaniṣads* and Buddha to Ramakrishna and Gandhi, men who strove successfully to realise this ideal.

If *adhyātma vidyā,* the science of spirituality, is the strongest element in the Indian heritage, positive sciences and technology form her weakest points. She had made splendid contributions in these fields for centuries. But drawn by the lure of the divine within, and following the technique of meditation and inner withdrawal, she comparatively neglected the world without and the technique of action and struggle in that outer world; and this neglect of man's outer life became almost cruel in succeeding centuries. This is the one single cause behind almost all the maladies afflicting modern Indian society, not only its poverty and ignorance, but also its piety-fringed worldiness and social harshness. A policy that produced a few spiritual giants, produced also millions of arrested and stunted personalities and any number of selfish crooks in between.

Vivekananda's Tackling of Our National Weaknesses

The experiences of ancient Greece and the modern West, on the one side, and India on the other, reveal the strength and weakness of all specialisations in the field of culture; it also demonstrates the partial character of all existing cultures, and their complementarity. This is particularly true of the Indian and Western cultural legacies. That these two are not antithetical but basically akin was brought home to our people by Vivekananda who traced the cause of our national degradation to our attitude of false superiority, to our considering ourselves as the 'chosen people', and to our consequent policy of national isolation from the rest of the world. Speaking on the subject of 'The Work Before Us' in Madras in 1987, Vivekananda said *(Complete Works,* Vol. III Eighth Edition, p.272):

> We cannot do without the world outside India; it was our foolishness that we thought we could, and we have paid the penalty by about a thousand years of slavery. That we did not go out to compare things with other nations, did not mark the workings that have been all around us, has been the one great cause of this degrtadation of the Indian mind. We have paid the penalty; let us do it no more.

In a letter written from Bombay in September 1892, the Swami writes *(Letters of Swami Vivekananda,* Fourth Edition, p.54):

> So you see, we must travel, we must go to foreign parts. We must see how the engine of society works in other countries, and keep free and open communication with what is going on in the minds of other nations, if we really want to be a nation again. And over and above all, we must cease to tyrannise.

Writing from Yokohama in July 1893, he exhorts the nation thus *(ibid.,* p.64):

> Come out of your narrow holes and have a look abroad. See how nations are on the march. Do you love man? Do you love your country? Then, come, let us struggle for higher and better things... India wants the sacrifice of at least a thousand of her young men... to struggle unto life and death to bring about a new state of things—sympathy for the poor and bread to their hungry mouths, enlightenment to the people at large, and struggle unto death to make men of them who have been brought to the level of beasts by the tyranny of your forefathers.

Writing from New York in November 1984, he says *(ibid,* p.148):

> To my mind, the one great cause of the downfall and the degeneration coming was the building of a wall of custom-whose foundation was hatred of others-round the nation, and the real aim of which in ancient times was to prevent the Hindu from coming in contact with the surrounding Buddhistic nations.
>
> Whatever cloak ancient or modern sophistry may try to throw over it, the inevitable result—the vindication of the moral law, that none can hate others without degenerating himself—is that the race that was foremost amongst the ancient races is now a byword and a scom among nations. We are object-lessons of the violation of that law which our ancestors were the first to discover and discriminate.
>
> Give and take is the law, and if India wants to raise herself once more, it is absolutely necessary that she brings out her treasures and throws them broadcast among the nations of the earth, and in return be ready to receive what others have to give her. Expansion is life, contraction is death. Love is life, hatred is death. We commenced to die the day we began to hate other races, and nothing can prevent our

death unless we come back to expansion, which is life.

'We must mix therefore with all the races of the earth.'

Assimilation of Western Values by Modern India

What India is dead-set to achieve in the modern age is the correcting of this centuries-old imbalance in her outlook and way of life. No more is she going to neglect her outer life. This mood and earnestness is writ large on her modern renaissance which has for its aim the all-round flowering of her national genius. All the movements of India's soul—political, economic or cultural—during the past sixty-five years of this century, have had for their one aim the awakening of our people to the realities of the modern age. The nation has been engaged in educating herself in the fundamental values, the strong points, of the modern Western culture. The first value to be absorbed was political freedom. To a people who has for centuries looked on political freedom and political slavery with an almost equal eye in their pursuit of a post-mortem salvation, political awakening was the necessary prelude to the correction of all other national imbalances. All the virtues and graces of man's social existence proceed from political freedom. Such freedom and the sense of responsibility that flows from it are the twin values that constitute the primary dignity of man. This is the modern concept of citizenship in which man achieves self-realisation in the context of a free society. The adoption by free India of a democratic republican constitution for herself marks a milestone in the political education of our people. The constitution is the first of a series of new documents, to be followed by others in due course, including a common civil code for all, which will eventually replace all existing religious codes of the country in so far as they deal with the secular life of the Indian people.

Nation-building in Modern India

These new documents will complete the process of nation-building in India out of her diverse racial, linguistic—and religious elements; they will constitute the new national *dharma-śāstra* of this age, and provide the necessary firm secular base for Indian spiritual life, allowing for the release of the truly spiritual forces of all her great religions, what one may call her national *mokṣa-śāstra* traditions, into creative and constructive channels. *It is only when the spiritual forces of the great world religions in India become fused into a unified current of a Godward passion and a manward love that she will achieve full nationhood.*

Citizenship in a democracy involves, as I said earlier, not only freedom but also responsibility. This sense of social responsibility releases the energies of the citizen for the service of his fellow-citizens, ensuring thereby the all-around development of society and its unity and integrity. If 'We, the People of India', have given ourselves a free constitution, as the preamble to our constitution proclaims, it is again we, the people of India, on whom lies the responsibility to ensure the dignity of the individual and the unity of the nation through hard work and mutual co-operation. In this sphere of practical politics, success depends upon the whole nation living down much of its own obsolete traditions, and assimilating the traditions of the modern West. Such assimilation depends upon the igniting of the Promethean spark in every one of our citizens, making him or her a reservoir of disciplined energy and resource.

This is what is being done in our country since our independence. During the last eighteen years after independence, India has achieved by way of economic development and social transformation more than what she had achieved in the hundred years before independence. This is a proof of the youthful vitality of the nation, and its assimilation of the spirit of energy and progress, action and endeavour, of the modern West. Under the pressure of mounting problems yet remaining to be solved, the nation should not fail to recognise its own solid achievements. Constant self-deprecation saps the vitality of a nation, says Vivekananda, by destroying its faith in itself. *Ajṇaśca aśraddadhānaśca saṁśayātmā vinaśyati*—'the ignorant, the faithless, and the doubting come to ruin', says the *Gītā* (IV. 40).

Modern India: The Meeting Ground of the Ancient Greek and the Ancient Hindu

Nation-building in the case of India, we should always remember, means nothing more than forging a new body-politic for her undying soul. That soul had so far been housed in a body inconsistent with its own majesty and glory. No other society in the world has exhibited such a contrast between ideals and realities as India in her spiritual vision and her body-politic. In the poignant words of Vivekananda *(Letters of Swami Vivekananda,* p.69):

> No religion on earth preaches the dignity of humanity in such a lofty strain as Hinduism, and no religion on earth treads upon the necks of the poor and the low in such a fashion as Hinduism.

For the first time in her long history, India has resolved to translate her vision of human excellence into reality by earnestly embarking on the creation of a free and egalitarian society offering opportunities for self-development to every one of her citizens.

Nivedita, in her book quoted earlier, refers to the words of Vivekananda, uttered during his second voyage to the West, giving this much-needed orientation to the Indian tradition (p.203):

> Hitherto, the great fault of our Indian religion has lain in its knowing only two words-renunciation and mu*kti* (salvation). Only *'mukti'* here! Nothing for the householder!

> But these are the very people whom I want to help.
>
> And so strength must come to the nation through education.

Pointing to the importance of this utterance, Nivedita remarks *(ibid):*

> I thought at the time, and I think increasingly as I consider it, that this one talk of my master had been well worth the whole voyage, to have heard.

Whatever success India has so far achieved in this adventure, in this war against poverty, social injustice, and general stagnation, is the fruit of her assimilation of the spirit of humanism and progress of the modern West. This is the tribute that our ancient nation is paying today to the spirit of ancient Greece and the modern West. It is the finest tribute that any culture can pay to another. It was Vivekananda, as I have already said, who first pointed out the basic kinship between the strong points of the two cultural legacies of India and the West. He foresaw that modern world conditions afforded the best opportunity for the evolution of a complete human civilisation by the cross fertilisation of these two legacies. He considered India to be the finest laboratory for this momentous cultural fusion; he preached the Indian national philosophy of Vedanta in East and West alike, in view of its synthesis of the inner and outer aspects of human life in its synoptic vision of a comprehensive spirituality; and he bent the energies of her modern renaissance in that high direction. Stressing this central feature of the Indian renaissance in his lecture on 'The Work Before Us', Vivekananda says *(Complete Works,* Vol. III, eighth edition, p.271):

> England, nay the whole of Europe (and America), has to thank Greece for its civilisation. It is Greece that speaks through everything (in the West). Every building, every

piece of furniture has the impress of Greece upon it; European (Western) science and art are nothing but Grecian. (Words within brackets not Vivekananda's).

Today the ancient Greek is meeting the ancient Hindu on the soil of India. Thus slowly and silently the leaven has come; the broadening, the life-giving, and the revivalist movement that we see all around us has been worked out by these forces together. A broader and more generous conception of life is before us; and although at first we have been deluded a little and wanted to narrow things down, we are finding out today that these generous impulses which are at work, these broader conceptions of life, are the logical interpretation of what is in our ancient books. They are the carrying out, to the rigorously logical effect, of the primary conceptions of our own ancestors. *To become broad, to go out, to amalgamate, to universalise, is the end of our aims.* And all the time, we have been making ourselves smaller and smaller, and dissociating ourselves, contrary to the plans laid down in our scriptures.

Spirituality and Evolution

In developing and perfecting its *adhyātma vidyā,* the science of the Self, India has given a spiritual direction to human evolution consistent with the dignity of man and his infinite potentialities. Twentieth-century biology, as I said before, enthrones quality over quantity as the criterion of evolution at the human stage, and upholds fulfilment as its goal, in place of numerical increase or mere survival. The *Upaniṣads* uphold that this search for fulfilment will take man progressively beyond his physical and sensate awareness which is finite and limited, and give him a glimpse of his infinite spiritual dimension. It is only through such spiritual growth that man can achieve fulfilment by realising his true dimension as the Atman, which is infinite and universal, and embrace his fellow-beings in bonds of love and service.

This is the strongest of the strong elements of the Indian heritage referred to in the remark of Vivekananda quoted in the earlier part of this lecture. It is an element needed to be fostered not only by India, but also by the modern world. As the modern West has posed a challenge to India, India in turn has thrown a challenge to the west. Both are healthy challenges, adequate response to which by each will ensure the steady march of man everywhere to the evolutionary goal of fulfilment. The West has need to find a remedy for what E.M. Forster, in the passage quoted earlier, refers to as those elements of her Greek legacy which *afflict* her. This malady that afflicts the modern West has been best described by the German philosopher, Schopenhauer *(The World as Will and Idea,* Vol. I, p.404):

> Almost all men who are secure from want and care, now that at last they have thrown off all other burdens, become a burden to themselves.

Since the two legacies are complementary, and since the Indian contribution refers to man indepth, the West may find in the Indian legacy that sought-for remedy for the weak points of her otherwise noble and dynamic cultural tradition. Vivekananda refers to this in his lecture on 'The Mission of the Vedanta' delivered in India in 1897. Though a bit long, it will be found relevant in the present context. Says the Swami *(Complete Works,* Vol. III, eighth edition, pp.181-2):

> We have, as it were, thrown a challenge to the whole world from the most ancient times. In the West, they are trying to solve the problem how much a man can possess, and we are trying here to solve the problem on how little a man

can live. This struggle and this difference will still go on for some centuries. But if history has any truth in it, and if prognostications ever prove true, it must be that those who train themselves to live on the least, and control themselves well, will in the end gain the battle, and that those who run after enjoyment and luxury, however vigorous they may seem for the moment, will have to die and become annihilated. There are times in the history of a man's life, nay, in the history of the lives of nations, when a sort of world-weariness becomes painfully predominant. It seems that such a tide of world-weariness has come upon the Western world. There, too, they have their thinkers, great men; and they are already finding out that his race after gold and power is all vanity of vanities; many, nay, most of the cultured men and women there are already weary of this competition, this struggle, this brutality of their commercial civilisation, and they are looking forward towards something better. There is a class which still clings on to political and social changes as the only panacea for the evils..., but among the great thinkers there, other ideals are growing. They have found out that no amount of political or social manipulation of human conditions can cure the evils of life. It is a change of the soul itself for the better that alone will cure the evils of life. No amount of force, or government, or legislative cruelty will change the conditions of a race, but it is spiritual culture and ethical culture alone that can change wrong racial tendencies for the better. Thus these races of the West are eager for some new thought, for some new philosophy; the religion they have had, Christianity, although good and glorious in many respects, has been imperfectly understood, and is, as understood hitherto, found to be insufficient. The thoughtful men of the West find in our ancient philosophy, especially in Vedānta, the new impulse of thought they are seeking, the very spiritual food and drink for which they are hungering and thirsting. And it is no wonder that this is so.

Practical Vedanta

The strong point of the Indian tradition is, as we have seen, its vision of the spiritual dimension of the human personality, and the scientific tradition of religion in which this vision is embodied. Stressing as it does the spirit of seeking and inquiry, and upholding experiment and experience as the criterion of true religion, the Indian tradition frees religion from all dogmatic and creedal limitations and blends with the spirit of modern science. This Indian spiritual tradition has within it the energy and the power to *deepen* the scientific humanism of the modern West. The Western tradition, similarly, has the energy and the power within it to *broaden* the scope of the Indian tradition, channelling its blessings from a small minority of the spiritually gifted to the millions of ordinary men and women. This synthesis of the inner and the outer, of the sacred and the secular, had already been achieved *in the plane of thought* in the unifying philosophy of Vedānta, and especially in its great formulation, namely, the *Gitā*. Its achievement *in the plane of the work-a-day world* is what Vivekananda gave to modern India as his unique contribution in his philosophy and programme of Practical Vedānta, and what the nation is engaged in ever since.

Our programme of material improvement of the country does not necessarily commit us to the philosophy of materialism. On the other hand, our spiritual philosophy, as Vivekananda pointed out, considers involuntary poverty to be unspiritual and commits us to the improvement of the material condition of the people with a view to improving their spiritual life. This is the meaning of his plea for what he terms a 'toned down materialism' for India. 'I do not believe in a religion,' says he, 'which cannot wipe the widow's tears or stop the orphan's wails'; again, 'even if a dog goes hungry in my country, my religion will be to find food for that dog.'

Our Youth and Our Emerging Nation

Such is the Indian society that is waiting to receive each and every one of our youths who complete their university education today. *It is a society of bubbling hopes and mounting problems, with an impressive past and a glorious future.* Every youthful generation of modern India owes it to itself and to the nation at large to strive to become strong and dynamic. Such strength is the product of faith in oneself and in one's country's heritage, reinforced by the *assimilation* of all available knowledge, national and international. This is the aim of all true education. Vivekananda defined the scope of our national education as the assimilation of the spirit of Vedānta and modern science. The *Chāndogya Upaniṣad* in a memorable passage (1.1.10) refers to the energy of character generated by education:

Yadeva vidyaya karoti, śraddhayā, upanisadā, tadeva viryavattaram bhavati—'Whatever is done through mastery of the know-how, through faith (in oneself and one's cause) and through inner meditation—that alone 'becomes charged with the highest energy.'

Revolution: The Indian Way

In the passage from Nivedita's book quoted at the beginning of this lecture, Vivekananda had told us that new India will be a *growth from within;* and that this growth from within will be the result of the assimilation by her children of the strong points of the ancient Indian and the modern Western traditions. This is a significant point to remember in studying the development of modern India. In these three words, namely, *growth from within,* Vivekananda has given to our nation its *national educational vision.* Nations have been shaped by impact from outside either by a military or an ideological invasion; in such cases, the energy within the nation succumbs to the outside impact. Nations have also been shaped by violent revolutions from within due to the explosion of long-thwarted social aspirations. But India in her long history has stood many such outside impacts, revealing thereby the presence of a tremendous core of inner strength. She has also avoided violent explosions from within by timely adjustments. But the inner strength demonstrated by India during the past several centuries was defensive in its posture and apologetic in its expression, when neither did the tree of Indian life put forth fresh shoots nor did it die. It was a period of general national stagnation. *But today our ancient motherland is bubbling with a new youthfulness; it is bursting with a new life, inner and outer, by the assimilation of all available nourishment of knowledge and ideas.* The process undoubtedly will be intensified in the coming decades. Nothing can hinder or stop it.

The growth of a new and dynamic India, effecting revolutionary changes within her own body-politic consistent with her vision of human excellence, and exerting her distinctive influence on the rest of the world, is the vision that should inspire all our education and politics, life and religion.

If this is the aim of the modern renaissance, who are the agents to work it out? The instruments of social change in any modern society are the educated youth of that society. Ever since India began to experience her modern renaissance over a century and a half ago in the wake of Raja Rammohun Roy, her educated youth have been the mainstay of all her revolutionary movements in the social, political, cultural, and spiritual fields.

Our Educational Stagnation

This is the national context, awareness on which will make our education purposive, not only during the formal schooling period, but throughout life. Most of the ailments of our present-day educational system, most of the maladies afflicting our students and teachers, proceed from educational objectives too narrowly conceived, namely, examinations and jobs. Our educational vision must assimilate the wisdom of Sri Ramakrishna's conviction: 'As long as I live, so long do I learn.' Education so conceived becomes continual growth of personality, steady development of character, and the qualitative improvement of life. A trained mind has the capacity to draw spiritual nourishment from every experience, be it defeat or victory, sorrow or joy. Education is *training the mind* and not *stuffing the brain.* Character efficiency is the fruit of the former while the latter produces mental stagnation and its attendant character deficiencies. Every country today is suffering from this undue stress on examinations and the stuffing-the-brain process behind it; but it is prevalent in its most harmful form in our education. The definition of current American education given by an American journal *(National Parent-Teacher Journal,* April 1955) as 'the mysterious process whereby information passes from the notes of the professor on to the notebook of the student, through his pen, without entering the mind of either of them,' is an apt description of much of what passes for education in India today.

Our Educational Vision

This educational stagnation can be removed only by treating education primarily as training of the mind and, as Vivekananda defines it, as 'the life-building, man-making, character-making *assimilation* of ideas.' The entire educational method and programme should keep this high objective in view. Vivekananda's writings make their own irresistible appeal,' as remarked by Gandhiji in his Foreword to *Education,* the little selection of Viveknanda's utterances on education. Here are some of these precious utterances:

> Getting by heart the thoughts of others in a foreign language, and stuffing your brain with them and taking some university degrees, you consider yourself educated? Is this education?... Open your eyes and see what a piteous cry for food is rising in the land of Bharata, proverbial for its food. Will your education fulfil this want? The education that does not help the common mass of people to equip themselves for the struggle for life, which does not bring out strength of character, a spirit of philanthropy, and the courage of a lion—is it worth the name?

> We want that education by which character is formed, strength of mind is increased, the intellect is expanded, and by which one can stand on one's own feet. What we need is to study, independent of foreign control, different branches of the knowledge that is our own, and with it the English language and Western science; we need technical education and all else that will develop industries, so that men, instead of seeking for service, may earn enough to provide for themselves and save against a rainy day.

Again:

> The end of all education, all training, should be man-making. The end and aim of all training is to make the man grow. The training by which the current and expression of will are brought under control and become fruitful is called education.

In the light of these ideas of Vivekananda, let us assess our developmental activities, in general, and education, in particular.

All our nation-building programmes should have two objectives—one short-term, the other long-term. Too much stress on the short-term, and too little or none at all on the long-term, is what is actually obtaining in our educational, political, and other fields. The short-term objective in politics is what we stress when we view it from one election to the next; this is the way of the *mere politician.* Its long-term objective is the political education of the Indian people so that every citizen becomes an intelligent participant in the national life, and the state becomes strengthened with the strength and efficiency of its 450 million awakened citizens; this is the way of the *statesman* who combines the short-term and long-term objectives in a synoptic vision of total human evolution. India had the recent example of such a statesman in Shri Jawaharlal Nehru, who never lost sight of the qualitative improvement of man. Education, similarly, has been viewed only in its short-term objective by most of the Indian students and, it is sad to note, by the Indian state as well. To the student, it means merely passing an examination and securing a job; to the state, it means largely turning out so many mechanics and fitters, doctors and lawyers, teachers and clerks, and a host of other social functionaries. The state has need of the services of thousands of well-trained technicians of all types for its developmental programmes; it is also imperative that, with a view to strengthening the democratic base of Indian life, universal compulsory education, up to the primary level to begin with and up to the school final level eventually, is achieved with the minimum possible delay. This is therefore a legitimate and urgent objective; what is not so legitimate is the ignoring of the long-term objective, which, as we have seen before, is the qualitative improvement of man through the qualitative improvement of education at all levels, which means the progressive assimilation by every citizen of the finest heritage of East and West; citizens in whom the diverse forces of the spirit-faith and reason, the sacred and the secular, and meditation and action—so long at loggerheads with each other, have achieved a happy synthesis, giving man an experience of complete fulfilment.

Conclusion

This is our educational vision. A nation without vision perishes. Since India has not perished, and shall not perish, let us cease to divorce our short-term objectives from the long-term ones, and make education the surest means to human fulfilment, individual and collective. Even while planning our institutional programmes of education through schools, colleges, and universities, let us also not lose sight of the fact that the highest education is gained not from institutions, however well conducted they be, but from ilṭlumined men and women. The former give us only *aparā vidyā* or supreme knowledge. Narendranath Datta was one of the brilliant students who blazoned the name of this University of Calcutta. But this student, let us never forget, became Vivekananda, who, in the words of Romain Rolland *(Life of Vivekananda,* Third Impression, p.192):

> Of all modern men achieved the highest equilibrium between the diverse forces of thought, and was one of the first to sign a treaty of peace between the two forces eternally warring within us: the forces of reason and faith.

Only after he secured a still higher education at the feet of Sri Ramakrishna at Dakshineswar, who himself, strange to note, did not undergo any institutional education.

India's educational vision whispers into the ears of every student who passes out of her institutions of higher learning that there is a still higher education which yields the knowledge of the infinite Self of man, the Atman. Surplus human energy accumulated at the secular or sensate level of life, if not channelled into this higher spiritual direction, will recoil on the personality and create emotional disturbances and inner tensions, leading man further and further away from his ideal of fulfilment, in spite of all the technological products of his wealth and power, knowledge and leisure. Our institutional education will be judged a complete success only if the students it turns out are not insensitive to these gentle whispers, but are moved, by the fascination of this deeper mystery, to continue their education throughout life through the medium of their life and work, to convert their very breadwinning into self-knowledge, until the highest spiritual knowledge is gained. In the passionate words of poet Tagore *(Lectures and Addresses,* pp.27-8):

> The object of education is to give man the unity of truth....
>
> I believe in a spiritual world, not as anything separate from this world, but as its innermost truth. With the breath we draw, we must always feel this truth, that we are living in God. Born in this great world, full of the mystery of the infinite, we cannot accept our existence as a momentary outburst of chance, drifting on the current of matter towards an eternal nowhere.

For all students of the modern age, ancient India presents the glowing example of Nārada of the *Chāndogya Upaniṣad* as the prototype of this spiritual sensitivity in a student of learning and talent, who was dissatisfied with institutional education and mere book knowledge, and who used both as spurs to spiritual knowledge and wisdom.

Let me conclude this discussion of our national educational vision with the clarion call given to us by Swami Vivekananda: 'Arise! Awake! and stop not till the goal is reached!'

Bhagvān Buddha and Our Heritage*

Introduction

IT is remarkable that our country which, unlike Ceylon or Burma, does not profess to be a Buddhistic country, has yet become very enthusiastic about the celebration of the 2500th anniversary of the birth of Bhagvān Buddha. A phenomenon like this can take place only in India, not in other countries—the celebration of the birthday of a great teacher whom we are not supposed to be following as professed adherents. But it is this very fact that invests this celebration with a significance which we would do well to understand—how India and the vast body of Hindus could enthusiastically enter into this great celebration and make it a nation-wide affair. The answer to this question will be found in the nature and scope of the faith of the Hindus and the place which Buddha holds in that faith.

---

*Speech delivered at the celebration of the 2500th birthday of Bhagvan Buddha at the Ramakrishna Math, Mylapore, Madras, on 30 May 1956, and later published in *Vedanta Kesari,* Madras, in its issues for September and October 1957.

Modern India's Recovery of the Buddhist Period of her Long History

For centuries together, we had entirely forgotten Buddha, and his doctrines and creed had become almost alien to us, while they had been taken up by peoples outside India and made the religion of their own countries and societies. It is only for the last hundred years, ever since the recovery of Buddhism and its literature by the Western scholars and of archaeological finds in India, that our people have begun to love and appreciate the great personality of Buddha and his teachings. But once the discovery was made that there was such a great period in Indian history which was dominated by the personality of Buddha, our national mind reacted to this fact with enthusiasm and devotion; we felt elated at the uncovering of a period of our ancient history which had been dark to us, but glorious at the time at which it was lived, and dominated by this great teacher and his sublime message of unity, holiness, renunciation, and love for one and all; and that period of our history is today accepted by us as one of the greatest periods of Indian history. When the great message of Buddha throbbed in the hearts of millions of our country, the whole nation rose morally, spiritually, as also politically; and with that accession of strength, our nation became the centre for a wide and rich cultural diffusion in the world outside.

Greater India of the historic period is the gift of Buddha to us and the world. Till then India was self-contained, though even then there are evidences of her thought and people influencing her neighbouring countries in an unorganised way; but organised work of this type was largely confined to India itself. Whatever cultural values we had evolved, whatever religions we had developed, we had tried to diffuse them only within the Indian continent But with Buddha started that organised expansion of Indian culture and Indian thought outside India, for which half the world is grateful to this country today. It is in this context that we are viewing the great work of Buddha and what it can do to enrich and ennoble our spiritual and cultural life in this age.

Swami Vivekananda and Bhagvān Buddha

Swami Vivekananda is one of the most prominent leaders of our country in recent times who has called our attention to the great work of Bhagvān Buddha in the past and the greater work that the Buddha spirit can do to us today. In his lectures and discourses, he has beautifully expressed his conviction that modern India requires to assimilate the great intellect of Śaṅkara and the great heart of Buddha, the great heart for which, somehow or other, in the later development of philosophy in this country, we had practically found no place. That the human mind cannot only think high, but also feel deeply, and work energetically from that high point of view, was something which was continually forgotten for centuries together; and it was Swamiji who pointed out to us that the origin of almost all the social maladies in our time, all those things which made us immobile as a people, leading to the accumulation of all sorts of evils in our body-politic-all these experiences of recent centuries can be traced back to the banishment of the Buddha spirit, of the Buddha heart, from the thought and practice of our country. In the same breath, he exhorted us to turn out back once again to that great heritage, to call back Buddha to our nation and to our hearts; and he also added that until we did that, our country could never hope to develop that internal strength which we all wish and pray for. This was the approach of all enlightened minds of India in recent decades. This positive approach to Buddha and his place in our history has gripped the minds of our people, so that today, after nearly sixty years of education by Swami Vivekananda and other leaders, the nation feels a sense of pride in owning Buddha as one of its glorious teachers and in being the children of a country which produced a Buddha. That is the context in which we are living and functioning today.

Buddha and the Indian Tradition

In what sense can we say that Buddha is intimate to us, that his contribution is of vital importance to us today? What is his place in our national tradition? Unless we answer that question, we shall not be able to accept him with that whole-heartedness with which we have accepted the other great teachers who preceded and succeeded him. We have responded with all love and enthusiasm and reverence to the celebration of his 2500th birthday, and yet we are not Buddhists. When we ask ourselves as to what are those traces of the teaching of Buddha in ourselves through which we are slowly and imperceptibly discovering our kinship with this great teacher, we are led to the realisation, through a study of his life and message, that he is closest to us in all the essential teachings that he gave, in all the greatness and depth of the holy dedicated life that he lived. We may have forsaken the creed which developed out of his teachings in later centuries as Buddhism; yet, even in the matter of that creed, many aspects of it are akin to our own; but our interest in Buddha today does not proceed from that source; it does not mean that we are going to become Buddhists in the political or sectarian or credal sense. Whether to become such a Buddhist or not is not a vital question with us; after all, if a man or a group changes the label of his or its creed, it will only result in removing his or its name from one column to another in the census register. It does not result in the increase of the moral or spiritual strength of the nation. But if the nation as a whole, or at least large numbers in it, can inspire themselves with the spirit of Buddha, can imbibe his spirit of love and compassion and tolerance, can imbibe that spirit by which knowledge can flow into love and service of the people, if that can be developed in us, resulting in a purer and a nobler mode of life, certainly the whole nation stands to gain and to benefit from that assimilation.

Buddha and the Upaniṣads

That is the line in which the country has tried to understand Buddha, and that is the line in which Swami Vivekananda taught it to accept this great teacher, who, according to him, *is the fulfilment of the spiritual thought of the* Upaniṣads *which had preceded him.*

Coming close upon the age of the *Upaniṣads,* wherein the foundations of the subsequent developments of culture and religion in India had been laid, Buddha stands closest to the spirit of the Upaniṣads. In fact, it is not possible to appreciate the life and teachings of Buddha adequately without understanding the spirit of the Upaniṣads. There are at least a few Western scholars who appreciate this fact. A large number of Western scholars, who have written books on Buddha, have been unduly harsh on the prevailing Vedic religion, often confusing their estimates of it with post-Buddhistic developments. It looks as if they sought the growth of the plant of the Buddha movement at the cost of the soil in which it was raised and reared, to trace its life development outside that soil and climate. But there have been, as I said, a few Western scholars who have realised that Buddha could not be understood except in the context of the spiritual soil and philosophical climate provided by the sages of the *Upaniṣads.*

Edmund Holmes on the Vedāntic Background of Buddhism

One such author whom I would like to quote, one who has made a sympathetic study of Buddha, is Edmund Holmes. In his book, *The Creed of Buddha,* he warns us that to understand Buddha without understanding the *Upaniṣads* is to miss the significance of Buddha and his teachings. The understanding of the *Upaniṣads* is absolutely essential, for it is against that Himalayan thought background that we can realise the significance of the new advances that Buddha made in the thought and practice of that great philosophy. Writes Edmund Holmes at the commencement of his fifth chapter entitled 'A Misreading of Buddha' (*The Creed of Buddha,* p.98):

> Those who have followed me thus far will, I think, admit that Buddha's scheme of life coincides, at all its vital points, with the scheme that I worked out by drawing practical deductions from the master ideas of that deeply spiritual philosophy which found its expression in the *Upaniṣads*.

Again (*ibid.,* pp.102-103):

> The cumulative evidence afforded by these facts, added to the internal evidence which has already been set forth in detail, seems to point with irresistible force to one conclusion, namely, that Buddha accepted the idealistic teachings of the *Upaniṣads*—accepted it at its highest level and in its purest form—and took upon himself as his life's mission to fill the obvious gap in it—in other words, to make the spiritual ideas, which had hitherto been the exclusive possession of a few select souls, available for the daily needs of mankind. If this conclusion is correct, we shall see in Buddhism, not a revolt against the 'Brāhminic' philosophy as such, but an ethical interpretation of the leading ideas of that philosophy—a following out of those ideas, not into the word-built systems of (so called) thought which the metaphysicians of the day were constructing with fatal facility, but into their practical consequences in the inner life of man.

Upaniṣadic Parallels in Buddha's Life

There are a few points in the teachings of Buddha which have always been points of controversy, wherein great interpreters have differed from one another. The most important of these are two: first, the well-known *Anatta* doctrine, the teaching that there is no permanent soul; this teaching is so pervasive of Buddhism that we can take it as part and parcel of the original Buddhism. In the second discourse delivered by Buddha at the very beginning of his public ministration at Sārnāth, entitled the *Anattalakkhaṇa Sutta,* we have an exposition of this *Anatta* doctrine; so that it is necessary for us to understand what Buddha meant by this *Anatta or Anātmā* doctrine, which *apparently* represents a fundamental point of departure from the great teachings of the Upaniṣads on the subject of the true nature of individuality. The second is with regard to the nature of the ultimate reality. When man attains *nirvāṇa,* what does he realise and what happens to him? Does he attain something positive or something negative? On this subject the language of the *Upaniṣads* is clear, in spite of all the prefaces with which they have expounded it, stating that ultimate Truth is that from which speech and thought recoil, that it transcends all specifications. In spite of this kind of reservation, the *Upaniṣads* leave us in no doubt that the ultimate Truth is a 'Yes' and not a 'No'. It is a positive something and not a negative nothing; the *Upaniṣads* speak of it as Brahman, the One without a second, the Self of all, beyond sense and thought, the Impersonal, the Transcendent as well as the Immanent. Even though it transcends specifications by speech and thought, yet it is a positive reality. The *Katha Upaniṣad* (VI. 3.12-13) says:

Naiva vācā na manasā prāptuṁ śakyo na cakṣuṣā;
Astīti bruvato' nyatra kathaṃ tad upalabhyate

This Self cannot be reached through the organs of speech or thought or sight. How can It be realised except through one who says 'It is?'

Asti ityeva upalabdhavyaḥ

It must be comprehended as "is" (and not as "is not").

The last category of thought can only be a position, and not a negation, according to the *Upaniṣadic* thought. On this basis when we proceed, we do not see in the teachings of Buddha any clear reference to the reality of a changeless Being behind the fluctuations of Becoming.

As in the case of the soul, it is something composite, impermaṭnent, and ultimately insubstantial, so in the case of the world, it is also impermanent and insubstanital; but with regard to the ultimate reality realised in *nirvāṇa,* Buddha did not say that it also is impermanent and insubstantial. He did not say anything about it at all. He was silent about it, as he was also silent about the nature of the individual in the state of *nirvāṇa,* and evaded giving direct answers to questions relating to them. That is a point which we shall have to discuss, the meaning of this silence of his on the subject of the ultimate Reality in man and in the universe, and to determine his position in the great philosophical tradition of the *Upaniṣads*.

The Parivrìjaka Movement

In the life of Buddha we can trace three eventful periods. The first is the period of his youth and early manhood when, as Siddhartha Gautama, he lived a life in the world, all the while yearning to gain the truth of all life and existence. Gifted as he was with a keen mind, a pure mind, a mind that questions and struggles to find the truth, the spirit of utter dispassion for the life of empty pleasures came upon him at the age of twenty-nine, and he entered the second stage of his career, namely, renunciation and whole-souled search after Truth. Gautama getting the spirit of dispassion and leaving the world of evanescent pleasures in search of Truth is not a new or strange phenomenon in Indian history. Hundreds and thousands of ordinary and gifted men and women had passed through the same experience. They had followed the path of renunciation to search for the meaning of life, so that at the time of Gautama, there were many wandering teachers who were also inspired by the great desire to penetrate the world of appearance and come in touch with Reality. They had renounced all sense pleasures and become wandering ascetics, *parivrājakas;* and these *parivrājakas were large in number at the time of Buddha. Thus, Gautama did not initiate something unique or new in turning a parivrājaka.* He himself was one of the *parivrājakas;* and when he left the world, he attached himself now to one teacher and then to another, each of whom was a *parivrājaka.* This tendency to go forth into the homeless state in search of Truth was well established in the age of the Aranyakas and the *Upaniṣads;* they give us arresting pictures of gifted men and women imbued with the spirit of renunciation and earnestness, with hearts pure and tranquil, leading lives of meditation and truth-seeking, alone or in groups, in forests and quiet retreats. This is a tradition which goes back to a very early period of Indian history. Says Rhys Davids *(Buddhist India,* pp.161-62):

> The career of such a wandering teacher seems to have been open to anyone, and even to women. And the most perfect freedom, both of thought and of expression, was permitted to them—a freedom probably unequalled in the history of the world.
>
> This curious state of things would only have been posssible among people of a very fair degree both of average general intelligence and of gentle manners.

So far as the renunciation of Gautama, the future Buddha, is concerned, so far as the steps that he took in this direction are concerned, he fully falls in line with the nationl tradition well established in the *Upaniṣads*.

Buddha's Search for a Guru

Following this established pattern, we find Gautama, in the wake of his renunciation, attaching himself now to one teacher, then to another, in his search for Truth. First he goes to Ālāra Kālāma. He was a famous teacher of the time, and to the last day of his life, Buddha held him in great respect. Learning what he could from Ālāra, we find Gautama attaching himself next to another famous teacher, Uddaka, the son of Rāma. These were his two teachers, themselves spiritually advanced souls, living in the forest near Rājagṛha with their groups of seeker-followers. Writes J.G. Jennings *(The Vedāntic Buddhism of the Buddha,* p.ixvi):

> Though Gautama ultimately rejected the teachings of both these ascetic thinkers, the Brahman doctrine of the *Parama-ātman* evidently remained as the basis of his own doctrine of the impermanence of the individual.

Thus the first step that Gautama took on entering the homeless life was to search for a *guru,* one from whom he could get guidance in his spiritual quest, and in this, again, he was on the trail blazed by the *Upaniṣads*. For we know from the *Muṇḍaka Upaniṣad* (1.2.7, 11) that the seeker after Truth, the seeker after spiritual excellence, forsakes all interests in rituals and ceremonials which had been elaborated by the ritualistic portion of the *Vedas*, knowing them to be useless in the search for the highest Truth:

Plavā hi ete adṛḍhā yajñarūpā
aṣṭādaśoktam avaraṁ yesu karma;

Etat śreyo ye abhinandanti mūḍhāḥ
jarāmṛtyum te punarevāp yanti

These paths of sacrifices and rituals are very frail boats; the fools who rate them high and indulge in them enter into the cycle of birth and death again and again.

Tapaḥ-śraddhe ye hi upvasanti araṇye
sāntā vidvāṁso bhaikṣyacaryāṁ carantaḥ

But the wise with tranquil minds live in the forest as mendicants practising austerity and faith.

Inadequacy of the Heaven Concept

The *Upaniṣad (ibid.,* 1.2.12) then proceeds to state that a person who wants to realise the ultimate Truth must examine all that can be gained by ritualistic acts in this world as well as in the next, whether in the earthly world or in a heavenly world; whatever pleasures and delights can be had in these, he must examine thoroughly with the eye of reason, of understanding, and, having examined, reject them as of no consequence at all, because Truth cannot be had by a life of pleasure here or elsewhere. Having rejected all these things, he must search for the Truth within himself, for which he approaches a great teacher and sits at his feet and learns the lessons of pure spirituality:

Parīksya lokān karmacitān brāhmaṇo
nirvedam āyāt nāsti akṛtaḥ kṛtena
Tadvijnānārthaṁ sa gurum eva abhigacchet
samitpāiḥ śrotriyam brahmanistham

Having examined all the worlds which are caused and conditioned by actions, a Brahmana shall conceive utter dispassion for all of them; for the Unconditioned cannot be had through the conditioned.

In order to realise the Unconditioned, let him approach, in all humility, a teacher who knows the spirit of the scriptures and is established in Brahman.'

'The Uncaused Cannot be had Through the Caused'

'The uncaused cannot be had through the caused', says the *Upaniṣad*. That is a great idea. What kind of dispassion does that person get? That this world as well as the world of heaven is the product of actions and that both are within the causal chain. Buddha also taught at a later period that what falls within the sphere of causality cannot be unconditioned and absolute.

The most reiterated formula in Buddhism refers to Buddha's knowledge of the entire range of conditioned things and their cessation:

Ye dharmā hetuprabhavā teṣām hetuṁ tathāgato hyavadat:
Teṣām ca yo nirodho evaṁ vādi hi mahāsramanaḥ

Whatever entities *(dhammas)* are produced from a cause, of these the *Tathagata* tells the cause *(hetu)*; and also that which is the cessation *(yo nirodho)* of these; thus declares the great recluse.

Therefore, says the *Upaniṣad,* to realise the unconditioned reality, taking the mind away from all conditioned things here or elsewhere, one should, in a spirit of questing humility, resort to a great teacher, a teacher who is a *brahma-niṣṭha,* one established in that Reality and thus embodying the spirit of the *sdstras* or scriptures (*Muṇḍaka Upaniṣad,* 1.2.13):

Tasmai sa vidvān upasannāya samyak
praśantacittāya śamānvitāya;
Yenākṣaraṁ puruṣaṁ veda satyam
provāca tāṁ tattvato brahmavidyām

To one who has so approached, and who has fulfilled all moral virtues, and become tranquil, the teacher shall impart that highest wisdom by which the Imperishable, the True, the Self, is realised.

Buddha's Asceticism in the Jungles of Uruvela

Thus, so far as the approach to the two great teachers is concerned, Gautama followed the tradition laid down by the Upaniṣads; having approached those great teachers, he learnt whatever they had to give. If the particular teachers could not give the highest teaching, that does not mean the highest teaching was not there. For, after all, teachers who have assimilated the highest teachings are not to be had in every generation; and this particular seeker was of a type that could not be satisfied by an ordinary teacher. He assimilated whatever his teachers could give and asked for more; but they could not satisfy the aspirations of his heart for the highest realisation. With all politeness, Gautama then left these two teachers and resolved to seek the highest truth for himself. It was in that mood, with that spirit, that he walked from Rājagṛha to the place which is today known as Buddha Gaya in the jungles of Uruvela. Having gone there, he established himself in a course of severe austerity, penance, and inward contemplation. Five other devotees were also engaged in the same pursuit in the place. They recognized the advanced spirituality of Gautama and accepted him as their spiritual guide and leader and followed him in his path of austerities. It was a path that was well defined and followed by various *sādhakas* of the time, a path consisting of severe austerity of body and mind. It was a form of extreme, rigorous asceticism. Gautama was a thorough-going person. If he accepted a procedure, he would not rest content till he thoroughly saw to the end of it. So he was foremost among the six seekers in the practice of austerity and mortification, until he became extremely happy and hoped that he would soon attain enlightenment.

Buddha's Illumination After Forsaking such Asceticism

But one day, when Gautama was getting up from his seat, he fell down unconscious from weakness; regaining consciousness, the following thought arose in his mind. 'What foolishness! I am in search of the highest Truth. It is a search that calls for the utmost courage and stamina, and yet I am weakening my body, weakening my senses, the only instruments I possess by which I can undertake this voyage of discovery; I shall not proceed on this path of foolish mortification any more.' So he immediately forsook the path of senseless austeriity, and proceeded to a nearby village to beg for a little food to strengthen himself. Seeing Gautama abandoning the path of asceticism, the five disciples felt that their leader had strayed into the path of luxury and ease and decided that he was not worthy of them; they deserted him and went away.

Gautama did not mind their desertion. He went to the village and received a bowl of *payasa* or sweetened milk-rice from a village girl by name Sujātā; he bathed in the nearby river, ate the *pāyasa* and rested during the afternoon; and towards the evening he proceeded to a nearby spot where there was a large banyan tree, and sat under it with the determination not to rise till he had realised the highest Truth.

All these were in the line of what the *Upaniṣads* had prescribed. Sitting under the tree, with senses and mind under control, Gautama entered into the depths of meditation. His naturally pure mind, which had become purer as a result of the discipline he had undergone for six years, was now so fine that with a little effort he soared to the heights of meditation. In the first three watches of the night, Gautama plunged deeper and deeper into the depths of his being, and the descriptions of his meditation given in the Buddhist scriptures tally with what the Vedānta describes as the process of entering into the *nirvikalpa* state of *samādhi,* the *samādhi* where the mind transcends the sphere of form, the sphere of consciousness, and the sphere of duality, and untimately goes to the highest realm where no personality exists, where existence is unconditioned and pure. Towards the fourth watch of the night, Gautama realised the highest Truth and attained *bodhi,* Enlightenment. He became Buddha, the Illumined.

Buddha's Own Account of His Illumination

What exactly is the nature of this illumination? As I said before, this question has been left unanswered by Buddha. It has not been answered by his immediate disciples either; but they have given some description of it in negative terms, as the cessation of craving, of the grasping ego, of ignorance and delusion; and this silence regarding the nature of the unconditioned, impersonal state and its description in negative terms, or even through silence, is perfectly Vedāntic. But it was sought to be answered in more positive language by later followers who had split up the movement on various grounds into eighteen sects within a century of the Master's death. Thus it was from the later followers' formulation of answers to a question on which Buddha himṭself, and also his immediate disciples, had kept silent that all the confusion and misunderstanding regarding Buddhism has arisen.

Let us try to understand the content of that realisation in the words of the Master himself. In his very first discourse at Sārnāth, Buddha expressed the content of that realisation in these few simple words (*Majjhima Nikaya, Sutta* 26, adapted from J.G. Jennings's translation):

> There (at Uruvela) I settled, *Bhikkhus,* there being everything needed for effort. And being myself subjected to earthly existence, I perceived the wretchedness of what is subjected to earthly existence, and seeking the supreme peace of *nibbānam* not affected by earthly existence. Being myself

> subjected to decay, to disease, to death, to grief, (and) defilement, I attained the supreme peace of *nibbānam* not affected by decay, disease, death, grief, (and) defilement.
>
> And the knowledge *(jñānm) now as a thing seen arose in me:* 'My liberation *(vimutti)* is established, separate existence *(jāti)* is terminated here; there is not now rebirth *(punna-bhavo).'*

Continuing further, Buddha said *(ibid., Sutta 36)*:

> Then I turned my mind to the knowledge of the destruction of the taints *(āsavās).* I knew verily *(yathābhūtam)* the four truths: " This is sorrow.' . . . 'This is the origination of sorrow'. . . .'This is the cessation of sorrow' . . . I knew verily: 'These are the taints (Āsavās).' . . . 'This is the origination of the taints.' . . . 'This is the path leading to the cessation of the taints.'
>
> When thus I perceived and understood, my mind *(cittam)* was liberated from the taint of lust (*Kama-āsava*); and . . . the taint of individuality *(bhava-āsava);* and . . . the taint of ignorance *(avijja-āsava);* and when I was liberated, there arose in me the knowledge of my liberation. I knew: 'separate existence *(jāti)* is ended *(khīnā);* the holy life *(branma-cariyam*) is lived, what must be done is done; there is nothing beyond this *(nāparam itthattāya)*.'

Buddha's Illumination: Its Upaniṣadic Ring

This is how Buddha described the content of his realisation; and it can easily be mistaken for a passage in any one of the Upaniṣads. Destruction of the separate ego sense, cessation of rebirth, attainment of perfect purity and insight—this is spiritual emancipation according to both the Upaniṣads and Bhagvān Buddha. Both term it *mukti* or *nirvāṇa,* a state which ensues when *avidyā,* spiritual blindness along with all its effects, is completely destroyed. Says the *Muṇḍaka Upaniṣad* (II2.8):

> *Bhidyate hṛdaya-granthiḫ chidyante sarvasaṁśayāḥ;*
> *Kṣiyante cāsya karmāṇi tasmin dṛṣṭe parāvare*

The knots of the heart are cut asunder, all doubts are dispelled, (the seeds of) all actions get exhausted, when the supreme truth of Oneness is realised.

Buddha's Initial Hesitation to Teach Mankind

The Buddha had attained *'bodhi',* enlightenment, which is *'bahukalpadurlabha',* difficult to get even by aeons of struggle. He enjoyed the supreme bliss of his attainment for seven weeks all alone in Bodh-Gaya or Buddha Gaya. Then a question arose in his mind: Should he or should he not share this treasure with the world? Initially, he was inclined to keep it to himself, and for good reasons; for the worldly-minded cannot comprehend it, and it would be mere vexation of spirit to teach it to them. But the god Brahma intervened on behalf of the world, and Buddha agreed to communicate his realisation out of 'compassion for the world' and the knowledge that there would be some at least who would be pure enough to comprehend so high a teaching. With this resolve, he entered the third and most significant phase of his eventful life. To put the matter in his own words *(Majjhima Nikāya, Sutta 26,* Jennings's translation):

> Thus, O Bhikkhus, as I pondered, my mind inclined me to inaction and to refrain from explaining the *Dharma.* Then, because of compassion for living beings, I gazed over the world and I saw (beings with natures) scarcely tainted, . . . much tainted, with keen faculties, with dull

> faculties, well-disposed, ill-disposed, docile, indocile, and a few who lived perceiving a world beyond sin and danger—just as in a pond of blue lotuses or pink lotuses, some lotuses bom and springing up in the water do not emerge from but are nourished under the water, others . . . reach the surface of the water; and others . . . rise above and are untouched by the water.

His Final Overcoming of that Hesitation

Though he felt that the world, so much given to sensuality and ordinary pleasures, might not understand him, still there might be a few whose minds were not so full of the dust of ignorance and attachment and who, with a little effort, could be made to see the truth; he decided to search them out and share his experience with them. That was the difficult choice before Buddha, and his compassion decided for him. Every teacher who has reached very high levels of spirituality is in the same quandary. The higher the attainment, the more difficult it is to find people capable of sharing that attainment. We know in the case of Sri Ramakrishna how he could not share with one and all some of his innermost experiences. That was why he yearned for the arrival of those pure-minded disciples headed by Narendra, later Vivekananda, to whom he could communicate whatever he had experienced.

Thus we find Buddha looking out for those to whom he could communicate his realisation. The thought of his two venerable teachers, Ālāra Kālāma and Uddaka, came to his mind and, out of gratitude for them, he resolved to seek them out and impart his realisation to them. He said to himself *(ibid.)*:

> There is Ālāra Kālāma, wise, intelligent, and learned, his nature has so long been scarcely tainted. What if I should first declare the *Dharma* to him? He will quickly comprehend it. . . . and the knowledge clearly came to

> me: 'Ālāra Kālāma died seven days ago.' Then, *Bhikkhus,* this thought came to me: 'Nobly born was Ālāra Kālāma. If he had heard the *Dharma,* he would quickly have comprehended it. Then the thought came to me: 'There is Uddaka, the son of Rāma, wise, intellegent, and learned; his nature has long been scarcely tainted' . . . and knowledge clearly came to me: 'Uddaka, the son of Rāma died yesterday evening.' Then, *Bhikkhus,* this thought came to me: 'Nobly bom was Uddaka, the son of Rāma. If he had heard the *Dharma* he would quickly have comprehended it.'

Buddha Walks to Vārāṇāsi from Buddhagaya

Then the thought came to him of the five disciples who had been with him, had later deserted him, but who were also advanced spiritually. He decided to seek them out; and learning that they had gone to Isipaṭṭaṇā or Sārnāth near Vārāṇāsi or Banaras, he decided to go there, a distance of 114 miles from Buddha Gaya. Reaching Isipaṭṭaṇā, he saw from a distance the five disciples sitting in a park there. And enfolding them in the love of his pure mind, he approached them. 'But at first they were not inclined to greet him and show due courteises, because they had decided that he had fallen from the path. They addressed him by name calling him 'friend'; yet there was something compelling in the demeanour, in the dignity, in the poise of Buddha that made them receive him with love and reverence. He then said to them *(ibid.)*:

> Hear me, *Bhikkhus,* the Immortal has been gained by me. I teach, I show the *Dharma.* If you walk as I teach, you will ere long and in the present life learn fully for yourselves, realize, and having attained, abide in the supreme fulfilment of the holy life, for the sake of which the clansmen rightly go from home to the homeless life.

Turning the Wheel of Dharma at Sārnāth

When they did not seem to have been convinced of his spiritual *bonafides,* he said again, in a gentle tone of authority: 'Are you conscious, O *Bhikkhus,* that I have not spoken to you in this manner before?' They understood that he spoke from the depth of personal realisation, and became receptive and attentive. The Master then imparted his realisation to them and, through them, to humanity, in two well-known discourses, the first of which is the *Dharmacakra-pravartana Sutra* and the second, the *Anatmalakṣaṇa-Sutra,* delivered five days later.

Addressing the five on the first occasion, the Buddha said (*Vinaya Piṭaka, Mahāvagga, Khandhaka* 1.6, J.G. Jennings's translation):

> These two extremes, O Bhikkhus, are not to be approached by him who has withdrawn (from the world). Which two? On the one hand, that which is linked and connected with lust through sensuous pleasures, and is low, ignorant, vulgar, ignoble, and profitless, and on the other hand, that which is connected with self-mortification, and is painful, ignoble, and profitless. Avoiding both these extremes, the middle road *(madhyama pratipada)* bringing insight, bringing knowledge, leads to tranquillity, to highest knowledge, to full enlightenment, to peace. And what middle road leads to peace? It is indeed this Noble Eightfold Path, namely, right outlook, right will, right speech, right action, right livelihood, right effort, right mindfulness, right absorption. This middle road leads to peace.
>
> Now again, this is the Noble Truth as to sorrow *(dukkham ariya saccam):* birth *(jāti)* is sorrowful, decay is sorrowful, disease is sorrowful, death is sorrowful, union with the unpteasing is sorrowful, separation from the pleasing is sorrowful, the wish which one does not fulfil is sorrowful

in brief, desire-ridden transient individuality *(panca-upādāna khandha)* is sorrowful.

Again, this is the Noble Truth as to the cessation of sorrow *(dukkha-samudayam ariya saccam)*: It is this recurring craving *(tanha)* associated with pleasure and attachment, seeking enjoyment everywhere, namely, the craving for sense-pleasure *(kāma tanha),* the craving for separate earthly existence *(bhava tanha),* the craving for heavenly existence *(vibhava tanha).*

Again, this is the Noble Truth as to the cessation of sorrow *(dukkha nirodham ariya saccam):* It is the cessation of this very craving, so that no remnant or trace of it remains, its abandonment, its renouncement, liberation *(mukti)* from it, detachment *(an-ālayo)* from it.

And this once more is the Noble Truth as to the road leading to the cessation of sorrow *(dukkha-nirodha-gāminī pati pada ariya saccam):* It is indeed that Noble Eightfold Path *(maggo).* . . .

As soon as my knowledge and insight *(nāna dassanam)* concerning these Four Noble Truths were pure, I knew that I had attained supreme and full enlightenment *(sarnmā-sambodhim)* . . . The knowledge now as a thing seen arose in me. The liberation of my mind *(me ceto vimutli)* is established, separate existence is here ended, there is not now re-birth.

In the second discourse, the Buddha stripped the notion of individuality of all its unreal elemennts *(ibid.):*

Rūpam (material form) is *an-atta* (not the self); *vedanā* (sensation) is *anatta* . . . *sanna* (perception) is *an-atta* . . . sankara (predisposition) is *anatta* . . . *vinnanam* (consciousness) is *an-atta* (not the self).

'Again what think you, Bhikkus? Is the material form permanent *(niccam)* or impermanent *(a-mccam) or* impermanent, revered sir.' 'But that which is impermanent, is that suffering *(dukham)* or happy *(sukḥham)?'* 'Suffering, revered sir.' 'That then which is impermanent, is suffering, and by nature changeable *(vipariṇāma dhammam),* is it proper to regard it thus: "This is mine, I am this, this is my self *(etam mama, esoíham asmi, eso me atta)."* 'No indeed, revered sir.' 'Is sensation permanent? . . . Is perception permanent? Is pre-disposition permanent? . . . Is consciousness permanent? . . . That then which is impermanent, suffering, and by nature changeable, is it proper to regard it thus: 'This is mine, I am this, this is my self?' 'No indeed, revered sir.'

And so, Bhikkhus, all material form whether past, future, or present, whether within us or external, whether gross or subtle, low or high, far or near, is to be regarded with right insight as it really is *(yathā bhūlam)* thus: This is not mine, I am not this, this is not my self . . . All sensation . . . gross or subtle, all perception . . . gross or subtle, . . . all predisposition . . . low or high . . . all consciousness . . . far or near, is to be regarded with right insight as it really is thus: This is not mine, I am not this, this is not my self.

Regarding them thus, O Bhikkhus, an instructed *ariyan* disciple becomes indifferent to *(nibbindati)* material form, becomes indifferent to sensation, becomes indifferent to perception, becomes indifferent to consciousness. Becoming indifferent, he becomes free from desire (*vi-rajjati*); through non-desire *(vi-rāgo)* he is liberated.

'When he is liberated, there arises in him the knowledge, "I am liberated." He knows "*jāti* (birth or separate existence) is ended *(khīna); brahmacariya* (the holy life) has lived; *karaṇīyam* (what ought to be done) has been done; there is nothing beyond *(nāparam)* this state (*itthattāya).*"

The above two discourses, and several others in the Buddhistic scriptures, can be easily mistaken for passages in any one of the several *Upaniṣads.*

'The Middle Path'

Buddha is the teacher of the *madhyama pratipada,* the middle path, in spiritual life, neither austerity nor indulgence, but a steady pursuit of truth with all the strength of body and mind. It is the exposition in the first discourse, repeated in his later expositions of the spiritual life, that has come down to us as the famous teaching of the Middle Path associated with Buddha. It was original only in the sense that he taught it with a force, he expounded it with such authority, that the country which had strayed into the extremes of sense indulgence and senseless asceticism accepted it and benefited from it. But it was there in the *Upaniṣads*, as it is there in any moral and spiritual system; for, if our pursuit is morality and spirituality, we gain nothing from senseless asceticism and much less from sensual indulgence. Such austerities have a place only in a religious discipline dominated by the idea of the magical. But moral and spiritual discipline has for its aim the reshaping of our character, the creation of a new pattern of human personality, through increase in inner purity and the overṭcoming of spiritual blindness. Training for such a character has nothing to do with any kind of magic or trick generally associated with such kind of austerity. *In giving the authority of his powerful personality to the Middle Path, Buddha helped to release the spiritual life from the grip of magic and mummery, and to direct human energies to fruitful channels, towards the cultivation of a moral and spiritual character.*

We are familiar with this emphasis on the middle path in the Gītā. In its sixth chapter (verses 16, 17) Śrī Kṛṣṇa says:

Nātyasnatastu yogosti na caikāntam anasnataḥ;
Na cātisvapnaśīlasya jāgrato naiva cārjuna—

Yoga is not for him who eats too much or does not eat at all, nor sleeps too much or does not sleep at all.

Yuktāhāravihārasya yuktaceṣṭasya karmasu;
yuktasvapnāvabodhsya yogo bhavati duḥkhahā—

But *yoga* becomes the discipline for the destruction of sorrow for him who is moderate in eating and recreation, moderate in work and sleep and waking.

Thus Vedānta and Buddha emphasise this Middle Path. In the case of Buddha there is this additional charm that his teaching on this subject issued out of his personal experience of austerity and its meaninglessness; it was not hearsay with him, which explains the tone of authority in his utterances on the subject.

'The Ārya Satyāni'

The Middle Path is meant to lead the seeker to a firm grip on experience and to the discipline leading to the realisation of the truth imbedded in experience. With this end in view, Buddha expounded the Four Noble Truths, or the *Ārya-satyāni,* and the Eightfold Path, to his five disciples. The first of the four truths is the truth of suffering, the universal experience of satisfactions falling short of desires. The Upaniṣads spoke of life ridden with sorrow till life detaches itself from the changing waves of surface-becoming and gets rooted in the changeless depth of being. The second relates to the origin of suffering; this is *tanha (tṛṣṇā)* or desire, the tendency of the ego to go out of itself to seek satisfactions, impelled by spiritual blindness. The *Upaniṣads* spoke of *avidyā* and *kāma* as the roots of relative existence, through them we forge links in the causal chain of existence, forget our own spiritual nature, and become cogs in the wheel of *samsdra;* that *tṛṣṇā* or desire, with its root, ignorance, must be eradicated. Therefore, the third truth is the recognition of the possibility that we can ovecome suffering. And the fourth truth is the path that leads to the cessation of suffering through the eradication of ignorance and desire; and this is the path that leads to the state of *nirvāṇa,* the state of enduring peace and emancipation.

'The Noble Eightfold Path'

This fourth truth which flowers into the Noble Eightfold Path with its stress on moral and spiritual endeavour, constitutes the essential teaching of Buddha. So far as the discovery that the world is suffering, that life is suffering, and that it proceeds from *tṛṣṇa* is concerned, there is not much difference between the *Upaniṣads* and Buddha. When we compare the teachings of the *Upaniṣads* with those of Buddha, we find very little difference so far as the content is concerned, but a good deal of difference in the way certain points were stressed or developed or ignored in the two teachings. For example, Buddha laid stress on the subject of suffering. He also developed the subject of the path to *nirvāṇa* in all its details; but he ignored defining the goal, the state of *nirvāṇa.* Buddha takes various examples to show that life is suffering. Thus the fact of suffering in life gets a good deal of emphasis in his teaching. This special stress on suffering is absent in the *Upaniṣads.* Though recognising the fact of suffering, the *Upaniṣads* lay stress on the state of bliss that transcends suffering and proclaim that as the true nature of man.

The Meaning of Buddha's Stress on Suffering

It is a question of stress, as I said. You can say that life is sorrow, if you look at it from the human end. You can say that life is joy, if you look at it from the ideal end. Both conclusions are true. The *Upaniṣads* also say that to live as a separate individual, as a finite individual, cut off from the vast ocean of Being around us and in us, is sorrow. The finite, separate individual is the focus of tension and strain; the world and the soul are in their essential nature the *Sat-Cit-Ānanda* Brahman, Existence-Knowledge-Bliss Absolute; cut off from that ocean of being, the finite separate individual becomes a zero, and yet fears to become a zero, and fears still more to shed its finitude. As Śaṅkara said: 'Cut off from that ocean of pure Being, the world gets reduced to a zero.' If life or the world is separated from the supreme Atman, which is the source of all joy, of all existence, and of all knowledge, it will become sorrow-ridden, fugitive, and dark. In the words of Sri Ramakrishna, zeros have value only when the figure '1' is behind them. Take the '1' away, they become mere nothingness. So also is human life; cut off from the Reality of the One, it becomes ridden with sorrow, reduced to darkness and nothingness. Buddha took this finite individual for his theme—the human soul subject to ignorance, desire, delusion, grief, and death. And his compassion went out to steady his feet, illumine his mind, and fill his heart with wisdom, peace, and joy; hence his stress on psychology and ethics but not on metaphysics.

Buddha's Practical Approach to Man's Spiritual Life

The finite, separate individual ever passes into something other than itself in the ceaseless flow of becoming. Spiritual teaching must proceed from this fact. This is the *doctrine of actuality* preached by Buddha. In revealing this, he was compelled to ignore studiously all metaphysical questions as to the existence or otherwise of a permanent self behind the fleeting ego, of an abiding reality behind the world of becoming, and of the nature of *nirvāṇa.* His silence on these questions is matched by his expressiveness on how man can wisely tackle the actual situation in which he finds himself. Man has forgotten his real self; he has grasped things other than himself. In so grasping, he has fallen into the endless chain of cause and effect, of *avidyā, tṛṣṇa,* and *karmā,* or ignorance, desire, and action, into the chain of *pratītyasamu-tapāda,* the whirlpool of *saṁsāra.* It is nothing but sorrow to be thus caught in the wheel of birth and death and change, to be merely a helpless thing worked upon by forces outside of oneself.

This is the meaning of the first and second Noble Truths, the actuality of sorrow. But, according to the Upaniṣads, it is only half the truth. Buddha also meant it to be taken only as half the truth. To both, there is also the state beyond sorrow and the path that leads us from the world of sorrow to the world of joy. But the Upaniṣads proclaimed in no uncertain terms that that ultimate state of bliss and peace is also the essential nature of each and every individual even now. This was not stresssed by Buddha. The Upaniṣadic Brahman or Ātman is peace, so is the *nirvāṇa* of Buddha. But the Upaniṣads stress the fact of bliss imbedded in our nature, while Buddha stressed the fact of sorrow which we actually see in and around us. In the case of Buddha, the stress on actuality was meant to focus that attention on ethical preparation and spiritual struggle which had been largely dissipated in defining metaphysical subtleties of the goal. This alone can explain his consistent silence on the subject of the nature of the goal. In the words of Dr. Radhakrishnan *(Gautama Buddha,* p.56):

> The Buddha warns us against the danger of assuming that, because we are divine in essence, we are not divided in actuality. To become actually divine is our goal.

This severely practical approach of Buddha to the problem of the spiritual life is expressed in the Nobel Eightfold Path, and finds repeated emphasis through parables and illustrations in all his teachings. To both the *Upaniṣads* and Buddha, Truth is not merely a thing to be intellectually known, but also a value to be inwardly realised; *moksa* and *nirvāṇa* are *puruṣārthas*. Both refer to spiritual realisation as *kṛtakṛtyatā,* doing what ought to be done. Neither intellectualism nor sentimentalism can help us. And both these aberrations have often vitiated Indian spiritual life, not only before Buddha, but also after him; his own movement became infected by this intellectualism five centuries after his time, and never recovered from the resulting stagnation. There is constant need to hearken to Buddha's stress on the path to be traversed, his insistence on the remaking of character through severe practical self-discipline in thought and conduct.

Vivekananda's Endorsement of this Approach Today

It has been a recurring experience in India that we talk high philosophy and live very low lives. In Buddha's time, probably, it must have been much more serious. We know that, in our own time, it is a very serious problem with our nation as a whole; we have the mood and the energy to discuss the highest philosophy or pressing national problems in our drawing-rooms, at our tea-tables, and at public meetings; but in day-to day life, we lapse into a spiritual lassitude and function largely at the bottom levels of existence. Swami Vivekananda was the first to diagnose this trait of ours in this age. And in great agony he said *(The Complete Works,* Volume V, p.15, seventh (enlarged) edition):

> No religion on earth preaches the dignity of humanity in such a lofty strain as Hinduism, and no religion on earth treads upon the necks of the poor and the low in such a fashion as Hinduism.

The highly sensitive mind of Swami Vivekananda felt this great disparity between the highest philosophical conceptions and the unspiritual, unsocial, and unethical practices of our people. And he strove to bring about harmony between our professions and our practices. If it is a desideratum in our own time, we may as well infer from Buddha's silence on the goal, and stress on the Eight fold Path, that it may have been more so in his own time.

Buddha's Silence of Ultimate Questions: Māluṅkyaputta

The silence of Buddha on ultimate metaphysical questions and his constant stress on conduct and character is clearly brought out in his replies to the questions put by the monk Māluṅkyaputta. Māluṅkya asked Buddha with a bluntness almost bordering on discourtesy to state whether or not the world is eternal, whether or not the perfect Buddha continues to exist after death, and demanded that if he did not know the answers, he should be straightforward and say that he did not know.

Budddha answered *(Majjhima Nikāya,* Discourse 63, Woodward's translation):

> Suppose, Maluṅkyaputta, a man were pierced with an arrow well steeped in poison, and his close friends and relatives were to summon a physician, a surgeon. Then suppose the man says; 'I will not have this arrow pulled out until I know of the man by whom I was pierced, both his name and his clan, and whether he be tall or short or of middle stature; till I know him whether he be a black man or dark or shallow-skinned; whether he be of such and such a village or suburb or town, I will not have the arrow pulled out until I know of the bow by which I was pierced, whether it was a long bow or a cross bow; till I know of the arrow by which I was pierced, whether it be a reed-shaft, or of a sapling. . .'

Well, Māluṅkyaputta, that man would die, but still that matter would not be found out by him.

'. . . But I am one who declares thus: Whether the world is eternal or not, nevertheless there is birth, there is decay, there is death, there are sorrow and grief, woe, lamentation, and despair; and it is the destruction of these things that I do declare.'

'. . .Wherefore, Māluṅkyaputta, do you bear in mind that what I have declared is declared, and what I have not declared is not declared. Bear that in mind.

And what, Malunkyaputta, have I not declared? That world is eternal or otherwise . . . that the Tathagata is beyond death or otherwise, and so forth.

And why, Māluṅkyaputta, have I. not so declared?

Because this thing is not concerned with profit; because it is not a principle of the holy life; because it does not lead to repulsion, to aversion, to cessation, to calming, to the super-knowledge, to the supreme wisdom, to *nibbana.* That is why I have not declared it.

And what, Māluṅkyaputta, have I declared?

I have declared, This is suffering; This is the arising of suffering; This the ceasing of suffering; This is the way leading to the ceasing of suffering.

And why, Māluṅkyaputta, have I so declared?

Because it is concerned with profit; because it is a principle of the holy life; because it leads to repulsion, to aversion, to cessation, to calming, to the super-knowledge, to the supreme wisdom, to *nibbana.* That, Māluṅkyaputta, is why I have declared it.'

Buddha's Silence on Ultimate Questions: Vacchagotta

Buddha's silence regarding the reality or otherwise of a permanent self is well brought out in his encounter with Vacchagotta the Wanderer *(Sutta Nipāta,* VI. 400. Woodward's translation):

> 'Master Gotama,' said Vacchagotta, 'what have you to say about the existence of the self?'
>
> At these words the Exalted One was silent.
>
> 'How now. Master Gotama? Is there no such thing as the self?'
>
> At these words the Exalted One was silent.
>
> Then Vacchagotta the Wanderer (in disgust) rose up from his seat and went away. Not long after he was gone, the venerable Ananda said to the Exalted One:
>
> 'How is it, Lord, that the Exalted One made no reply to the question asked by Vacchagoatta the Wanderer?'
>
> 'If Ananda, when asked, Does the self exist?' I had replied to him, "The self exists," then, Ananda, that would be to side with all those samanas and Brahmanas who are eternalists.'
>
> 'But if, Ānanda, when asked the question, "Does the self not exist then?" I had replied, "No, the self does not exist" that would be to side with those *samanas* and *brahmanas* who are amihilationists.'
>
> 'And, Ānanda, when asked by Vacchagotta the Wanderer, "Does the self exist?" I had replied, "The self does exist," would that reply be consistent with my knowledge that all things are impermanent?'

'No, Lord, it would not.'

'Again, Ānanda, when asked. Then, does not the self exist? if I had replied, "No, it does not exist," it would have added to the bewilderment of Vacchagotta the Wanderer, already bewildered. For he would have said, "Formerly I had a self, but now I have one no more."

The sage of the *Kena Upaniṣad* (1.3,4,6) had faced this problem earlier; Buddha shares his hesitncy to define the indefinable which is the true self in man:

> The eye does not go there, nor speech, nor the mind; we do not know or understand how this (knowledge of the Self) could be imparted. It is entirely different from the known: yet it is beyond the unknown. Thus have we heard from the teachers of old who explained It to us.
>
> That which cannot be apprehended by the mind (and the senses) but by which, they say, the mind itself is apprehendedóknow thou That alone as Brahman, and not that which people worship here.

The goal of the Eightfold Path is nibbāṇ; Buddha defined nibbāṇa only in negative terms, as the destruction of craving, of ignorance, of separate individuality, of delusion and sorrow.

Buddha's Silence on Ultimate Questions: The Monk Rādha

Addressing the monk Radha, the Buddha said that the five *skandhas*—(constituent factors of personality) should be regarded as the seat of Māra; then the following conversation ensued between the two *(Sutta Nipāta,* III. 187, Woodward's translation);

> 'What was the purpose of so regarding,' asked Rādha.
> 'For the sake of disgust,' replied Buddha

'But disgust. Lord, for what purpose is it?'
'Disgust, Rādha, is to bring about dispassion.'
'But dispassion. Lord, for what purpose is it?'
'Dispassion, Rādha, is to get release.'
'But release, Lord, what is it for?'
'Release Rādha, means *nibbāṇa.'*
'But *nibbāna,* Lord, what is the aim of that?'
'This, Rādha, is a question that goes too far You can grasp no limit to this question. Rooted in *nibbāna,* Rādha, the holy life is lived. *Nibbāna* is its goal. *Nibbāna* is its end.'

The Upaniṣadic *way of expressing this truth is contained in an arresting dialogue of the* Brhadāranyaka Upaniṣad *(11.4. 12-14).*

Addressing his wife Maitreyi, the sage Yajnavalkya said:

'As a lump of salt dropped into water dissolves with (its component) water, and no one is able to pick it up, but whencesoever one takes it, it tastes salt, even so, my dear, this great, endless, infinite reality is but pure Intelligence. (The self) comes out (as a separate entity) from these elements, and (this separateness) is destroyed with them. After attaining (this oneness), it has no more consciousness. This is what I say, my dear.'

Maitreyī said:

'Just here you have thrown me into confusion, sir, by saying that, after attaining (oneness), the self has no more consciousness.'

Yajnavalkya said:

'Certainly, I am not saying anything confusing, my dear; this is quite sufficient for knowledge, O Maitreyī.'

'Because, when there is duality, as it were, then one smells something, one sees something, one speaks something, one thinks something, one knows something But, when to the lcnower of Brahman everything has become the Self, then what shoufd one smell, and through what? What should one see, and through what. What should one think, and through what? What should one know, and through what? Through what should one know That through which all this is known—through what, O Maitreyī, should one know the knower?'

Buddha's Silence on Ultimate Questions: Yamaka and Sāriputta

The teachings of Buddha on the subject of self involve the distinction between the true Self and the false Self. When we are asked to deny self-hood to all the constituent elements of personality, the *pañca upādāna skandhas,* we are not left to believe that we are empty nothings.

That Buddha, and also his immediate disciples, kept in view this distinction between the false Self and the true Self is brought out in the episode of Yamaka's heresy (adapted from H.C. Warren, *Buddhism in Translation):*

> Not understanding the true import of Buddha's teaching on the subject of *nibbāṇa,* Yamaka the monk came to the belief that, 'on the dissolution of the body, the monk who has lost all depravity is annihilated, perishes, and does not exist after death.' His fellow monks, after trying in vain to make him give up what they considered a wicked heresy, requested Sariputta to tackle him.
>
> Sāriputta asked Yamaka whether the report about his views was true.
>
> Yamaka replied:
>
> 'Even so, brother, do I understand the doctrine taught by the Blessed One, that on the dissolution of the body, the

monk who has lost all depravity is annihilated, perishes, and does not exist after death.'

Sāriputta then asked him whether the five *skandhas* of form, sensation, perception, predispositions, and consciousness were permanent or transitory.

Yamaka admitted they were transitory.

'And that which is transitory, is it evil or is it good?' asked Sariputta.

'It is evil brother,' replied Yamaka.

'And that which is transitory, evil, and liable to change-is it possible to say of it: This is mine; this am I; this is my self?' asked Sariputta.

'No, brother', said Yamaka.

'Accordingly, brother Yamaka, as respects all form whatsoever, as respects all sensation whatsoever, as respects all perception whatsoever, as respects all predispositions whatsoever, past, future, or present, be it subjective or existing outside, gross or subtle, mean or exalted, far or near, the correct view in the light of the highest knowledge is as follows: This is not mine; this am I not; this is not myself.'

'Perceiving this, brother Yamaka, the learned and noble disciple, conceives an aversion for form, conceives an aversion for sensation, conceives an aversion for perception, conceives an aversion for predispositions, conceives an aversion for contsciousness. And, in conceiving this aversion, he becomes divested of passion, and by the absence of passion, he becomes free, and when he is free he becomes aware that he is free; and he knows that rebirth is exhausted, that he has lived the holy life, that he has done what it 'behoved him to do, and that he is no more for the world.'

Sāriputta then asked him whether the *arhat* who has achieved *nibbāṇa* can be comprised in form, sensation, perception, predispositions, and consciousness, or distinct from them. Yamaka replied in the negative.

'Considering now, brother Yamaka, that you fail to make out and establish the existence of the *arhat* in the present life, is it reasonable for you to say: Thus do I understand the doctrine taught by the Blessed One, that, on the dissolution of the body, the monk who has lost all depravity is annihilated, perishes, and does not exist after death?'

'Brother Sāriputta, it was because of my ignorance that I held this wicked heresy; but now that I have listened to the doctrinal instruction of the venerable Sāriputta, I have abandoned that wicked heresy and acquired the true doctrine.'

Buddha's Silence on Ultimate Questions: King Pasenadi and Nun Khema

The conversation between King Pasenadi and the Nun Khema further elucidates the point (Oldenberg, quoted by Edmund Holmes in his *The Creed of Buddha):*

To the question of King Pasenadi of Kosala regarding the existence or otherwise of Buddha after death, the nun Khema replied that Buddha had not revealed this subject.

The king was astonished and asked:

'What is the reason, venerable lady, what is the ground on which the Exalted One has not revealed this?'

She asked the king in reply whether he had an accountant who could count the sands of the Ganga or measure the water in the great ocean.

The king replied in the negative.

'And why not?,' the nun replied, and continued: 'The great ocean is deep, immeasurable, unfathomable. So also, O great King, if the existence of the Perfect One be measured by the predicates of corporeal form: these predicates of the corporeal form are abolished in the Perfect One, their root is severed, they are hewn away like a palm tree and laid aside, so that they cannot germinate again in the future. Released, O great King, is the Perfect One from this, that his being should be gauged by the measure of the corporeal world; he is deep, immeasurable, unfathomable, as the great ocean.'

The 'Bodhi' of Buddha versus the 'Jñāna of Vedānta'

Jñāna and *bodhi* are indefinable; so are the ways of the *Jñāni* and that of the Buddha. The following verse quoted by Śāṅkara in his *Māṇḍukya-kārikā-bhāsya* (IV. 95) reinforces and clarifies nun Khema's view:

Sarvābhūtatmābhūtasya sarvābhūtāhitasya ca
Devā api mārge muhyanti apadasya padaiṣiṇaḥ;
Śakunīnām iva ākāśe gatirnaivopapadyate

'Even the gods feel puzzled while trying to follow the footsteps of those who leave no track behind, of those who realise themselves in all beings and who are always devoted to the welfare of all; they leave no track behind like the birds flying through the sky.'

The Nirvāṇa of Buddha versus the 'Brahman' of Vedanta

The attainment of *nirvāṇa* in Buddha's teachings tallies in all essential respects with the attainment of the impersonal, formless Brahman in the *Upaniṣads*. By the negation of self-hood to the five *skandhas,* the second discourse at Sārnāth did not explain *away* the self, but pointed to this Impersonal Brahman, the Universal Self, as the true Self of all; for, in the words of the *Upaniṣads, Brahmavit brahmaiva bhavati*—'the knower of Brahman becomes Brahman' *(Muṇḍaka Upaniṣad, III. 2.9);* again *Ayam ātmā brahma* —'this Self is Brahman' *(Maṇukya Upanisad,* 1.2); and *Brahmavi āpnotiparam; tadeṣābhyuktā: satyam jñānam anantam brahma*—'the knower of Brahman attains the Highest; on this, there is the following declaration: Brahman is Truth, Knowledge, and Infinity *(Taittirīya Upaniṣad,* II. 1).

In the course of one of his addresses to the monks on the subject of *nibbāṇa* in the Jeta grove at Sāvatthi, the Buddha uttered these solemn words *(Udāna, Woodward's transition):*

> There is, brethren, an unborn, a not-become, a not-made, a not-compounded. If there were not brethren, this that is unborn, not-become, not-made, not-compounded, there could not be made any escape from what is bom, become, made, compounded.
>
> But since, brethren, there is this unborn, not-become, not-made, not-compounded, therefore is there made known an escape from what is bom, become made, and compounded.

Common Teachings of Buddha and the Upaniṣads

It will be clear from the above extracts from the teachings of Buddha and the *Upaniṣads* that the goal of spiritual life in both is the destruction not of self as such, but of all limited and false notions of the self which treat it as separate from the other selves; the realisation of the true Self ensues when ignorance and delusion, leading to attachment and identification with the body and other constituents of personality, are overcome. This realisation is deep and immeasurable as the ocean, because the individuality loses himself in the universal, the Jiva in Brahman, which is *advaita,* 'the One without a second'. The *Taittirīya Upaniṣad's* analysis of individuality through the negation of the five *kosas* or sheaths leads to the same conclusion; the self that manifests through each of the *kośas,* or through all of them, is unreal and shadowy, finite and fugitive. When the *kośas* are negated, the one true Self, which is the Self of all, shines in all its glory in the *nirvikalpa samādhi.* This is *prajñā* or *bodhi* in both the teachings.

When the *Upaniṣads* tell us that the Ātman should be realised through hearing, reflection, and meditation, it is not the finite, separate, changeful, personal self of man that is meant, but the impersonal, universal, changeless Self which is the Self of all. And nowhere does Buddha negate the reality of this Self which is the theme of the *Upaniṣads;* nor does he ever negate the reality of the impersonal Brahman of the *Upaniṣads,* though Buddha's discourses often refer to Brahma, the personal Creator, as paying homage to Buddha and as a being falling within the world of change. His Sārnāth discourse, entitled *'Anattalakkhaṇa-Sūtta',* is acceptable to the *Upaniṣads* in its entirety, and can be correctly understood only in the light of the *Upaniṣadic* exposition of the subject.

Sri Ramakrishna held the view that Buddha's teachings were on the lines of the *jñāna-yoga* of the *Upaniṣads*. The *Vedas* and the Vedic path, often criticised in the Buddhist scriptures, mean, in every instance, only the Vedic *karmā-kāṇḍā,* the ritualistic portion; but never the *jñāna-kāṇḍā,* the philosophic portion comprised in the *Upaniṣads*. These *Upaniṣads* themselves contain criticisms and evaluations of the Vedic *karmā-kāṇḍā,* almost exactly on the lines of the Buddhist criticisms and evaluations. And even the *Gītā (II. 42,43)* speaks disparagingly of the *vedavādaratas,* those who indulge in Vedic ritualism impelled by desire and attachment. Sankara's Advaita is a severe critique of the *karmā-kāṇḍā* as well as the philosophy behind it. The *Upaniṣads* and the *Gītā* prescribe for the spiritual seeker dispassion and other moral virtues on the lines of Buddha's Eightfold Path. Buddha's final exhortation to Ānanda to work out his salvation with diligence, depending on himself and not on any personal god or other external aids, is equally applicable to the *jñāna-yoga* of the *Upaniṣads,* which also advocates the three stages of *sīla, saṁādhi,* and *prajñā* prescribed by Buddha for the spiritual life. Also common to both is the notion of the 'ten fetters' and their destruction, characteristic of spiritual progress and realisation.

Buddha's silence on the subjects of a permanent Self and of the nature of *nirvāṇa,* and his studious disapproval of metaphysical discussion, did not have the results he anticipated. Silence on questions of deep import acts as a spur to speculation.

Buddha and Śaṅkara

This was what happened to Buddhist thought in subsequent centuries. A flood of metaphysical speculation of these forbidden themes ensued. And such speculation, without any guidance from the Master or his first disciples, and without any guidance from the *Upaniṣads,* which were not to become widely known till Śaṅkara, a thousand years later, split up the Buddhist movement into sects upholding views many of which were clearly considered as heresies in the Master's own time. Yamaka had a Sāriputta to conect him of his nihilistic views. But Yamaka's views did not die with his correction. What Buddha wanted to avoid in the case of Vacchagotta—bewildering his mind by saying there is no permanent Self-became the source of bewilderment and confusion to his later followers. These wrong views steadily penetrated the later Buddhist movement at the intellectual levels and, in the eyes of many Buddhist and all non-Buddhists, became the main characteristic of that thought.

This later intellectual movement found no point of contact with the vast masses of the Buddhistic population, which sought solace not in *nirvāṇa,* or its metaphysical formulations, but in the worship of the Buddha through the idols, temples, processions, and pilgrimages of popular Buddhism; cut off from its intellectual sustenance, popular Buddhism slowly decayed and withered and got absorbed in the reviving Vedic religious movements of later Hinduism. And intellectual Buddhism found its challenge in Sankara in the eighth century, who succeeded in reuniting Indian philosophic thought with the thought of the *Upaniṣads.* Unlike the other post-Buddhistic movements which were merely revivalist and sectarian, Śaṅkara's was synthetic and constructive and inclusive.

The Advaita Vedānta of Śaṅkara has absorbed all the essential elements of Buddhist thought; it is becoming increasingly clear that if Buddha's teachings are to be provided with a metaphysical support, we have to search for it in Śaṅkara's Advaita. In the Buddhist philosophy (as presented to us in the Buddhist scriptures), we have, in the words of Dr Oldenberg, only 'a fragment of a circle, to complete which and to find the centre of which is forbidden, for it would involve an inquiry after things which do not contribute to deliverance and happiness', (quoted by Edmund Holmes, *The Creed of Buddha,* p.64). If Buddhism had continued in the spirit in which Buddha had meant it to proceed, if it had not indulged in metaphysical speculations, but propagated only the Four Noble Truths and the Noble Eightfold Path, Śaṅkara need not have appeared. But when, against the exhortations of the Master and without his guidance, metaphysical attempts to 'complete the circle' miscarried, resulting in intelllectual confusion and spiritual anarchy, Śaṅkara appeared and gave to humanity the priceless thought of Advaita Vedānta, which, in the words of Thibaut ('Introduction' to *The Vedānta-Sūtras,* p.xiv):

> is, from a purely philosophical point of view, and apart from all theological considerations, the most important and interesting one which has arisen on Indian soil; neither those forms of the Vedānta which diverge from the view represented by Śaṅkara nor any of the non-Vedantic systems can be compared with the so-called orthodox Vedānta in boldness, depth, and subtlety of speculation.

Writes Dr. Radhakrishnan *(Indian Philosophy,* Vol. II, p.446):

> It is impossible to read Śaṅkara's writings, packed as they are with serious and subtle thinking, without being conscious that one is in contact with a mind of a very fine penetration and profound spirituality. With his acute feeling of the immeasurable world, his stirring gaze into the abysmal mysteries of spirit, his unswerving resolve to say neither more nor less than what could be proved, Śaṅkara stands out as a heroic figure of the first rank in the somewhat motley crowd of religious thinkers of the medieval India. His philosophy stands forth complete, needing neither a before nor an after.

Vivekananda on the Decay of Indian Buddhism

Commenting on the decay of Buddhism in India, Swami Vivekananda said sixty years ago ('Sages of India', *Complete Works,* Vol. Ill, Ninth Edition, pp.263-65.):

> The earlier Buddhists, in their rage against the killing of animals, had denounced the sacrifices of the Vedas; and these sacrifices used to be held in every house. There was a fire burning and that was all the paraphernalia of worship.

> These sacrifices were obliterated and in their place came gorgeous temples, gorgeous ceremonies, and gorgeous priests, and all that you see in India in modern times. I smile when I read books written by some modern people, who ought to have known better, that the Buddha was the destroyer of Brahmanical idolatry. Little do they know that Buddhism created Brahmanism and idolatry in India. . . .
>
> Thus, in spite of the preaching of mercy to animals, in spite of the sublime ethical religion, in spite of the hair-splitting discussions about the existence or non-existence of a permanent soul, the whole building of Buddhism tumbled down piecemeal; and the ruin was simply hideous. The most hideous ceremonies, the most horrible, the most obscene books that human hands ever wrote or the human brain ever conceived, the most bestial forms that ever passed under the name of religion, have all been the creation of degraded Buddhism.

And referring to the legacy which Buddhism, in its state of degradation, left for Śaṅkara, and his great work of synthesis, Swami Vivekananda continued:

> But India had to live, and the spirit of the Lord descended again. . . . the marvellous boy Śaṅkarāchārya arose. The writings of this boy of sixteen are the wonders of the modern world, and so was the boy. He wanted to bring back the Indian world to its pristine purity, but think of the amount of the task before him. I have told you a few points about the state of things that existed in India. All these horrors that you are trying to reform are the outcome of that reign of degradation. The Tartars and the Balucis and all the hideous races of mankind came to India and became Buddhists, and assimilated with us, and brought

their national customs, and the whole of our national life became a huge page of the most horrible and the most bestial customs. That was the inheritance which that boy got from the Buddhists, and from that time to this, the whole work in India is a re-conquest of this Buddhistic degradation by the Vedānta. It is still going on, it is not yet finished, Śaṅkara came, a great philosopher, and showed that the real essence of Buddhism and that of the Vedānta are not very different, but that the disciples did not understand the Master and have degraded themselves, denied the existence of the soul and of God, and have become atheists. That was what Śaṅkara showed, and all the Buddhists began to come back to the old religion.'

Conclusion

It is this combined legacy of the two great architects of Indian thought and culture—Buddha and Śaṅkara—that modern India is learning to appreciate and to cherish, discovering, after centuries, the deep kinship between them. Behind them both stand, like the Himalayan background, the eternal visions of the sages of the *Upaniṣads* which found their undying expression, in a later period, through Śrī Kṛṣṇa in the *Bhāgavad Gītā*.

The self-transcending ethics of unselfish love and compassion of Buddha and his movement, united to the philosophy of the transcendent Self of Śaṅkara's Vedānta, is the new thought—the New Vedānta which is energising and stimulating India's mind and heart today. It is no wonder, then, that India as a whole has responded with enthusiasm and devotion to the message of the 2500th birthday of Bhagavān Buddha.

The Christ We Adore*

Introduction

We, in India, have learnt, through our religion, to look upon great teachers with a heart open to the inspiration which they hold for all humanity. The approach of our people to the lives of all teachers has something refreshingly beautiful about it; it is hard for non-Hindus to understand how we, professing a different religion, can open our hearts, with equal fervour, to receive the inspiration of this great Son of Man, Jesus. India's approach to religion is experiential and not dogmatic. It is spirituality that India seeks in its religious quest and not a creed or dogma. This is also the approach of Jesus Christ to religion, as we shall presently see. It is this approach that explains the spiritual hospitality of the Indian mind. This, broad, all-inclusive, approach will be increasingly appreciated and accepted by the thinking people of the world in the coming years. *What is now the cherished possession of a national culure will eventually become an integral part of*

---

*Speech delivered at the Christmas celebration held at the Ramakrishna Mission Institute of Culture, Calcutta, in 1954, and later published in the December 1955 issue of the *Bulletin* of the Ramakrishna Mission Institute of Culture, Calcutta.

human culture and civilisation. Such a consummation will help to release the Christ-spirit from the shackles of a narrow sectarian creed in which it has been stifled for centuries. This will be the service that the spirit of India will render in this age to the religion of this great Master.

Birth and Boyhood of Jesus

We are familiar in our country with the idea that, at the birth of divine personalities, there is joyous co-operation of man and nature to welcome them; for it is an event heralding universal joy. In the words of one of our sacred books: The ancestors rejoice, the gods dance in joy, and this world gets a saviour—*Modante pitaro, nṛtyanti devatāḥ, sanāthā ceyaṁ bhūrbhavati (Nārada Bhakti-Sūtra, V. 5).*

Very similiar is the account of the birth of Jesus Christ, as given in the various Gospels of the New Testament. Deeply touching is the description of the episode in Luke. The parents, Joseph and Mary, had come to Bethlehem in Judea, from Nazareth in Galilee, to be taxed according to the newly promulgated Roman law. Mary was expecting her first child. The couple took shelter in an inn, where Mary gave birth to an infant who was destined to become a great spiritual teacher. For want of accommodation in the inn, the mother wrapped the baby in swaddling clothes and laid him in a manger. At this time, a group of shepherds, keeping watch over their sheep nearby, received, in the stillness of the night, in an extraordinary way, the intimation of the birth of this wonderful infant.

> And, lo, the angel of the Lord came upon them, and the glory of the Lord shone round about them; and they were sore afraid. And the angel said unto them, Fear not; for, behold, I bring you good tidings of great joy, which shall

> be to all people. For unto you is bom this day in the city of David, a Saviour, which is Christ the Lord. And this shall be a sign unto you; ye shall find the babe wrapt in swaddling clothes, lying in a manger. (Luke, II. 14).

The shepherds were amazed. Hardly had they time to recover from this amazement, when they heard a multitude of angels singing, praising God: 'Glory to God in the highest, and on earth peace, goodwill, toward men' *(ibid.,* II. 14).

The shepherds proceeded to Bethlehem in search of the babe as indicated, and found Mary and Joseph and the babe lying in a manger, and they offered him loving worship and homage.

Next, we get a glimpse, a tender and pleasing glimpse, of him as a boy of twelve. He was accompanying his parents to the Holy temple in Jerusalem for the Passover feast. After the ceremonies, the parents started homeward; they expected Jesus to be in the party but after a day's journey when they found him missing, they searched for him here and there and, finaly, retracing their steps, found him after three days, in the courtyard of the Holy temple dicussing with the learned doctors points of law and faith. When his mother, piqued, told him how much she and his father had been worried over his disappearance, he gave a characteristic answer: 'How is it that ye sought me? Wist ye not that I must be about my father's business?' His parents could not make anything of this enigmatic reply, but they were satisfied when they found him willing to return home with them.

We get hardly any account of Jesus during his youth and early manhood. 'And Jesus increased in wisdom and stature, and in favour with God and man,' says the Gospel in a compressed narrative (ibid., II.52).

But we have enough references to show that Jesus, very early in life, had become aware of the great purpose of his advent and set about it with a thoroughness that nothing could thwart. He must have also spent long hours in silence and aloneness in the nearby mountains and communed with himself. Later, when we meet him next, he is already a young man of about thirty. Moving from place to place, Jesus heard of another teacher who was creating a stir by his way of life and preaching. This was John the Baptist, who went about in the wilderness of Judea, and later in the Jordan area, proclaming: 'Repent ye: for the kingdom of heaven is at hand' (Matthew, III. 2).

Semitic Religious Tradition

The lives and works of John the Baptist and Jesus introduce us to a new chapter in Semitic religious history. There is something extraordinary, something refreshingly striking, in their contribution, which has made religion in the West flow into a new channel of God's intimacy with man, with love as the bond between both. In the old Semitic tradition, this was not the central idea. The idea there was that God was far away; His distance from man was the measure of His majesty; man was called upon to conduct his life here below with faith and fear, and the fruit of such faith was to be reaped after death. Such a religion tends to be largely this-worldly, increasingly bound to time and the historical process. As a socio-political faith, with a slight flavour of the otherworldly, it constantly tends to be bound in a rigid creed which leads to dogmatism, bigotry and intolerance, on the one hand, and formalism and stress on correct ritualistic behaviour, on the other.

The New Testament contains a vivid description of such a situation in the field of religion at the advent of John the Baptist and Jesus. Its pages reveal the birth-pangs of a new spiritual *Weltanschauung* at once universal and human, the recurring conflicts of this new ideology with the entrenched monotheistic exaggerations, the deep aspirations of the people for release from the rigidities of a lifeless tradition as represented by the priesthood, and the shining figures of John and Jesus proclaiming through life and teaching a compelling message of hope and assurance.

Man, as spiritual seeker, transcends the sphere of law and commandments of a religion. Whereas law and commandments relate him to parochial and temporal interests, spirituality relates him to the eternal and the infinite. Jesus came to offer this to man, to give the bread of life to the spiritually hungry. Insistence on correct ritualistic behaviour does not bring satisfaction to man at this stage. They are as stones to a hungry man, as the New Testament puts it. Jesus proclamind a religion of wide and deep horizons; brought God near to man and bound both with the cord of love; he eliminated fear as the medium of their relationship. With love implanted in his heart in place of fear, man emerged as the lover of his fellow-men; he learnt to find fulfilment in a life of love for God and service to man, to God in man. This love for God, this intimate communion with Him, is the fulfilment of the righteous life; it is the only means of satisfying the soul's spiritual hunger. This is the *essential* of religion. It holds that man has a higher dimension which transcends his physical and social personality; he is essentially spiritual; in that inmost being of his lies his intimacy with and closeness to the divine, and his kinship to all creation. Religion is the realisation of this spiritual fact and its expression in life and behaviour.

This is the approach of Jesus to religion. And this is the approach which India has learnt from the *Upaniṣads*, the *Bhagavad Gītā,* the *Srimad Bhāgavatam,* and other scriptures, and has made it part and parcel of our national awareness. These scriptures have taught us that *religion is realisation;* it is not creed or dogma or mere believing; it is not merely the good life, the moral life, the righteous life, though all these are necessary for the flowering of religion in spiritual realisation.

Thanks to the *Upaniṣads,* religion in India, unlike religion in Palestine, learnt to understand and appreciate this mood of spiritual earnestness, this passion for the spiritual as distinct from the merely socio-religious and moral, and to welcome it This is the meaning of our national idea that *Śruti* is more binding than *Smṛti,* that life according to the *Smrti* is only a prelude to life according to the *Śruti.*

Jesus Came to Fulfil, Not to Destroy

For the first time, a glimpse of this great idea came to the Semitic world through John and Jesus; it was not that this idea was entirely absent from the older tradition; a few gifted individuals had borne witness to it. But theirs were forlorn voices incapable of making any impression on the tradition. This was the case even with John the Baptist, who was compelled to refer to himself as 'the vioce of one crying in the wilderness'. But with Jesus the idea became a force, which inevitably came into conflict with the traditional religion. In the New Testament, we can see these two currents flowing side by side. The conflict was all a one-way affair; it was the old in conflict with the new, and not the new in conflict with the old. A spiritual message is large enough to accommodate all forms of faith. Its approach is synthetic and inclusive. Love and grace do not negate law and commandment, but fulfil them. Jesus himself never desired to exclude the old religion. He claimed to have come to fulfil and not to destroy. In this broad and generous spirit, which is the mark of a deeply spiritual religion, we find him endeavouring to effect a synthesis of the old and the new.

The New Testament gives us glimpses of this attempt at synthesis between the message of Moses and the message of Jesus. 'For the law was given by Moses, but grace and truth came by Jesus Christ! (John, 1.17).

To the rich man who wanted to know the way to inherit eternal life, Jesus gave the advice to fulfil the commandments before proceeding higher in the spiritual quest. It was in this sphere of the higher spiritual life that Jesus had somethig new to give. It was not merely new, it was also startling to the people who. heard him. 'They were astonished at his doctrine,' records the New Testament in several places.

Baptism of Jesus

The appearance of John the Baptist on the horizon was the first surprise to the people. John was an ascetic and lived a celibate life. Asceticism and celibacy were foreign to the Semitic tradition. John burst upon the people's attention with the startling proclamation: 'Repent ye: for the kingdom of heaven is at hand.' The people were familiar with the notion of a kingdom of heaven. So there was nothing startling in that; it was a far-away thing in time and space, and they could afford to wait till death and take things leisurely till then. But John proclaimed that the kingdom of heaven was *at hand:* not far away, but *here, now.* To a people suffering from Roman oppression, this was a happy announcement; and they naturally interpreted it in political terms. He asked the people to prepare themselves to enter into it by inner purification through baptism in the Jordan river.

Hundreds of people flocked to John to be baptised; a few among them who were wicked at heart, he sent away hurling after them words of rebuke and threat. He exhorted the baptised to practise charity, justice, mercy, and honesty. The crowds took John to be the promised Messiah; but he divined their thoughts and proclaimed in clear language:

> 'I indeed baptise you with water unto repentance; but he that cometh after me is mightier than I, whose shoes I am not worthy to bean he shall baptise you with the Holy Ghost, and with fire,' (Matthew, III. 11).

Presently, Jesus, who was still an unknown figure, went to him to be baptised by him. John eyed Jesus for a minute and then remonstrated, saying that he was not fit to baptise him, but that he had need to be baptised by Jesus, but Jesus replied: 'Suffer it to be so now: for thus it becometh us to fulfil all righteousness' *(ibid.,* III. 15). John baptised him, and, coming out of the water, Jesus had his first recorded spiritual experience; and a voice from heaven proclaimed: 'This is my beloved Son, in whom I am well pleased' *(ibid.,* III. 17).

Jesus now began his mission. John was arrested and beheaded shortly after, for the fault of being far ahead of his time. Immediately after baptism, Jesus retired to the silence of the mountains nearby and passed through a tense inner struggle and, coming out victorious over the 'temptation', moved to the coast of the lake of Galilee to enter into the period of his public ministry.

His Spiritual Mission

The first act of this ministry was the gathering of his disciples. There is something very fascinating in this process, in the call he sends forth and the response he receives; its simplicity and directness are charming. Finding Peter and his brother Andrew, both fishermen, casting their nets into the sea Jesus went up to them and summoned: 'Follow me and I will make you fishers of men. And they straightway left their nets, and followed him' *(ibid.,* IV.19-20). Two other fishermen, James and John, he similarly gathered, and later Mathew, the customs clerk, and the rest of the twelve.

This is something we understand well in India: the tremendous magnetism of a spiritual teacher who finds and gathers round him those who are to be his spiritual intimates and the bearers of his message, the pure ones who have the capacity to share his inmost thoughts and relieve his loneliness. Buddha, after his illumination, went to Vāraṇāsi to gather his five disciples. We are reminded, in this connexion, of the words which Sri Ramakrishna (1836-86) spoke at the close of the period of his *sādhanā,* describing the longing of his heart for his disciples *(Ramakrishna: The Prophet of New India* by Swami Nikhilananda, p.38):

> A mother never longed so intensely for the sight of her child, nor a friend for his companion, nor a lover for his sweetheart, as I longed for them. Oh! it was indescribable. Shortly after this period of yearning, the devotees began to arrive.

Jesus now began to move about with his disciples, preaching the kingdom of heaven in the synagogues and performing various miracles of healing. But the congregations of the synagogues could not understand or appreciate him. They were certainly looking for the advent of a heavenly kingdom; but it was one largely political in complexion, tribal in scope, and intended to free the Jews from the hated Romans. One who claimed to be the promised Messiah had to fulfil this national demand. Jesus did claim to be the Messiah in direct and indirect references, but made only vague mystical references to the kingdom. He merely incurred the displeasure of the orthodox. But the masses followed him, fascinated by his personality and the miracles he wrought. Although he delivered his message in the famous 'Sermon on the Mount' to his disciples alone, it has provided spiritual nourishment to vast masses of mankind these nineteen hundred years.

The Sermon on the Mount

The 'Sermon on the Mount' expounds moral and spiritual ideas which are universal; they do no breathe the air of Jewish exclusiveness. They are the G.C.M of the inner life of spirit, and will not sound strange to any spiritual seeker nourished on the ideas of the Upaniṣads and the *Bhagavad Gītā.* But it sounded strange to the ears of those who listened. There was newness in them, and there was a ring of authority in their utterance. It was not an authority deriving from any sacerdotal office; it took its force from inner realisation. The New Testament has put it pithily: 'And it came to pass, when Jesus had ended these sayings, the people were astonished at his doctrine. For he taught them as one having authority, and not as the scribes' (*Matthew*, VII.28-29).

The Sermon was a tremendous departure from the accepted ideas of the time; it was a mighty attempt to release the life of the spirit from the shackles of tribal morality and dogmatic religion. Old familiar words were used, but they were given new meanings; old moral codes were invoked, but they received an inward content and. direction; old familiar hopes were mentioned, only to be filled with new spiritaul meanings. And all these innovations had been prefaced with a 'but I say unto you,' conveying a sense of authority. It was no wonder that the people were astonished at his doctrine.

There is a continuity from John to Jesus. John preached baptism unto repentance with a view to preparing man for the kingdom of heaven; and Jesus took up this idea, in spite of its background of Jewish dogma, for, as he expressed it, he came not to destroy, but to fulfil the law and the prophets. Repentance is based on the Jewish dogma of original sin; but whatever be the dogma behind it, it has its significance for spiritual life, in so far as it initiates the inner cleaning process; it leads to humility and receptivity of heart. As a moral act, it steels the mind against further evil doings. Without this resolve, no spiritual life is possible. But repentance is not everything; there are further steps to be taken before we can achieve the kingdom of heaven which, though near at hand, is yet far. It was these further steps that Jesus elucidated in his impressive Sermon.

Jesus opened the Sermon with a reference to repentance and its fruit: 'Blessed are the poor in spirit: for theirs is the kingdom of heaven' (*ibid.*, V.3).

But he struck a new note thereafter: not only was the kingdom of heaven at hand, but it was also *within* us not outside; and we can realise it. This was a revolutionary conception that spiritual realisation was to be had then and there, *in this very life,* here and now, not after death. And so he added: 'Blessed are the pure in heart: for they shall *see* God' *(ibid.,* V. 8).

Thus purity of heart is the one condition for spiritual realisation. It follows that everything else-acts of piety, morality, and social service-is but the means to attain this purity. This was entirely new language for his listeners—that we can *realise* God, become intimate with Him, and be blessed in this very life. *And here we have his unique message, a spiritual religion of inward realisation.* We are reminded of the ringing proclamation of the *Upaniṣads:*

'Ātmā vā are draṣṭavyaḥ—The Self, O dear, must be realised' *Brhadharanyaka Upaniṣad, II. 45); 'Tam akratuh paśyati vīta-śoko dhātu-prasāadāt mahimanam atamna'*— He who is humble and pure realises the glory of the Ātman and becomes free from grief. (*Kaṭha Upaniṣad,* II, 20).

The farthest that Judaism had gone till then was to make man hear the voice of God; the idea of *seeing* God was thus an innovation which, with all its corollaries, was the main point of departure from the prevailing tribal god and faith. These corollaries are set forth in the succeeding passages dealing with the inwardness of morals, rituals, and pietistic acts, indicating the clear departure from the old in the emphatic words in refrain: 'Ye have heard that it was said by them of old time . . . *But I say unto you.'* The moral and ethical demands of a spiritual religion are far more exacting than those of a socio-political faith; hence he said: 'That except your righteousness shall exceed the righteousness of the Scribes and Pharisees, ye shall in no case enter into the kingdom of heaven' (*Matthew* V. 20).

The departure became complete when he exhored his listeners to strive for perfection: 'Be ye therefore perfect, even as your Father which is in heaven is perfect' *(ibid.,*V. 48).

This exhortation sounds strangely Vedantic in significance. He then wound up the Sermon with a ringing statement on the need for the *practice* of the teaching, and not merely the hearing of it or *believing* in its truth, and illustrated the nature of wisdom and folly through a beautiful parable *(ibid.,* VII. 24-27):

> Therefore whosoever heareth these sayings of mine, and doeth them, I will liken him unto a wise man, which built his house upon a rock. And the rain, descended, and the floods came, and the winds blew, and beat upon that house; and it fell not; for it was founded upon a rock. And every one that heareth these sayings of mine, and doeth them not, shall be likened unto a foolish man, which built his house upon the sand: And the rain descended, and the floods came, and the winds blew, and beat upon that house, and it fell; and great was the fall of it.

How akin this sounds to the exhortaion of an earlier teacher, Śrī Kṛṣṇa, in our own country!

> Those devotees who practise, in a converging life endeavour, this teaching of mine which fulfils all righteousness and leads to immortality, endowed with faith and a godward passion, are extremely dear to me.' *(Bhagavad Gītā,* XII. 20)

Here is a refreshing statement of the scope and goal of religion. The emphasis is on *sādhana,* the *pratice* of religion, with a view to attaining *anubhava,* realisation. 'Religion is realisation; it is being and becoming,' in the words of Swami Vivekananda; it is character. It is not a cosy belief, but an adventure, something that sets the soul on fire, the carrying, as Jesus would say, of one's cross by oneself and not by proxy. It reminds us of Buddha's last words addressed to his dear disciple, Ānanda:

> Be a lamp unto yourself, O Ānanda; depend not on any external refuge: work out your emancipation with diligence.

Perfection is a complete transformation of character through the realisation of the kingdom of heaven which is within. *It is the fruit of lived religion.* This conception frees religion from all elements that are magical and misty, materialistic and primitive. The strength that comes to a life through the realisation of the ever-present Ātman within is something palpable. It is the rock-bottom of experience, which ensures steadiness of wisdom and character; it is the *sthitaprajña,* the life of steady wisdom, of the *Bhagavad Gītā.*

The Healing Touch of Jesus

With the 'Sermon on the Mount' closed, once for all, the chapter of obscurity in the life of Jesus. Multitudes thronged round him, many of them victims of serious bodily and mental ailments, some of whom were endowed with deep faith in his spiritual power. They sought his blessing which was given, and they were cured. Some he touched; some just touched the hem of his garment; and some he just blessed, saying 'Be thou whole.' In all cases, the effect was immediate. Jesus had the power within him, and he had compassion in his heart. But he did not like to exhibit this power or make it known wide. Accordingly, he exhorted the cured not to make a fuss about it. He asked them to mollify orthodoxy by making customay gifts to the synagogue in thankfulness for the healing. He gave the credit for all healing to the faith in the heart of the healed: 'Thy faith hath made thee whole.'

From now on, the events in his life move ever faster; and the shadow of tragedy, arising from the conflict with established religious authority, becomes darker and darker, until it reaches its final act in the crucifixion. But within this brief period of about two and a half years, we are introduced to events and episodes and personalities which have the touch of the immortal about them. They form the bright and cheerful scenes of an otherwise gloomy drama. We find Jesus moving from place to place, a picture of alertness and vigour, compassion and humanity, humour and laughter. We watch him in his dealings with the rich and the poor, the good and the sinful, the lowly and the lost; we are amazed at the piose, self-assurance, and versatility which he manifests in these varying situations.

Mary and Martha

The touching episode of Mary and Martha of Bethany has entered into world literature. The two sisters were deeply devoted to Jesus. The death of their brother Lazarus made them grief-stricken. They heard that Jesus was in the neighbourhood. Martha went out to call Jesus. She expressed her faith in his divinity, and then rushed home to call her sister, Mary, saying: 'The Master is come and called for thee' (*John*. XI. 28).

Both then rushed out to welcome the Master. Mary fell at his feet weeping. Jesus was moved:

> When Jesus therefore saw her weeping, and the Jews also weeping which came with her, he groaned in the spirit, and was troubled. . . . Jesus wept *(ibid.,* ix. 33, 35).

He then went up to the grave of Lazarus and, after deeply communing with God for a moment, commanded Lazarus to come forth. And forthwith he rose alive.

In another touching scene, we find the same Mary doing a loving service to Jesus at Bethany, just before his last supper.

She brought an alabaster box of precious ointment and poured it on the head of Jesus, as he sat at his meal. When a disciple protested at the waste and said that it could better have been utilised to help the poor, Jesus made the significant and ominous remark.

> Why trouble ye the woman? For she hath wrought a good work upon me. For ye have the poor always with you; but me ye have not always. For in that she hath poured this ointment on my body, she did it for my burial. Verily I say unto you, wheresover this gospel shall be preached in the whole world, there shall also this, that this woman hath done, be told for a memorial of her. (*Matthew*. XXVI. 10-13).

There was also a third occasion when the two sisters met Jesus; it is a story full of mystical import. They received Jesus into their house. Mary was sitting at his feet and hearing his inspiring words; whereas Martha was busy in the kitchen. She complained to Jesus about her sister Mary:

> Lord, dost thou not care that my sister has left me to serve alone? Bid her therefore that she help me. And Jesus answered and said unto her: Martha, Martha, thou art careful and troubled about many things. But one thing is needful; and Mary hath chosen that good part, which shall not be taken away from her. (*Luke* X. 40-42).

Divine Life Demands Total Renunciation

During his wanderings in Judea, Jesus was approached by a certain man who knelt before him and, addressing him 'Good Master,' asked him what he should do to inherit eternal life. Jesus reprimanded him for calling him good, saying that none except God deserved the epithet, and asked him to keep the ten moral commandments. The man replied that these he had been keeping from his youth; he woud like to know what else he should do.

> Then Jesus beholding him loved him, and said unto him, one thing thou lackest; go thy way, sell whatsoever thou hast, and give to the poor and thou shalt have treasure in heaven; and come, take up the cross, and follow me.
>
> And he was sad at that saying, and went away grieved: for he had great possessions. (Mark. X. 21-22).

Seeing him thus go away, Jesus made the famous remark that it was easier for a camel to pass through the eye of a needle than for a rich man to enter into the kingdom of God.

This episode illustrates the distance that separates mere social ethics from divine life, and proclaims total renunciation as the watchword of the latter. The young man of the story went away grieving; but the story itself has inspired many a young man and woman of later generations, of the type of St. Antony and others, to fulfil to the letter the demands of Jesus and scale the heights of holiness and blessedness.

The Compassionate Jesus

The compassion of a divine incarnation and his power to redeem shine remarkably through two anecdotes, which also reveal the way purity views sin.

A Pharisee, Simon by name, invited Jesus for a meal one day. Jesus accepted and sat down to eat. A woman in the city, who was a sinner, hearing that Jesus was in the house of the Pharisee, bought an alabaster box of ointment and washing his feet with her tears and wiping them with her hair, kissed them and anointed them with the ointment.

Seeing this, the Pharisee was angry that Jesus should have allowed a sinner to do all this. Jesus, addressing Simon, said:

> There was a certain creditor which had two debtors: the one owed five hundred pence, and the other fifty. And

> when they had nothing to pay, he frankly forgave them both. Tell me, therefore, which of them will love him most? Simon answered and said, I supose that he, to whom he forgave most. And he said unto him, thou hast rightly judged. And he turned to the woman, and said unto Simon, seest thou this woman? I entered into thine house, thou gavest me no water for my feet: but she has washed my feet with tears, and wiped them with the hairs of her head. Thou gavest me no kiss: but this woman, since the time I came in, hath not ceased to kiss my feet. My head with oil thou didst not anoint: but this woman hath anointed my feet with ointment. Wherefore I say unto thee, her sins, which are many, are forgiven: for she loved much: but to whom little is forgiven, the same loveth little. And he said unto her: Thy sins are forgiven. And they that sat at meal with him began to say within themselves: Who is this that forgiveth sins also? And he said to the woman: Thy faith hath saved thee; go in peace. (Luke. VII.41-50).

Jesus was teaching in the temple in Jerusalem. The Scribes and Pharisees brought before Jesus a woman taken in adultery and, announcing that, according to Mosaic law, she had to be stoned, asked him for his opinion, just to entangle him unawares. The Gospels give a fine picture of Jesus stooping down and writing on the ground with his finger, as if he did not hear them. But when they pestered him, he lifted up his head and, turning to them, declared:

> He that is without sin among you, let him first cast a stone at her. And again he stooped down, and wrote on the ground. And they which heard it, being convicted by their own conscience, went out one by one, beginning at the eldest, even upto the last; and Jesus was left alone, and the woman standing in the midst When Jesus had lifted

> up himself, and saw none but the woman, he said unto her: Woman, where are those thine accusers? Hath no man condemned thee? She said; 'No man, Lord.' And Jesus said unto her: Neither do I condemn thee; go and sin no more. (*John*. VIII. 7-11).

The power behind the words 'Thy sins are forgiven' is the power of God working through an incarnation only; it is beyond the reach even of saints. This divine power working through Jesus is specially revealed in his famous declaration.

> Come unto me, all ye that labour and are heavy laden, and I will give you rest Take my yoke upon you, and learn of me; for I am meek and lowly in heart; and ye shall find rest unto your souls. For my yoke is easy, and my burden is light. (*Matthew*. XI. 28-30).

We are reminded of an identical promise given by an earlier incarnation, Śrī Kṛṣṇa (*Bhagavad Gītā,* XVIII. 66):

> Renounce all your duties and take refuge in me alone, I shall redeem you from all sins; grieve not.

The Teachings of Jesus

Trials and tribulations began to confront Jesus. Various attempts were made by the priests to entangle him in some remark of treason or blasphemy. But his intelligence and ready wit baffled their attempts. A group of priests brought a Roman coin and asked him whether it was lawful to give tribute to Caesar or not; on his asking whose image and superscription the coin bore, the priests answered, that it was of Caesar. Then he answered, to the amazement of the clever priests:

> Render therefore unto Caesar the things which are Caesar's; and unto God the things that are God's. (*Matthew*. XXII. 21).

Then a lawyer came forward to entangle him with a clever question, as to what constituted the great commandment in the law; *and the world got in the answer of Jesus a compressed statement of spiritualiy and social ethics:*

> Jesus said unto him, Thou shalt love the Lord thy God with all thy heart, and with all thy soul, and with all thy mind. This is the first and great commandment. And the second is like unto it: Thou shalt love thy neighbour as thyself. On these two commandments hang all the law and the prophets. *(ibid.,* XXII. 37-40)

This great enunciation gave rise to a very practical question: Who is my neighbour? In answering it, through the famous parable of the good Samaritan, Jesus contrasted the universality of the spirit and temper of spiritual ethics with the narrow and parochial temper of credal and sectarian morals.

A certain man went down from Jerusalem to Jericho and fell among thieves; and they stripped him of his raiment, wounded him, and departed, leaving him half dead. A priest and a Levite chanced to pass that way; seeing the helpless man, they, instead of going to his help, went away by the opposite side of the road. Narrating the above, Jesus continued:

> But a certain Samaritan, as he journeyed, came where he was; and when he saw him, he had compassion on him, and bound up his wounds, pouring in oil and wine, and set him on his own beast, and brought him to an inn, and took care of him. And on the morrow when he departed, he took out pence, and gave them to the host, and said unto him: Take care of him; and whatsoever thou spendest more, when I come again, I will repay thee. (*Luke*. X.33-35).

After narrating this, Jesus asked his questioner as to who really behaved as neighbour to the one that fell among the thieves. 'And he said: He that showed mercy on him. Then said Jesus unto him: 'Go, and do thou likewise' *(ibid.,* X. 37).

In between the harassments of the priests, Jesus did a lot of teaching; first to the simple masses and then to his close disciples. To the former he spoke in parables, making thereby difficult subjects easy to comprehend. Each one of these parables, like the parable of the good Samaritan, elucidates one or other aspect of his central theme, the life of godliness. Some of them, like the parable of the Ten Virgins, are full of mystical significance. He spoke to the disciples about the service of man, the poor, the sick, the homeless, the naked, and the forlorn, in the spirit of the worship of God:

> Verily I say unto you, inasmuch as ye have done it unto one of the least of these my brethren, ye have done it unto me. (*Matthew*. XXV. 40)

He charged the disciples to go forth and preach his gospel among the people, and he prescribed a way of life and behaviour for the preachers, which breathes the spirit of renunciation, dependence on God, non-possession, peacefulness, and humility, echoing the exhorttation of Buddha to his diciples. *It is a tragedy of history that subsequent Christian preachers, unlike the Buddhists, have largely strayed from the strait and narrow path shown by their great Master.*

To his chosen disciples, Jesus gave his spiritual teaching directly and without the aid of parables. He revealed to them, a few days before his death, his true personality as the Christ, the anointed One, and charged them not to tell it to anyone else till the day of resurrection:

> I am the way, the truth, and the life: no man cometh unto the Father, but by me. If ye had known me, ye should have known my Father also. He that hath seen me hath seen the Father. . . . Believest thou not that I am in the Father, and

> the Father in me? The words that I speak unto you, I speak not of myself: but the Father that dwelleth in me, he doeth the works. (*John.* XIV.6-10)

He asked all those who would choose to follow him to be prepared to deny themselves and take up their crosses; it was not a cosy and comfortable religion that he offered, but a heroic path of adventure, a life of total renunciation in the love of God:

> For whosoever will save his life shall lose it; and whosoever will lose his life for my sake shall find it. For what is a man profited, if he shall gain the whole world, and lose his own soul? Or what shall a man give in exchange for his soul? (Matthew. XVI.25-26).

The Betrayal and the Trial

The preachings, movements, and miracles of Jesus had stirred up by now a good deal of hostility from the priests, who now began to take steps to apprehend him and bring him before the law. They picked up stray bits of remarks made by Jesus and built up a case for blasphemy against the faith. The tragedy deepened with the last supper in the company of all his disciples, when Jesus made the ominous remark that one of his disciples would betray him and hinted at Judas. When Peter protested against it, he made the still more ominous remark that even Peter would deny him thrice before the next morning. Feeling the end near, and with a heavy heart, Jesus moved to Gethsemane and sat down to pray, asking Peter and two of his other disciples to watch and pray in the meantime. But Peter fell asleep, and Jesus, annoyed, rebuked him:

> What, could ye not watch with me one hour? Watch and pray, that ye enter not into tempation: the spirit indeed is willing, but the flesh is weak. *(ibid.,* XXVI. 40-41).

This happened three times; but the third time he allowed them to sleep and, after prayer, waited for the betrayal by Judas, who had been bribed by the priests to do so with thirty pieces of silver. Judas came up soon after with the priests and soldiers, and betrayed Jesus to them through a kiss of the Master's hand for identification, and the soldiers took Jesus into custody. Peter, in defence, cut off the ear of a soldier with his sword. Jesus reproved him saying.

> Put up again thy sword into its place: for all they that take the sword, shall perish with the swords. *(ibid,* XXVI, 52).

Henceforth, it was mounting pathos to the end. Jesus was taken to the high priest, Caiphas; all the disciples deserted him. Peter, however, attended the trial from a distance; and during the trial he denied thrice, before passers-by who asked, that he had anything to do with Jesus. The operations of an inexorable fate left Peter sad and weeping. The priests decided, though without much evidence, that Jesus was guilty, and they hauled him up before Pontius Pilate, the Roman governor.

Pilate asked Jesus whether he took himself to be the king of the Jews. Jesus remained silent, which amazed Pilate. Pilate found Jesus was not guilty, but the priests demanded his crucifixion amid tumultuous scenes. Pilate, finding no other way, yielded to their demand and, washing his hands with some water symbolically, said that he was innocent of the blood of Jesus, whom he referred to as a just man. The people assembled there cried out that they were willing to take his blood on themselves and on their descendants. What a tragic statement, and what tragic consequences have followed therefrom ever since!

The Crucifixion and the Resurrection

The doleful procession, with Jesus adorned with a scarlet robe and a crown of thorns and carrying his heavy cross, proceeded to

Golgotha. He was attended by soldiers who jeeringly hailed him king of the Jews and spat upon and smote him; then they removed the scarlet robe and put his own raiment upon him and nailed him on the cross on the mount of Calvary between two thieves similarly crucified. They placed over his head a taunting signboard: This is Jesus, the king of the Jews.

After hours of intense agony, Jesus cried with a loud voice:

> 'My God, my God, why hast thou forsaken me?' (*Matthew*. XXVII.46), and then in an appealing voice:
>
> 'Father, forgive them; for they know not what they do' (*Luke*. XXII.34).

It was a Friday. The mother of Jesus was a witness of this pathetic scene from a distance; with her was her sister and Mary Magdalene and John. Before he finally expired, Jesus pointed to his mother and asked John to treat her as his own mother, and asked her to treat him as her own son. After this expression of tenderness, Jesus bent his head and expired, after nine hours of intense torture.

The tragedy was complete. Forsaken by the world, for whose redemption he had come, Jesus ended his earthly career when he was hardly thirty-three. But his spirit triumphed in the resurrection. Joseph of Arimathea, a silent but influential devotee, took his body for burial with the permission of the Roman governor. He laid the body in a new tomb and, placing a heavy stone over it, departed. The two Marys, however, remained near the sepulchre. After three days, on Monday, they had a shaking spiritual experience; and they learnt about the resurrection of Jesus through the angels. They rushed to convey the news to the disciples at Galilee in fear and joy. On the way, the radiant form of Jesus appeared before them, and they fell at his feet and worshipped him. Directed by him, they informed the disciples of the glad tidings, and Jesus appeared to all of them on a hill in Galilee, blessed them, spoke to them commanding them to teach the gospel to all the world and, before disappearing, assured them that he would be with them always unto the end of the world.

In this moving story of the resurrection, there is one touching episode relating to one of the disciples, Thomas, who was absent at that time. When they related the vision to him, he refused to believe them until he had a direct experience. Exactly eight days after, Jesus again revealed himself to all of them, including Thomas, and invoked his peace on them. Calling to Thomas, Jesus asked him to feel his wounds with his fingers, which he did in amazement and sorrow and joy. Jesus admonished him to believe and not be faithless, and added a significant remark:

> Thomas, because thou hast seen me, thou hast believed: blessed ate they that have not seen, and yet have believed. (*John.* XX.29).

As a sequel to the above episode, the expression; 'doubting Thomas' passed into the world's vocabulary of banter.

It is interesting for us to recall the tradition that our country first heard the message of Jesus from this direct disciple of his, and a group of Christians of our Kerala state trace their spiritual descent from him.

These are, then, some of the salient features of the life and teachings of this arresting personality, whom the Hindus spontaneously recognise as a divine incarnation. As we have seen, his life is full of sweetness and tenderness, tragedy and pathos; it is spiritually inspiring. *To us in India, however, the end is just a tragedy, bereft of any special spiritual beauty.* It is the life that is, in our view, spiritually beautifull and elevating. The deaths of our own spiritual heroes, Śrī Rāma and Śrī Kṛṣṇa were *near tragic;* but we did not build our religion on them. India treats the manner of their death most casually, while she seeks to build her religion on their lives and teachings.

It is no wonder that ordinary people do not understand the depths of a divine incarnation's personality; they can at best appreciate his miracles, while missing his character. Too much insistence on these miracles, converts religion into a sort of magic, and degrades the content of the life-giving message to cheapness. All great teachers, including Jesus, therefore, discountenanced them. The difficulty of recognising an incarnation has been well expressed by Śrī Kṛṣṇa in the *Bhagavad Gītā;* only a few can understand him; the rest will deride him or just ignore him.

Avajananti maṁ mūdhā manuṣīṁ tanum āśritam;
Paraṁ bhāvamajānanto ṁama bhūtamaheśvaram

'Fools deride me when invested with a human body, not being able to grasp my transcendent nature as the supreme Lord of all beings.' (*Bhagavad Gītā,* IX.11).

The trial and crucifixion of Jesus is the measure of the intolerance and folly of the contemporary society. There is pathos in the lament of Jesus over Jerusalem:

> O Jerusalem, Jerusalem, thou that killest the prophets, and sons which are sent unto thee, how often would I have gathered thy children together, even as a hen gathereth her chickens under her wings, and ye would not! (*Matthew.* XXIII.37).

Persecution is the outcome of intolerance, which is a social malady arising out of the limitations of its *Weltanschauung*. India was, and is, fortunately free from this malady, thanks to its generous spiritual outlook which finds beautiful elucidation in several of our sacred books:

'Knowers of Truth declare that it is the same non-dual Reality that is spoken of as Brahman (Absolute) by the philosophers, as Paramātman (Supreme Self) by the mystics, and as Bhagavān (God) by the devotees'

Vadanti tat tattvavidaḥ tattvaṁ yat jñānam advayam; Brahmeti Paramātmeti Bhagavān iti sabdyate—(*Śrimad Bhagavatam,* I. 2.11).

The New Movement

To teach the world faster than it can learn is to court disaster, as Bertrand Russell has put it. The teachings of Jesus relating to the kingdom of God and the resurrection were just incomprehensible to most of his hearers. There is the typical instance of the Pharisee demanding Jesus to state when the kingdom of God should come. Jesus answered:

> The kingdom of God cometh not with observation: Neither shall they say, Lo here! or lo there! for, behold, the kingdom of God is within you. (*Luke*. XVII.20-21).

This statement that the kingdom of God is within us can hardly be squared with the dogma of the innate vileness of human nature. How beautifully have the Upaniṣads expressed the above sentiment of Jesus.

Na sandṛśe tiṣṭhati rūpamasya
na caksusā paśyati kaścanainam;
Hṛdā manīṣā manasābhiklṛpto
ya etadviduramṛtāste bhavanu

The form of the Self is not an object of vision;
None can behold Him with the fleshy eye;
One can know Him when, by constant meditation
And free from doubt,
He is revealed by the heart.

'Those who know thus become immortal.' (*Katha Upaniṣad,* VI.9).

The crucifixion was a tragedy of the first magnitude; *but a greater tragedy was the way it was handled.* Woven into the prevailing dogmas, it slowly became central to the new movement. The man of joy, which Jesus undoubtedly was in real life, became transformed into the man of sorrows, in dogma. We may find a forbidding austerity in John the Baptist; but the Son of Man, as he himself has said, came eating and drinking, trailing clouds of humour and laughter. By transforming him ino a man of sorrow, dogma has helped to turn his religion into grim and cheerless aspects, with serious consequences for the emotional life of its followers. Only a few great saints have been able to penetrate through this spiritual heaviness. 'A sad nun is a bad nun,' wrote St. Theresa; and she exclaimed: 'O Lord, save us from sullen saints!'

The dogma of one man's sin affecting all humanity gave rise to its logical corollary of the dogma of one man's blood washing away the sins of all; such an approach led inevitably to a chain reaction of such tragedies involving the lives of Stephen and Joseph, Peter and Paul, immediately after, and of countless other good and noble and innocent souls, thereafter. The theory that the blood of the martyr is the seed of the Church developed out of this dogma; and, in place of calm reason and generous love, frenzy, fanaticism, intolerance, and bigotry gripped the propagation of the life-giving message of Jesus down the centuries, destroying as many lives as it undoubtely helped to build, with groups interchanging places as persecutor and victim.

It is interesting to speculate how the message would have spread, like a little leaven leavening the whole bread, from one good soul to another in comparative peace and goodwill, if the divine life and sublime teaching of Jesus had found the central place, instead of the popular and striking dogmas of 'the scapegoat' and 'the atonement,' physical resurrection and the second advent, earthly kingdom, and the imminence of the Day of Judgement.

These dogmas were purely tribal in their scope, including the prevalent concept of the monotheistic god. They were the nurseries of contemporary Jewish patriotism and national cohesion, sectarian intolerance and political frenzy.

This fettering, in cast-iron dogmas, of the universal message of Jesus—the ideas of the indwelling diviniy, of divine race, universal ethics, and spiritual realisaton—caused the distortion of its universality through bigotry and intolerance, and the dilution of its peace and love content with hatred, violence, and war.

Judaism represents an impressive human movement of ethical fervour and faith in the divine; but its scope was severely limited to the Jewish community which, in response to the challenge of a hostile world, had tightened its moods and ways, life and laws. The radiant faith in a living God and the laws and commandments which nursed that faith in the hearts of its people, made it the only steady spiritual island in the sea of the moral and religious confusions of the Roman world. As such, it had justification for its faith in its world mission; it was also fitted to be the nursery of the new message of John and Jesus, which had brought with it the vision, the energy, and the character to translate that faith into reality. The only impression that the Gospels warrant us to carry is that Jesus meant his movement to be at first a deepening and, eventually, a broadening of his people's heritage. He took in much before he gave out in ample measure; he came to fulfil and not to destroy the law and the prophets.' Here was an attempt at a lofty synthesis by an equally lofty spiritual character.

But history records the tragedy of its failure; the word 'fulfil' was slowly interpreted, not in its spiritual sense as meant by Jesus, but in its prevailing socio-political significance; and this not merely by the Jews, but also by the new movement, which led to the dissatisfaction of Jews against the new movement with its tragic consequences, on the one hand, and the strait-jacketing of the soaring spirit of the movement itself in the 'letter' of the dogmas of the old faith, on the other.

The new movement thus began as an uneasy combination of the universal and the tribal, the spiritual and the dogmatic, the peaceful and the passionate. The latter elements in their original context, which was consciously parochial and limited, were constructive and creative; but in their new context of the universal, they became largely negative and destructive. The former elements, however, became the source of the high spiritual, mystical, and humanitarian temper of the new movement. The history of Christianity, in its twin records of persecution, violence, and war, on the one side, and lofty mysticism, moral passion, and humanitarianism on the other, bears the impress of this inner division, which also explains its recurrent conflicts with sciṭence. A successful synthesis needs the guidance of an adequate Well tanschauung, which was not available at the time. The successful synthesis of thought elements, each one of which is vital and powerful, flowering as they do from human experience at various levels—the ethical passion of Judaism, the mystical and humanitarian fervour of Christianity, and the rational temper of science—calls for the guidance of a philosophy or world-view such as that of Vedānta, which is not afraid of any aspect of experience, but seeks truth in all of them with zestful detachment and devotion.

The Future of Indian Christianity

It is against this background that we view with hope the future of Indian Christianity. Under the guidance of the philisophy of Vedānta, the Christian message in India can achieve that synthesis by which it will flow as an entirely constructive force with its universal elements functioning free in the spirit of the universal, and its dogmatic elements digested and retained to accord with the spirit of the universal and human.

Our people have the genius, inherent and active, to appreciate a truly spiritual message; our minds are hospitable to spiritual ideas, however new or startling they may be. *The message of Jesus and his life divine have found their lodgement in the Indian soul through the irresistible appeal of their beauty and charm.* It is our earnest hope that the Christian message, passing through Indian experience, will bear in its look a new charm and force of tolerance and gentleness, peace and fellowship, capturing thus the Master's spirit in full.

Conclusion

The gospel of Jesus is a gospel of spiritual redemption. That gospel has a meaning only when we feel the bondage of worldliness irksome and heavy, and seek for freedom in the freedom of God. There is the assurance given by the Master that we shall then get what we seek. To ask and seek and knock is our share, and to give and reveal and open is the Lord's. That is the mood and attitude in which we adore Christ. That is the Hindu way of acceptance and assimilation.

The Message Of Prophet Muhammad*

The Character of Prophet Muhammad

The character of Prophet Muhammad has been misrepresented, not only by many prejudiced non-Muslim critics, but also by the violent, ambitious, and worldly-minded faithful Muslims as well. In his personal life, the prophet shines as a man of high character, integrity, and humanity. He lived a simple spartan life, exemplifying the truth of the dignity of labour. In his later life, he felt that he had a mission to deliver to humanity in general, and to his own Arab people in particular, and he set about implementing this mission and succeeded, before his death, in uniting the Arab people through a religio-political ideology and making them conscious of their destiny to be a civilising force in the world.

---

*Based on a public lecture delivered, on the occasion of the celebration of the Prophet's birthday by the Musliim Students Society, Rangoon, at the City Hall, Rangoon, Burma, on 21 April 1940.

He also instilled love of knowledge in the Arab people. His inspiration soon transformed Arabia from a backward bedouin-inhabited desert area into the political and cultural hub of Eurasia for four centuries, marked by advancement of science and learning, trade and commerce, and dynamic international contacts. This is the period when the universal spiritual message of Islam and its rational and scientific temper dominated the Muslim mind, which endowed them with an insatiable spirit of curiosity, which inspired them to learn from contemporary civilisations like the Indian, the Chinese, and the Greeco-Roman, and which stimulated them to advance science, philosophy, and the arts in many directions.

But, after the Mongolian invasion of the thirteenth century after Christ and the complete destruction of Baghdad in 1258, when many millions were killed, whole areas were laid waste, and political rule in the centre of the Islamic world passed into the hands of barbarian infidels, leaving only Egypt and Spain to nourish Arab culture for another two centuries, there set in the slow and steady erosion of these universal and rational elements and the rising, to dominance, of its dogmatic and intolerant elements. The Mongol invaders, and later the Turks, were soon converted to Islam and became the carriers of Islamic religion, culture, and political power. With some great exceptions, these new Muslim groups came under the influence, less of Islam's rational and universal, and more of its dogmatic and intolerant, elements. This led to the increasing exploitation of the name of Islam by several military conquerors to destroy and rob and pillage other countries and cultures, which has given a bad name to this great religion.

The Message of the Prophet: Its Universal Elements

As in the case of every religion, there is, in the message of Prophet Muhammad also, a mixture of the eternal and universal ethical and spiritual elements along with the temporary and local socio-political elements. These represent the two aspects of every religious tradition, firstly, as a path of God, and next, as a socio-political ordering of human life. The followers of Islam derive their inspiration primarily from the Quran and secondarily, as deriving from the Quran, from the *Ṣarīah* and the *Hadith.* All the three contain elements, what the Indian *Sanātana Dharma,* or Hinduism calls, *śruti,* representing the first, *smṛti,* representing the second, in varying proportions. The stagnation and decay of Islam commenced, as in the case of *Sanātana Dharma* in recent centuries, with the dominance of the *smṛti* over the *śruti* elements. It was a dominance of the fundamentalist group over the ever-diminishing rational and humanist group which advocated the scientific approach and the stressing more and more of the eternal, universal, spiritual elements and the soft-pedalling of the temporal and local elemens, in response to the advance of history.

The following select passages of the Quran breathe the spirit of the *śṛuti* or the eternal and the universal:

> (We commence) with the name of God
> The most Merciful (to begin with),
> The most Merciful (to the end).
>
> All praise belongs to God,
> Lord of all the worlds,
> The Most Merciful (to begin with),
> The most Merciful (to the end).
>
> Master of the day of Judgement.
> Thee alone do we serve,
> And Thee alone do we ask for help.

The Quran speaks of Muhammad and the universal elements of his mission in these words:

'We have not sent thee but as a mercy and blessing for the world.'

The second Sura of the Quran commands us to believe, in not only what was revealed to Muhammad, but also in what was revealed to those who went before him. This clearly indicated the Prophet's acceptance of many true religions of which Islam is one. The universality of the Prophet's message is also revealed in his teaching, that only those are nearest to his heart and to God who do what is right. In several *Suras* of the Quran, we come across this universal approach:

'To every one have we given a law and a way. And if God had pleased, He would have made you all one people (believers in one religioin); but he has done otherwise that He might try you in that which He hath severally given unto you. Wherefore press forward in good works. Unto God shall ye return and He will tell you that concerning which ye disagree.'

'Shall I not inform you of a better act than fasting, alms, and prayer? Making peace between one and another; enmity and malice tear up rewards by roots.'

'It is not righteousness that ye turn your faces to the east and the west; but righteous is he who believeth in Allah and the Last Day and the angels and the scripture and the prophets; and gives his wealth, for love of Him, to kinsfolk, and to orphans, and to the needy, and to the wayfarer, and to those who ask, and set slaves free, and observeth proper worship and payeth the poor-due; and those who keep their treaty when they make one, and the patient in tribulation and adversity and time of stress. Such are they who are sincere. Such are the God fearing.'

'Say (O Muslims): We believe in Allah and that which is revealed unto us, and that which was revealed unto Abraham, and Ishmael, and Issac, and Jacob, and the tribes, and that which Moses and Jesus received, and that which the prophets received, from their Lord. We make no distinction between any of them and unto Him we have surrendered.'

'Lo! religion with Allah (is) the Surrender (to His will and guidance).'

'Oh ye who believe! Be steadfast witnesses for Allah in equity, and let not hatred of any people seduce you that ye deal not justly. Deal justly, that is nearer to your duty. Observe your duty towards Allah. Lo! Allah is informed of what ye do.'

In the course of his farewell sermon before his passing away, the Prophet gave the message of a universal and humanistic ethics:

'And hearken, o mankind! An Arab has no superiority over a non-Arab and a non-Arab is not superior to an Arab, a white man is not superior to a black man nor a black man superior to a white man, except by virtue of his conduct. The noblest in the sight of Allah is he who is noblest in conduct.'

Says the Quran elsewhere:

'Man's actions are judged by his intention.'

'He is not of us who sleeps with his stomach full while his neighbour is hungry.'

There is an oft-quoted saying in the Quran which also has the ring of universality:

'Let there be no compulsion in religion.'

That God is one and that He is beyond man's sensory experience, is highlighted in another beautiful verse of the Quran:

'Sight perceives Him not. But He perceives men's sights; for He is the knower of secrets, the Aware.'

This teaching is exactly similar to the teaching of the *Kena Upaniṣad* (1.7):

Yaccakṣusā na paśyati
yena cakṣūṁṣi paśyati;
Tadeva brahma tvaṁ viddhi
nedam yadidam upāsate

'That which cannot be seen by the eye but through which the eye itself sees, know That to be Brahman and not what people worship here (in the mainfested world).'

Islam in the Light of the 'Śruti' and the 'Smṛti' Concepts of India's Sanātana Dharma

Some Muslim thinkers have made a distinction between Islam and Muhammadanism and they have preferred the word Islam to Muhammadanism. The former is a more universal concept than the latter, the truths taught in it being impersonal in origin. This is the meaning of *Śruti* in the Hindu or the *Sanātana Dharma* tradition of India; the sages of the Upaniṣads, or of the *Śrutis,* were only discoverers of eternal spiritual truths which can be re-discovered by any one else also at any time. But the latter, namely, Muhammadanism, refers to a person as the sanction for the teachings it expounds. Without the personal founder, the teachings cannot stand. Such teachings constitute, as I said earlier, the *Smṛti* dimension of a religion, which is limited by place, time, and history. The Hindus consider even their *Bhagavad Gītā* as a *Smṛti* in form though a *śruti* in content, since it deals with ethical and spiritual truths only and not social rules and regulations.

In the Hindu tradition, unlike in all other religious traditions, there is a clear distinction between its *śruti* and its *smṛti* elements. The *śruti* stands for the body of eternal and impersonal truths valid for all times and peoples. And the *Smṛti* stands for the temporal and the local elements; and because they are temporal and local, they cannot be universal. And Hinduism emphasises that they need to be changed age after age, in response to changing socio-economic conditions. The *śruti* is represented by the *Vedas* generally, and by the *Upaniṣads* particularly. They contain truths of the spiritual dimension of life discovered by different sages, among whom were many women also. These truths, like any truth about the physical world, are eternal and are capable of being re-discovered by any human being equipped with moral purity and mental penetration. Among these truths are the innate divinity of man, the unity of God as infinite and non-dual consciousness which is the Self of man and nature, man's capacity to realise this truth in life, and the availability of different paths to realise God, The Hindu mind discovered the presence of these truths in every world religion. And the mystics of every religion, including the Sufi mystics of Islam, apart from the Prophet himself, have borne witness to these eternal spiritual truths. This is what India calls the *Sanatana dharma* dimension of any religious tradition.

The *smṛti* is represented by the various law books of the Hindu tradition, like *Manu Smṛti, Yājnavalkya Smṛti, Āpasthamba dharma-sūtras* etc. They deal with rules to regulate the day-to day life of people individually and collectively; they deal with subjects such as food, dress, marriage, inheritance etc. This is what India calls the *yuga dharma* dimension of any religious tradition, the *dharma* relevant for a particular *yuga,* age or epoch. The Hindu tradition, even in its orthodox form, provides for the giving up of old *smṛtis* and the creation and adoption of new *smṛtis.* That is why, in the long history of the Hindu tradition, there have been many *smṛtis,* but only one *śruti;* and, in this modern period, the most arresting fact of Hindu life is the rejection of the authority of the old *smṛtis,* and the free and fearless adoption of new *smṛtis* by the people, in response to the onward march of history and the demands of the modern age. The age-old experience of the Hindu tradition demonstrates the truth that the changing of these *smṛti* elements of any tradition, which become at a later age, what in Greek mythology is called, *procrustean beds,* not only will not harm that tradition but, on the contrary, will or strengthen that tradition, and make it better fitted to achieve human development. The Hindu tradition recognises the fact that, with respect to human development and fulfilment, these *smṛti* elements of a tradition are like the bark of a tree; as the tree grows, the bark also must grow side by side; if not, the bark will choke the tree and destroy it. But a living tree will cast off its old bark and create for itself a new bark suitable to its growth. With regard to *smṛtis,* in general, the following pithy observation of Sri Ramakrishna (1836-86) presents the essence of Hindu wisdom aptly:

> The Mughal coins have no currency under the (British East India) Company's rule.

One of the features that helped to sustain the impressive millennia-long continuity of the Hindu tradition is the general acceptance of this dominance of the *śruti* over the *smṛti.* This produced two great results, namely, the emergence of a galaxy of mystics and saints and reformers, and the high respect they commanded from the people, even though some of them preached openly against several aspects of the teachings of the current Hindu *smṛtis.* If, on the other hand, the *smṛtis,* what in Islam is called the *Sariyah,* had dominated the Hindu tradition, these mystics and saints and reformers would have been silenced or destroyed. In our own time, a Vivekananda (1863-1902) appeared, and he preached strongly against several beliefs and practices advocated by the Hindu *Smṛtis,* showing them to be obsolete and enemies of human development and fulfilment; and yet he was accepted, respected, and honoured even by the orthodox tradition. This stands in sharp contrast to the tragic fate of several lovable saints and innovators in the wide spectrum of the Semitic tradition.

Islam: Creative versus Stagnant

Islam has produced some of the most lovable men and women of God, the Sufis. The Prophet's teachings contained inspiration for this God-ward direction of human life, and mystics began to appear in Islam within a century of his death. The earliest outstanding Sufi mystic was a woman, Rabia of Basra (717-801 AD), who has inspired most of the later Sufis. She and several other Sufis were monastics, a state of life condemned by Islamic *Ṣarīyah* or law books. Many of them had a hard time to express their deep-felt spiritual urges and experiences, for fear of offending the rigid *Ṣarīyah* or fundamentalist orthodoxy of Islam, which has even put to death some of the noblest among them. This is the bitter fruit of a stagnant Islam. If Islam were dominated by its creative, by its eternal and universal, elements, this would not have taken place. In the first four centuries of Islam, when it was creative, these dogmatic and rigid fundamentalist elements had been held in check by the rational, universal, and expansive spirit of Islam, which made for the flowering of the Islamic culture and civilisation. Since the destruction of Baghdad, there has been an increasing dominance by its rigid and intolerant *Ṣarīyah* or *Smṛti* elements, and the consequent exploitation of Islam, as referred to earlier, by power-hungry worldly-minded individuals to cover their own greed and blood-thirstiness.

If Islam is to become creative once again, and help in the human development and fulfilment of its followers, it has to capture once again the rational and universal temper of its early period, by taking inspiration from the *spirit* of Islam and not from its *letter.* This rational approach is found in many early Muslim thinkers. It is expressed in a famous verse by Jalāluddin Rūmi, in his *Masnavi,* which is treated as only second to the Quran in importance and reverence (quoted by Dr. Bhagawan Das in his *Essential Unity of All Religions,* Bharatiya Vidya Bhavan edition, 1960, p.100):

Man ze Qurān maghz rā bardāṣṭam,
Ustukḥāṇ peṣe sagāṅ andakḥtam

The marrow from the Quran have I drawn,
And the dry bones unto the dogs have cast.

Conclusion

Such a creative Islam alone will be able to establish happy and fruitful relations with its sister world religions, and also to become a progressive force in its own secular field. Islamic conquerors and missionaries have a bad reputation as idol breakers with respect to other religions. If this is accepted as an essential element of Islam, it will have to be engaged in this fruitless task till the end of time; and consequently, it will never be able to establish happy and peaceful relations with other religions, many of which will continue to use images and symbols. It is good for Islam to engage in another type of idol-breaking, namely, idols of the mind, consisting of prejudices and prepossessions. This is one of the important disciplines of the scientific method as expounded by Francis Bacon, who refers to the need for every scientific seeker to free the mind from the 'idols of the cave,' from the 'idols of the theatre,' etc. In a famous poem, the great Jalāluddin Rūmi protests vigorously against this idol-breaking programme, which applies to all Semitic religious missionaries generally, and to all Islamic conquerors and non-Sufi missionaries specially. *(Masnavi,* quoted in Claude Field's *Mystics and Sufis of Islam,* p.154):

Moses, to his horror, heard one summer day
A benighted shepherd blasphemously pray:
'Lord,' he said, 'I would I know Thee, where Thou art,
That for Thee I might perform a servant's part,
Comb Thy hair, and dust Thy shoes, and sweep Thy room,
Bring Thee every morning milk and honeycomb.'

Moses cried, 'Blasphemer!
Curb thy blatant speech!
Whom art thou addressing? Lord of all and each,
Allah the almighty? Thinkest thou He doth need
Thine officious folly? Wilt Thou all bounds exceed?
Miscreant, have a care, lest thunderbolts should break
On our heads, and others perish for thy sake.
Without eyes He seeth, without ears He heareth,
Hath no son nor partner through the endless years;

Space cannot contain Him, time He is above.
All the limits that He knows are Light and Love.'
Put to shame, the shepherd, his poor garment rent,
Went away disheartened, his ardour spent.

Then spake God to Moses: 'Why hast thou for
Me Driven away My servant, who goes heavily?
Not for severence it was, but union
I commissioned thee to preach, O hasty one!
Hatefullest of all things is to me divorce (of man from man),
And the worst of all ways is the way of force;
I made not creation, self to aggrandise,
But that creatures might with Me communion prize.

What though the childish tongue trip? 'tis the heart I see, if it really loves Me in sincerity.'

Sri Ramakrishna and Universal Religion*

Introduction

It is an undeniable fact of history that one of the most potent factors in the evolution of humanity has been the force which manifests itself as religion and the religious motive. From earliest times it has supplied the motive for social cohesion and social progress. Besides satisfying the individual's spiritual needs, it has also been the power to unite individuals into groups and communities.

Religion: A Curse as Well as a Blessing in the Past

But it is a strange paradox that this same impulse which has contributed to human unity and welfare has also been the cause of much strife and disunion among mankind. It seems as though religions are closed systems and the only relation they can have

---

*Contributed to the *Prabuddha Bharata,* January 1936.

towards one another is that of antagonism. The powers for blessing which they exhibit in their narrow spheres of sect and community turn into curses when applied to the large world outside. Every system has appealed to the religious susceptibilities of its votaries to goad them either to war, persecution, or murder. Thus some of the most atrocious crimes and inhuman practices in all history have been perpetrated in its name. These are some of the blackest pages of all religious history. Whatever blessing it has conferred in private has thus been nullified in public.

Indian Religious Thought: Its Unique Feature

The only country where religious wars and persecutions have been comparatively negligible is India. This, let us note, is not because there is no deep religious feeling in India, as some critics would think, to whom love for one's religion is achieved only by hating other religions; neither is it due to any absence of variety in the religious outlook. History shows, and even today it is a fact, that both in point of spiritual fervour and the variety of its expression, India stands foremost in the world. The science of comparative religion tells us that the evolution of religious ideas has been, to a great extent, identical throughout the world. But whereas, outside India, this evolution stopped at the tribal stage and the monotheistic conception, Indian spiritual genius soared higher and yet higher and discovered the Unity behind all the gods. This is a great landmark in the history of religions in general, for it marks the stage at which religion turns out to be the messenger of *all peace* and *all blessing* to the *whole* of humanity, instead of being partially good and partially evil, as it has been in its earlier stages. For India herself, this discovery was momentous; for through this she has been spared from endless travails of religious persecution. This idea carries with it a certain universal outlook, being based on a highly rational philosophy, which later Vedic thought, especially the Upaniṣads, developed into its logical conclusion by discovering the Unity behind all existence.

Sectarianism: Its Evils and Their Remedy

The relationship between religion and religion has been anything but happy. Religions which seemed to have worked well in the places of their birth are found to be failures in their careers outside. Sentiments like love, brotherhood, and peace give place to those of hatred, scorn, and strife. In the name of religion, countries have been devastated, great cultures have been destroyed, and masses of men have been massacred—all with the 'pious' idea of extending the empire of the 'One God.' Little does the fanatical religionist realise that that is not the way to establish the 'Kingdom of Heaven' on earth. There is no doubt that the destruction of old cultures like those of Peru, Mexico, etc. really leaves such a 'Kingdom of Heaven' poorer in spiritual content. The sectarian spirit of religion is manifestly antagonistic to the very spirit of modern times which is scientific through and through, and which appeals not to sects and sections but to humanity at large. Consequently, the prestige of religion itself has suffered much in modern times. If religion is to be a living force in the modem world and contributes its share for the ushering in of a future civilisation of humanity, it requires to be restated and cast into rational and scientific moulds. The solidarity of mankind is the ideal for which science stands. The immense possibilities which the scientific advancement of the last three centuries holds in its bosom for the realisation of the great hopes of poets and philosophers of the past ages, require for their consummation a new spirit, a new outlook, and a new message, universal in its appeal, which will mediate between religion and religion on the one hand, and science and religion on the other. Where is this message, this quickening impulse, to come from? To this insistent question, the eager minds of thinking men, both in East and West, turn towards India and the invaluable treasure of her spiritual and philosophic thought, the Vedānta.

Vedānta: Its Contribution to Indian Thought and Life

This is no audacious claim. We have seen already how Indian thought took a great step towards religious harmony when it discovered the one God of whom all other gods are but manifestations. This is the great idea embodied in the famous verse of the *Ṛg-Veda* (I.164.46): *Ekaṁ sat viprā bahudhā vadanti*—'Truth is One; sages call It by various names,' such as Indra, Mitra, Varuna, etc. Not only this; no new thought has ever suffered suppression in India—be it in science, religion, or philosophy. Where all knowledge is held as sacred, how is it possible to suppress any aspect of it? The *Muṇḍaka Upaniṣad* (1.2.4) speaks of the *parā* and *aparā* kinds of knowledge: *Dve vidye veditavye iti ha sma yad brahmavido vadanti parā caiva aparā ca.* All sciences including even the holy Vedas are only *aparā* knowledge. Let us note, in this connection, that *aparā does not and cannot mean here anything inferior in kind. That knowledge which is derived from human experience in parts and aspects is aparā,* while that which is the fruit of a study of experience as a whole, of life in its totality, is *parā.* And all knowledge of the *aparā* kind is only an expression of the *parā vidyā,* Philosophy. This is the same as *Brahmavidyā,* Brahman standing for the totality of existence and experience.

This is the famous Vedānta philosophy, which is the very kernel and core of Indian culture, the fairest flower of its thought—the one which has given Indian culture its distinctive character and uniqueness. It is the spirit of Vedānta which has moulded all forms of Indian life and which has mediated between sect and sect, imparting to the rich variety of Indian thought its synthetic unity. This is the mesmerism of Indian thought which is slowly gripping the minds of many a serious thinker of the West. Those who speak of Hinduism as a bewildering mass of confused religious and social ideas and practices have not yet grasped Vedānta. To understand India and Hinduism requires, first of all, an intimate acquaintance with the spirit of Vedānta. It is in virtue of this Vedānta that we are enabled to speak of the fundamental unity of India. It will be in virtue of this same Vedānta that we will be enabled not merely to speak about, but achieve, the fundamental unity of humanity itself. And if religious harmony, social progress, and national solidarity are lacking in present-day India, the quickening impulse must come from this Vedānta alone, for it is the storehouse of all wisdom.

Indian Thought and Sri Ramakrishna

The oneness of all existence is the message which Vedānta teaches. The immediate implication of this message in life and thought is another great idea which seems to run counter to the very spirit of religious sectarianism, but which breathes truly the scientific spirit. As Swami Vivekananda expresses it *(Complete Works,* Vol. I, eleventh edition, p.15):

> Man is not travelling from error to truth, but from truth to truth, from lower truth to higher truth.

If truth is like a pyramid, the philosophical understanding of Unity is its apex. Viewed from this supreme height, no aspect of life or effort can appear as false or erroneous; for truth itself is the goal of all paths. It is chiefly in the application of this great idea to the pressing problems of modern life that the life and message of Sri Ramakrishna and Swami Vivekananda are supremely significant. Through them we find Indian thought, especially Vedānta, speaking to the modern world for composing its distractions and ushering in on earth an era of what the *Taittirīya Upaniṣad* (I. 6) calls *Satyātma prāṇārāmaṁ mana ānandam śānti samṛddham amṛtaṁ*—Truth, the solace of life and bliss of the mind, exuberant with the wealth of peace and immortality.

Universalism: Old and New

The idea of universal religion is not something new in the world. There have been two senses in which it has been understood. When a religion steps out of its local boundaries and starts on a career of conquest and annexation, adding new recruits, much in the same way as an empire extends by the accession of new territories, it styles itself a universal religion. Such a religion keeps before itself the alluring ideal of becoming a world-religion sooner or later and believes itself to be the only fit candidate to that estate. The outstanding examples of this type are Christianity, Islam, and Buddhism. The last one differs from the other two both in its methods and motives of such extension. Unlike Christianity and Islam, the spread of Buddhism has been singularly characterised by the spirit of peace and non-violence. This is undoubtedly due to the influence of Indian thought wherein Buddhism has its roots and from which it has sprung. Christianity and Islam, on the other hand, have followed a relentless course of destruction and persecution with the ostensible purpose of 'saving' the 'damned souls.'

Now this idea of universal religion is self-destructive. Not through conquest and the use of might is the way to universal religion. It breathes the spirit of the Old Testament, where, when a tribe conquers another tribe, it also destroys the latter's god and imposes its own god over it It is this same spirit which is working now when, in the place of tribes, we have alien cultures and religions. And when there are two claimants, both equally strong, zealous, and fanatical, this idea of universalism is seen to defeat itself. The fact is, there is a world of difference between the two assertions—'My god is the only true god and you must accept Him' and 'My god and your god are one and the same, differing at best only in name.' When a single religious belief, sincerely held, is disturbed and destroyed, the purpose of universal religion defeats itself.

The second idea of universal religion is seen expressed in the eclecticism of Akbar and some modern sects and movements.

Eclecticism is like a bouquet of choice flowers, and like a bouquet it has not any enlivening principle in it and is bound to wither away. A still greater criticism is that it has a tendency to become a closed system in itself, which defeats its very purpose. It says, 'There is so much sectarianism in the world; it must be destroyed; so let us start a new sect.' This sounds like the famous wartime sentiment—a war to end all wars. But just as not one among the older sects is entitled legitimately to claim universality, by the same inexorable logic, no new sect also can lay claim to that position.

Sri Ramakrishna's Ideal of Universal Religion

From the previous analysis we have come to this—that no religion can aspire individually to become universal. Unity in variety is the test of universality and not a dull and dead uniformity. In sharp contrast to the previous two conceptions stands Sri Ramakrishna's ideal of universal religion. The very first principle of this ideal is: 'If one religion is true, then by the very same logic all other religions are also true,' the verifiction of which is found in the fact that 'holiness, purity, and charity are not the exclusive possessions of any church in the world and that every system has produced men and women of the most exalted character' *(Complete Works of Swami Vivekananda,* Vol. I, eleventh edition, p.22). Hence this great teacher left every religion undisturbed; neither did he start a new religion. Yet his life was the greatest vindication of true religion. Nay, it was a veritable Parliament of Religions. He traversed the various paths of the Hindu faith and attained perfection in each. Not content with this, he lived the life of a pious Christian and a devout Muslim reaching the goal of the respective paths. As a result of all his experiments, he realised that all relgions are at bottom one, they all teach the same truth and lead to the same goal. In his own words *(Sayings of Sri Ramakrishna,* 1954, p.152):

> Many are the names of God, and infinite the forms that help us to know Him. By whatsoever name or form you desire to know Him, in that very form and under that very name will you see Him. Different creeds are but different paths to reach the one God; various and different are the ways that lead to the temple of Mother Kali at Kalighat (in Calcutta). Similarly various are the paths that take men to the house of the Lord, Every religion is nothing but one of these paths.

Again *(ibid.,* p.155):

> As a mother in nursing her sick children gives rice and curry to one, sago and arrowroot to another, and bread and butter to a third, so the lord has laid out different paths for different men suitable to their natures.

What follows? To quote Sri Ramakrishna again *(ibid.,* p.156)

> Every man should follow his own religion. A Christian should follow Christianity, a Mohammedan should follow Mohammedanism. For the Hindu the ancient path, the path of the Āryan *ṛṣis,* is the best. A truly religious man should think that other religions are also so many paths leading to the Truth. We should always maintain an attitude of respect towards other religions.

Thus, in Sri Ramakrishna's view, the existence of many sects and religions not merely does not stand as obstacles in the way, but actually helps the realisation, of universal religion. Let sects multiply until each individual will have a religion for himself. As no two individuals can be exactly similar in respect of taste, outlook, and capacity, so no one religion can perfectly satisfy the needs of all. Thus sects ought to multiply until they coincide with humanity itself. But *sectarianism* will disappear. And with its disappearance will be realised the ideal of a universal religion. In fact, it is already existing, no one has to create it, only one has to discover it for himself. But its symphony is marred and distorted by the sharp and dissonant note of sectarianism. And sectarianism will disappear only when the world understands this new ideal of religious harmony taught by Sri Ramakrishna, when men will learn to see truth in every sincere longing of the human heart, knowing it to be an urge towards light and truth.

Conclusion

This ideal of universal religion accords most with the modem spirit and temper. It enables religions to work for human welfare as co-operating parts instead of remaining as colliding units. And religious fellowship will bring in the sense of human kinship and brotherhood and enable the collective wisdom and effort of man to work towards the evolution of a complete human civilisation and a world culture.

The Message of Sri Ramakrishna*

The Uniqueness of Ramakrishna Temples

There is a uniqueness about a temple to Sri Ramakrishna. We are not lacking in temples in India. We have had plenty of them; we are having plenty of them even today. But a temple bearing Sri Ramakrishna's name has a special significance. I should like to expound this theme this evening. Take, for instance, this Raipur Ramakrishna temple. Behind it are years of work in the service of the people of this area—work not merely spiritual or cultural, but also humanitarian. Two years ago, in fact, the work on this temple was suspended while the time and energies of the monks and devotees were diverted to urgent drought relief work in this state. Thousands and thousands of poor people were fed, were employed in test relief works, and were rendered many other types of service, including house-building. Earlier, too, similar services

---

*Presidential Address on the occasion of the Sri Ramkrishna Temple Dedication Public Meeting, on 3 February 1976, at the Ramakrishna Mission Vivekananda Ashram, Raipur, Madhya Pradesh.

had been given to other suffering people. During the large-scale influx of migrants from East Pakistan in the sixties, much effective relief was rendered by the Ramakrishna Mission with this Raipur ashrama as the base of operations.

So a Ramakrishna Ashrama and a Ramakrishna Temple have a unique message to the people of our country today. And it is this: this ashrama and this temple are meant to be a source of inspiration to make our people love other human beings, and even animals, and serve humanity, without distinction of cast, creed, or sex. To see God in man is a great teaching of *sanātana-dharma* (eternal religion). Sri Ramakrishna puts it in a beautiful formula: 'Every *jīva* (soul) is Śiva (God). *Service of the jīva* is the worship of Siva. 'This is an extraordinary teaching. We have not practised it much in our country in the past, though it has been there all along in our holy books—in the *Upaniṣads,* in the *Gītā,* in the *Śrimad Bhāgavatam.* We did not apply it effectively till now. We constructed temples; but these did not have, and still mostly do not have, any vital relation with the rest of the world, with the rest of our life and work in the world. That was the wrong direction we took in the past. But now we shall correct it. We shall go to a temple, we shall worship the image there—it is a living presence of the Divine; it is what we call in our *bhakti-śāstras* (devotional scriptures) an *arcāvatāra*—God incarnated as an *arcā,* which means an image. But we shall also not neglect God in His incarnation as living human beings. He who is there in the temple as the *arcā,* is also present in your heart as the *antaryāmin,* inner self. So, when we see the image and worship it, our worship should not stop there; we should also, on coming out of the temple, worship God residing in all living beings. That makes our worship whole, and that makes our life and character integrated.

Integration of Life and Religion

But, unfortunately, till the coming of Sri Ramakrishna and Swami Vivekananda, we had been keeping this whole idea of temple worship away from the practical life of man. We thought we could have any type of life here—we could be selfish, we could be quarrelsome and litigious, we could be exploitative of other human beings, we could even cheat the state about our tax dues—and yet things would be all right with us if we only went to a temple, just worshipped an image there, and put some money in its offering box! But with the advent of Sri Ramakrishna, we are taught again, for the first time after a lapse of ages, the true meaning of temple worship. We are taught that this temple worship—this image worship in a temple—is mainly to inspire us to see God in ourselves and in every living being. We should derive that inspiration from our temples. This has been said in many passages in our great spiritual literature. But now, to help awaken you to this truth, you will find as the background of this temple project, the great record of human service by this ashrama, and by our other ashramas in various parts of India—service rendered through hospitals and schools, and special service to people in distress during famine, flood, earthquake, and other calamities. *All these constitute an integral part of this temple worship in a Ramakrishna Centre.* The two—service of the people outside in society and worship of God inside a temple—are not different things standing apart, but they form one integral whole of a comprehensive philosophy of life. It is, as taught by Sri Ramakrishna, to see God with eyes closed in meditation and see Him with eyes open in daily life. Go to the temple and worship Him; and then pour out what you gain therefrom in loving dedicated service outside.

Now, this is a teaching which our people had for ages entirely failed to grasp and live by. We need therefore to understand and implement this great teaching today. We do want more temples;

but we want temples which will give us strength, which will make us grow *spiritually,* which will make us manifest the Divine that is within us, and which will generate humanist impulses in our hearts and make them flow out into channels of love and service of beings. That is the purpose of these temples. And the sooner we convert all our temples, all our churches, all our mosques, into that kind of worship-places, the better for us, the better for all religions. Indeed it is for this purpose, ecially, that India produced Sri Ramakrishna in the modern age.

The Twin Message of Sri Ramakrishna

Most of us know about the various *sādhanās* (spiritual disciplines) that Sri Ramakrishna performed, crossing the barriers of individual Hindu sects, and even of our whole Hindu religion, and embracing also Christianity and Islam, and creating thereby a benign pattern for unity and harmony among the world's religions. That is one of the greatest contributions of *Sri Ramakrishna.* No doubt, the teaching of such a message of unity and harmony appears from the very beginnings of our culture, in our philosophy, in our *Vedas* of over five thousand years ago; but this is the first time the world has seen a person teaching and *living* the harmony of all religions.

Two great ideas especially shine in Sri Ramakrishna's life and message: one, the deepening of man's spiritual life, and the other, the harmony among the religions of the world. Swami Vivekananda, closing his famous lecture on 'My Master,' summed up Sri Ramakrishna's message in these words. *(The Complete Works of Swami Vivekananda,* Volume IV, p.187, eighth edition):

> This is the message of Sri Ramakrishna to the modern world: 'Do not care for doctrines, do not care for dogmas, or sects, or churches, or temples; they count for little compared with the essence of existence in each man,

> which is spirituality; and the more this is developed in a man, the more powerful is he for good. Earn that first, acquire that, and criticise no one, for all doctrines and creeds have some good in them. Show by your lives that religion does not mean words, or names, or sects, but that it means spiritual realisation. Only those can understand who have felt Only those who have attained to spirituality can communicate it to others, can be great teachers of mankind. They alone are the powers of light.'
>
> The more such men are produced in a country, the more that country will be raised; and that country where such men absolutely do not exist is simply doomed, nothing can save it. Therefore my Master's message to mankind is: 'Be spiritual and realise truth for yourself.' He would have you give up for the sake of your fellow—beings. He would have you cease talking about love for your brother, and set to work to prove your words. The time has come for renunciation, for realisation; and then you will see the harmony in all the religions of the world. You will know that there is no need of any quarrel. And then only will you be ready to help humanity. *To proclaim and make clear the fundamental unity underlying all religions was the mission of my Master.* Other teachers have taught special religions which bear their names; but this great teacher of the nineteenth century made no claim for himself. *He left every religion undisturbed because he had realised that, in reality, they are all part and parcel of the one eternal religion.'*

The Vision of Harmony Behind Indian Culture

So, we who seek to follow Sri Ramakrishna must realise the spiritual dimension of our personality, the Ātman that is the immortal and inalienable birthright of one and all; and show respect to every other path that men and women follow to realise this truth. Depth of spirituality and breadth of understanding and sympathy must go side by side. That is the only way to make religion a creative and dynamic force in human life. We in India need both these teachings today. To take up the subject of harmony first, and only briefly here, I would particularly stress that in this Bhārata-bhūmi-this vast land of Indiait has been an integral feature of our religious and state policy from ancient times, to respect one's neighbour's religion and enhance the spirit of harmony among different religions. Our great teachers, from the Vedic times to Sri Ramakrishna, have taught us this lesson. Our saints and devotees have also exemplified it in their lives; and our political states have further upheld the same great policy of harmony, the spirit of active toleration, of acceptance, in their dealings with the world of religions. The great Mauryan Emperor Asoka, in the third century BC, upheld this as an article of political faith, and in his vast empire from Afghanistan in the northwest to Kamataka in the south, we find his edicts on rocks and pillars proclaming far and wide this great idea: *samavāya eva sādhuḥ—samavāya,* that is, concord, alone is just and fair—in the world of religions. That is an article of faith still, so far as the people of India and the state policy of India are concerned. The famous British historian, author of a ten-volume book: *A Study of History,* the late Arnold Toynbee, has said that, unlike all Semitic religions and cultures the Hindu religion has been distinctive for its great idea of harmony between different religions and cultures. One goes to a church, another goes to a temple, and a third goes to a mosque; what does it matter? The same God is being worshipped everywhere, says Hinduism.

This capacity to sense the underlying unity behind the different religions is natural and easy to the Hindu from ancient times. Now you have to give it to the Christians; you have to give it to the Muslims. They have never had it. Their Semitic tradition has been exclusive, and not inclusive like that of the Hindus, as shown especially well by Toynbee in his book *A Historian's Approach to Religion.* But slowly they are coming to understand this truth today. We find now that a Catholic and a Protestant are able to come closer to each other in friendship. How? Is it not because of the Hindu influence, the Vedantic influence, which says that the truth behind all the different religions is the same? So, why hate each other? Why not come togehter in friendship? Instead of mutual confrontation, practise what they call today mutual dialogue; try to understand each other, and pool all the spiritual resources to serve man, instead of dissipating them in mutual suspicion and hatred, which only bring religion itself into contempt.

The Spiritual Basis of Harmony

This is the message of Vedānta to all the religions of the world. Therefore we, in India, must all the more cherish and protect this ideal and practice of harmony as our special heritage. In our country, we find our six hundred million people, belonging to various cults and various religions, living in harmony, living in peace—except the groups that come occasionally under the grip of narrow political frenzies in the garb of religion. Why? Because our sages have taught this lesson to receptive minds, our great and far-seeing political leaders of past and present also have taught us this lesson. And in order to help us retain this great ideal in the modern age, and diffuse it all over the world, Sri Ramakrishna came, experimented with the whole range of man's religions, lived a luminous life, and became, as it were, a parliament of religions in himself, years before the meeting of the World Parliament of Religions in Chicago in 1893.

Here is a beautiful and inspiring verse from the *Śrīmad Bhāgavatam.* Such verses are also found in the *Ṛg-Veda,* in the *Gītā,* and other books among our scriptures (I. ii. 11):

Vadanti tat tattva-vidaḥ
tattvaṃ yat jñānam advayam;
Brahmeti, paramātmeti,
Bhagavān iti, śābdyate

'That one and the same non-dual *Jñāna* (Pure Consciousness) is variously called by the knowers of Truth as Brahman (The Absolute, in philosophy), as Paramātman (the Supreme Self, in mysticism), and as *Bhagavān* (the Blessed Lord, in the religion of *bhakti* or devotion).'

This teaching, that the same God is approached by various people through various ways, must become dynamic again in India today, so that India may continue to grow in her spiritual strength as a centre of harmony, of understanding, and of cooperation among her diverse religions, and also between her believers and her non-believers. For a contrast, look at Ireland: just now how much fighting is going on between the Catholics and the Protestants, in spite of the fact that both belong to the same great Christian religion! Again, currently we find this type of fighting erupting in Lebanon also, between its two sections of the same Arab race and common Semitic traditions, namely, Muslims and Christians. We too had, till recent years, a lot of suffering here—our Hindus and our Muslims fighting with one another. We had of course a foreign government till lately, which did much to divide us and make us fight with and weaken one another. But today, we are realising that we can become true to ourselves only by assimilating the teaching of the broad and deep, positive and creative, elements of our philosophical and spiritual tradition, as exemplified for us in the life and message of Sri Ramakrishna.

This then is the first part of the twofold message of Sri Ramakrishna.

What is True Religion?

The second part of that message of Sri Ramakrishna relates to what is spiritual life, what is true religion. For centuries, we had thought that going to temples, to churches, or to other holy places, or taking baths in holy rivers, or performing some rituals, constituted spiritual life. But Sri Ramakrishna taught us that these were not the essentials of religion: they were only acts of piety, means for the culture of true religion-means which certainly help some in the cultivating of true religion, but which, if made ends in themselves, may also injure true religion. This is ritualism, in the harmful sense. For religion means spiritual growth; it is that which makes you grow spiritually; it is *ādhyātmika vikāsa* (spititual expansion). Have your acts of piety achieved for you that spiritual growth? If they have, or are beginning to do so, then they are fine; they are welcome. But if they have not, then that piety has become reduced to a static religiosity, a piety-fringed worldliness. Our history shows what a fund of piety we always had; how many temples, how much of worship, have been there; and yet for centuries now, we have failed to develop national health and strength, character and public spirit, and the elevation of our millions to the levels of human dignity and equality. Static piety, increasingly noisy and showy, on the one side, and widespread human exploitation and degradation on the other, have made for poverty and suffering and continual foreign invasions and oppressions. These brought our country down and down, century after century. If true religion were there, how could these things have happened? So, we need to understand what is true religion, and then live it.

What is true religion? *The essence of religion is spirituality,* inner growth or realisation, says Sri Ramakrishna. Achieve spiritual growth; that is the message of true religion. Merely being pious won't be enough. Piety is easy; you can get external piety cheaply.

But what is needed is your inner growth. Sūrdās, Mīrābāi, Guru Nānak, Tulsidās, all these and other saints have taught us to be spiritual, to manifest the Divine that is within man. *To grow spiritually is the real purpose of religion: it is the science of religion.* Go to the temple, spend even five minutes there, and, when you come out from there, you should feel that you are one step nearer to God, one step nearer to your own infinite Self, that you have manifested the Divine in yourself at least a little. That is the criterion of spiritual growth. Every act of religion, every act of piety—in fact every action in life—must be directed to make you grow spiritually. That is the true test of religion. If this growth is not there, all this going about in piety becomes absolutely meaningless.

What does the Hindu religion teach? It teaches, first, that God is present in every human being, in all beings: *aham ātmā Guḍākeśa sarvabhūtāśaya-sthitah*—'I am present in the hearts of all beings, O Arjuna,' says Śrī Kṛṣṇa in the *Gītā* (X.20). Secondly, if God is in the hearts of all, should we not manifest Him in our life, conduct, and action? Should we not become aware of Him, and also see His presence in every other human being? Let me try to *realise* God who is always within me—that is the mood in which to face the first challenge of the Hindu religion. Then, let me try to see the same God in all other beings, and thus love other people, serve other people, and not exploit them or fight with them, or be jealous of them—this is the mood in which to face the second challenge. With our slave type of minds, all these centuries, we have not responded to these two challenges. But, today, forsaking that static way, and freeing our minds, we must see that mutual love and concern, spirit of service and dedication, great efficiency and strong character, come out of our religion. Character is the test, the fruit, of true religion; it alone is the true measure of the spiritual growth of man. Sri Ramakrishna emphasises this again and again.

Static Piety versus Dynamic Spirituality

Sri Ramakrishna never liked showy religion; and much of religion today is showy and also noisy. That is why Swami Vivekananda wrote in a letter *(The Complete Works,* Vol. VII (1958), p.489):

> Religions of the world have become lifeless mockeries. What the world wants is character. The world is in need for those whose life is one burning love, selfless. That love will make every word tell like thunderbolt.

The more character you have, the more religion you have. Showy religion is no religion at all. Sri Ramakrishna warns us against such a religion. We read this saying of his in the *Gospel of Sri Ramakrishna:*

> Beware of the man who wears *tulasi* leaves in his ears!

Some people pose as being very pious by wearing holy *tulasi* leaves in their ears, and the next moment they go out and cheat somebody, or do other evil acts; both these can go, and have gone, together in India. But the truly spiritual man will never do such things. Show that you are spiritual by your love, by your human concern, by your spirit of service. That is a central teaching of Sri Ramakrishna; and it is also a central teaching of all our *śāstras,* or books of the science of religion. They exhort us to live religion and thus manifest the Divine that is within. Swami Vivekananda therefore defines religion thus:

> Religion is the manifestation of the Divinity already in man.

When that Divinity manifests even a little, concern for other individuals will come, a spirit of service will come, efficiency will come. And exploitation, litigiousness, weakness, fear, and inefficiency—these things will disappear. The Hindus have been, and still are, among the most litigious people in the world. We are very fond of quarrelling, fighting, and going to the courts—formerly even up to the British Privy Council, but now to our own Supreme Court—for flimsy causes. Why? Because we have had only piety-fringed worldliness, or in other words, religiosity only, but very little true religion. That piety of ours did not reveal any spiritual growth. Now that Hindu must change and a new Hindu must emerge, who will sense the presence of God in himself or herself and in every other human being, and will make his or her love of God flow into the channels of love and service of man.

Temples are meant to inspire you with this vision. *What you take in by worship and contemplation, that you must pour out in love and service.* When that vision, and conduct in the light of that vision, are not there, then temples and worship and rituals, which in our *Sanatana Dharma* are aesthetically and spiritually beautiful, become increasṭingly reduced to *static pietistic* forms, bereft of all spiritual meaning and fruits. This is the glowing theme of a passage in the *Śrīmad Bhāgavatam,* which our people will do well to understand and assimilate today, so that our temples, and all other forms of worship, may become fruitful in terms of character and *dynamic spirituality* for which they are meant. Contrasting static piety with dynamic spirituality, God in his incarnation as Kapila, addressing His mother Devahūti, says *(Śrīmad Bhāgavatam,* III. xxix. 21-6):

Ahaṁ sarveṣu bhūteṣu
Bhūtātma-vasthitah sodā;
Tam avanjñāya māin martyaḥ
Kurute'rcā viḍaṃbanam.

Yo māṃ sarveṣu bhūteṣu
santamātmānam iśvaram;
hitvāracāṁ bhajate mauḍhyāt
bhasmanyeva juhoti saḥ

Dviṣatah parā-kāye mām
mānino bhinna-darśinaḥ;
Bhūteṣu baddha-vairasya
na manaḥ-śāntiṁ ṛcchati.

Aham uccavacaiḥ dravyaiḥ
Kriyayo't pannyānaghe;
Naiva tuṣye' rcito-'rcāyām
bhūta-grāmā-vamāninaḥ.

Arcādau arcayet tāvat
īśvartaṁ māṁ sva-karmā-kṛt;
Yāvat na veda sva-hṛdi
Sarvā-bhūteṣvavasthitam.

Ātmanāsca parasyāpi
yaḥ karotyantarodaram;
Tasya bhinna-dṛśo mṛtyuḥ
vidadhe bhayam ulbaṇam

'I am present always, in every being, as the very Self of all; but mortal man, by insulting Me in man, makes his worship of Me in images a mere farce.'

'He who worships Me in images, foolishly ignoring My presence in all beings as their Self and Lord, his worship is in vain, like pouring oblations of ghee (clarified butter) in ashes (instead of in the fire).'

'That man can never attain peace of mind who, out of pride and a (wrong) sense of separateness, and practising inveterate enmity to other beings, really practises enmity towards Me who exists in other bodies.'

'O sinless one, I am not at all pleased with the worship, accompanied (though it be) with big and small offerings and rituals, offered to Me, in images, by him who insults the dignity of all beings.'

'Let worship be offered to Me, the Lord, in images, accompanied with meticulous discharge of one's duties (to society), till one leams to see Me in one's own heart.'

'He who makes the slightest difference between himself and others—he who thus dwells on this (false) sense of separateness—spiritual death shall be his terrible reward.'

The Philosophy of Service

The verse, coming immediately after the above six, can be considered as the scriptural inspiration behind Swami Vivekananda's great message of 'Renunciation and Service' and he quite likely had it in mind when he uttered these words in 1897 on *The Future of India (The Complete Works,* Vol. Ill (1960). pp. 300-1):

> So give up being a slave! For the next fifty years, this alone shall be our keynote-this, our great Mother India. Let all other vain gods disappear for the time from our minds. This is the only god that is awake, our own race, everywhere his hands, everywhere his feet, everywhere his ears, he covers everything. . . . What vain gods shall we go after and yet cannot worship the god that we see all around us, the *Virāt? When we have worshipped this, we shall be able to worship all other gods. Before we can crawl half a mile, we want to cross the ocean, like Hanuman! It cannot be. Everyone going to be a yogi, everyone going to meditate! It cannot be.* The whole day mixing with the world, with *Karmā Kānda,* and in the evening sitting down and blowing through your nose! Is it so easy? Should *ṛṣis* come flying through the air, because you have blown three times through the nose? Is it a joke? It is all nonsense. What is needed is *Citta-suddhi,* purification of the heart. And how does that come?

> The first of all worship is the worship of the *Virāt . . . of* those all around us. Worship it. *Worship is the exact equivalent of the Sanskrit word, and no other English word will do.* These are all our gods-men and animals, and the first gods we have to worship are our countrymen. These we have to worship, instead of being jealous of each other and fighting each other. It is the most terrible *karmā* for which we are suffering, and yet it does not open our eyes!

Now listen to that next verse of the *Śrīmad Bhāgavatam:*

> *Atha mām sarveṣu bhūteṣu*
> *bhūtātmānaṁ kṛtālayam;*
> *Arhayet dānamānābhyām*
> *maitryā abhinnena cakṣuṣā*

'Therefore, worship Me, who am the Self of all beings and who have already built a temple (for Myself in them), by giving gifts and showing respect (removing the felt privations of all beings and protecting their dignity and self-respect while so doing); (and do all this) in a spirit of friendliness and attitude of non-separateness.'

The whole of the above teaching of Swami Vivekananda may be said to be a commentary on this sloka.

Worship Me in all beings, says the Lord. But how? asks the devotee. The Lord replies: *dānamānābhyām*—by *dāna* and *māna. Māna* means respect. Show respect to the other individual. He may be poor; he may be ignorant; he may be of a lower social or economic status; but show respect to him, for 'I am present in him', says the Lord. *Dāna* means giving, or gift. If the other is hungry and is in want, provide him with food and employment. If he is ignorant, provide him with education. If he is down with frustration, give him peace and consolation; and, removing the felt needs of humanity and all beings thus, 'worship Me'—*mām arhayet.*

What should be my attitude? *Maitryā*—with intense friendliness. What a beautiful idea! But the next and last phrase is still more wonderful: *abhinnena cakṣuṣā* —with the eye (or vision) of non-separateness. We are essentially one. You may be rich; the other person may be poor; you may be highly educated while the other may be ignorant. Still, do not see merely these variable externals, but focus your attention on the invariable and inalienable truth within all beings, namely, the Lord; for 'I, the one Lord, am present in all as their very Self.' This is the meaning of *abhinnena cakṣuṣā*—looking upon all with the same eye of equality. This *abhinna-cakṣu, or abhinna-dṛṣṭi,* is highly praised in the Vedānta; and its opposite, *bhinna dṛṣṭi,* is always condemned as unethical and harmful, because it is untrue. But, unfortunately, what we have had all these centuries, in our Indian society, was the devil's play of *bhinna dṛṣṭi*—you are separate; I am separate; I get a hundred rupees more salary than you; I am a Brahmin and you are a Harijan, and so on *ad infinitum.*

But today, with the advent of Sri Ramakrishna and Swami Vivekananda, we are re-taught this great message of our Vedānta philosophy, of equality and human dignity. This is what India needs; it is also what the world needs—this teaching of how to see the same Ātman in every being. When we implement this great philosophy, then alone will we be able to build a united integrated nation in our country-strong and creative, progressive and human. Then and then alone will the full development of India become an accomplished fact.

So, as I said in the beginning, behind this Ashrama and Temple is this great philosophy of healthy inter-human relationships-service in place of exploitation, worship in place of even service. Through service of God in man, we can realise God that is ever within us, and stimulate the same creative process in the recipient of our service also. Through this process of service itself, the *kācā āmi,* or 'unripe I,' will become the *pākā. āmi,* or 'ripe I,' says Sri Ramakrishna. He gives the description of the 'unripe I' as being that which says: I am a Hindu or I am a Muslim; I am a man of wealth, a man of power, a man of position. Transform this *kācā* 'I' into the *pākā* 'I,' exhorts Sri Ramakrishna. The *pākā* 'I' says: I am the servant of all; I am the friend of all; I am a child of God, a devotee of God. Till now, though we have had plenty of piety, our T has been of the 'unripe' variety; therefore we could not do much good, and did much harm instead. Sri Ramakrishna now exhorts us to convert this 'unripe I' into the 'ripe I.' That is the meaning of being spiritual—the manifestation of a little of the inherent divine dimension of man. That is spiritual growth, spiritual expansion—*ātma vikāsa;* the spiritual growth of individuality *(vyaktitva)* into personality *(vikāsita-vyaktitva).* It is only with the onset of this unique type of growth that men and women become capable of working with other men and women, in a cooperative spirit-without fighting and quarrelling with each other and pulling down, not only each other, but also the institutions concerned and the nation.

Sri Ramakrishna gives another illustration to illumine this subject of man's spiritual growth:

> 'Live in the world: there is no harm in that; but don't allow the world to live in you. A boat will be on the water; that is the right place for the boat; but the water should not be in the boat. If water enters a boat, it will either sink or gradually decay and become unfit for the purpose for which it is meant. Similarly, when the world—that is, worldliness-enters into a man, he becomes stagnant.'

Saṁsāra (relative existence), in its evil sense, means this stagnation. Living in *samsara,* or in the world, is not the same thing as being a *saṁsāri or a worldly individual. We are all in saṁsāra.* Śrī Kṛṣṇa and Sri Ramakrishna were also in *saṁsāra.* The teaching is not against *saṁsāra* or the world, but against the *saṁsāric* attitude, against worldliness. We Hindus really have had too much *saṁsāra* within us. That was why we quarrelled and fought, lost our political freedom, and made our society a den of exploitation, corruption, human distortions of the worst type. And now, with the inspiration of these great teachers, a new India is emerging, with creative ideas and progressive humanistic attitudes increasingly influencing our thought, action, and behaviour. Swami Vivekananda wanted us to develop *character,* 'deep as the ocean and wide as the sky'; he wanted us to combine, in our character, the intensity of the fanatic and the extensity of the materialist. *(The Complete Works,* Vol. V (1959), p.227; Vol. III, p.174)

This is a far-reaching message of Sri Ramakrishna and of the institutions bearing his name.

Life is Itself Religion

These Ramakrishna institutions, again, are not like the usual type of religious organisations where there is a gulf between life and religion. Sri Ramakrishna came to bridge that gulf and to teach us that *life is itself religion.* He exhorts us to see life in its unity and wholeness. This is the *vyavasāyātmika buddhih* (one-pointed intelligence) spoken of in the *Bhagavad Gītā* (11.41), where there is a unity of vision and unity of purpose and endeavour, external and internal. This is the basis of all character development. Young people today want to see character coming out of religion; if they do not see this, they are not going to be inspired by religion or religious people. If you profess religion and show no character, they will respect neither religion nor you; and they will grow cynical as a result. But when you show character along with your religious belief, they respect it. This is true here; it is also true abroad—in America, in Europe, everywhere. So, this is the challenge before all religion: can it and does it show character? Just as the food that you take in must show its effect in the strength of your body, so also the religion that you profess and live by must show its effect in your inner riches, in your character, in your spirit of service, in your day-to-day life.

The Spiritual Fascination of Sri Ramakrishna

So, this is the message, to spread which Sri Ramakrishna and Swami Vivekananda came. And in this context, I must mention also a third personality, namely, Sri Ramakrishna's life companion, Sri Sarada Devi, the Holy Mother, who was simple and unassuming and yet an embodiment of purity, love, and compassion. These three spiritual giants are at the back of this Ramakrishna Movement, the mission of which is to spiritually illumine and energise not only India, but also the rest of the world. There is a remarkable spiritual and human fascination about Sri Ramakrishna. I have seen how people all over India, and also abroad, listen with the greatest interest and reverence to talks about him. Wherever the name of Sri Ramakrishna is uttered, that place becomes holy and elevating. These experiences help me to understand the truth of what the *Śrīmad Bhāgavatam* has said about Śrī Kṛṣṇa. Here are two beautiful verses from that great book *(Śrīmad Bhāgavatam* I. i. 19; X.31.9):

Vayam tu na vitr]pyamah
uttama-śloka-vikrame;
Yat sṛṇvatāṁ rasajñānām
svādu svādu pade pade

'We are not satiated listening to words relating to the heroic deeds of the supremely famous (Śrī Kṛṣṇa). The more we listen, the more becomes the appetite in us to hear more and more of the same.'

Tava kathāmṛtaṁ tapta jīvanam
kavibiriditaim kalmaṣapaham;
Sravaṇa-maṇgalaṁ śrīmadatam
bhuvi gṛṇanti te bhūridā janāḥ

'Your (i.e., Śrī Kṛṣṇa's) words are a divine elixir, bringing life to scorched souls, highly praised by poet-saints, auspicious to listen to, and productive of expanding *Sri* (wealth and welfare). Those who spread them wide on earth are the most generous of persons.'

What a beautiful sentiment! The words of, and words relating to, Śrī Kṛṣṇa are nectar to parched souls, says the text. The same can be said of Sri Ramakrishna. The story of his life is nectar; his words are nectar. Thousands and thousands of people, in all parts of the world, read at least a few pages daily from that great book, *Sri Ramakrishna Kathamṛta— The Gospel of Sri Ramakrishna.*

I cannot do anything better, in closing, than to recall a simple beautiful verse on Sri Ramakrishna composed by Swami Vivekananda. The time and occasion, when this verse first came from his lips, are reminiscent of the event we are now celebrating. Yesterday, we installed an image of Sri Ramakrishna in the temple here. There was a somewhat similar occasion about a year after Swami Vivekananda's return in 1897 from the West. A householder devotee of Sri Ramakrishna, Mrs Navagopal Ghosh, had constructed a small shrine in her new house in Howrah. She had approached Swamiji and asked him: 'Naren, you please come and establish Sri Ramakrishna's picture in my shrine.' Swamiji agreed. He took his bath in the Ganga and reached the house at the appointed time. He entered the shrine; it was a small room but it had marble flooring. He reverentially placed the picture of Sri Ramakrishna on the altar and prayed: 'Be Thou present in this home, and bless this family.' His installation worship was very simple and informal, for, to him, Sri Ramakrishna was a living presence. Then, while saluting the Master at the close of the worship, this *sloka* (or verse) burst forth from his mouth—a verse which is now recited during the *arati* (morning and evening service) in all our centres in East and West:

Sthāpakāya ca dharmasya
sarva-dharma-svarūpiṇe;
Avatārā variṣṭhāya
Rāmakrishnāya te namaḥ

'Salutation to Thee, Sri Ramakrishna, who came (into the world) to establish *dharma* (religion), the embodiment of all the *dharmas* (of the world), and the best of the divine incarnations.'

Conclusion

This verse portrays the real character of Sri Ramakrishna as a spiritual teacher, and conveys the infinite scope of his mission in the world. He came to establish *dharma*—religion or spirituality. But not any new religion bearing his own name, not a Ramakrishna religion or sect: no, nothing of the sort, but he is *sarvadharma-svarūpin*—'the embodiment of all religions.' Through him each and all of the world's religions will thrive as true spiritual forces; a Christian will become a better Christian, a Muslim a better Muslim, a Hindu a better Hindu, through the influence of his all-embracing spirituality. And therefore, *avatāra-variṣṭhāya*—'to the best of divine incarnations,' *Rāmakṛsnāya te namaḥ*—'to that Ramakrishna be our salutations.'

Sarada Devi, The Holy Mother*

Introduction

In recent years, the name of Sarada Devi, the Holy Mother, is becoming increasingly known among the people, and her birth centenary celebrations have hastened the process of lifting the veil of obscurity behind which she had remained hidden so far. This knowledge has roused an amazing degree of spiritual enthusiasm in men and women, and an eagerness to know more about this great woman of our age who, as the disciple and helpmate of *Bhagāvān* Sri Ramakrishna, played the roles of wife and nun and mother and *guru* in one.

Sarada Devi: The Mesmerism of Her Personality

What is the source of the mesmerism of this name and personṭality? Even a slight acquaintance with her life will make us realise that

---

*Lecture delivered at the Ramakrishna Mission Society, Rangoon, Burma, at a public meeting held on 4 December 1954, on the occasion of the Holy Mother's Birth Centenary Celebrations.

this mesmerism does not proceed from any aspects of her personality which the modern world recognises as significant in women. To all outward appearances, the Holy Mother was just ordinary, or even less than ordinary. Rustic in simplicity, almost unlettered, and shy and modest, she was far removed from the educated, self-conscious, active type of modern women. And yet, her life finds powerful responsive echoes from the hearts of all men and women, rustic and modern alike. It is evident that she has captured, in her life and being, the fundamental value which lies at the back of the womanliness of woman and which transcends all distinctions based on mere sex and the attractions thereof. This fact alone explains her universal appeal, representing, as she does, not a mere national or racial type, but the fulfilment of woman as woman, the realisation, in flesh and blood, of the *Eternal Feminine.*

Her Life-Career: A Brief Sketch

No greatness has sprung up and got reared and even flowered in greater obscurity and silence than that of Sarada Devi. She was born in the obscure village of Jayrambati in West-Bengal, India, on 22 December 1853. Her advent coincided with the brightening of the family fortunes of her poor but pious parents, who enfolded her in tender love and care. Even as a child, she was active and hard-working, and helped her mother in her household chores. She was hardly six when she was betrothed to Sri Ramakrishna who was then twenty-three and who was passing through the stormy period of his spiritual *sādhanās* and realisations. Through this betrothal, little Sarada entered into the current of the life of one who, in his God-intoxication, passed most of his life in divine ecstasies and visions, and the rest in soul-stirring conversations with earnest souls, conveying a message of radiant spirituality to the modem world.

It was a strange betrothal; for it remained unconsummated in the physical plane, but found its spiritual consummation in a union of souls on the occasion of the *Soḍaśī-pūjā* in 1872. This was the culminating act of Sri Ramakrishna's spiritual *sādhanās* when he worshipped the Divine Mother of the universe in the person of his wife, at the end of which the worshipped and the worshipper entered into deep *samādhi* and realised their spiritual identity. Thenceforth they became as one soul functioning in two bodies, and Sarada Devi assumed her equal role in the fulfilment of the mission of Sri Ramakrishna.

Sarada Devi: Her Spiritual Eminence

Sri Ramakrishna himself recognised the spiritual eminence of Sri Sarada Devi. Unlike the general run of spiritual aspirants who forsake all worldly connections on entering the religious life, for which there is the sanction of religious law and custom behind them, Sri Ramakrishna welcomed Sarada Devi to his side when she, coming of age, came to claim her rights over him. It is a deeply moving episode in their lives, which helps to reveal the stuff of both. Sri Ramakrishna was in Dakshineswar, passing through storms of spiritual moods and experiences; except on the two occasions of his brief visits to his native village, he had not met his wedded wife these twelve long years and seemed apparently to have forgotten her.

Sarada Devi, now about eighteen, entered his room late at night after an arduous journey from her native village in the company of her father. She had her fears in her heart proceeding from the gossip she had heard in her village about the deranged condition of her husband's mind, and her own knowledge of his utter indifference to worldly concerns. But Sri Ramakrishna, though a bit surprised at her sudden arrival, welcomed her very cordially, and accommodated her in his own room for facility of medical attention, and arranged for the medical care of her body which had been ravaged by illness and fatigue during the long trek. She found in him the same loving divine husband whom she had known during his previous visits to the village. When she had settled down, Sri Ramakrishna one day addressed her thus:

> 'As for me, the Divine Mother has shown me that She resides in every woman, and so I have learned to look upon every woman as Mother. That is the one ideal I can have about you; but if you wish to drag me into the world, as I have been married to you, I am at your service.'

To this challenging question of her divine husband, Sarada Devi gave a straightforward answer:

> 'Why should I desire to drag your mind down to the worldly plane? I have come only to help you in your chosen path. I desire only to live with you and serve you and to learn of you.'

This reply of his pure and spotless wife pleased Sri Ramakrishna immensely and he experienced a great accession of spiritual strength. His mission, in the world, of calling humanity back to an awareness of its inborn divine nature is not to be a lonely struggle; he recognised in Sarada Devi a companion in his noble mission; within a year of her arrival, he verified the truth of this exalted view of his wife through the *Soḍaśī-pūjū* experience referred to above.

From now on till the end of his life, for full fourteen years, Sarada Devi served the person of Sri Ramakrishna and the large number of disciples and devotees visiting him, with a rare devotion and self-effacement unrivalled in human history. It was also the period of her intense spiritual education under her divine husband. She has referred to this period as a continuous experience of intense bliss. Months together they lived in the same room and slept in the same bed, with no trace of carnal thought in the mind of either. Their minds constantly soared in the region of divine awareness and bliss; each stood transfigured to the other; and both became instruments for the working out of the divine will. The immense store of spiritual energy-divine *sakti*—which was generated by the *sādhanās* of Sri Ramakrishna and Sarada Devi contains the promise of the spiritual evolution of modern humanity which keenly feels its own tragic aspiritual poverty in the midst of abundant material wealth.

Her Role as Spiritual Teacher

Sri Ramakrishna passed away in 1886. Sarada Devi was thirty-three at the time. Having lived in a non-physical plane of relationship with her husband, she did not experience the feeling of widowhood at his death. To her he continued to be a living reality to the end of her days. And for the next thirty-four years, she lived a life, complex in its roles and varied in its riches, and withal silent and sweet, that gained for her the endearing title of *'Sri Ma,'* 'the Holy Mother,' by which she is known ever since.

The Holy Mother was called upon to be the spiritual guide of the monks of the Ramakrishna Order, constituted initially of Sri Ramakrishna's direct disciples under the leadership of Swami Vivekananda and to be the *guru* of an ever-increasing circle of spiritually hungry men and women. Her spiritual eminence and the divine power of her personality enabled her to fulfil this mighty role with ease and naturalness. But it was in the role of a household woman, in the midst of her own family circle consisting of her worldly—minded brothers, sisters-in-law, and their children, that the Holy Mother manifested a unique facet of her character and personality. It is this aspect of her personality that provides a shining example of practical spirituality capable of inspiring all men and women. The nun shone through the householder, and both through the heart of an all-loving mother. Far from shunning a distracting world, she embraced it and enfolded it in her love. And in the midst of a thousand distractions, she preserved the naturalness and peace of her personality.

The Manifestation of Divine Motherhood in Sarada Devi

Verification is the proof of a theory or a claim. The test of life alone proves the genuineness of a moral virtue or a spiritual value; virtues are tested more in ill-fortune than in good fortune. To maintain poise and grace in good weather is easy enough; but it is only bad weather that tests their genuineness. The calmness, poise, and grace, and the spirit of unobstructed love and self-effacing service, which Sarada Devi expressed in her day-to-day life in the context of a highly distracting environment of sheer worldliness, proclaims the supremely uplifting power of godliness and spirituality. The possession of this power by a man or a woman makes him or her pure and holy. The expression of this power in life is love. Sarada Devi was the very personification of this purity, holiness, and love which is the meaning of the ideal of motherhood at its highest and best. This power lies imbedded in the heart of every woman. An ordinary woman captures in her life only a fraction of this ideal by which she shines in her loving kindness and holiness. A merely biological function becomes elevated through the infilling of a spiritual value. But this spiritual value shone in its fullness, even outside the biological context, in the personality of the Holy Mother, demonstrating thereby the ideal in its pure form. Out of the abundance of her heart Sarada Devi gave of her love to one and all without any distinction and, by so doing, justified the endearing epithet of 'the Holy Mother.'

Herself out of the ordinary in all basic values of character and personality, but hiding these under the mantle of the simple and the ordinary in social and physical make-up, the Holy Mother eludes the grasp of ordinary minds, but reveals her true form to all seekers of basic values. Did not Sri Ramakrishna say of her: 'She is Sarasvati, the goddesss of Wisdom, come to give spiritual knowledge to humanity.' And had she not also said of herself: 'Sri Ramakrishna has left me to manifest the ideal of divine Motherhood.'

In her life and in her teachings she has left a balm for suffering humanity in search of light and peace. Her love knew no distinctions of sex, creed, or race. It enfolded and uplifted the Muslim labourer Amjad as much as the *sannyasin* Saradananda, the gifted Sister Nivedita as much as the simple 'mother of Annapurna.' The Holy Mother's death-bed advice to the latter is typical of her universal personality and depth of insight. To the 'mother of Annapurna,' sorrowing at the thought of Holy Mother's imminent passing away, she said these words of uplifting consolation and strength:

> 'If you want peace of mind, do not look for faults in others. Rather look out to discover your own weaknesses. Leam to make the whole world your own. No one here is an alien or a stranger, my child. The whole world is your own.'

Conclusion

Let me conclude this tribute with the beautiful Sanskrit verse composed by Swami Abhedananda, a direct disciple of Sri Ramakrishna, in praise of the Holy Mother's pure nobility:

Pavitraṁ caritaṁ yasyāḥ pavitram jīvanaṁ tathā;
Pavitratā-svarūpinyai tasyai devyai namo namaḥ

'Whose character is all pure and whose life is similarly pure; who is the embodiment of purity divine; that shining goddess I salute again and again.'

Sarada Devi: The Crowning Glory of Indian Womanhood*

Introduction

In the course of her five-thousand-year-old history, India has experimented with human life from various angles and at various levels, and has discovered many truths about human life and human destiny, some of which she also later proved and verified, through the lives of some of the greatest, as well as some of the commonest, among her people, down to our own times.

Her great philosophy, the Vedānta, discovered ages ago that the object of human life is not pleasure and organic satisfactions, much less pain, but knowledge, *jñānam,* through a detached scrutiny of both. Pleasure and pain, and all experience, provide the opportunity to man to awaken himself or herself to the world of knowledge, both secular and spiritual, for which nature has provided

*Contributed to the book: *Beacon Light of Eternity,* published by The Ramakrishna Centre of South Africa, Natal, in February 1979, on the occasion of the 143rd birthday of Sri Ramakrishna.

him or her with the necessary organic capacities. Young immature cultures, like immature minds, fail to grasp this vital truth and proceed to build the edifice of their culture and character on the shaky basis of the sole pursuit of organic satisfactions; and all such edifices decay and fall, unable to stand the pressures from without and within. But Indian culture has endured these thousands of years, surviving dark periods of challenges from without and within, because of its stable foundations, its mature *Weltanschauung,* provided by her great sages and seers.

Man's Innate Divinity

Among the truths that *Weltanschauung* has placed before India and the rest of humanity, the most significant is the shining truth of the innate divinity and purity of man. Men and women, nay, in fact, all beings, are divine in their essential nature. And Vedānta views social and cultural evolution as the process of the unfoldment of this great value in the context of inter-human relationships, from which alone are derived the cherished human values of freedom, equality, and the dignity of personality. Vedānta presents this as the measuring rod of cultural and social progress. Swami Vivekananda, accordingly, presents religion in precise scientific language as: 'the manifestation of the divinity already in man.'

Equality of Man and Woman

Among the various types of human inter-actions for the manifestation of this innate human divinity, that between man and woman is most important. Unlike in the Semitic tradition, where woman is presented as produced from a *dispensable* rib of man, the *Upaniṣads* present man and woman as the equal halves of a divine unity, each the complement of, and incomplete without, the other *(Bṛhadāraṇyaka Upaniṣad,* 1.4.3):

> *Sa imam eva ātmānam dvedhā apātayat: tataḥ patiśca patnī ca abhavatam. Tasmāt idam ardhabrgalam iva sav iti*
>
> 'He (the divine Person) divided Himself into two halves: thus was the origin of husband and wife. Therefore, this (the body of man) is only like the one half of a split pea.'

The *Upaniṣads* also discovered that the real nature of man and woman as the Ātman, as the sexless Self, is ever pure, perfect, and free. Associated with body and mind, it becomes conditioned as organic individuality with its sex and other differentiations. This is *man* or *woman,* the *known,* the subject of sociology and other empirical sciences, behind which is man or woman, the *unknown,* the subject of the science of spirituality.

Man the known is limited, imperfect, and helpless; and he or she strives to become whole, through associations and relationships with individuals and groups and objects, outside of himself or herself. The satisfactions proceeding from such associations range from the purely animal and organic to the deeply spiritual, passing through the intermediate stages of the primitive, the cultured, and the refined. It is discipline and restraint, followed by creative onward movement, that characterises progress from one stage to the other. And all such discipline and restraint involves checking of the lower self, man the known, and progressive manifestation of the higher self, *man the unknown,* the Ātman, the transcendent sexless Self.

Women in Indian Culture

This spiritual vision of man, realised by the sages of the Upaniṣads, became the rock foundation for the later development of the vast and varied Indian cultural edifice. It had a profound impact on India's theories of marriage and morals, inter-personal and inter-religious relationships, and attitude to God and the world. Thanks to it, India has always upheld, *in theory,* the spiritual equality of man and man, and man and woman. But in *actual social practice,* India has often failed to live up to this great vision. And the fullest social impletmentation of this great vision, on a nation-wide scale, constitutes the meaning and significance of the modern period of Indian history, through the lived experiences and teachings and examples of the greatest of her modern teachers, namely, Sri Ramakrishna, Holy Mother Sarada Devi, and Swami Vivekananda.

Swami Vivekananda was the first Indian leader and teacher to point out the great harm done to the Indian nation and its culture by the neglect and suppression of women and the common people. And since his time, she has, through powerful socio-political movements, deliberately set about the great task of regaining the social balance, by giving back to her women and the common people their individual freedom and worth and dignity, to enable them to grow to their full stature and to take their equal place in home and society.

In this connection, it is worthy of note that, unlike several other highly developed societies of the modern period, India has not experienced a violent political revolution or a feminist movement. It is only when a worldview goes rigidly counter to the claims of women for a status of dignity and honour as *persons,* and men uphold such a limited worldview as against the spirit of the times, that a feminist movement or a woman's liberation movement explodes in a society. But in modern India, men themselves came forward to uphold the claims of women, and also of the commom people, and move onward with the times; such men arose not only in social and political movements, but also in religious movements; and they worked hand in hand with awakened Indian women as well, imbued with the passion to evolve a progressive social order in modem India. And, in this effort, they were sustained, as much by the ancient Indian philosophical and spiritual tradition, as by the modern teachers and leaders of the nation along with the modern Western humanistic socio-political thought and experience.

The aspirations of modern Indian women have to be viewed against this background. Free to seek the most advanced intellectual development or pursue any social or political avocations, the Indian woman of today does not feel herself as a competitor of man but as his comrade and helper, whose good wishes and active help she also values.

Woman as Wife to Grow into Woman as Mother

This has led to important consequences for the Indian ideal of womanhood. For the first time after several centuries, marriage is becoming a comradeship of equals, a joint adventure in the development of society and the enjoyment of its delights. And India's spiritual heritage today gently whispers to every woman, as also to every man, to utilise the marriage context to achieve the increasing liberation of the tremendous value of the Ātman, the sexless Self, behind man and woman. Vedānta upholds this as the goal and direction of social evolution, or of evolution at the human stage.

So far as woman is concerned, this is achieved by the wife growing into the mother, not merely, or even necessarily, biologically, but certainly spiritually. Motherhood is a spiritual transformation of wifehood. If woman as wife is socially significant woman as mother is spiritually glorious. If the spiritual is more than coterminous with the biological, then woman as mother of a little genetic group would have remained the highest possible moral and spiritual development for her sex. But Vedānta sees the spiritual as transcending the merely genetic and the biological, and even the social, and finding expression in an ideal of motherhood, where love and service break the barriers of family, race, and creed, and assume a universal aspect. It is this spiritual elevation in self-transcendence that enables woman, *even us wife,* to function effectively as a citizen of a free socio-political order, embracing with her mother-heart the millions of its body-politic. If this is called *finding life*—larger and fuller life—then the path to it lies through self-development by self-effacement. That is what a woman does when she *grows* from wifehood to motherhood. In this, no human value is neglected or negated, but there is only a growth from a smaller to a larger personality, and a progressive manifestation of the inherent divinity.

The Glory of Mother in Indian Culture

And this is, as I have pointed out earlier, the Vedāntic criterion of progress of an individual or a culture. This motherhood ideal is the highest reach of womanhood, according to Indian culture. This symbol of self-effacing love and service, namely, the mother, has revealed to the Hindu mind the presence of a divine reality within, over and above the limited personality of the visible mother. To the Hindu, even God is revealed as the Mother of all creation. A people and a philosophy that has educated itself to look upon God as Mother, has also learnt to invest its view of woman with the utmost tenderness and reverence. The very hoary culture of the Hindu trains him to look upon all women, nay, to look upon the female of all species, as forms of the one Divine Mother. In the words of the *Manu Smṛti* (11.145):

> *Upādhyāyāt daśā-cāryah,*
> *ācāryaṇaṁ sataṁ pitā;*
> *Sahasraṁ to pitṛn mātā*
> *gauraveṇātiricyate*

'From the point of view of reverence due, a teacher is tenfold superior to a mere lecturer, a father a hundredfold to teacher, and a mother a thousandfold to a father.'

And what constitutes this abundant glory in the mother is her self-effacing love and compassion which, to the Hindu, is the mark of high spirituality and true culture. And men in general, and women in particular, have the privilege to attain to this high spirituality and true culture by growing beyond the limitations of mere sex, even while living and functioning physically at that level in all dignity and freedom. It is this vision that India has always held up before all men and women, and which her women, more than her men, have passionately struggled to realise in their lives.

Indian Ideal of Womanhood: Ancient and Modern

The ideals of chastity and purity, unselfishness and service, simplicity and modesty, exemplified in great women like Sita, Savitri, and Damayanti, have been pursued by the Indian women, drawn by that vision of innate and inalienable divinity of man and woman. Millennia of historic experience have made these the warp and woof of their being. And modern Indian women cannot jump out of this age-old inheritance of theirs. In his lecture on *The Sages of India,* Swami Vivekananda pointed out this truth over eighty years ago *(The Complete Works of Swami Vivekananda,* Vol.III, eighth edition, p.256):

> Any attempt to modernise our women, if it tries to take our women away from that ideal of Sita, is immediately a failure, as we see every day. The women of India must grow and develop in the footprints of Sita, and that is the only way.

Women in old India were nourished on the ideals of Sita, Savitri, and Damayanti. But women in modern India, even while responding to these ideals and examples, are in search of a newer inspiration to sustain them in the wider opportunities for self-expression offered by the modern age, compared to their sisters of previous ages.

Modern Indian women are in search of an adaptation of the ancient spiritual values to the vastly expanded modern conditions and opportunities of life and work. And it is this authentic sanction that the modern Indian women receive from Sri Ramakrishna, Holy Mother Sarada Devi, and Swami Vivekananda.

The Uniqueness of Sri Ramakrishna

Among spiritual teachers, Sri Ramakrishna is unique in several respects, even in the impressive context of India's age-old religious history. He worked as a priest, performed all his spiritual experiments, communicated his universal spiritual message to humanity, and trained his disciples—all in the precincts of a temple, the Kali Temple of Dakshineswar, near Calcutta, built and sustained by a distinguished woman, namely, Rani Rashmani; his first spiritual guru was another distinguished woman saint and intellectual, namely, the intrepid and freely-wandering Bhairavi Brahmani; in the temple, he was the worshipper of God conceived as the Divine Mother of the Universe, namely, *Bhavatāriṇī Kalī;* and, in spite of being an ascetic, he agreed to his mother's proposal of marriage and took as wife a remarkable woman, Sarada Devi; and both lived a unique married life together, in mutual love and service and respect, and in the service of all humanity, without a trace of the physical in their relationships, but manifesting a unique union of souls even while living as separate individuals at the physical level.

A Great Ancient Myth Recreated as Lived History

In the mutual relationship of Sri Ramakrishna and Sarada Devi, modern India once again experienced that purest love, untouched by any trace of the carnal, manifested in the relationship of Siva and Uma of her ancient tradition, whom her greatest classical poet and dramatist Kālidāsa describes as 'the parents of the universe'—*Jagatah pitarau.* In his epic poem *Kumāra-saṁbhavam,* Kālidāsa vividly describes Umā's, or Pārvatī's, pure love winning Śiva as her husband, after Śiva, on his part, had burnt to ashes *Kāmadeva,* Indian Cupid, who had tried, through his various arts, to rouse carnal love in Śiva. Kālidāsa presents Umā, or Pārvatī, as the embodiment of all beauty (1.48):

Sarvopamā-dravya-samuccayena
yathā-pradeśam viniveśitena;
Sā nirmitā visvasṛjā prayatnāt
ekastha saundarya didṛkṣayeva

'Gathering all excellent things of beauty, and fixing them in their appropriate places, the Creator of the universe created her, with the desire, as it were, to see all beauty centred in one person.'

When this Pārvatī expressed a wish to serve the ascetic Śiva who was then performing *tapasya* (spiritual practices) in the Himālayās, Kālidāsa describes Śiva's response in a great verse, the sentiment of which, and the situation it describes, had found a profound recreation, in our own time, in a really historical event of Sri Ramakrishna's hearty response to his young wife Sarada Devi's request to be allowed to serve him at the Kālī Temple at Dakshineswar *(Kumārasaṁbhavaṁ,* 1.58):

Pratyartha-bhūtām api tāṁ samādheḥ
ṣuṣrūsamāṇām Giriśo' umene;
Vikārahetau sati vikriyante
yeṣāṁ na cetāṁsi ta eva dhīraḥ

'Even though (her presence nearby) would be an obstruction to his (practice of) *samādhi,* Śiva agreed to her (Pārvatī's) request to serve him; those persons alone are *dhīrās,* i.e., heroes, whose minds do not get disturbed even when circumstances to disturb them are present.'

And, finally, Śiva's pure love surrenders to the pure love of Pārvatī, says Kālidāsa in a great verse *(ibid.,* V. 86):

Adya-prabhṛtyavanatāṅgi tavāsmi dāsaḥ
kritaḥ tapohiriti vādini Chandramaulau;
Ahnāya sā niyamajaṁ kiamam utsasarja
kleśaḥ phalena hi punaḥ navatāṁ vidhatte

'From how onwards, O Beautiful One, I am your salve; you have purchased me through your *tapas,* i.e. spiritual practices!'— when Śiva said this, all her tension and tiredness arising from her holy penance vanished immediately; it is well known that all tension and tiredness become creatively renewed when they yield (their expected) fruits.'

This ancient and ever-living Śiva-Umā *myth* of India became *real history* when, in our modern age, Sarada Devi, now in the bloom of her youth and arriving at Dakshineswar from her far-away village at Jayarambati, presented herself before her ascetic husband Sri Ramakrishna, late at night on a day in May 1872. Sri Ramakrishna received her cordially and, when she had settled down, he addressed her thus:

> 'As for me, the Mother has shown me that She resides in every woman, and so I have learned to look upon every woman as Mother. That is the one idea I can have about you. But if you wish to drag me into the world, as I have been married to you, I am at your service.'

To this challenging remark of her divine husband, Sarada Devi gave an equally straight-forward and conclusive answer:

> 'Why should I desire to drag your mind down to the worldly plane? I have only come to help you in your chosen path. I desire only to live with you and serve you and to learn from you.'

Sri Ramakrishna and Sri Sarada Devi

This unambiguous reply of his pure and spotless wife pleased Sri Ramakrishna immensely and he experienced a great accession of spiritual strength. He became convinced that his mission in the world—of calling humanity back to an awareness of its inborn divine nature—is not to be a lonely struggle; he recognised in Saradda Devi a companion in this noble mission; and within a year of her arrival at Dakshineswar, he verified the truth of this exalted view of his wife through the historically unique *Ṣoḍasī-pūja* experience when, unlike in the past when wives worshipped their husbands and looked upon them as divine, Sri Ramakrishna worshipped his wedded wife Sarada Devi as *Ṣoḍasī,* or *Tripura sundarī,* or *Lalitā*—the Divine Mother of the universe personified as Beauty.

From then on till the end of his life, for full fourteen years, Sarada Devi served the person of Sri Ramakrishna, and the large number of disciples and devotees visiting him, with a rare devotion and self-effacement unrivalled in human history. It also saw her intense spiritual education under her divine husband. She has referred to this period as a continuous experience of intense bliss. Months and months they lived together in the same room, and slept in the same bed, with no carnal thought arising in the mind of either. Their minds constantly soared in the region of divine awareness and bliss; each stood transfigured to the other; and both became instruments for the working out of the Divine Will in the modern world. The immense store of spiritual energy-divine *Śakti*—which was generated by the *sādhanās* of Sri Ramakrishna and Sarada Devi contains the promise of the spiriṭtual evolution of modern humanity, which keenly feels its own tragic aspiritual poverty in the midst of abundant material wealth.

The Mesmerism of the Eternal Feminine

After the passing away of Sri Ramakrishna in 1886, Sarada Devi continued his spiritual ministration, for the remaining thirty-four years of her life, to an ever-increasing number of men and women from India and abroad. What is the source of the mesmerism of her name and personality? Even a slight acquaintance with her life will make one realise that this mesmerism does not proceed from any aspects of her personality which the sophisticated modern age recognises as significant in women. To all outward appearances, the Holy Mother was just ordinary, or less than ordinary. Rustic in simplicity, almost unlettered, and shy and modest, she is far removed from the contemporary educated, self-conscious, active type of women; and yet, her life finds powerful and responsive echoes from the hearts of all men and women, rustic and modern alike. It is evident that she has captured, in her life and character, the essence of the modern spirit of truth and humanism, and the fundamental value which lies at the back of the womanliness of woman and which transcends all distinctions based on mere sex and the attractions thereof. This fact alone explains her universal appeal, representing, as she does, not a mere national or racial type, but the fulfilment of woman as woman, the realisation, in flesh and blood, of what the German poet Goethe, in his immortal *Faust,* presents as *The Eternal Feminine.*

Sarada Devi and Sister Nivedita

Readers of her biography will obtain glimpses of the modern mind and outlook and sympathy, shining through her external rustic personality, in several human situations, be it in scolding an old -fashioned mother not to ruin the life of her teen-age daughter through early marriage but to arrange for her further education and personality development, or in her overcoming all caste distinctions in a natural human way and treating Muslims and Christians as her own children as she treated Hindus. Her ready acceptance of the Irish intellectual Miss Margaret Noble, later famous as Sister Nivedita, as her own spiritual daughter, is specially significant in this context. Swami Vivekananda wondered how to make Miss Margaret Noble, who had become his devoted disciple in England and who had offered to dedicate her enormous energies and her shining intellect to the furtherance of his mission in India in 1898, acceptable to the Indian people, in the context of the then prevailing social exclusiveness and distrust of the Western people. He decided to introduce her first to the Holy Mother and, through her, to the Indian people. And, to the great satisfaction of the Swami, and to the immense joy of Margaret herself, the Holy Mother gave her a motherly welcome as soon as the Swami introduced Margaret to her and the Holy Mother made her sit on her own cot and conversed with her with loving intimacy; and to the end of her days, Niveditā considered herself as the Holy Mother's *khooki,* i.e., little daughter.

Swami Vivekananda's Vision of the Future Indian Woman

Conveying Vivekananda's vision of the woman of the future, Sister Niveditā says in her great book: *The Master as I Saw Him (Complete Works of Sister Niveditā,* edited by Pravrājika Atmaprāna, Vol.1, p.195):

> He could not foresee a Hindu woman of the future, entirely without the old power of meditation. Modern science, women must learn; but not at the cost of the ancient spirituality. He saw clearly enough that the ideal education would be one that should exercise the smallest possible influence for direct change on the social body as a whole. It would be that which should best enable every woman,

> in time to come, to resume into herself the greatness of all the women of the Indian past.

Again, highlighting, in the same book, the Swami's stress on the need, for both men and women, to outgrow their physical limitations by their steady spiritual growth and closer and closer approach to the realisation of the Ātman, the sex-less Self, she remarks *(ibid.,* pp.196-97):

> He saw plainly enough that what was wanted was a race of women-educators, and this was how he contemplated making them. Strength, strength, strength was the one quality he called for in woman as in man. But how stem was his discrimination of what constituted strength! Neither self-advertisement nor over-emotion roused his admiration. His mind was full of the grand old types of silence and sweetness and steadiness, to be attracted by any form of mere display. At the same time, woman had as large an inheritance as man in all the thought and knowledge that formed the peculiar gift of the (modern) age to India. *There could be no sex in truth. He would never tolerate any scheme of life and polity that tended to bind tighter, on mind and soul, the fetters of the body, The greater the individual, the more would she transcend the limitations of ferminity in mind and character, and the more was such transcendence to be expected and admired.* (italics not by Niveditā).

Conclusion

Sarada Devi: the Link between the Ancient and the Modern

Sarada Devi stands as an inspiring example to the modern woman in her efforts to steady her steps through the currents and cross-currents of the revolutionary modern age. Herself an ideal wife and nun, it was the mother that shone through her varied roles, including that of the guru. She never assumed the airs of a guru; in spite of her immense spiritual status and stature, she always made her innumerable disciples, Eastern and Western, feel that she was their mother and not guru. Accordingly, on many occasions, after initiating her disciples in the divine *mantra,* she would cook for them, feed them, and wash their dishes. When they naturally protested that it was not proper for them to have their guru serve them, she would reply that she felt it a privilege, as their mother, to serve them.

The following revelation of her personality given by Sister Niveditā in The Master as I Saw Him may form a fitting conclusion to this brief exposition of Sarada Devi's status as the crowning glory of Indian womanhood, (ibid., pp.147-48):

> But is she the last of an old order, or the beginning of a new? In her one sees realised that wisdom and sweetness to which the simplest of women may attain. And yet, to myself, the stateliness of her courtesy and her great open mind are almost as wonderful as her sainthood. I have never known her hesitate in giving utterance to large and generous judgement, however new or complex might be the question put before her. Her life is one long stillness of prayer. Her whole experience is of theocratic civilisation. Yet she rises to the height of every situation. Is she tormented by the perversity of any about her? The only sign is a strange quiet and intensity that comes upon her. Does one carry to her some perplexity or mortification bom of social developments beyond her ken? With unerring intuition, she goes straight to the heart of the matter, and sets the questioner in the true attitude to the difficulty. Or is there

need for severity? No foolish sentimentality causes her waver. . . .

And yet is she, as one of her spiritual children said of her, speaking literally of her gift of song, 'full of music,' all gentleness, all playfulness. And the room wherein she worships, withal, is filled with sweetness.

Swami Vivekananda: His Central Theme*

Introduction

Swami Vivekananda can be looked upon as a great organiser or a great orator, as one whose heart bled for the poor in this country and abroad or as one who successfully carried the message of Vedānta to foreign lands; he can also be looked upon as an intellectual giant who built a bridge between the East and the West, as also between reason and faith. But behind all these, there was that fundamental basic inspiration, his spiritual realisation.

Sri Ramakrishna's Estimate of Young Narendra

Swami Vivekananda derived all the inspiration for his work from that touch with the spiritual depths of his own being. It is this aspect of his personality that gives nourishment to all that he said and all that he did. When he came to Sri Ramakrishna as a young

---

*Speech delivered at the Ramakrishna Mission, New Delhi, on 17 February 1952, on the occasion of the celebration of the ninetieth brithday of Swami Vivekananda.

boy, Sri Ramakrishna marked in him the eyes of a *yogi* and told the other disciples that Vivekananda, or Naren as he was then called, was a spiritual personality of a high order. He added (Swami Saradananda: *Sri Ramakrishna the Great Master,* Sri Ramakrishna Math, Madras 4, 1952, p.720):

> I found that his eyes were indrawn; half his mind was looking to something within and only the other half was aware of the outside world.

This, said Sri Ramakrishna, was the characteristic feature of the eyes of great *yogis.* Naren had this characteristic of inwardness which constantly drew him close to the Spirit within. Sitting at the feet of Sri Ramakrishna, he developed this trait and became a man of the highest spiritual realisation.

Narendra's Transformation into Vivekananda

When he had realised this spiritual amplitude and fullness, the question arose in his mind as to what he should do thereafter. As it often happens in the life of spiritual aspirants, when they get the vision of the spiritual ideal, they get immersed in that realisation. They have little sympathy for or interest in the world of struggling souls around them. Swami Vivekananda would have become one such among the, great spiritual luminaries that have come to this country. But his path was to be otherwise, and the fate of India was to be otherwise; for Swami Vivekananda appeared on the scene at a crucial period of our history as a man with a message, and with the necessary spiritual authority and power to impart that message. In that transformation of Swami Vivekananda from a self-absorbed saint to a compassionate teacher is contained the story of modern India's spiritual and cultural regeneration.

When Vivekananda wanted to enjoy spiritual bliss, it was Sri Ramakrishna who told him that he was meant for a different purpose and that he was not to be like an ordinary saint enjoying spiritual beatitude for himself. He was a person who was meant to be a source of inspiration to millions of people in India and abroad; and it was Sri Ramakrishna who gave that turn to Swami Vivekananda's spiritual energies and purposes. With this touch of his Master, Swami Vivekananda burst upon the world not as a passive saint, but as a dynamic world-mover. If Swami Vivekananda exerted so much influence on the contemporary world, and continues to exert that influence in ever increasing measure in the East and the West, it is because he realised the eternal imperishable truth in his own being, and sought inspiration from that in his work to compose the distractions of our age. The edifice of his character was built on the rock foundation of spirituality which found expression in a vigorous personality of scintillating intellect and measureless heart. I wish to emphasise this point because Swami Vivekananda was a many-sided personality and can appear to us in various hues, but his greatness had something eternal about it unlike the passing greatness familiar in the world of achievements. The flow of time affects such greatness in a strange way; it augments it instead of diminishing and destroying it. Rooted in the Ātman and drawing nourishment therefrom, the personality and work of such men and women carry something compelling in it and possess an enduring character.

The Mesmerism of a Truly Spiritual Message

Great teachers of the world like Jesus Christ, Bhagavān Buddha, Sri Ramakrishna, and Swami Vivekananda derive their strength and inspiration not from the muscles or mind or intellect, but from the deepest reality in man and nature.

That is why they speak a language which goes straight into the hearts of the people, not only of their own generation but for centuries thereafter. That is how they stand before us, these spiritual giants, in spite of passing time, as the timeless witnesses of what is permanent and eternal in man. It is this that flavours the message which Swami Vivekananda gave to India, on the one side, and the West, on the other.

Vivekananda's Central Theme: Spirituality

It is significant that though he had dived deep into the ocean of spiritual realisation, he did not give the same message, or rather the message in the same form, to India as he gave to the West. He varied his message to suit the needs of the people; but all these variations were expressions of one central theme-spirituality. In the Indian context, he saw that the path to spirituality lay through material and social amelioration. To this end, he drew out of Vedānta a social philosophy and outlook, at once dynamic and practical. To India which sorely needed it, he gave the message of a man-making religion and a nation-making faith and resolve.

While Swami Vivekananda felt proud at the glory of old India, he was deeply afflicted to see her in the depths of degradation and misfortune. The sufferings of his countrymen, their age-old starvation, ignorance, and social disabilities, moved him deeply. Confronted with this situation, his abundant spirituality and dynamic philosophy flowed into a stream of compassion and love, into a national message of, renunciation and service; Vedānta once again became dynamic and practical. It is this that makes Vivekananda not merely a great *ṛṣi* or sage but also a patriot and epoch-maker. From him proceeded a wave of national awareness and patriotism, issuing in a great struggle to improve the lot of the common man. Whatever we have achieved by way of political independence, by way of social awareness and national solidarity, has come from that orientation of the ancient message of India's spirituality given by Swami Vivekananda.

Going to foreign countries, in America and England, he was confronted with a different situation. There were people who were lacking in nothing by way of social or material amenities; but they were lacking in something fundamental which had turned their very material advancements into ashes in the mouth. Outer wealth and glory had been achieved at the cost of inner richness and peace. The modern man was in search of a soul, a search in which his science and wisdom just failed him.

Spirituality: Its many-sided Expression

Swami Vivekananda stood before the Western world as an authentic voice of the spirit in man and the spirit in the universe. To them he went as the teacher of Vedānta, of the inward contemplative life, the teacher of active tolerance and fellowship, the teacher of universal love. There, in the West, he stood forth as the representative of the *ṛṣis* of India and imparted their ancient message in keeping with the spiritual needs of the modem West. That is why Vivekananda is respected in the Western world as a spiritual teacher and world thinker of a rare calibre. To the average youth of our country, he makes an irresistible appeal as one who taught patriotism and national service in ever-memorable words, as one who worked and asked others to work for uplifting the vast millions in this country who are sunk in ignorance and poverty. To the nation at large, he shines as the emblem of purity, spirituality, love, and energy through whose inspiration it hopes to build its body and mind anew.

These are the various aspects of his personality directly derived from the supreme strength of realised Vedānta. The richness and strength of this Vedantic realisation accounts for the many-sidedness of his character and message. He brings down Vedānta to fertilise the fields of common life, so that life may be raised to uncommon heights and made capable to taste Vedānta at its purest source.

Through him once more Vedānta spoke in accents of human happiness and welfare. He keenly felt the truth that the purer delights of spiritual life can be experienced only after man has been able to meet the demands of life's immediate and pressing needs. 'Religion is not for empty bellies', he said, and he found India full of empty bellies and naked bodies; he considered it a mockery to preach religion to a hungry man. Hence he became a teacher of love; of love of God flowing into service of man, of faith flowing into works, and both forging character which is manṭliness and manliness which is spirituality.

Its Expression in Modern India as Practical Spirituality

His message has great practical utility today; the political and social policy of India has to bear the impress of that spirituality which Swami Vivekananda gave to the nation out of the fullness of his realisation. The nation wanted a teacher who would guide its thoughts so as to humanise its religion and spiritualise its social purposes and activities; and the nation got Swami Vivekananda at the right time.

He made Indian philosophy concern itself with the problems of the common man. *But he has also warned us that all our politics and policies, our social developments and economic improvements, in short, all our deepest cravings for betterment, must be subordinated to the one fundamental national theme of spirituality.* In this emphasis on the fundamental theme of Indian life, Swami Vivekananda stands as a unique figure among the great leaders who have come to this country in recent times.

At the time of Vivekananda, political subjection was lying heavy on the shoulders of India. Today it has been lifted; but along with political subjection there has been social decay, and it looked as if an old and rich civilisation had ceased to grow. Swami Vivekananda wanted to make this civilisation take a new shape and stand forth as a fresh, energetic, and vigorous civilisation before the modern world. For that purpose, he wanted India to assimilate the spirit and technique of modern science which has come to us from the West; but this capacity to assimilate the dynamic scientific culture of the West depended upon a prior energising of the national tradition in the minds of his countrymen. Without this strengthening of the national heritage, India's response to the West, he held, will result in a patchy imitation instead of a healthy assimilation. He warned us against that temptation and danger. He visualised a new India in which the spirit of equality, social awareness, and practical efficiency of the modern West would get happily blended with the mature gentleness and tolerance of Indian tradition, with its deep spiritual awareness and passion which has made Indian history a saga of spiritual aspiration and realisation. He wanted India to be young, vigorous, and progressive; and yet he wanted all these to be achieved as the fulfilment of the spiritual ideal and purpose.

Therefore, he placed before us his great message of nation-building based on spirituality. He wanted that all improvements to be effected in this country should be effected not at the cost of the national asset which is spirituality, but as flowing from it and leading up to it. He interpreted Indian history to demonstrate to us that progress in social and other lines is the fruit of the strengthening of the nation's spirituality, whatever other lessons the histories of other nations may teach. He gave that warning because he found a tendency around him to relegate religion to second place, or even to treat it as an enemy of social progress, and concentrate on material improvement and social progress so as to lead India on absolutely secular lines. This kind of tendency, useful within limits, might yet create mischief in our country and rob the nation of its spiritual stamina. It was, therefore, necessary that the warning should be issued, and the nation got it in time through the powerful and authentic voice of Swami Vivekananda.

He warned us that if India gave up spirituality and her age-old way of life, she would perish. It is this spiritual asset which has made India a continuing concern, unlike other civilisations which have passed away. Taking the lessons of world history, he told us that if India gave up spirituality and took to any other ideal of life, she would be an extinct culture in three generations. Ancient Greece and Rome and some of the European states which had flourished for a time are nowhere to be seen in the world today. Even some of the nations of the contemporary world, though lacking in nothing by way of material advancement and worldly power, are finding their foundations shaken and are struggling to discover spiritual values to stabilise themselves. They find that something fundamental is lacking in the edifice of their civilisation based upon the mere intellect of man, on the achievements of science and technology, and on the advancement of material prosperity. India discovered long ago that if there is to be stability in the structure of a civilisation, it shall have to seek for other forces than the forces of muscle or brain or mere intellect. That is how some of the thinkers of Europe and America today are also thinking, and they are in search of that stabilising force of spirituality of which they view India to be the representative and voice. We see all around us that, in spite of material prosperity, in spite of social improvements, in spite of all that are based on sense values, there are forces that are trying to destroy civilisation itself. In such critical periods of world history, India has ever been a source of spiritual strength and sustenance to humanity. She has played that historic role in spite of her own disasters and sufferings and the vicissitudes that befell her. Her continued existence and vitality in spite of these national disasters, a fraction of which has wiped away other civilisations, imparts to her voice and message the compelling quality of lived and tested experience.

Insufficiencies of the Modern Welfare State Ideologies

This wisdom tells humanity today through Swami Vivekananda that man's true welfare is basically spiritual and that material and social welfare is but a means to this end. Spirituality is the fundamental good in which are true peace and happiness. There are nations in the West today who have gone far in establishing a welfare state but whose citizens are far from being happy or secure. It is a tragedy that the more advanced a state is, the more insecure and unhappy are its people.

Among modern states, Sweden may be taken as an example of a state which has gone farthest in material advancement and social progress; some have called it not merely a welfare state, but a welfarest state. According to a dispatch published recently (31 December 1951) in the American *Time* from its Stockholm correspondent, the people in this welfarest state are anything but happy. The correspondent found that the state has provision for all its citizens from the womb to the tomb, and even to salvation, for the state has provided paid preachers to care for the souls of the dead. He found the municipal services perfect, social amenities extensive, wealth plenty, and life easy, with no conceivable cause for unhappiness, insecurity, or worry. Is everything all right with the people of this welfarest state? he asked himself; and he went about to see if there was anything lacking. He found an undercurrent of unrest and unhappiness. A government official told him, 'In a country that has established an orderly society, there comes a time when one begins to ask oneself 'What next?' He found a lot of Swedes asking this question 'What next?' *tatah kim?* as our own Śaṅkara expressed it long ago, and finding and receiving no answer; the resultant undercurrent of emotional unrest is giving rise to a variety of social maladiess like—alcoholism, juvenile delinquency, unhappy marriages, and loose morals. Sweden presents the picture of a society where man has all the good things of life and yet feels a gnawing vacancy in his heart. This inner emptiness becomes the cause of the instability of the outer structure/ or *to gain the whole world by losing the soul is to lose the world so gained.* The hunger for God, the desire for spirituality, the craving for inner richness and fullness is a fundamental and basic urge in man; and a civlisation that does not take note of it and provide for it will be building itself on sand. The philosophy that stands sponsor to such a civilisation is naive and shallow, having not dared to plumb man and nature to their depths.

India's Vision of Total Human Welfare

The great sages of India knew man and his possibilities and needs most intimately and fully, and provided for them in their scheme of life through the twofold values of *abhyudaya* and *nihsreyasa*—social welfare and spiritual emancipation. Their maturest thought, Vedānta, is pervaded by a deep passion for truth and a deeper passion for human happiness and welfare. It takes man gently by the hand in his primitive state of childish exuberance and leads him through the delights and restraints of culture and civilisation to the peace and fullness of perfection. With such a philosophy to sponsor it and sustain it, India has built an enduring edifice of culture in the life of a seventh of the human race with spiritual freedom as its watchword and tolerance and gentleness as its motto. It was this culture in all its force and charm that found living expression in our time in the lives and message of Sri Ramakrishna and Swami Vivekananda. They represent the Vedantic passion for human welfare—welfare in all its phases, material and moral, cultural and spiritual. This explains the variations in Swami Vivekananda's message and programme in the East and the West. To India's millions he gave out of Vedānta a message of hope through social security and welfare leading to a purer form of renunciation and spirituality. To the materially advanced West he gave out of the same Vedānta a message of renunciation and self-realisation as a value to be sought after directly and immediately.

Our country has been provided in Vedānta with a rational philosophy and religion which will answer every quest and thirst of the human intellect and heart. Swami Vivekananda preached a religion which is emotionally satisfying and rationally convincing. Its rationality is creative and inspires faith in life and its values, unlike modern rationalism which destroys hope after first destroying faith. Western man learned to swear by this rationalism from the time of the Renaissance. In the first three centuries it succeeded in withering his faith in God in the name of the faith in man. But in the first half of this twentieth century it has succeeded in whittling his faith in man also, leaving modem man like a rudderless boat in the storm-tossed sea of the modern world, without a faith to sustain him or hope to inspire him, but with enough cynicism yoked to animal vigour which seeks expression in a fantasy of self-and-world-destruction.

If the thinking people of America and England gave a spontaneous response to the message of Swami Vivekananda fifty years ago, it was because he had sensed this inner tension of the modern mind and had conveyed in his message the needed spiritual pabulum. The appeal of Vedānta to the modern man has been steadily deepening and widening since then. It inspires him with a rational faith and a realisable hope and restores to him in a purer form that zest in life which his cynicism had shattered. *To the earnest, seeking, storm-tossed souls of the modern world, a study of Swami Vivekananda's Vedānta has been, and is bound to be, like a bath in the Ganga for a weary pilgrim, a refreshing experience, a spiritual rebirth.*

Conclusion

Swami Vivekananda has left us a rich legacy of thought and inspiration. If India assimilates them, she will become the hope of the nations. That is the historically acquired role of India, according to Swami Vivekananda. He preached nation-building with this world-objective in view, to prepare India to discharge her world responsibility. *And nation-building in India, according to him, is the gathering up of the nation's scattered spiritual forces.* And because he found her present economic and social maladjustments thwarting this higher expression of the national will and purpose, he became the first monastic advocate of what he happily termed 'a toned-down materialism' for his country. He had the fullest faith in the capacity of his people to assimilate moral and spiritual ideas. This assimilative power will gather momentum as the nation succeeds step by step in composing the distractions of its battered body-politic.

An India, physically healthy, socially stable and strong, and morally and spiritually resurgent, will confront the modern world with a challenge of goodwill and sincerity, fellowship and peace. It will be an utterly new experience to the world after centuries of experience of a different type of challenge, that of hatred, violence, and war. The world is waiting for that new experience with bated breath. And that experience will be vouchsafed to the world by an India fashioned and shaped by the ideas and ideals of Swami Vivekananda. The spirit of India brought him forth and fashioned him for this very purpose.

Swami Vivekananda: His Life And Mission*

Introduction

Today, India is celebrating, with the rest of the world, the first birth centenary of Swami Vivekanada. He came in the unbroken line of spiritual teachers who brightened the sky of India from the Vedic period to the modern age. It is they who imparted the spiritual energy and direction characteristic of Indian culture. It is because they came, age after age, that India is still alive in spite of invasions, subjections, and devastations, while a fraction of such calamities has destroyed many a nation and many a culture in world history. The periodical touch of these master minds gave India renewed strength and hope every time.

The Modern Indian Awakening

By the end of the eighteenth century, India had become old and effete, broken and dispirited, and awaited either dissolution and

*Talk broadcast over the National Programme of All India Radio, on 17 January 1963, on the occasion of the celebration of the Birth Centenary of Swami Vivekananda.

death or reintegration and life. Her innate spiritual strength burst forth at the prospect of this danger, and a new life came to her by the beginning of the nineteenth century. She accepted the challenge of the age and resolved to meet the challenge in a creative, constructive manner. This rejuvenation process was spearheaded by a mighty and far-sighted personality, Raja Rammuhan Roy, who strove to awaken his country-men, purify and strengthen the age-old culture of his people, and to effect a synthesis of the ancient Indian heritage and the modern Western heritage. This process of reawakening continued throughout the century, throwing up great leaders and movements. And towards the end of the century, it found its full maturity and consummation through the lives and teachings of its most dynamic and authentic representatives, Sri Ramakrishna and Swami Vivekananda. Though born in India they represented the spiritual hopes and aspirations of all mankind. They were 'Universe Souls' in the language of Romain Rolland *(The Life of Ramakrishna,* Third Impression, p. 22).

Vivekananda and Modern India

Vivekananda took India out of her isolation of centuries and brought her into the stream of international life and thought. He awakened the people of India to the realities and demands of the modern age. Says Romain Rolland in his *The Life of Vivekananda (ibid.,* pp.316-18):

> So India was hauled out of the shifting sands of barren speculation wherein she had been engulfed for centuries, by the hand of one of her own *sannyasins;* and the result was that the whole reservoir of mysticism, sleeping beneath, broke its bounds and spread by a series of great ripples into action. . . . This 'greater India,' this new India, . . . is

> impregnated with the soul of Ramakrishna. The twin star of the *Paramahamsa* and the hero who translated his thought into action, dominates and guides her present destinies. Its warm radiance is the leaven working within the soil of India and fertilising it.

Swami Vivekananda was a spiritual teacher of a rare type. Himself immersed in the bliss of God, he came down to the ordinary levels of men and women. To him, these were not two separate fields, but one; and he expressed this truth in his great equation 'work is worship'. He taught humanity a philosophy which combines external action in a spirit of service for the enrichment of society, with internal action, for the spiritual enrichment of the individual. In the language of the *Gītā,* action and inaction, *karmā and jñ āna,* become one. This equation is the essence of Swami Vivekananda's spiritual message, a message which has been left to us in the eight volumes of his *Complete Works.* The spirit of that message has been beautifully summarised for us by his gifted Western disciple, Sister Niveditā in a powerful passage in her 'Introduction' to *The Complete Works of Swami Vivekananda.* Says she (Vol.1, 1962 Edition, p.XV):

> If the many and the One be indeed the same Reality, then it is not all modes of worship alone, but equally all modes of work, all modes of struggle, all modes of creation, which are paths of realisation. No distinction, henceforth, between sacred and secular. To labour is to pray. To conquer is to renounce. Life is itself religion. To have and to hold is as stem a trust as to quit and to avoid.

The Intensity of Vivekananda's Brief Life

Swami Vivekananda's span of earthly life was hardly forty years, but within this short period, he lived an intense life, first as a student in school and college, then as the foremost disciple of his great Master, Sri Ramakrishna, then as a wanderer across the length and breadth of India, and lastly as the spiritual teacher of West and East. His public teaching commenced with his speeches at the World's Parliament of Religions at Chicago in 1893; and he passed away on 4 July 1902. He spent four intense years in the United States and England, and five equally intense years in India delivering his message of a universal and practical spirituality, and setting in motion a movement as an effective conduit for the furtherance of his message.

Everywhere, he taught man to realise his divine heritage. The innate divinity of man was the constant theme of all his teachings. *This teaching cuts across all divisions based on political or religious affiliations.* Its assimilation by man will make for a character at once deep and broad. He held that spirituality was the core of every religion; dogmatic exclusiveness and intolerance are no part of true religion. The more spiritual a man, the more universal he is. He held that the modern age stood in urgent need of this education from religion, by which men will learn to make their love of God flow into the love and service df all men. He worked hard to give this spiritual orientation to the world's religions, so that they may be transformed into wholly constructive forces and become capable of redeeming modern man from his inner impoverishment in the context of external enrichment.

Vivekananda's Message in His Own Words

While speaking on Vivekananda, it is best to let Vivekananda speak for himself. There is a beauty and a power in his words which fascinate the listener. Referring to this, Romain Rolland says in his *The Life of Vivekananda* (Third Impression, p.62):

> His words are great music, phrases in the style of Beethoven, stirring rhythms like the march of Handel choruses. I

> cannot touch these sayings of his, scattered as they are through the pages of books at thirty years' distance, without receiving a thrill through my body like an electric shock. And what shocks, what transport must have been produced when in burning words they issued from the lips of the hero!

In a letter to an American lady written on 21 March 1895, Swami Vivekananda says *(Letters of Swami Vivekananda,* fourth edition, p.211):

> My Master used to say that these names as Hindu, Christian, etc. stand as great bars to all brotherly feelings between man and man. We must try to break them down first. They have lost all their good powers and now only stand as baneful influences under whose black magic even the best of us behave like demons. Well, we will have to work hard and must succeed.

The closing words of his address on Hinduism delivered to the Chicago Parliament of Religions breathe the spirit of the universal and human, characteristic not only of him and of his great Master, but also of the Indian spiritual tradition, and express his appreciation of the universality of the American mind, which conceived and realised such an international assembly of world religions. In his 'Paper on Hinduism' read at the Parliament, and addressing the American nation with deep feeling, Vivekananda said *(Complete Works,* Vol.1, 1962 Edition, p.19):

> . . . If there is ever to be a universal religion, it must be one which will have no location in place or time; which will be infinite, like the God it will preach, and whose sun will shine upon the followers of Kṛṣṇa and of Christ, on saints and sinners alike; which will not be Brahmanic or Buddhistic, Christian or Mohammedan, but the sum total

> of all these, and still have infinite space for development; which in its catholocity will embrace in its infinite arms, and find a place for, every human being, from the lowest grovelling savage not far removed from the brute, to the highest man towering by the virtues of his head and heart almost above humanity, making society stand in awe of him and doubt his human nature. It will be a religion which will have no place for persecution or intolerance in its polity, which will recognize divinity in every man and woman, and whose whole scope, whose whole force, will be centred in aiding humanity to realise its own true, divine nature.
>
> Offer such a religion and all the nations will follow you. Aśoka's Council was a council of the Buddhist faith. Akbar's, though more to the purpose, was only a parlour-meeting. It was reserved for America to proclaim to all quarters of the globe that the Lord is in every religion.

Pointing to the profound significance of the universal sentiments pervading Vivekananda's speeches at the Chicago Parliament of Religions, Romain Rolland observes *(The Life of Vivekananda,* third impression, pp.42-43):

> Each time he repeated with new arguments but with the same force of conviction his thesis of a universal religion without limit of time or space, uniting the whole *Credo* of the human spirit, from the enslaved fetishism of the savage to the most liberal creative affirmations of modem science. He harmonised them into a magnificent synthesis, which, far from extinguishing the hope of a single one, helped all hopes to grow and flourish according to their own proper nature. There was to be no other dogma but the divinity inherent in man and his capacity for indefinite evolution.

He elucidated still further his conception of universal religion in two of his subsequent lectures delivered in California in 1900. Speaking on 'The Way to the Realisation of Universal Religion', at Pasadena, he said (*Complete Works,* Vol.11, ninth edition, p. 377):

> I accept all religions that were in the past, and worship with them all; I worship God with every one of them, in whatever form they worship Him. I shall go to the mosque of the Mohammedan; I shall enter the Christain's church and kneel before the crucifix; I shall enter the Buddhistic temple, where I shall take refuge in Buddha and his Law. I shall go into the forest and sit down in meditation with the Hindu, who is trying to see the Light which enlightens the heart of every one.
>
> Not only shall I do all these, but I shall keep my heart open for all that may come in the future. Is God's book finished? Or is it still a continuous revelation, going on? It is a marvellous book—these spiritual revelations of the world. The Bible, the Vedas, the Koran, and all other sacred books, are but so many pages, and an infinite number of pages remain yet to be unfolded. I would leave it open for all of them.

Speaking in San Francisco a month later on 'The Ideal of a Universal Religion', he said *(ibid.,* pp.387-88):

> 'What I want to propagate is a religion that will be equally acceptable to all minds; it must be equally philosophic, equally emotional, equally mystic, and equally conducive to action. . . . And this combination will be the ideal of the nearest approach to a universal religion. Would to God that all men were so constituted that in their minds *all* these elements of philosophy, mysticism, emotion, and of work

were equally present in full! That is the ideal, my ideal of a perfect man. Everyone who has only one or two of these elements of character, I consider "one-sided;" and this world is almost full of such "onesided" men, with knowledge of that one road only in which they move; and anything else is dangerous and horrible to them. To become harmoniously balanced in all these four directions is *my* ideal of religion.'

Vivekananda's Mission in His Own Words

Swami Vivekananda defined his life's objective as twofold; firstly, to place before man in East and West a comprehensive message of man's spiritual development and realisation in clear simple language; and secondly, to set in motion the wheel of such a spiritual message, to set in motion the wheel of *dharma, dharmacakra pravartana,* in the expressive words of Buddha.

Writing to an Indian disciple from America on 17 February 1896, Vivekananda expounded his first objective thus *(Letters of Swami Vivekananda,* fourth edition, p.302):

> To put the Hindu ideas into English and then make out of dry philosophy and intricate mythology and queer startling psychology, a religion which shall be easy, simple, popular, and at the same time meet the requirements of the highest minds—is a task only those can understand who have attempted it The abstract Advaita must become living—poetic—in everyday life; out of hopelessly intricate mythology must come concrete moral forms; and out of bewildering yogism must come the most scientific and practical psychology—and all this must be put in a form so that a child may grasp it. That is my life's work.

Readers of Vivekananda's works know how great was his success in this field. Apart from his other books, his books on the four *yogas—Yoga, Bhakti-yoga, Jnana-yoga,* and *Raja-yoga*—have become classics on spiritual life and realisation. The reader is impressed by their simplicity of language and profundity of thought. Above all, they carry the impact of the man behind the message, the powerful impact of realised truth.

On his second objective, he writes thus on 24 January 1894 in a letter from America to an Indian disciple *(ibid.,* p.,83*):*

> My whole ambition in life is to set in motion a machinery which will bring noble ideas to the door of everybody, and then let men and women settle their own fate. Let them know what our forefathers as well as other nations have thought on the most momentous questions of life. Let them see specially what others are doing now, and then decide. We are to put the chemicals together, the crystallisation will be done by nature according to her laws.

The Sri Ramakrishna Order

Before his passing away, Sri Ramakrishna had formed a new Order of monks out of his young disciples, with Vivekananda as their leader.

The Order had taken on itself the responsibility to protect and to enhance the deep spirituality and the spirit of universality which had found such a glowing expression in the life of the Master. Vivekananda now added to the inward spiritual life of the Order an outward programme of cultural and humanitarian activities, in which the Order sought the co-operation of laymen also. These two inseparable aspects of the movement initiated by him in the name of his Master became the Ramakrishna Math (Monastery) and the Ramakrishna Mission, with their headquarters just outside

Calcutta at Belur Math, near Howrah, West Bengal. He gave the movement the inspiring motto: *Ātmano mokṣārthaṁ jagadhitāya ca*—'for the freedom of oneself and for the welfare of the world.'

The Vivekananda Literature

Swami Vivekananda's lectures, letters, and discourses run into eight published volumes in English. They are also being made available during this centenary year in ten-volume editions in several of the Indian languages, and selections of them in several foreign languages as well. This vast literature can be aptly described as literature immortal; it is a strengthening, purifying, broadening, and illumining literature. It will educate the youth of today in the problems of the modern world and help him to solve them in the light of the eternal elements in the spiritual heritage of the East and the West. To the Indian youth, in partiular, this literature carries the message of a man-making, character-building education and religion. Says Vivekaṭnanda *(Complete Works,* Vol. V. seventh edition, p.228):

> The national ideals of India are renunciation and service; intensify her in those *channels, and the rest will take care of itself.*

His literature will inspire our youth with these great national ideals of renunciation and service, intensifying which in their awareness and character they will acquire the necessary strength of will and purpose to build a free and egalitarian society in their beloved motherland. It will educate them in the compelling message of international fellowship, co-operation, and welfare, and shape, them into world citizens.

'Arise, Awake, O man!'

This is the type of awakening that he personally imparted to thousands of spiritually sensitive souls in East and West alike during his brief earthly career. The same work of awakening he has continued to impart to an ever-increasing circle of men and women through his literature since his death. Freely rendering the message of the Upaniṣadic verse, *Uttiṣṭhata! Jāgrata! Prāpya varān nibodhata,* he summoned humanity to 'Arise! Awake! And stop not till the goal is reached'. It is the awakened alert man, he said, that achieves science and civilisation, morality and social welfare. It is the same awakening process carried still deeper that brings man to the feet of God and confers on him the fruit of spiritual realisation and complete life fulfilment. He held this as the mission of Vedānta in the modern age.

Says he in ringing words *(Complete Works,* Vol. III, Fourth Edition, p.193):

> Teach yourselves, teach everyone, his real naure; call upon the sleeping soul and see how it awakes. Power will come, glory will come, goodness will come, purity will come, and everything that is excellent will come, when this sleeping soul is roused to self-conscious activity.

The Message of Eternal India

It was this message of eternal India, the eternal music of the human soul, that Vivekananda broadcast in India and abroad. He loved India, because he realised that India had lit the lamp of spiritual knowledge early in her history, and had kept it burning bright and pure thtough good and evil fortune for the service of the whole world. A large component of India's foreign policy as revealed by her history, he held, had always consisted of this diffusion of spiritual knowledge in the contemporary world. She had conquered half the world through Buddha's wisdom and love. Her long cultural and spiritual education had so conditioned her that her expansion outside her borders can and will always be only of an intellectual and spiritual character.

In a letter from America to an Indian disciple dated 31 August 1894, we find Vivekananda referring to this conviction of his. He writes *(Letters of Swami Vivekananda,* Fourth Edition, p.121):

> The whole world requires Light. It is expectant! India alone has that Light, not in magic, mummeries and charlatanism, but in the teaching of the glories of the spirit of real religion—of the highest spiritual truth. That is why the Lord has preserved the race through all its vicissitudes unto the present day. Now the time has come.

Vivekananda summoned his countrymen to prepare morally and spiritually to render this same service now to the modern world *(Complete Works,* Vol. III, p.277):

> Up, India, and conquer the world with your spirituality.

And he warned his countrymen against the temptation to substitute the age-old spiritual idealism of India with the lesser ambitions for material or military glory. Says he:

> India is immortal if she persists in her search for God. But if she gives it up and takes to politics and social conflict, she will die.

Conclusion

The current celebrations of the birth centenary of Vivekananda will acquaint India and the rest of the world with the life and work of one who represented in himself *a condensed India* and a synthesis of the best in the human heritage of East and West.

The Meeting of East and West In Swami Vivekananda*

Ramakrishna and the Indian Renaissance

Sri Ramakrishna's life span was barely fifty years, but it was an intense life devoted to the search for spiritual truth, in the first part, and its dissemination among eager seekers, in the second. Such an intense life which re-lives the spiritual life of a whole people is the most dynamic force in history. It ceases to be just an individual-life and becomes a world-moving force. Human history is the product of forces, partly arising from external nature and partly from man himself. The ratio of this combination will vary according to the stage of cultural development reached by a society. The higher the stage of development, the more the human contribution. And among such human contributions, there is one that is dynamic and significant. That comes from the hero, the specially gifted individual in society. He fuses in himself the

---

*Based on the public lecture delivered at the Ramakrishna Vedanta Centre, 68, Duke's Avenue, Muswell Hill, London, on 23 April 1963, during the Swami's four-month lecture tour of seventeen European countries and later re-delivered at the Ramakrishna Mission Institute of Culture, Calcutta, on 9 January 1962.

values, aspirations, and wills of his people, and marches onward carrying other members of the society with him, immediately or in due course. And the most dynamic among such heroes are the God-men, ablaze with divinity. Indian history has felt the impact of several such heroes who became her history's epoch-makers; and the most outstanding of them all were spiritual men. Each one of them represented in varying degrees a gathering up of the past national heritage, a fusing of the historical and the contemporary urges and aspirations in themselves, and the setting in motion of a dynamic force for human betterment. Indian cultural history, in contrast to her political history, owes much to these epoch-makers. The first of such, of the pre-historic period, is Śrī Kṛṣṇa, whose great thought and energy are palpable even today. His is the most pervasive influence on Indian culture and thought; next come Buddha and Śaṅkara, in the historic period.

And in our own time, there appeared Sri Ramakrishna. The mass of spiritual energy which he manifested in his lifetime did not vanish with the death of his body. Its power of impact has continued and will continue for centuries to come. Physical death has no significance in the case of personalities such as Sri Ramakrishna; they hardly lived in the physical plane even when they were alive. Each one of them is like an atom-smashing cyclotron which generates and holds immense energies within itself, the range and quality of which cannot be explained in terms of the size of the machine itself. Sri Ramakrishna's body was frail; but within that frail body was contained enormous energy—energy which was released by his penetration into the spiritual depths of his being. It was a mass of spiritual energy consisting of wisdom and purity, love and compassion. Sri Ramakrishna was ablaze with divinity. It was the play of this tremendous divine energy that was witnessed in a little room in the temple of Daksineswar, near Calcutta, away from the rush and turmoil of the modem civilisation which was centred in that city, the then capital of India. And yet, the energies released in the precincts of that temple had their powerful impact first, on Calcutta, and, later, on other parts of India and abroad. This diffusion was accomplished by his foremost disciple, Swami Vivekananda, whose training and outlook were the opposite of his master's, and yet complementary to his, for which reason the master chose him as his effective conduit. In the words of Romain Rolland *(Life of Vivekananda,* 1947 Edition, p.3):

> The great disciple whose task it was to take up the spiritual heritage of Ramakrishna and disseminate the grain of his thought throughout the world was both physically and morally his direct antithesis.

The Profile of Narendra

Vivekananda's pre-monastic name was Narendranath Dutta, Narendranath or Naren, for short. Unlike Ramakrishna, whose wisdom and enlightenment owed nothing to institutional education, traditional or modern, Vivekananda was a full-fledged modern youth in education and upbringing, when he first met Ramakrishna towards the end of 1881. In his views and outlook, he represented young India in transition. India had, by then, been exposed to the powerful influence of modern Western culture for over half a century through the new education introduced by the British government, which was avidly sought after by the Indian youths. Modern science, Greeco-Roman history, English literature, modern Western history, and modern sociopolitical thought, opened the mind of India to the rich culture heritage of the Western peoples and roused in it a mood of questioning, self-criticism, and a general spirit of restlessness. Narendra drank freely of this education; he was a keen student of Western thought with its scientific spirit and its philosophy of rationalism and humanism. This philosophy had already dominated the Western mind for nearly a hundred years, and now it found a fertile soil in India also. At college, Narendra was a handsome youth, intelligent, vivacious, and energetic. He was a keen physical culturist, a devotee of music, a student of science, and a lover of philosophy. He opened himself up to the influences of all the best elements in the Western heritage and became a dynamic representative of that heritage. He was a picture of strength and manliness; he possessed the *promethean* spirit. And yet, this education and achievement did not satisfy his heart; it was restless with a nameless spiritual thirst and a yearning to realise truth. It was to quench this thirst that he went to Sri Ramakrishna.

His English and Indian professors as well as his fellow-students were impressed by his intellectual brilliance. His English principal, William Hastie, a great scholar, said of him (*The Life of Swami Vivekananda by His Eastern and Western Disciples,* fourth edition, p.26):

> Narendranath is really a genius. I have travelled far and wide, but I have never yet come across a lad of his talents and possibilities even in German Universities amongst philosophical students. He is bound to make his mark in life.

In spite of the intellectual agnosticism which modern education bred in him, he held fast to the ideals of purity and renunciation, which he had imbibed from his childhood days. He was a past-master in meditation; and his passion for spiritual life grew with the years.

It was from a chance remark of Principal Hastie during a lesson on Wordsworth's poem, *The Excursion,* that Narendra heard the name of his future master for the first time. Explaining the poet's reference to trance, Principal Hastie had said that such religious ecstasies were the result of purity and concentration, that it was a rare phenomenon in modern times, and that he had known only one person who had experienced that blessed state, and that person was Ramakrishna of Daksineswar.

Narendra's Search for Truth

Narendra soon realised the inadequacies of modem rationalism and humanism. Religion may have its faults; it may have blundered into dogmatism and intolerance; but it has a spiritual core which mankind cannot ignore without making itself poorer, said he to himself. The endeavours and conclusions of the sense-bound intellect cannot be the last word in man's search for truth. An intellectual approach to truth will end only in agnosticism; and often even in cynicism. But the whole being of man seeks to *experience* truth, to *realise* it. And he found that modern thought had no message to give to man on this *theme. This rising above rationalism to direct experience and realisation, this growth of man from the sensate to the super-sensual dimension, is the special message of the Indian spiritual tradition;* and Ramakrishna embodied it in himself in its fullness.

Man may sharpen his reason and intellect; he may have the best of wealth and power; he may enjoy the delights of art and literature; yet his heart will continue to be a vacuum, and a prey to tension and sorrow, till he discovers his own spiritual dimension, till he realises God. This is the testament of Indian thought. Says the *Śvetasvatāra Upaniṣad* (VI. 19):

Yadā carmavadākāśaṁ veṣṭayiṣyanti mānavāḥ;
Tadā devam avijñāya duhkhasyānto bhaviṣyati

'Even if men (through their technical efficiency) will roll up all space like a piece of leather, they will not experience the end of sorrow without realising God.'

Vivekananda felt the pang of this vacuum as a university student.That made him restless; he could have silenced his heart's craving for truth, learnt to live with his intellectual agnosticism, and made the best of the world with his undoubted talents. But he was made of a different stuff, and meant for a different role.

His passion for truth would not allow him to compromise with a humdrum life. So like a 'hart that panteth after the water-brooks', in the words of the Psalm, his heart became restless for truth, and in this mood he went from place to place, from teacher to teacher, until an inexorable destiny took him to Sri Ramakrishna. 'Is there a God?' And, if there is, 'Have you seen Him?' were the questions that this young seeker put to every teacher. The history of religion tells us that when this question has been seriously put by any seeker, he has received a positive answer. The very soul of religion lies in the yearning behind this question. None of the teachers gave him satisfactory replies. None, except one; and that was Sri Ramakrishna.

The Profile of Sri Ramakrishna

At the suggestion of a friend that he might get a satisfactory answer from Sri Ramakrishna, Vivekananda wended his way to the Daksineswar temple on the left bank of the Ganga, where lived Ramakrishna in a small room facing the holy river. He was a strange person. He had passed through a stormy period of hankering and search for God and had realised Him, first through one path, then through another, until he traversed not only all the recognised paths of the Hindu religion, but also of Christianity and Islam. He had realised that it is the same God that is worshipped in all the religions and that 'the paths are many, but the goal is one.' This realisation had made him universal in outlook and sympathy with a deep love for man everywhere. He saw man in a new light; for he saw God in the hearts of all men. *He saw God both with his eyes closed and with his eyes open.* He was God-intoxicated and yet intensely human; with a smile on his face, he greeted every visitor and enfolded him in his pure love; and hundreds visited him—men and women, rich and poor, university students and pious householders, philosophers and artists, agnostics and holy men. He also, on his part, sought out the great and the holy. He conversed with all with infinite tenderness and sympathy. In the midst of serious conversations on God and the spiritual life, a chance divine suggestion would send him into divine ecstasy. Coming down from that state, he would become simple and playful like a child, and enjoy much fun and frolic with his listeners, especially the youthful ones.

This combination of the divine and the human in him fascinated all who went to him, and his words held them in thrall. His room was 'mart of joy,' in the words of 'M,' the author of *The Gospel of Sri Ramakrishna.* 'When the lotus opens', Sri Ramakrishna used to tell his young listeners, giving a parable to illustrate the magnetic influence of a man of God, 'bees come to it from all quarters on their own accord to seek its honey; it has not to send out an invitation.' This was literally true in his own case. He had prayed to the Divine Mother: 'Mother, don't get any creeds expounded through my mouth.' They are, as Jesus had expressed it, as *stones* to a hungry man. What he gave to all seekers without distinction was the *bread* of spirituality. The main theme of his conversations was man growing spiritually through the manifestation of the Divine within. A procession of seekers, which included such distinguished men as the great religious leader of the Brahmo Samaj, Keshab Chandra Sen, went to him from Calcutta and nearby villages; it began as a trickle in 1875 and became a flood by the time he passed away in 1886. We get an arresting account of this pilgrimage of spiritually hungry souls to this unique teacher in that great book above referred to, *The Gospel of Sri Ramakrishna* by Mahendranath Gupta, the highly gifted and intimate householder disciple of the Master, who was the headmaster of a Calcutta school, and who hides his persontality under the pseudonym 'M'.

Referring to this book and its author in his Foreword to the English edition of the book, Aldous Huxley says:

> Making good use of his natural gifts and of the circumstances in which he found himself, 'M' produced a book unique, so far as my knowledge goes, in the literature of hagiography. No other saint has had so able and indefatigable a Boswell. Never have the small events of a contemplative's daily life been described with such a wealth of intimate detail. Never have the casual and unstudied utterances of a great religious teacher been set down with so minute a fidelity.

Narendra at the Feet of Sri Ramakrishna

The Master gave of his realisations to all who came to him; each received according to his or her need and capacity; the central theme of all his talks was spirituality and the way to achieve it; the same teaching was not given to any two seekers. No creed was expounded; no belief was criticised; but the spiritual life of the seeker was stimulated and deepened, and his vision and sympathy broadened. Thus he poured out a stream of truth and wisdom almost eighteen hours of the twenty-four. And to him went Narendra, his steps guided by a divine destiny, who asked the question which was agitating his heart for years and for which he could not get any satisfactory answer from any teacher till then: 'Sir, have you seen God?' 'Yes, my boy, I have seen Him,' replied the Master with calm and loving assurance and added: 'I see Him more intensely than I see you here; and you can also see Him.'

This was new language indeed! It is difficult to express the powerful impact which these simple words made on the mind and heart of Narendra. He felt in the depth of his being that these words came from the depths of the Master's realisation; and he decided to learn more of him and from him; every day brought him to a clearer awareness of the profound spirituality of the Master and the significance of his life and realisations.

Narendra grew into full spiritual maturity under the loving guidance of Sri Ramakrishna. Unlike other disciples, Narendra tested every word of the teachings of his Master by his keen intellect and critical reason, and literally fought every inch of his way to spiritual truth and conviction. The Master on his part encouraged his gifted disciple in this. 'Test me as the money changers test their coins', the Master used to tell Narendra.

Narendra was to allude to this fact later when, as Swami Vivekananda, he had to deal with his own highly gifted but sceptical and rebellious disciple, Miss Margaret Noble, who later became famous in the East and West as Sister Nivedita. Says she in her *The Master as I Saw Him* (sixth edition, pp.12-13):

> Referring to this scepticism of mind, which was well known at the time to the rest of the class, a more fortunate disciple, long afterwards, was teasing me, in the Swami's presence, and claiming that she had been able to accept every statement she had ever heard him make. The Swami paid little or no attention to the conversation at the time, but afterwards he took a quiet moment to say: 'Let none regret that they were difficult to convince! I fought my Master for six long years, with the result that I know every inch of the way! Every inch of the way!

This training of Narendra at the hands of Sri Ramakrishna, by which the young dynamic intellectual became a man of God, one who saw God in himself and in all beings, one who became, like his Master, universal in his sympathy for man in the East and the West, is a momentous chapter in modern history, fraught with great consequences for the future.

Vivekananda sitting at the feet of Sri Ramakrishna is an arresting phenomenon. No two people could have been more opposite in temperament, up-bringing, and mental make-up than these two; and yet no two people have been so intimate and attuned to each other as these. One was the complement of the other; the Master continuing his being in the disciple and the disciple fulfilling the life-work and mission of the Master. Before he passed away on 16 August 1886, Sri Ramakrishna banded the handful of his young disciples, fifteen in number, into a monastic order under Narendra's leadership. In due course, they assumed monastic names, he taking the name Vivekananda, meaning the 'bliss of discrimination', before his departure to the West in 1893.

The Meeting of Two Master-minds

Ramakrishna represented the eternal soul of India, calm and majestic, 'with a unifying, pacifying love for all living things,' in the words of Will Durant. In his Foreword to the *Life of Sri Ramakrishna,* (sixth edition), Mahatma Gandhi writes:

> The story of Ramakrishna Paramahamsa's life is a story of religion in practice. His life enables us to see God face to face. None can read the story of his life without being convinced that God alone is real and that all else is an illusion. Ramakrishna was a living embodiment of godliness. . . . His love knew no limits, geographical or otherwise. May his divine love be an inspiration to all who read the following pages.

Vivekananda, on the other hand, represented the modern spirit of freedom and equality, manliness and energy of action. *The intimate communion of the Master and the disciple demonstrated the basic unity of godliness and manliness.* True godliness is the very consummation of manliness; true manliness, similarly, is an expression of godliness. As held in Indian spiritual thought, Narayana (God) is the *sakha* (friend) of *Nara* (man). As held in Christian spiritual thought, the Son of God is also the Son of man. This close communion between the ancient Indian legacy of godliness and the modern Western legacy of manliness in Ramakrishna and Vivekananda is what I have taken as the theme of tonight's lecture: *The Meeting of East and West in Swami Vivekananda.*

Ramakrishna gave himself to the world in Vivekananda. The coming together of any two gifted souls as teacher and student has always been an event of creative significance of varying measure in world history. In this case, the two souls were not merely gifted but uniquely outstanding and creatively original; each was a complement to the other, and both together represented the totality of human outlooks and aspirations, tastes and temperaments. The creative significance of such a confluence is bound to be deep, abiding, and world-wide. In the words of the *Kaṭha Upaniṣad* (II. 7):

> *Āścaryo vaktā kuśalosyalabdhā āścaryo jñātā*
> *kuśalānuśiṣṭaḥ*

'Wonderful the teacher and very competent the disciple; wonderful becomes the seeker of knowledge when taught by a competent teacher.'

This confluence witnessed the emergence of a glorious vision of truth, of a more perfect excellence of character than achieved hitherto in East or West, and the striving for universal human happiness and welfare. Knowledge is a powerful force. Love is another powerful force. The more universal and pure the knowledge and love, the more dynamic they become. In Ramakrishna and Vivekananda, knowledge and love shed all their limitations and became a mighty force-pure, positive, and dynamic.

This supreme consummation cannot, and will not, remain confined to an individual like Vivekananda. Modern world conditions and the urges and needs of modern man make its achievement in some measure, by every man and woman in the present age, a desirable ideal and an imperative necessity. *Modern education needs to be shaped to that end.* Education should convey the heritage of the whole world to every man and woman, so that unlimited character-efficiency may be achieved and a global outlook may be realised, to complement the global physical unity achieved by modern technology. Here is the world significance of Sri Ramakrishna and Swami Vivekananda, and the movement initiated by them. They have set in motion a powerful energy of spiritual vision dedicated to the forging of human unity through God—God dwelling in the heart of man, the God in man beckoning him to continue his evolution by going beyond his sense-bound personality to realise his divine dimension and his spiritual solidarity with all existence. *It is a vision backed by the intellectual and moral vigour of Vedānta and fulfilling the urges and aspirations of modern scientific and social thought.*

The education of Vivekananda in this universal vision and sympathy at the hands of his great master is a fascinating theme for all students of education and religion. There are two landmarks in this education which I would like specially to refer to. The first relates to the acceptance, by Vivekananda, after much struggle, of the truth of Śakti, the immanent aspect of Reality, the personal aspect of the impersonal Brahman; and the second relates to his acceptance of its positivistic corollary, namely, 'seeing God with eyes open', in the words of Sri Ramakrishna.

Narendra's Inner Conflicts

When he came to his master, Narendra was a votary of the personal but formless God as presented in the Brahmo Samaj, of which he was then a member. He did not relish the idea of God either as the impersonal Absolute or as the personal sakti, the one source of all nature and its energies. These two represented the age-old conflict between the two schools of *jñāna* (the path of the impersonal God) and *bhakti* (the path of the personal God), with the God of the Brahmo Samaj partaking of the abstractions of both. The first is the path of negation, while the second is the path of affirmation, which latter, in its full and robust forms, involves also the path of *karmā* or action. The differences in approach between these cannot and should not annul the unity of their common goal. But this was what happened in India in later ages, weakening both the paths and narrowing the minds of their followers. This had meant in effect that there were two Gods—one that of the *jñāni,* and the other that of the *bhakta.* The *jñāni* dismissed the world as *māyā,* the God of the *bhakta* as a product of this *māyā,* and the *bhakta* himself as a weak sentimentalist. The *bhakta,* on his part, dismissed the transcendent God of the *jñāni* as a pure nothingness and the *jñāni* himself as a dry intellectual. The modern votaries of secular rationalism and scientific humanism, on the other hand, to whom the world itself is their god and reality, dismissed both the *jñāni* and the *bhakta* as vain dreamers and their gods as products of a pious wish-fulfilment.

Into this murky atmosphere of contemporary thought came the luminous vision of Sri Ramakrishna, who realised the fundamental unity of the God of *the jñāni* and the God of the *bhakta,* and the complementary character of the two paths of affirmation and negation. Romain Rolland opens his preface entitled 'To My Eastern Readers' to his *Life of Ramakrishna* with the following utterance of Sri Ramakrishna suffused with this unifying vision:

> Greeting to the feet of the *jñāni!* Greeting to the feet of the *Bhakta!* Greeting to the devout who believe in the formless God! Greeting to those who believe in God with form! Greeting to the men of old who knew Brahman! Greeting to the modern knowers of Truth. (Ramakrishna, October 28, 1882).

Sri Ramakrishna gently educated Narendra in this unifying vision during the six years of his discipleship. In the early stages, Narendra reacted violently to the concept of the impersonal and formless

Brahman, as he had all along reacted to that of the personal God with form. To him and to many seekers of the personal God like him, the impersonal meant something inert and abstract, equivalent to the physicist's primordial nature, and the personal meant crude anthropomorphism and superstition. Sri Ramakrishna slowly made him understand the *spiritual* character of the impersonal Absolute through a convincing presentation of the philosophy of the path of negation. Brahman as the *Self* of all beings cannot be impersonal in the sense in which scientists present nature, or the cosmic dust, or the cosmic background material. Neither can Brahman, the one behind the many, be a person to be designated either as masculine or feminine; hence the preference of the neuter term 'It' to describe Brahman. The path to It is the path of negation, the path of *neti, neti;* by negating all objects and entities, all predicates and concepts, and even the ego, as belonging to the world of *māyā,* the seeker approaches Brahman as the transcendental Absolute, the Unconditioned, 'from which all speech and thought recoil, not being able to grasp It,' the experience of which is best expressed only through silence. Sri Ramakrishna had earlier followed this path under the guidance of his *guru,* Totāpuri, and attained its consummation in the experience of *nirvikalpa samādhi.*

Narendra and the Critical Spirit in Religion

Narendra soon became fascinated with this path of the 'abysmal God'. He became eager to experience *nirvikalpa samādhi.* And he had it with the gracious help of his *guru.* But when he desired to pursue this path and its bliss of the unconditioned Brahman exclusively, Sri Ramakrishna reproved him and pointed out to him the path and goal of a comprehensive spirituality, in which the paths of affirmation and negation merge, and which he was to follow, and of which he was to be the teacher and exemplar to millions of people in the modern age.

Before meeting Narendra, Sri Ramakrishna had been heard to pray: 'O Mother, send me some one who will doubt my realisations.' Narendra's arrival at Daksineswar signified the granting of this prayer. He was unlike all his other disciples. A staunch follower of the Brahmo Samaj cult of the personal God without form, he could not tolerate the worship of the personal God through various forms upheld in the Hindu religion and practised by his own master, Sri Ramakrishna. He used to criticise even Sri Ramakrishna's visions of divine forms and his worship of Kālī, the Divine Mother, before whom Narendra not only refused to bow down himself, but also criticised other fellow disciples for doing so. Sri Ramakrishna's reaction to this critical and even hostile attitude and conduct of his disciple was unusual and refreshingly modern. He told Narendra: 'Do not accept anything because I say so. Test everything for yourself.' Further, as mentioned earlier, the Master told him: 'Test me as the money changers test their coins.' This unique relationship is revealed in the following passage of the *Life of Sri Ramakrishna* (Sixth Edition, p.345):

> The liberty which Narendranath enjoyed in his association with Sri Ramakrishna was unusual, as will be gathered from the following incident. He often argued with the Master against image-worship. One day, when the latter could not convince him, he said: 'Why do you come here if you won't acknowledge my Mother?' Narendra replied; 'Must I accept Her simply because I come here?' 'All right', said the Master, 'are long you shall not only acknowledge my blessed Mother, but weep in Her name.' Then addressing the other devotees he said: 'This boy has no faith in the forms of God and tells me that my supersensuous experiences are hallucinations; but he is a very fine boy, of pure instincts. He does not believe in

anything unless he gets direct proof. He has studied much, and is possessed of great judgement and discrimination.'

Kāli, the Divine Mother

What did Sri Ramakrishna mean when he referred to Kāli as my 'Divine Mother?' What did he mean when he spoke about the worship of God with form? Why did he desire that Narendra should accept his Divine Mother?

To the unthinking observer, Kālī worshipped in the temple of Daksineswar may be nothing more than an idol, like several other idols of gods and goddesses, 'superstitiously' worshipped by ignorant devotees! When such an unthinking observer becomes a thinking seeker, he will begin to discover meaning and significance behind all such worship, he will learn to pierce the outer crust and reach the inner truth visualised by the outer symbol. He will also understand that what a seeker seeks is spiritual growth and realisation and not mere intellectual formulation.

A Fellow-Student's Estimate of Narendra

One of Vivekananda's own fellow-students in college, the distinguished intellectual and scholar, and author of *The Positive Sciences of the Ancient Hindus,* Dr. Brajendra Nath Seal, felt at first scandalised when he saw Narendra, the rationalist and iconoclast, fallen under the influence of an idolatrous teacher. Says he in a penetrating article published in *The Prabuddha Bharata* five years after Vivekananda's death in 1902 *(The Life of Swami Vivekananda by His Eastern and Western Disciples,* pp. 81-82):

I watched with intense interest the transformation that went on under my eyes. The attitude of a rampant Vedāntistcum-Hegelian-cum-revolutionary like myself towards the cult of religious ecstasy and Kālī-worship may be easily imagined; and the spectacle of a born iconoclast and free-thinker like Vivekananda, a creative and dominating intelligence, a tamer of souls, himsel caught in the meshes of what appeared to me as uncouth, supernatural mysticism was a ridddle which my philosophy of the Pure Reason could scarcely read at the time. But Vivekananda 'the loved and lost' was loved, and mourned most in what I could not but then regard as his defection; and it was personal feeling, after all, the hated pathological element of individual preference and individual relationship, which most impelled me, when at last I went on what to a home-keeping recluse like myself was an adventurous journey to Daksineswar, to see and hear Vivekananda's Master, and spent the greater part of a long summer day in the shady and peaceful solitudes of the temple-garden, returning as the sun set amidst the whirl and rush and roar and the awful gloom of a blinding thunder-storm, with a sense of bewilderment as well moral as physical, and a lurking perception of the truth that the majesty of Law orders the apparently irregular and grotesque, that there may be self-mastery in apparent self-alienation, that sense even in its errors is only insipient Reason, and that faith in a Saving Power *ab extra* is but the dim reflex of an original act of self-determination. And a significant confirmation of all this came in the subsequent life-history of Vivekananda, who, after he had found the firm assurance he sought in the saving Grace and Power of his Master, went about preaching and teaching the creed of the Universal, and the absolute and inalienable sovereignty of the Self.

Sri Ramakrishna's Divine Mother

The image of Kālī worshipped by Sri Ramakrishna as *Bhavatāriṇī,* the Saviour of the Universe, is made of basalt and stands on the chest of a white marble image of the prostrate body of Her divine consort, Śiva, the symbol of the Absolute. She wears a golden garland of severed human heads, and a girdle of human arms. She has four hands. The lower left hand holds a severed human head and the upper one grips a blood-stained sword. One right hand offers boons to Her children; the other offers them protection from fear. The majesty of Her posture combines the terror of destruction with the tender assurance of motherly love. She is the primordial cosmic Power, the totality of all existence, the glorious harmony of the pairs of opposites. She creates, preserves, and destroys. She has three eyes, the third, on the forehead, being the symbol of divine wisdom. She is Nature, *aparā* as well as *parā,* physical as well as spiritual, cosmic as well as divine; the Universal Mother, who reveals Herself to Her children under diverse aspects and under different divine incarnations; the visible God who leads the seeker to the heart of the divine Mystery; the gracious Mother who, if it so pleases Her, takes away the last trace of the finite ego from a seeker and merges it in the infinite and absolute consciousness of Brahman, the impersonal and formless God.

Idolatry is religion that *starts* and *ends* with the worship of an idol. An idol is a form of God visible and tangible to the senses. *If such an idol, on the other hand, inspires the worshipeer to go beyond the sense-bound world and realise the primordial divine spiritual energy behind the universe, it ceases to be idolatry; it then becomes the essential first lesson in the grand book of spiritual knowledge and experience.* This is the Hindu approach to image worship; *and Sri Ramakrishna re-explored this path from the starting point to the goal, from the base to the summit.* His worship *started* with the image of Kālī; but *it did not end* there.

It soon penetrated the outer crust of reality revealed to the senses as an idol, as a sensual form, the *mrnmayi mūrti,* and reached the heart of reality, the *cinmayī Śakti,* the supreme energy of Consciousness behind the whole universe of man and nature. Sri Ramakrishna called this Reality by the sweet name of 'My Divine Mother', whom he approached through the path of affirmation, and who, he held, is the *Śakti* or primordial divine Energy, of that Brahman, the Absolute of stillness and quiescence, which is the goal of the path of negation and which he had later attained through his *nirvikalpa samādhi* experience.

The Old Testament also sings in its Psalms the glory of this impersonal-personal God (Psalm 139, 7-10):

> Whither shall I go from Thy spirit or whither shall I flee from Thy presence? If I ascend up into heaven, Thou art there; if I make by bed in hell, behold, Thou art there.
>
> If I take the wings of the morning and dwell in the uttermost parts of the sea; even there shall Thy hand lead me and Thy right hand shall hold me.

The nature of Kālī or Śakti realised by Sri Ramakrishna shines through his several expositions on the subject, as can be gleaned from the following passages of *The Gospel of Sri Ramakrishna* (New York Edition, p.106):

To explain the nature of Kālī to the scholar Iswar Chandra Vidyasagar, Sri Ramakrishna sang the following song of poet-saint Ramaprasad:

> Who is there who can understand what Mother Kālī is?
> Even the six *darsanas* (Indian philosophical systems) are powerless to reveal Her.
> It is She, the scriptures say, that is the inner Self
> Of the *yogi,* who in Self discovers all his joy;
> She that, of Her own sweet will, inhabits every living thing.

The macrocosm and microcosm rest in the Mother's womb;
Now do you see how vast it is? In the mu*ladhara* (sacral plexus)
The *yogi* meditates on Her, and in the *sahasrāra* (the brain);
Who but Śiva has beheld Her as She really is?
Within the lotus wilderness (heart) She sports beside Her Mate, the Swan (Śiva, the Absolute).
When man aspires to *understand* Her, Ramaprasad must smile!
To think of knowing Her, he says, is quite as laughable
As to imagine one can swim across the boundless sea.
But while my mind has understood, alas! my heart has not;
Though but a dwarf, it still would strive to make a captive of the moon!

Unity of Brahman and Śakti

Explaining to the Brahmo Samaj leader, Keshab Chandra Sen, the difference in approaches between the paths of negation, *jnana,* and affirmation, *bhakti,* Sri Ramakrishna says (*ibid.,* p.134):

> The *jñānīs,* who adhere to the non-dualistic philosophy of Vedānta, say that the acts of creation, preservation, and destruction, the universe itself and all its living beings, are the manifestations of Śakti, the divine Power (known also as *Māyā*) . If you reason it out, you will realize that all these are as illusory as a dream. Brahman alone is the Reality, and all else is unreal. Even this very Śakti is insubstantial, like a dream.
>
> But though you reason all your life, unless you are established in *samadhi,* you cannot go beyond the jurisdiction of Śakti. Even when you say, 'I am meditating',

> or 'I am contemplating', still you are moving in the realm of Śakti, within Its power.
>
> Thus Brahman and Śakti are identical. If you accept the one, you must accept the other. It is like fire and its power to bum. If you see the fire, you must recognise its power to burn also. You cannot think of fire without its power to bum, nor can you think of the power to bum without fire. You cannot conceive of the sun's rays without the sun, nor can you conceive of the sun without its rays. . . .
>
> Thus one cannot think of Brahman without Śakti, or of Śakti without Brahman. One cannot think of the Absolute without the Relative, or of the Relative without the Absolute.

Unity of the Impersonal and the Personal

Instructing the Brahmo Samaj leader, Vijay Krishna Goswami, in the dual nature of God as with form and without form, Sri Ramakrishna says *(ibid.,* p.634):

> That which is Brahman is also Kālī, the Mother, the primal Energy. When inactive, It is called Brahman. Again, when creating, preserving, and destroying. It is called Śakti. Still water is an illustration of Brahman. The same water, moving in waves, may be compared to Śakti, Kālī. What is the meaning of Kālī? She who communes with Mahākāla, the Absolute, is Kālī. She is formless, and, again. She has forms. If you believe in the formless aspect, then meditate on Kālī as that If you merely on any aspect of Her with firm conviction, She will let you know Her true nature. Then you will realize that not mereloy does God exist, but He will come near you and talk to you as I am talking to you. Have faith and you will achieve everything. Remember

> this, too. If you believe that God is formless, then stick to that belief with firm conviction. But don't be dogmatic; never say emphatically about God that He can be only this and not that. You may say: ' I believe that God is formless. But He can be many things more. He alone knows what else He can be. I do not know; I do not understand.' How can man with his one ounce of intelligence know the real nature of God? Can you put four *seers* of milk in a one-*seer* jar? If God, through His grace, ever reveals Himself to His devotee and makes him understand, then he will know; but not otherwise.

Narendra's Education in the Vision of the Impersonal God

Sri Ramakrishna led Narendra slowly and steadily to this truly Advaitic (non-dual) vision of the impersonal-personal God. Apart from instruction and discourse, his powerful spiritual influence helped to soften the hold of one or two obstinate dogmas over Narenda's mind and make it a free and untrammelled instrument for the vision of Truth and his mission to humanity. At the very commencement of his discipleship, during his second visit to Sri Ramakrishna, Narendra, then about nineteen, received a glimpse of the impersonal God in *nirvicalpa samādhi* through the touch of the Master. Narendra's reaction to this unexpected and unprepared-for experience puzzled Sri Ramakrishna In the words of Narendra himself *(Life of Sri Ramakrishna,* pp.333-34)

> I found him sitting alone on the small bedstead. He was glad to see me and, calling me affectionately to his side, made me sit beside him on the bed. But the next moment, I found him overcome with a sort of emotion. Muttering something to himself, with his eyes fixed on me he slowly drew near me. I thought he might do something queer as

on the preceding occasion. But in the twinkling of an eye, he placed his right foot on my body. The touch at one gave rise to a novel experience within me. With my eyes open, I saw that the walls, and everything in the room, whirled rapidly and vanished into nought, and the whole universe, together with my individuality, was about to merge in an all encompassing mysterious void! I was terribly frightened and thought that I was facing death, for the loss of individuality meant nothing short of that. Unable to control myself, I cried out: 'What is this that you are doing to me? I have my parents at home!' He laughed aloud at this and stroking my chest said: 'All right; let it rest now. Everything will come in time!' The wonder of it was that no sooner had he said this than that strange experience of mine vanished. I was myself again and found everything within and without the room as it had been before.

All this happened in less time than it takes me to narrate it, but it revolutionised my mind. Amazed, I thought what it could possibily be. It came and went at the mere wish of this wonderful man! I began to question if it were mesmerism or hypnotism. But that was not likely, for these acted only on weak minds, and I prided myself on being just the reverse. I had not surrendered myself to the stronger personality of the man. Rather, I had taken him to be a monomaniac. So what might this sudden transformation of mine be due to? I could not come to any conclusion. It was an enigma, I thought, which I had better not attempt to solve. I was determined, however, to be on my guard and not to give him another chance to exert a similar influence on me.

. . . My rationalistic mind received an unpleasant rebuff at this failure in judging the true state of things. But I was resolved to fathom the mystery somehow.

Sri Ramakrishna knew in his heart of hearts that Narendra would eventually grasp the truth of the unconditioned Brahman. He made him read books like *Aṣṭāvakra Saṁhitā* on the subject. To Narendra's mind, trained in the theology of the Brahmo Safnaj, these writings appeared to be heretical. He would often rebel saying: 'It is blasphemy, or there is no difference between such philosophy and atheism. There is no greater sin in the world than to think of oneself as identical with the Creator. I am God, you are God, these created things are God—what can be more absurd than this? The sages who wrote such things must have been insane.' Sri Ramakrishna, amused at the bluntness of his disciple but desiring to lead him to a more comprehensive spiritual vision, would gently admonish: 'You may not accept the views of these seers. But how can you abuse them or limit God's infinitude? Go on praying to the God of truth and believe in that aspect of His which He reveals to you.'

Narendra's Experience of the Nirvikalpa Samādhi

One day, the Master tried to bring home to Narendra the identity of Ātman, the Self of man, with Brahman, the Self of the universe, but could not convince him. Narendra went out of the room .and discussed the topic with Hazra, another devotee of Sri Ramakrishna; and amidst derisive laughter, both dismissed the teaching as preposterous. Hearing the remark and laughter, Sri Ramakrishna came out of his room in a semiconscious state and, touching Narendra, went into *samadhi.* That holy touch revolutionised Narendra's mind, which began to see and realise that there was nothing but God in the universe. In the words of Narendra, closing his narration of the incident *(ibid.,* pp.344-45):

> This state of things continued for some days. When I became normal again, I realised that I must have had a glimpse of the Advaita state. Then it struck me that the

> words of the scriptures were not false. Thenceforth, I could not deny the conclusions of the Advaita philosophy.

Uptil now, Narendra had achieved the experience of Brahman through the grace of his Master, unsought and unprepared. But while, to the earlier two experiences, he had reacted, first, with fear and, then, with hostility, he reacted to the third experience with understanding and appreciation. And, during the last year of Sri Ramakrishna's life, we find Narendra consumed with a raging spiritual passion and seeking with restless yearning for this very experience of Brahman from the Master. In the words of the author of *The Life of Sri Ramakrishna* (p.588):

> We have seen Narendranath's aspirations for the highest truth and his struggle to attain it. Yet, one evening, as he was meditating, it came to him quite unexpectedly. At first, he felt as if a light had been placed behind his head. Then he passed beyond all relativity and was lost in the Absolute. He had attained the *nirvikalpa samādhi!* When he gained a little consciousness of the world, he found only his head, but not his body. He cried out 'Ah, where is my body?' Hearing his voice, Gopal Senior came into the room. Naren repeated the query. 'Here it is, Naren,' answered Gopal. When that failed to convince Narendra, Gopal was terrified and hastened to inform the Master. The latter only said: 'Let him stay in that state for a while! He has teased me long enough for it!'

You Have the Mother's Work To Do'

Romain Rolland narrates the same incident, quoting from a letter written to him by Swami Śivananda, a fellow disciple of Narendra, on 7 December 1927 *(Life of Ramakrishna,* p.268):

One day, Swami Sivananda told me, he was present in the garden of Cossipore, near Calcutta, when Naren really attained this state. Seeing him unconscious, his body as cold as that of a corpse, we ran in great agitation to the Master and told him what had happened. The Master showed no anxiety; he merely smiled and said: 'Very well!' and then relapsed into silence. Naren returned to outward consciousness and came to the Master. The Master said to him: 'Well, now do you understand? This (highest realisation) will henceforward remain under lock and key. You have the Mother's work to do. When it is finished. She will undo the lock.' Naren replied: 'Master, I was happy in *samādhi.* In my infinite joy, I had forgotten the world. I beseech you to let me remain in that state!' 'For shame!' cried the Master. 'How can you ask such things? I thought you were a vast receptacle of life, and here you wish to stay absorbed in personal joy like an ordinary man! . . . This realisation will become so natural to you by the grace of the Mother that, in your normal state, you will realise the One Divinity in all beings; you will do great things in the world; you will bring spiritual consciousness to men, and assuage the misery of the humble and the poor.'

Narendra's Experience of the Personal God

'You have the Mother's Work to do,' said Ramakrishna. We had seen earlier that Narendra had a poor opinion of His Master's worship of Kālī and of his various spiritual visions and experiences. But his seeking for *nirvikalpa samādhi* from the Master, referred to above, had been preceded by his understanding and acceptance of Sri Ramakrishna's vision of the truth of Kālī. This transformation, though coming on gently and steadily, was registered by an important event which occurred less than two years earlier, when Narendra experienced the delight of pure *bhakti* centred in the personal God.

In 1884, Narendra's prodigal father died suddenly of heart failure throwing the family into utter financial ruin. Being the eldest son, the burden of earning for the family of six or seven fell on Narendra. This introduced him for the first time to life's alter-face of sorrow and misery, and violently upset his erstwhile convictions as to the existence and truth of the benign personal God of monotheism. His biography by his Eastern and Western disciples contains, in its chapter entitled 'Trials and Hardships,' a vivid account, much of it in his own words, of his intimate contact with the tragic element in human life and of the tremendous reactions it produced in him. Facile philosophies and shallow beliefs become shattered under its impact, leaving man, in ordinary circumstances, cynical and sour, with heart dried up and mind empty, and in extraordinary circumstances, dynamic and cheerful, with heart warmed up with love and compassion and mind steady and pure. Such circumstances refer not to the presence or absence of intellect or wealth or power, but to the presence or absence of inward spiritual resources, to the presence or absence of the spiritual capacity to *digest* all experience. Narendra had these inner resources in abundance—he had zealously cultivated them even in the midst of intellectual storms and stresses—and he had the additional advantage of a supremely powerful resource outside of himself in the person of his extraordinary Master.

When he was in the very midst of this trial and hardship, Narendra had a transforming vision which brought him instant peace of heart and mind. To give it in his own words *(The Life of Swami Vivekananda,* pp.93-94):

> The summer was over and the rains set in. The search for a job still went on. One evening, after a whole day's fast and exposure to rain, I was returning home with tired limbs and a jaded mind; over powered with exhaustion and unable to move a step forward, I sank down on the outer plinth of a house on the roadside. I can't say whether I was insensible for a time or not. Various thoughts crowded into my mind, and I was too weak to drive them off and fix

> my attention on a particular thing. Suddenly, I felt as if by some divine power the coverings of my soul were removed one after another. All my former doubts regarding the co-existence of divine justice and mercy, and the presence of misery in the creation of a blissful Providence, were automatically solved. By a deep introspection, I found the meaning of it all, and was satisfied. As I proceeded homewards, I found there was no trace of fatigue in the body, and the mind was refreshed with wonderful strength and peace. The night was well nigh over.
>
> Henceforth I became deaf to the praise and blame of worldly people. I was convinced that I was not bom like humdrum people to earn money and maintain my family, much less to strive for sense-pleasure.

Unable to earn enough to keep his family above starvation, rebuffed everywhere, Narendra turned his mind to Sri Ramakrishna's blissful Mother and decided to ask him to intercede with Her on behalf of his starving family. To quote Narendra again *(ibid.,* p.95):

> One day the idea struck me that God listened to Sri Ramakrishna's prayers; so why should I not ask him to pray for me for the removal of my pecuniary wants-a favour the Master would never deny me? I hurried to Daksineswar and insisted on his making the appeal on behalf of my starving family. He said: 'My boy, I can't make such demands. But why don't *you* go and ask the Mother yourself? All your sufferings are due to your disregard for Her.' I said: 'I do not know the Mother; you please speak to Her on my behalf. You must.' He replied tenderly: 'My dear boy, I have done so again and again. But *you* do not accept Her; so She does not grant my prayer. All right, it is Tuesday—go to the Kālī temple

> tonight, prostrate yourself before the Mother, and ask Her any boon you like. It *shall* be granted. She is Knowledge Absoilute, the Inscrutable Power of Brahman, and by Her mere will has given birth to this world. Everything is in Her power to give.'

Narendra waited for the night. At about nine, he walked across the courtyard and reached the temple. To continue the narration in his own words *(ibid)*:

> As I went, I was filled with a divine intoxication. My feet were unsteady. My heart was leaping in anticipation of the joy of beholding the living Goddess and hearing Her words. . . . Reaching the temple, as I cast my eyes upon the image, I actually found that the Divine Mother was living and conscious, the perennial fountain of Divine Love and Beauty. I was caught in a surging wave of devotion and love. In an ecstasy of joy, I prostrated myself again and again before the Mother and prayed: 'Mother, give me discrimination! Grant me renunciation! Give unto me knowledge and devotion! Grant that I may have an uninterrupted vision of Thee!' A serene peace reigned in my soul. The world was forgotten. Only the Divine Mother shone within my heart!

He returned to Sri Ramakrishna's room. The Master asked him whether he had prayed for the removal of his worldly wants. 'No, Sir, I forgot all about it. But is there any remedy now?' The Master asked him to go again. He went; but, at the very sight of the Mother, he again forgot his mission and prayed only for love and devotion. The Master sent him a third time with the reprimand: 'How thoughtless! Couldn't you restrain yourself enough to say those few words?' He went again; but on entering the temple, a terrible feeling of shame overpowered him when he thought: What a trifle I have come to pray to the Mother for! It is like asking a gracious king for a few vegetables! What a fool I am!' He prostrated again and again and prayed for knowledge and devotion. He reported everything to Sri Ramakrishna and requested, him to grant the boon himself. The Master replied: 'Such a prayer never comes from my lips. I asked you to pray for yourself. But you couldn't do it. It appears that you are not destined to enjoy worldly happiness. Well, I can't help it.' When Narendra insisted, the Master said in an exalted mood: 'All right, your people at home will never be in want of plain food and clothing.'

A heavy burden was lifted from Narendra's heart; subsequent events proved the truth of the Master's blessing with respect to his family. Sri Ramakrishna was in a state of ecstasy that night, for his beloved disciple had accepted his Divine Mother. Narendra also spent the night in an ecstasy of devotion and joy singing the song on the Divine Mother glorifying Her omnipresence, and beginning with the lines: *Mā tvaṁ hi tārā*—'Mother, Thou art verily the Redeemer', which the Master had just then taught him at his request. *From that day onwards the disciple became one in spirit with the Master who, on his part, had always treated him as non-separate from himself.*

The rational mind of Narendra grasped the truth of Nature in a new dimension that night; it is not only energy—*śakti;* but also spiritual energy—*cit śakti,* of which all other energies are but manifestations. The Divine Mother of Sri Ramakrishna is this *cit śakti.* Long after, in a talk recorded by Sister Niveditā, Vivekananda confided to her his conviction in the profundity of the truth of Kālī, the Divine Mother, whose image he viewed as the symbol of the book of experience which the soul turns page after page, and, in whose name, men and women will find strength to sound many experiences to their depths *(The Master as I Saw Him,* p.170):

> You see, I cannot but believe that there is somewhere a great Power that thinks of Herself as feminine, and called Kālī, and Mother. . . . And I believe in Brahman, too.

Goethe expresses a similar conviction when he ends his *Faust* with the words:

> The Eternal Feminine leads us on and on.

In a few touching lines, Walt Whitman sings the invocation of the Divine Mother *(Leaves of Grass,* Everyman's Library Edition, 1927, p.279):

> Dark Mother, always gliding near with soft feet,
> Have none chanted for Thee a chant of fullest welcome?
> Then I chant it for Thee, I glorify Thee above all,
> I bring Thee a song that, when Thou must indeed come, come unfalteringly.

'By Their Fruits Ye Shall Know Them'

The philosophic and spiritual vision which Ramakrishna imparted to Vivekananda had a profound impact on the subsequent career of the latter and the history of modern India. For it soon began to translate itself into action with a pervasive sweep, unprecedented in the five-thousand-year history of India. As it unifies the divergent approaches of affirmation and negation, of Śakti and Brahman, it also synthesises the diverse paths of action and contemplation, work and worship, the secular and the sacred, in a comprehensive spirituality. In it, the God-ward passion pours out also as a man-ward love and service. 'By their fruits ye shall know them,' said Jesus about the truth or otherwise of man's ideological convictions. Such convictions have produced, as history has shown, in religious, political, and other fields of human life, character-fruits of diverse quality, from the sweetest to the bitterest, with any number of strands in between. Apathetic withdrawal or energetic action, pessimistic resignation or optimistic struggle, egoistic self-assertion or spiritual self-denial, intolerance or universal acceptance, violence and aggressiveness or non-violence and gentleṭness, universal love or blind hatred, selfishness and exploitation or renunciation and services—all these are the character-fruits of man's phiṭlosophies, well thought-out or ill.

Sri Ramakrishna has coined a new term for this comprehensive philosophic and spiritual vision, namely, *vijñāna. The fruit of this vijñāna in a character signifies the rare synthesis of the virtues and graces of the cultures of the East and the West. This was the extraordinary achievement in the character and personality of Swami Vivekananda. This explains the unprecedented sweep and range of its energy resources. This alone explains also its tremendous intensity and the explosive impact of its brief ten-year ministry.* Vivekananda was the supreme example of what Herbert Spencer *(Study of Sociology,* Eighth Edition, p.403) characterised as *uniting philanthropic energy with philosophic calm* which, in the Vedāntic terminology, means the union of Śakti and Śiva, or Kālī and Brahman.

Sri Ramakrishna: The Man And The Power

Romain Rolland, among several other sensitive thinkers, sensed the impact of these two dynamic spiritual leaders of modern India in a profound way. Says he in his preface, entitled To My Western Readers', to his *Life of Ramakrishna* (p.8):

> For a century in new India, Unity has been the target for the arrows of all archers. Fiery personalities throughout this century have sprung from her sacred earth, a veritable Ganges of peoples and thought Whatever may be the differences between them, their goal is ever the same—human unity through God. And through all the changes of workmen. Unity itself has expanded and gained in precision.

> From this magnificent procession of spiritual heroes whom we shall survey later, I have chosen two men, who have won my regard because, with incomparable charm and power, they have realised this splendid symphony of the universal Soul. They are, if one may say so, its Mozart and its *Beethoven-Pater Seraphicus* and Jove the Thunderer—Ramakrishna and Vivekananda.

The modern West is specially noted for its power of organisation, with the help of which it has developed a dynamic and progressive society. It has imbibed this power from the philosophy of man developed in the Greeco-Roman tradition, which had tested and verified its philosophy in its socio-political fields of endeavour. It was later amplified by Christianity passing through, first, the Greeco-Roman and, next, West European, experiences. *The capacity for organisation is the fruit of a disciplined man-ward awareness.* This awareness gets its sustenance from a philosophy of man which treats him essentially as a member of a community or society, and which upholds the significance of that inter-acting social *milieu* for man's education, for his full growth and development.

This may be termed the *political* view of man as different from the *religious* view of him which inspired Eastern cultures generally, arising from a different philosophy of man. This philosophy, which arose out of the several world religions, all of which had their birth in the East, viewed man primarily in his relation to God, and only secondarily in his relation to brother man. These religions also view man as possessing a higher dimension over and above his physical and sensate dimension; they also relate him to an eternal order over and above the time order. The mystical aspects of the world religions emphasise this transcendental view of man. All these elements in religion tend to put increasing stress on man as an individual in search of his other-worldly aspirations and goals, and correspondingly decreasing emphasis on his man-ward awareness in a collective *milieu.* If the path of the latter is action in the world of time, in the world of other fellow human beings and in co-operation with them, which is the essential field of character training, the path of the former is contemplation and the 'flight of the alone to the Alone,' which is the mother of all the gentler virtues and graces.

The impact of the mystical element in religion has been most pronounced on India. When it had for its base a strong man-ward awareness and social feeling, India remained strong and healthy. When that base was weakened, especially during the past thousand years, she became the prey to successive foreign invasions through internal divisions and the neglect and oppression of the common man. *The philosophic and spiritual vision of Ramakrishna and Vivekananda is dedicated to the strengthening of this social base through the effective organisation of the nation's material, moral, and spiritual resources, with a view to enhancing the one supreme quest of the Indian mind, namely, spirituality.*

Sri Ramakrishna exhorted his disciples to avoid being one-sided and develop an all-round character, in which contemplation and action stand harmoniously reconciled. And he held before them the example of Vivekananda as the perfectioin of such reconciliation. *One-sidedness has been the most serious drawback of the Indian character, proceeding from the limitations of the prevailing religious outlook of her people.* Ramakrishna showed the way to the removal of this limitation and the weakness of character resulting from it. Centuries earlier, the *Gītā* had shown the way, but the people had failed even to grasp it properly, and, even more, to implement it effectively.

When engaged in the world of action, unlike in the world of conttemplation, we have to reckon with other persons. A man with a purely mystical attitude becomes a failure in the field of actiion; he does not develop character-efficiency; for he has no place for the objective in his subjective vision; this limitation is highlighted by Sri Ramakrishna in one of his parables:

A *guru* taught his young disciples the truth that God is in all beings. One day, when the disciples were in the forest gathering fuel, a mad elephant came their way. Hearing the shout of the driver on the elephant asking all to run away for safety, all the disciples ran away for safety, except one who, remembering the *guru's* teaching of the presence of God in all, recognised His presence in the elephant and began to sing hymns of praise to the 'God in the elephant.' The elephant rushed at the youth and, taking him by its trunk, threw him aside and went its way. His fellow disciples came in search of him and found him bruised and unconscious. They restored him to consciousness and brought him before the *guru.* When asked by the *guru* why he, like his fellow disciples, did not run for safety, the disciple replied that, following his teaching that God is in all beings, he tried to see God in the elephant. The *guru,* on hearing this, exclaimed: What a fool you are! God is certainly in the elephant; but is He not also in the driver of the elephant? And why did you not listen to 'the driver God' when he asked you to run for safety?

Sri Ramakrishna the man passed away in 1886. But Sri Ramakrishna the power, all-beneficent and luminous, continued, and still continues, to affect in a fundamental way the life and destiny of man in increasing numbers in East and West. Before he passed away, he felt the need for an organisation, which would be an effective channel for the flow of his unifying vision to fertilize human life everywhere. And he set up such an organisation, a *saṅgha,* with Vivekananda at its head. His deep concern to see that the organisation remained intact is evident in his exhortation, a few days before his passing away, to Vivekananda to see that his young disciples were held together in a common dedication to the vision that he had imparted to them. To quote the biography of Vivekananda by his Eastern and Western disciples *(The Life of Swami Vivekananda,* p.147):

> It so happened that Naren had been called to the side of the Master some days earlier, when he was suffering intensely and could scarcely speak. The Master wrote on a piece of paper: 'Narendra will teach others.' Naren hesitated and said: 'I won't do that.' But the Master replied. 'You *shall have* to do it.'
>
> Now that the last days were approaching, the Master set himself with greater energy than ever to mould, in a calm and silent way, the spiritual life of these boys, particularly that of Naren. Every evening, he would call Naren to his room and, for two or three hours at a time, would impart final instructions to him on various spiritual subjects and advise him to keep his brother disciples together, how to guide and train them so that they would be able to live the life of renunciation.

Referring to what Ramakrishna himself gained by coming into contact with the Brahmo Samaj and its leaders, Romain Rolland says *(The Life of Ramakrishna.* p.186):

> It is easy to see what India gained from the meeting of Ramakrishna and the Brahmo Samaj. His own gain is less obvious, but no less definite. For the first time, he found himself brought into personal contact with the educated middle class of his country, and through them with the pioneers of progress and Western ideas. . . .
>
> He was not a man to react like a strict and narrow devotee, who hastens to put up the shutters of his cell. On the contrary, he flung them wide open. He was too human, too insatiably curious, too greedy for the fruit of the tree

> of life not to taste tnese new fruits to the full. His long searching glance insinuated itself, like a creeper through the chinks of the house, and studied all the different habitations of the same Host, and studied all the different spirits dwelling therein, and, in order to understand them better, he identified himself with them. He grasped their limitations (as well as their significance), and proportioned to each nature its own vision of life and individual duty. He never dreamt of imposing either vision or action alien to his proper nature on any man. He, to whom renunciation both then and always, so far as he was personally concerned, was the first and last word of truth, discovered that most men would have none of it, and he was neither astonished nor saddened by the discovery.

Pointing out the truth of the utility of organisation discovered by Ramakrishna through his contact with the westernised Brahmo Samaj, Romain Rolland says *(ibid.,* p.188):

> The ascendency he exercised over some of the best minds in India revealed the weakness and needs of these intellectuals, their unsatisfied aspirations, the inadequacy of the answers they gained from science, and the necessity for his intervention. The Brahmo Samaj showed him what strength of organisation, what beauty existed in a spiritual group uniting young souls round an elder brother, so that they tendered a basket of love as a joint offering to their Beloved, the Mother.
>
> The immediate result was that his mission, hitherto undefined, became crystallised; it concentrated first in a glowing nucleus of conscious thought wherein decision was centred, and then passed into action.

Vivekananda: The Man And The Power

Vivekananda was extraordinarily gifted with the powers of both vision and action. In his Master and within himself, apart from the philosophy he had imbibed, he had seen and experienced the greatness and glory of man. But within a short time after his Master's passing away, he saw, at close quarters, the tragedy of man in India when he wandered over the length and breadth of his beloved motherland, mixing with its princes and peasants, intellectuals and untouchables. On the eve of thie great and unique pilgrimage, he declared at Banaras in 1890: 'I am going away; but I shall never come back until I have burst on society like a bomb, and make it follow me like a dog.' And within three years of this utterance, he had burst upon the attention of the international world through his speeches at the Chicago Parliament of Religions, followed by whirlwind lecture tours in the U.S.A. and U.K. and, in another four years, on the horizon of modern India through his famous speeches, later collected in the book *Lectures from Colombo to Almora.* About the impact of his speeches and utterances, Romain Rolland writes *(The Life of Vivekananda,* p.162):

> His words arc great music, phrases in the style of Beethoven, stirring rhythms like the march of Handel Choruses. I cannot touch these sayings of his, scattered as they are through the pages of books at thirty years' distance, without receiving a thrill through my body like an electric shock. And what shocks, what transports must have been produced when, in burning words, they issued from the lips of the hero!

Vivekananda: A Social Revolutionary

Upholding the supremacy of the Indian ideal of spirituality in his life and teaching, Vivekananda was yet appalled to see the poverty and degradation of masses of his countrymen; and he proclaimed in anguish: 'I do not believe in a religion which cannot wipe the widow's tears or stop the orphan's wails;' and he quoted his Master's pungent words: 'Religion is not for empty bellies.' And for the first time in her long history, India got in him an outstanding spiritual leader tackling vigorously the pressing problems of the *secular* life of man, and pleading for what he terms a 'toned down' *materialism* for his country. *He traced the down-fall of India to the forcing down the throats of one and all the mystical heights of religion with its neglect of social feeling and action and emphasis only on renunciation and contemplation.* Says he *(The Complete Works,* Vol. III, pp.149-150):

> Yet, perhaps, some sort of materialism, toned down to our own requirements, would be a blessing to many of our brothers who are not yet ripe for the highest truths. This is the mistake made in every country and in every society, and it is a greatly regrettable thing that in India, where it was always understood, the same mistake of forcing the highest truths on people who are not ready for them, has been made of late. . . . There has been ample provision made for them in our books; but unfortunately, in later times, there has been a tendency to bind every one down by the same laws as those by which the *sannyāsin* (monk) is bound, and that is a great mistake. But for that, a good deal of the poverty and the misery that you see in India need not have been.

Vivekananda was not a 'revivalist,' but a social revolutionary. Reporting an important conversation with him during his second voyage to the West, Sister Niveditā records *(The Master as I Saw Him,* pp.201-202):

> 'I disagree with all those,' he said, 'who are giving their superstitions back to my people. Like the Egyptologist's

interest in Egypt, it is easy to feel an interest in India that is purely selfish. One may desire to see again the India of one's books, one's studies, one's dreams. My hope is to see again the strong points of that India, reinforced by the strong points of this age, only in a natural way. The new state of things must be a *growth* from within.

So I preach only the *Upaniṣads*. And of the *Upaniṣads,* it is only that one idea of *strength.* The quintessence of *Vedas* and Vedānta and all lies in that one word. . . .

But you may ask—what is the place of Ramakrishna in this scheme?

He is the method, that wonderful unconscious method! . . .

Hitherto the great fault of our Indian religion has lain in its knowing only two words— renunciation and *mukti* (spiritual emancipation). Only *mukti* here! Nothing for the householder!

But these are the very people whom I want to help. For are not all souls of the same quality? Is not the goal of all the same?

And so strength must come to the nation through education.

I thought at the time, and I think increasingly, as I consider it, that this one talk of my Master had been well worth the whole voyage, to have heard.'

Vivekananda: A Practical Visionary

Cornelia Conger, who had intimate association with Vivekananda during her childhood when her grandmother, Mrs. John B. Lyon of Chicago, had played host to him on behalf of the World

Parliament of Religions, narrates an interesting incident in her memories of him, which brings out his keen desire to help the Indian people imbibe the Western talent for organisation *(Reminiscences of Swami Vivekananda,* 1961, p.138):

> Once he said to my grandmother that he had the greatest temptation of his life in America. She liked to tease him a bit and said, 'Who is she, Swami?' He burst out laughing and said, 'Oh, it is not a lady; it is *organisation!'* He explained how the followers of Ramakrishna had all gone out alone and when they reached a village, would just quietly sit under a tree and wait for those in trouble to come to consult them. But in the States he saw how much could be accomplished by organising work. Yet he was doubtful about just what type of organisation would be acceptable to the Indian character, and he gave a great deal of thought and study how to adapt what seemed good to him in our Western world to the best advantage of his own people.

In a letter written from Massachusetts, USA, on 20 August 1893, to a disciple in India, after visiting a modern women's prison, the swami poured out his agony at the condition and treatment of human beings in India *(The Complete Works,* Vol.V. seventh edition, pp.13-14):

> They don't call it prison but reformatory here. It is the grandest thing I have seen in America. How the inmates are benevolently treated, how they are reformed and sent back as useful members of society. . . . And, Oh! how my heart ached to think of what we think of the poor, the low, in India. They have no chance, no escape, no way to climb up . . . Religion is not at fault. On the other hand, your religion teaches you that every being is only your own self

multiplied. But it was the want of practical application, the want of sympathy—the want of heart.'

It was to provide this practical application, this sympathy, this heart, that he felt the need for the Indian people to cut out a new channel of practical efficiency from their national reservoir of spirituality, to strive to achieve character, and learn the secret of organised action. In a letter written from the USA, on 11 July 1894, to a young disciple in India, he says:

> Go to work, my boys; the fire will come to youl The faculty of organisation is entirely absent in our nature, but this has to be infused. The great secret is absence of jealousy. Be always ready to concede to the opinions of your brethren, and try always to conciliate. That is the whole secret.

Speaking on the 'Future of India' in Madras, on his return from the West in 1897, he says *(ibid.,* Vol.III, Eighth Edition, pp.299-300):

> Why is it that organisations are so powerful? Do not say organisation is material. Why is it, to take a case in point, that forty millions of Englishmen rule three hundred millions of people here? What is the psychological explanation? These forty millions put their wills together and that means infinite power, and you three hundred millions have a will each separate from the other. Therefore, to make a great future India, the whole secret lies in organisation, accumulation of power, co-ordination of wills.
>
> Already before my mind rises one of the marvellous verses of the *Atharva Veda Saṁhitā* which says: 'Be thou all of one mind, be thou all of one thought; for in the days of yore, the gods being of one mind were enabled to receive

oblations. That the gods can be worshipped by men is because they are of one mind.' Being of one mind is the secret of society. . . . And the more you go on fighting and quarrelling about all trivialities . . . the further you are off from that accumulation of energy and power which is going to make the future India. For, mark you, the future India depends entirely upon that That is the secret-accumulation of will-power, co-ordination, bringing them all, as it were, into one focus.

Writing to the prime minister of an Indian princely state from Chicago in Novemeber 1894, he says *(ibid.,* Vol. VIII, Third Edition, p.328):

> The secret of success of the Westerners is the power of organisation and combination. That is only possible with mutual trust and co-operation.

The swami knew that over-organisation was as bad as no organisation. He felt that the West had inclined the former way where even religion had become overwhelmed, with ninety per cent energy spent on church organisation and only ten per cent left for spiritual striving. Yet he keenly felt the need for this faculty in the Indian context.

Writing to Mrs. Ole Bull of USA on 21 March 1895 from New York, he says *(ibid.,* Vol. VI, Sixth Edition, p.303):

> Organisation has its faults, no doubt, but, without that, nothing can be done.

The swami exhorted his countrymen to learn from the English people their capcity for *obedience with self-respect,* which is the secret of collective action. Writing to his brother disciple, Swami Akhandananda, from London in 1895, he says *(ibid.,* pp.322-23):

> Your idea is grand but our nation is totally lacking in the faculty of organisation. It is this one drawback which

> produces all sorts of evil. We are altogether averse in making a common cause for anything. The first requistie for organisation is obedience. I do a little bit of work when I feel so disposed, and then let it go to the dogs-this kind of work is of no avail. We must have plodding industry and perseverance.

Again, writing to the same on 13 November 1895, he says *(ibid.* pp.350-51):

> It is not at all in oar nature to do a work conjointly. It is to this that our miserable condition is due. He who knows how to obey, knows how to command. Learn obedience first. Among these Western nations, with such a high spirit of independence, the spirit of obedience is equally strong. We are all of us self-important, which never produces any work. Great enterprise, boundless courage, tremendous energy, and above all, perfect obedience-these are the only traits that lead to individual and national regeneration. These traits are altogether lacking in us.

The modern Western *promethean* spirit of energy and progress finds shining expression in the letter he wrote from Chicago on 24 January 1894 to the group of young disciples in Madras, in which he expounds his mission *(ibid.,* Vol. V, pp.29-30):

> Caste or no caste, creed or no creed, any man, or class, or caste or nation, or institution, which bars the power of free thought and action of an individual-even so long as that power does not injure others—is devilish and must go down.
>
> My whole ambition in life is to set in motion a machinery which will bring noble ideas to the door of everybody and then let men and women settle their own fate. Let them know what our forefathers as well as other nations have

> thought on the most momentous questions of life. Let them see specially what others are doing now, and then decide. We are to put the chemicals together, the crystallisation will be done by nature according to her laws. Work hard, be steady, and have faith in the Lord. Set to work; I am coming sooner or later. Keep the motto before you—'Elevation of the masses without injuring their religion.'
>
> Remember the nation lives in the cottage. But, alas! nobody ever did anything for them. . . . Can you raise them? Can you give them back their lost individuality? Can you become an occidental of occidentals in your spirit of equality, freedom, work, and energy, and at the same time a Hindu to the very backbone in religious culture and instincts? This is to be done and we *will do it.* You are all *born to do it.* Have faith in yourselves, great convictions are the mothers of great deeds. Onward for evert Sympathy for the poor, the downtrodden, even unto death—this is our motto. Onward, brave lads!

Referring to the synthesis of East and West sought to be achieved for his country by Swami Vivekananda, Sister Nivedita, his Western disciple, says *(The Master as I Saw Him,* p.45):

> His view was penetrative as well as comprehensive. He had analysed the elements of the development to be brought about. India must learn a new ideal of obedience. . . . The energy which had hitherto gone into the mortification of the body, might rightly, in his opinion, under modern conditions, be directed to the training of the muscles.
>
> To the Western mind, it might well seem that nothing in the Swami's life had been more admirable than this. Long ago, he had defined the mission of the Order of Ramakrishna

as that of realising and exchanging the highest ideals of the East and of the West.

Vivekananda on Man-making Education

It is specially in his ideas and programmes relating to the education of the Indian people that Vivekananda reveals his spiritual kinship with the finest in the traditions of East and West. His utterances on this vital subject, scattered in the eight volumes of his *Complete Works,* are available in a small book entitled *Education,* which carries the following brief Foreword from Mahatma Gandhi:

> Surely, Swami Vivekananda's writings need no introduction from anybody. They make their own irresistible appeal.

The swami defines education as 'the manifestation of the perfecttion already in man.' Viewing the prevailing educational system against the background of the pressing problems of his nation, he said *(Education,* p.7):

> Getting by heart the thoughts of others in a foreign language and stuffing your brain with them and taking some university degrees, you consider yourself educated! Is this education? . . . Open your eyes and see what a piteous cry for food is rising in the land of Bharata, proverbial for its food. Will your education fulfil this want? The education that does not help the common mass of people to equip themselves for the struggle for life, which does not bring out strength of character, a spirit of philanthropy, and the courage of a lion—is it worth the name?

> We want that education by which character is formed, strength of mind is increased, the intellect is expanded, and by which one can stand on one's own feet. What we need is to study, independent of foreign control, different branches of the knowledge that is our own, and with it the

> English language and Western science; we need technical education and all else that will develop industries, so that men, instead of seeking for service, may earn enough to provide for themselves and save against a rainy day.
>
> The end of all education, all training, should be man-making. The end and aim of all training is to make the man grow. The training by which the current and expression of will are brought under control, and become fruitful, is called education.'

Vivekananda on Man-making Religion

The swami defines religion almost exactly as he defines education. Religion, to him, is 'the manifestation of the divinity already in man.' So defined, religion ceases to be a formal subscription to a creed or a dogma, or a round of rituals, or end up in the membership of a church or a congregation; it becomes an educative process; it becomes continued education.

Tracing the downfall of India to the continued sapping of the faith of the Indian people in themselves through a wrong understanding of religion, and to the sad neglect, by them, of their physical selves, he said *(ibid.,* pp. 42-44):

> The old religions said that he was an atheist who did not believe in God. The new religion says that he is an atheist who does not believe in himself. But it is not selfish faith. It means faith in all because you are all. Love for yourself means love for all, love for animals, love for everything, for you are all one. . . . If the ideal of faith in ourselves had been more extensively taught and practised, I am sure a very large portion of the evils and miseries that we have would have vanished. Throughout the history of mankind, if any ny motive power has been more potent than another

> in the lives of great men and women, it is that faith in themselves. Bom with the consciousness that they were to be great, they became great. . . .
>
> Physical weakness is the cause of at least one-third of our miseries. We are lazy; we cannot combine. We speak of many things parrot-like, but never do them. Speaking and not doing has become a habit with us. What is the cause? Physical weakness. This sort of weak brain is not able to do anything. We must strengthen it. First of all, our young men must be strong. Religion will come afterwards. Be strong, my young friends, that is my advice to you. You will be nearer to Heaven through football than through the study of the *Gītā*. You will understand the *Gītā* better with your biceps, your muscles, a little stronger. You will understand the mighty genius and the mighty strength of Kṛṣṇa better with a little strong blood in you. You will understand the Upaniṣads better and the glory of the Atroan, when your body stands firm upon your feet, and you feel yourselves as men.'

Vivekananda's Concern for Women and the Common Man

Vivekananda is the first monk and outstanding spiritual teacher in all history to uphold, without any reservation, the cause of women and the common people. 'In India there are two evils,' he said, 'trampling on the woman and grinding the poor through caste restrictions.' Revealing his resolve to undo this injustice, Sister Nivedita writes (*The Master as I Saw Him,* pp.287-88):

> Our Master, at any rate, regarded the Order to which he belonged as one whose lot was cast for all time with the cause of Woman and the People. . . . It was the one

> thought, too, with which he would turn to the disciple at his side, whenever he felt himself nearer than usual to death, in a foreign country, alone, 'Never forget!' he would then say, 'the word is 'Woman and the people!'

His far-seeing mind grasped the significance of the modern age in the sure awakening of the suppressed millions everywhere. He called the present age the age of the Śudra, the age of the proletariat.

Stirring the conscience of his countrymen, he said about their proletariat fellow-countrymen *(Education,* pp.73-74):

> Engrossed in the struggle for existence, they had not the opportunity for the awakening of knowledge. They have worked so long like machines and the clever educated section have taken the substantial parts of the fruits of their labour. But times have changed. The lower classes are gradually awakening to this fact, and making a united front against this. The upper classes will no longer be able to repress the lower, try they ever so much. The well-being of the higher classes now lies in helping the lower to get their legitimate rights. Therefore I say: Set yourself to the task of spreading education among the masses. Tell them and make them understand: 'you are our brothers, a part and parcel of our bodies.' If they receive this sympathy from you, their enthusiasm for work will be increased a hundredfold.

Vivekananda on India's British Connection

Even while detesting the British subjugation of India, Vivekananda, in his creative role as the prophet of acceptance, as Tagore said of him, saw in it an opportunity to rescue India from its centuries-long stagnation, and utilised it accordingly. In one of his famous essays on 'Modern India', contributed to his Bengali monthly *Udbodhan* in 1899, Vivekananda said *(The Complete Works,* Vol. IV, eighth edition, pp.472-73):

> The present government of India has certain evils attendant on it, and there are some very great and good parts in it as well. Of highest good is this, that, after the fall of the Pātalīputrā (Maurya) Empire, till now, India was never under the guidance of such a powerful machinery of government as the British, wielding the sceptre throughout the length and breadth of the land. And under this *Vaiśya* (commercial) supremacy . . . the ideas and thoughts of different countries are forcing their way into the very bone and marrow of India. Of these ideas and thoughts, some are really most beneficial to her, some are harmful, while others disclose the ignorance and inability of the foreigners to determine what is truly good for the inhabitants of this country.
>
> But piercing through the mass of whatever good or evil there may be, is seen rising the sure emblem of India's future prosperity—that, as the result of the action and reaction between her own old national ideals, on the one hand, and the newly introduced strange ideals of foreign nations, on the other, she is slowly and gently awakening from her long deep sleep. Mistakes she will make; let her, there is no harm in that. In all our actions, errors and mistakes are our only teachers. Who commits mistakes, the path of truth is attainable by him only. Trees never make mistakes nor do stones fall into error; animals are hardly seen to transgress the fixed laws of nature. But man is prone to err, and it is man who becomes God-on-earth.

Vivekananda's Vision of Awakened India

And in an inspiring poem entitled *'To the Awakened India'* contributed to his English monthly, *Prabuddha Bhārata,* for its first issue after its transfer from Madras to its new home in the Himalayas, Vivekananda summoned India to wake up from her long sleep and resume her march for the welfare and happines of all humanity *(The Complete Works,* Vol. IV. p.387)

> Once more awake!
> For sleep it was, not death, to bring thee life
> Anew, and rest to lotus-eyes, for visions
> Daring yet the world in need awaits, O Truth!
>
> Resume thy march,
> With gentle feet that would not break the
> Peaceful rest, even of the roadside dust
> That lies so low. Yet strong and steady,
> Blissful, bold, and free.
> Awakener, ever Forward!
> Speak thy stirring words.

Inviting the attention of the West to the new India that is rising on the horizon of the modern world out of the energy of Vivekananda's vision. Romain Rolland says *(Life of Vivekananda,* p.316):

> So India was hauled out of the shifting sands of barren speculation wherein she had been engulfed for centuries, by the hand of one of her own *sannyasins;* and the result was that the whole reservoir of mysticism, sleeping beneath, broke its bounds, and spread by a series of great ripples into action. The West ought to be aware of the tremendous energies liberated by these means.

Tagore on Vivekananda

Rabindranath Tagore, himself a man of vision, recognised the depth and sweep of Vivekananda's vision and programme and its creative role in bringing out the best out of man. Pointing out the limitations of the message of the spinning wheel, which Gandhiji was then conveying to the Indian people, as a *bāhya kriyā,* 'external act', liable to be reduced in due course to a static *acara or 'observance,'* 'which has been a recurring experience in India's past', and 'incapable, therefore, of rousing the spirit of man to full creative life and action', Tagore said *(Prabasi,* Vol. 28, p.286):

> In recent times in India, it was Vivekananda alone who preached a great message which is not tied up with any do's and dont's. Addressing one and all in the nation, he said: In every one of you, there is the power of Brahman (God); the God in the poor desires you to serve (Him). This message has roused the heart of the youths in a pervasive way. That is why this message has borne fruit in the service of the nation in diverse ways and in diverse forms of renunciation. His message has, at one and the same time, imparted dignity and respect to man along with energy and power.

Vivekananda's Central Theme: Man's Inherent Divinity

Anyone reading the eight volumes of Vivekananda's published works and Sister Niveditā's masterly study of him in her *The Master as I Saw Him* cannot but be struck by the sweep of his thoughts and the depth of his convictions. The one running theme of all his utterances is *man*—his growth, his development, his fulfilment. Referring to this theme, in his study of Vivekananda's speeches at the World Parliament of Religions at Chicago, Romain Rolland says *(The Life of Vivekananda,* pp.42-43):

> Each time he repeated with new arguments but with the same force of conviction his thesis of a universal religion without limit of time or space, uniting the whole *credo* of the human spirit, from the enslaved fetishism of the savage to the most liberal creative affirmations of modem science. He harmonised them into a magnificent synthesis, which, far from extinguishing the hope of a single one, helped all hopes to grow and flourish according to their own proper nature. There was to be no other dogma but the divinity inherent in man and his capacity for indefinite evolution.

The Greeco-Roman Cultural Legacy

In his studies of the human cultural heritage, Vivekananda saw, what I had referred to earlier, two distinct approaches to the problem of human development, one as cultivated by the East and the other by the West These can be broadly stated, using the language of biology, as stress on the *environment* in the West and that on the *organism* in the East From Greeco-Roman times, the West has been specialising in the manipulation of the physical and social environments of man for ensuring his growth and fulfilment. The whole gamut of ideas and processes arising from this approach is conveyed to us by the rich modern words 'positivism' and 'humanism,' which, in the wake of modem technological advances, are often qualified by the word 'scientific'. It is the conviction of positivism that human development is ensured by understanding, controlling, and manipulating the environment, natural and social, in which man's life is cast. Through technology and socio-political processes, man suitably disciplines and manipulates his environment, which is sometimes tractable, often intractable, with a view to ensuring his own self-expression. The product of such manipulation is civilisation. There is, in this, a sense of a fight with an external enemy. Such a challenge calls forth from the spirit of man the qualities of courage, faith, and confidence in himself, and the capacity for co-operation and team-work. It disciplines his senses and mind in precision of observation and communication. It helps to endow him with a zest for life and for action and achievement All these constitute, for man, the school for the development of character and practical efficiency. Here is a distinct philosophy of man, which Vivekananda called the philosophy of *manliness* and which he saw as the fundamental stimulus of the West from the Greeco-Roman to modern times.

The Greek religion was an integral part of its positivistic philosophy, and it was essentially this-worldly and pragmatic. Though Socrates and the Greek Mystery Religions rise above the positivistic level, they were not integrated with the distinctively Greek outlook and thought, being foreign to both. This explains the disowning of Socrates by the Greek state and his trial and death. Their own great dictum, 'Man, know thyself,' was not pursued by the Greek beyond his social personality; neither did the Greeks experience the urge to subject these religious mysteries to that rational scrutiny which they so diligently and passionately applied to social and political phenomena, and in which their contributions were to become unique and lasting.

The Indo-Asian Cultural Legacy

But what the Greeks neglected became the one ruling passion of the East and, especially, of India. This registers the other approach, which stresses the *organism* and comparatively neglects the external environment. This is the approach of religion, specially in its higher mystical aspects; and all the higher religions of the world are Eastern contributions to total human culture. It asks man to strengthen his 'within' and *bear* with the environment and, if strong enough, even to ignore it. It instills the virtues of patience and endurance in place of struggle and advance in the external world, enhances the capacity for renunciation and suffering in place of action and enjoyment, and generally upholds the line of least resistance in the external world. There is, in this also, a sense of fight with an enemy, but that enemy is within man and not outside of him. This approach gives man 'intimations of immortality': it brings him into communion with a timeless order of existence within himself and in the world outside. This is also human fulfilment Śaṅkara but of a transcendental order. Its specific expression is found in the monastic life: and the mystical heights of all higher religions are monastic in mood and temper and approach. Herein is revealed another philosophy of man, the philosophy of *godliness or saintliness,* which Vivekananda recognised as the distinct message of the East Asia, generally, and India, particularly, have upheld this philosophy of man and sought to nourish their cultures and civilisations with it. It has profoundly affected Western culture and civilisation also, through Christianity, but has failed to become an integral part of it, just as the Western philosophy of manliness has failed to become an integral part of most Eastern cultures and civilisations. It uncovers a divine core in man, which makes him greater than all his external possessions and achievements; it reveals an inalienable spiritual focus within him, which proclaims his *intrinsic value* and dignity over and above his *value for society.* Herein is found the culmination of the Greek dictum: 'Man, know thyself.'

The dignity so revealed finds expression not only in the renunciation practised by spiritual seers and seekers, but also in the incidents of ordinary life; one such episode, relating to one of his great elder contemporaries, Pandit Iswar Chandra Vidyasagar, was a favourite with Vivekananda. After referring to his high regard for Vidyasagar as a hero of social reform, Sister Niveditā says in her charming book: *Notes of Some Wandering with Swami Vivekananda* (third edition, pp.35-36):

But his favourite story about him was of that day when he went home from the Legislative Council, pondering over the question of whether or not to adopt English dress on such occasions. Suddenly, some one came up to a fat Mogul (Muslim nobleman) who was proceeding homewards in leisurely and pompous fashion, in front of him, with the news: 'Sir, your house is on fire!' The Mogul went neither faster nor slower for this information, and presently the messenger contrived to express a discreet astonishment, whereupon his master turned on him angrily, 'Wretch!' he said, 'Am I to abandon the gait of my ancestors, because a few sticks happen to be burning?' And Vidyasagar, walking behind, determined to stick to the *chudder, dhoti,* and sandals, not even adopting coat and slippers.

Need for a Synthesis of Saintliness and Manliness

As the Greeks and others specialised in the subject of man in society, man in lateral extension, India specialised in the subject of man in depth, man in vertical elevation. Each has its glory and grandeur; each also has its limitations, which exactly render one the complement of the other.

In his own life, Vivekananda had plumbed the depths of both these philosophies; he had assimilated in his own personality the *manliness* of the West and the *saintliness* of the East. He saw clearly the excellences and limitations of each of these two human legacies which he embraced as two integral elements of a total human culture, *and proclaimed the modern age as the era of their synthesis.* In his philosophy of man, proceeding from Sri Ramakrishna's comprehensive spirituality of *vijñāna* referred to earlier, they cease to be contradictory and become complementary. He comprehended the Western concept of manliness and the

Eastern concept of saintliness in a newly defined philosophy of manliness, which dares to study man from his physical periphery to his spiritual core and to plumb life from the surface to the depths.

History reveals the insufficiency of each of these philosophies taken by themselves. The bitter lessons of the Eastern neglect of the *environment* are writ large in the arrested development of millions of its human beings. Vivekananda demonstrated to the people of Indian the lesson of their history that to neglect the body and to concentrate on the soul is to court disaster for both soul and body. On the other hand, he demonstrated to the people of the West the lesson of their own history in the reverse. Positivism and humanism, even scientific humanism, are perfectly valid, he said, if they do not reduce the human soul to a mere function of the environment, if they do not lead to the swamping of the spirit of man by worldliness, by, what one may call, over-civilisation. Man has an interior depth over and above his social personality, as he has a social personality over and above his individual egoistic self. The latter has to be surpassed and the former realised in each case, if he is to achieve fulfilment. 'In the last stages of life's journey,' says Dr. Radhakrishnan, 'man walks in single file.' This surpassing of man constitutes both his death and resurrection. 'He that findeth his life shall lose it; and he that loseth his life for my sake shall find it,' says Jesus (*Mathew,* 10.39). So long as this is not attempted and achieved, physical death, which is inevitable, will appear to him an unpleasant enigma and an unwelcome intruder, to which he shall ever remain unreconciled. *No philosophy can achieve depth without tackling the problem of death.* This has been the main weakness of the Western philosophy of man from Greeco-Roman times to this day. This basic tragedy of Western man is noticed by Western thinkers themselves. We have Schopenhauer telling us a hundred years ago, in what sounds as an apt critique of the modern welfare state, that the end of a sense-bound life is boredom *(The World as Will and Idea,* Translated by Haldane and Kemp, Vol. I, p.404)

> Almost all men who are secure from want and care, now that at last they have thrown off all other burdens, become a burden to themselves.

We have C.G. Jung discussing modern man in search of a soul. Making a distinction between worldly *achievement* and inner *culture,* and showing the undesirability of the modem pursuit of the first alone throughout life, he says *(Modern Man in Search of a Soul,* pp.118-26):

> Nature cares nothing whatsoever about a higher level of consciousness; quite the contrary. And then society does not value these feats of the psyche very highly; its prizes are always given for achievement and not for personality—the latter being rewarded, for the most part, posthumously. . . .
>
> Achievement, usefulness, and so forth are the ideals which appear to guide us out of the confusion of crowding problems. They may be our loadstars in the adventure of extending and solidifying our psychic existences—they may help us in striking our roots in the world; but they cannot guide us in the development of that wider consciousness to which we give the name of culture. . . .
>
> The nearer we approach to the middle of life, and the better we have succeeded in entrenching ourselves in our personal standpoints and social positions, the more it appears as if we had discovered the right course and the right ideals and principles of behaviour. For this reason, we suppose them to be eternally valid, and make a virtue of unchangeably clinging to them. We wholly overlook the essential fact that

> the achievements which society rewards are won at the cost of the diminution of personality. Many—too many—aspects of life which should also have been experienced lie in the lumber room among dusty memories. . . .
>
> The afternoon of human life must also have a significance of its own, and cannot be merely a pitifui appendage to life's morning. The significance of the morning undoubtedly lies in the development of the individual, our entrenchment-in the outer world, the propagation of our kind, and the care of our children. This is the obvious purpose of nature. But when this purpose has been attained—even more than attained—shall the earning of money, the extension of conquests, and the expansion of life go steadily on beyond the bounds of all reason and sense? *Whoever carries over into the afternoon the law of the morning—that is, the aim of nature—must pay for so doing with damage to his soul, just as surely as a growing youth who tries to salvage his childish egoism must pay for this mistake with social failure.* Moneymaking, social existence, family, and posterity are nothing but plain nature—not culture. Culture lies beyond the purpose of nature. Could by any chance culture be the meaning and purpose of the second half of life? *(italics, not the author's*)

Treating this as the major drawback of Greek culture, which, it is being increasingly recognised, is also the major drawback of modern Western culture, Lowes Dickinson says *(The Greek View of Life,* p.68):

> The more completely the Greek felt himself to be at home in the world, the more happily and freely he abandoned himself to the exercise of his powers, the more intensely and vividly he lived in action and in passion, the more

> alien, bitter, and incomprehensible did he find the phenomena of age and death. On this problem, so far as we can judge, he received from his religion but little light and still less consolation. The music of his brief life closed with a discord unresolved; and even before reason had brought her criticism to bear upon his creed, its deficiency was forced upon him by his feeling.

In his Preface to the above book, E.M. Forster refers to Greece as the land which 'encompassed within the tiny circuit of her city states much that *affects* and *afflicts* the modern man in his relationship to society' (italics not the author's).

While welcoming the truly positive elements of modern positivism, Vivekananda protested against its exaggerations, its negative features, in a pregnant utterance, when he said to Sister Niveditā *(The Master as I Saw Him,* pp.220-21):

> Remember! The message of India is always net the soul for nature, but nature for the soul.

Vivekananda had noticed the Western tragedy referred to by Lowes Dickinson. Comparing it with Indian experience, he said *(ibid.,* p.116):

> Social life in the West is like a peal of laughter, but Underneath it is a wail. It ends in sob. The fun and frivolity are all on the surface; really, it is full of tragic intensity. Now, here it is sad and gloomy on the outside, but underneath are carelessness and merriment.

Niveditā refers to another such contrast expressed by the Swami 'with some exaggerations,' but which 'is nevertheless essentially correct,' as she puts it (*ibid.,* p.110):

> 'Nothing,' said the Swami, 'better illustrated to his own mind the difference between Eastern and Western methods of thought than the European idea that a man could not

> live alone for twenty yean and remain quite sane, taken side by side with the Indian notion that, till a man had been alone for twenty years, he could not be regarded as perfectly himself.'

Thus viewing man integrally in his physical, social, and transocial dimensions, and with a view to ensuring his total fulfilment, Vivekananda expounds a philosophy of man in which man, whether Eastern or Western, can feel at home and find the inspiration to achieve total life fulfilment philosophy finds expression in a brief statement of his, in which *even positivism and secularism become integral elements of a comprehensive spirituality (The Complete Works,* Vol.1, p.124):

> Each soul is potentially divine.
>
> The goal (of life) is to manifest this divine within by controlling nature, external (by science, technology, and socio-political processes) and internal (by ethics, art, and religion).
>
> Do this either by work, or worship, or psychic control, or philosophy-by one, or more or all of these, and BE FREE.
>
> This is the whole of religion.
>
> Doctrines, or dogmas, or rituals, or books, or temples, or forms, are but secondary details.

The Advaitic Vision Behind such a Synthesis

At the back of this comprehensive spirituality stands his Advaitic vision, the vision of the unity of Brahman and Śakti, of the Impersonal-Personal God, which I had dealt with earlier. Referring to this vision and its corollary, Sister Niveditā says ('Introduction' to *The Complete Works of Swami Vivekananda,* Vol.1, pp. xv-xvi):

> It is this which adds its crowning significance to our Master's life, for here he becomes the meeting point, not only of East and West, but also of past and future. If the many and the One be indeed the same Reality, then it is not all modes of worship alone, but equally all modes of work, all modes of struggle, all modes of creation, which are paths of realisation. No distinction, henceforth, between sacred and secular. To labour is to pray. To conquer is to renounce. Life is itself religion. To have and to hold is as stern a trust as to quit and to avoid.
>
> This is the realisation which makes Vivekananda the great preacher of *karmā* (action) not as divorced from, but as expressing *jñāna* and *bhakti.* To him the workshop, the study, the farmyard, and the field are as true and fit scenes for the meeting of God with man as the cell of the monk or the door of the temple. To him, there is no distinction between service of man and worship of God, between manliness and faith, between true righteousness and spirituality. All his words, from one point of view, read as a commentary upon this central conviction. 'Art, science, and religion,' he said once, 'are but three different ways of expressing a single truth. But in order to understand this, we must have the theory of Advaita.'

It is this unifying vision that he imparted to India. *As the most outstanding creator of modern India, he conceivea of her as a mighty human laboratory to test and verify his vision and programme of a comprehensive spirituality in the life of a seventh of the human race.* He called it his 'domestic policy;' and he called the channelling of the energy of such an India in the spiritual service of the rest of the world his 'foreign policy.'

The Meeting of East and West in Modern India

The India that has emerged during the last sixty years, since Vivekananda's passing away in 1902, bears the unmistakable impress of this great teacher. Within three years of his passing away, the first collective action of organised masses shook Bengal in the political field. The struggle for political freedom soon entered on a dynamic phase under the leadership of Mahatma Gandhi and the Indian National Congress, creating a tremendous political and social awakening in the nation and hastening the entering of India into the modern age. Political independence came in 1947. A constitution for a sovereign democratic republic was proclaimed in 1950. Since then, this process has been intensified; and vast energies, long dormant in the people, have been released, and are being increasingly released, which are having their impact in all fields of national endeavour. India is steadily learning from the West, as Vivekananda had taught, the capacity for organised work, and using that capacity to remove the poverty and cultural backwardness of masses of her population. She is cultivating science and technology and modem socio-political processes in a big way. All these form part and parcel of Vivekananda's message of *Practical Vedānta;* they are part and parcel of his scheme of a *toned-down materialism to suit our purposes,* with a view to strengthening the age-old spiritual and cultural tradition of the nation.

In this mighty adventure, India, along with other Afro-Asian nations, is receiving all kinds of technical and other forms of assistance from the advanced nations of the East and West. This was one of the aims which Vivekananda had cherished when he undertook his historic mission to the West in 1893. He had constantly emphasised, as I have mentioned earlier in this lecture, the international context and dimension of human problems and relationships in the modern age.

Vivekananda had assimilated the spirit of the West so thoroughly that any Westerner would feel quite at home in his thought-horizon. But he represented within himself something more, namely, the resolution of the ever-present inner contradictions obtaining within Western culture and thought. *This something more in him is the precious gift of his great Master, Sri Ramakrishna.* Pointing to these dimensions of Vivekananda's personality in his penetrating study of his thought, Romain Rolland says *(Life of Vivekananda,* p.192):

> I shall try to show how closely allied is the aspect of Vivekananda's thought to our own, with our special needs, torments, aspirations, and doubts, urging us ever forward, like a blind mole, by instinct, upon the road leading to the light Naturally, I hope to be able to make other Westerners, who resemble me, feel the attraction that I feel for this elder brother, the son of the Ganges, *who, of all modern men, achieved the highest equilibrium between the two diverse forces of thought, and was one of the first to sign a treaty of peace between the two forces eternally warring within us: the forces of reason and faith.* (italics not author's)

The work which Vivekananda started in the field of dissemination of Indian spiritual thought in the West, under his programme of international commerce of ideas, has continued with increasing vigour since his passing away. The spiritual, cultural, and humanitarian movement which he had started in 1897 in the name of his Master, the Ramakrishna Math and the Ramakrishna Mission, upholding the twin ideals of renunciation and service, has grown and is flourishing in India and abroad as a meeting ground of the tested culture values of the East and the West. This is revealed even in the inspiring motto in Sanskrit given to it by Vivekananda: *Ātmano mokṣārtham jagat hitāya ca*—'For one's own spiritual liberation and for the welfare of the world.'

Vivekananda: The Great Awakener

What, in short, the world sees in India today is the capturing of a new youthful vitality and dynamism by one of the ancient living nations of the world, constituting about a seventh of the human race. Therein we witness the energy of the vision of Vivekananda, expressed in his first public lecture on the Indian soil at Ramnad, near Rameswaram, on his return from the West, in 1897, getting translated into national achievement *(The Complete Works,* Vol. III, pp.145-46):

> The longest night seems to be passing away, the sorest trouble seems to be coming to an end at last, the seeming corpse appears to be awaking, . . . India, this motherland of ours—from her deep long sleep. None can resist her any more; never is she going to sleep any more; no outward powers can hold her back any more; for the infinite giant is rising to her feet.

Opening his lecture on 'The Work before Us' delivered in Madras a few days later, Vivekananda referred to the divergent paths which two gifted peoples of the ancient world took—the one, the ancient Greek, who studied the outer world, and the other, the ancient Hindu, who studied the inner world. The first has influenced most of the subsequent developments of culture and thought in the West, and the other has done the same in the East. And drawing his countrymen's attention to the scope of the modern renaissance in India as the assimilation, by Indian culture, of the culture values of the West, with a view to correcting the imbalances in her own heritage, he said *(The Complete Works,* Vol. II, p.271):

> Today the ancient Greek is meeting the ancient Hindu on the soil of India. Thus slowly and silently, the leaven has come; the broadening, the life-giving, and the revivalist movement that we see all around us has been worked out

> by these forces together. A broader and more generous conception of life is before us; and although at first we have been deluded a little and wanted to narrow things down, we are finding out today that these generous impulses which are at work, these broader conceptions of life, are the logical interpretation of what is in our ancient books. They are the carrying out, to the rigorously logical effect, of the primary conceptions of our own ancestors. To become broad, to go out, to amalgamate, to universalise, is the end of our aims. And all the time, we have been making ourselves smaller and smaller, and dissociating ourselves, contrary to the plans laid down in our scriptures.

India's Spiritual Conquest of the World through Love

In the same lecture, he declared his conviction that the undoubtedly rich Western culture stands in urgent need of the spiritual message of Indian culture *(ibid.,* pp.276-77):

> There have been conquering races in the world. We also have been great conquerors. The story of our conquest has been described by that noble Emperor of India, As'oka, as the conquest of religion and spirituality. . . . The best work that you ever did for yourselves was when you worked for others, trying to disseminate your ideas in foreign languages, beyond the seas, and this very meeting is proof how the attempt to enlighten other countries with your thoughts is helping your own country. . . . Ay, as has been declared on this soil first, love must conquer hatred, hatred cannot conquer itself. Materialism and all its miseries can never be conquered by materialism. Armies, when they attempt to conquer armies, only multiply and make brutes of humanity. Spirituality must conquer the West. Slowly

> they are finding out that what they want is spirituality to preserve them as nations. They are waiting for it; they are eager for it.

Vivekananda exhorted the educated youth of India to imbibe the modern spirit, become dynamic agents of social change, and fearlessly cut out and remove all the dead wood in their national heritage. At the same time, he drew their attention to the imperishable element in their national heritage, namely, a scientific spiritual tradition, free and fearless, amplified and reauthenticated in this age by his own illustrious Master, and to the modern world's hunger for the same *(The Complete Works,* Vol. V, Seventh Edition, p.43):

> The whole world requires Light. It is expectant! India alone has that Light, not in magic, mummeries, and charlatanism, but in the teaching of the glories of the spirit of real religion—of the highest spiritual truth. That is why the Lord has preserved the race through all its vicissitudes unto the present day. Now the time has come.

Vivekananda's Mankind-Awareness

Vivekananda's love for India was the product of his love for man. To awaken men and women everywhere to their divine birthright was his life's mission. He saw man in the light of his own vision, and the vision of the Indian sages, as the Ātman, ever pure and ever free and infinite, assuring the infinite possibility of his or her growth, development, and realisation. Speaking on 'The Mission of the Vedānta', at Kumbakonam in 1897, he summoned humanity to this spiritual adventure (*ibid.,* Vol. III, p.193):

> Arise, awake! Awake from this hypnotism of weakness. *None* is *really weak;* the soul is infinite, omnipotent, and omniscient Stand up, assert yourself, proclaim the God

> within you, do not deny Him!. . . Teach yourself, teach everyone, his real nature; call upon the sleeping soul and see how it awakes. Power will come, glory will come, goodness will come, purity will come, and everything that is excellent will come, when this sleeping soul is roused to self-conscious activity.

When pressed by his Indian disciples to return to India to serve the cause of his own people, he replied to them from New York on 9 August 1895 in these clear words, embodying his glorious vision of human divinity and unity *(ibid.,* Vol. VIII, Third Edition, pp.349-50):

> Doubtless I do love India. But every day my sight grows clearer. What is India, or England, or America to us? We are the servants of that God who by the ignorant is called Man. He who pours water at the root, does he not water the whole tree?
>
> There is but one basis of well-being, social, political, or spiritual, to know that I and my brother are one. This is true for all countries and all people. And Westerners, let me say, will realize it more quickly than Orientals, who have almost exhausted themselves in formulating the idea and producing a few cases of individual realisation.

This vision of unity finds eloquent expression in a verse by the Indian philosopher Gaudapada of the seventh century AD, in which he expounds the scope of the Advaitic vision of India's Vedānta *(Mandukya Karika, IV. 2):*

> *Asparśa-yogo vai nāma sarva-sattva sukho hitaḥ;*
> *Avivado aviruddhaśca deśtastam namānyahaṁ*

'I salute this well-known unifying philosophy, which teaches the solidarity of all existence, which strives for the happiness and welfare f all beings, and which is free from strife and contradiction.'

Vivekananda's Vision of the Future World Order

In a luminous passage in his lecture on 'My Master,' delivered in New York in 1896, Vivekananda refers to the limitations of each of the cultural types, developed and conditioned by religion in the orient, and by the physical sciences and the positvistic outlook in the Occident. He *points out their complementarity* and says that the modern age will witness the emergence of a culture, neither oriental, nor occidental, but human, through a healthy interaction and assimilation among cultures; and he presents Ramakrishna as the powerful initiator of such a process in India. Though a bit long, it bears reproduction in this context. *(The Complete Works,* Vol. IV. pp.155-56):

> Each of these types has its grandeur, each has its glory. The present adjustment will be the harmonising, the mingling, of these two ideals. To the Oriental, the world of spirit is as real as to the Occidental is the world of senses. In the spiritual, the Oriental finds everything he wants or hopes for, in it he finds all that makes life real to him. To the Occidental, he is a dreamer; to the Oriental, the Occidental is a dreamer playing with ephemeral toys, and he laughs to think that grown-up men and women should make so much of a handful of matter which they will have to leave sooner or later. Each calls the other a dreamer. But the Oriental ideal is as necessary for the progress of the human race as is the Occidental, and I think it is more necessary. Machines never made mankind happy and never will make. He who is trying to make us believe this will claim that happiness is in the machine; but it is always in the mind. That man alone who is the lord of his mind can become happy, and none else. And what, after all, is this power of machinery? Why should a man who can send a current of electricity through a wire be called a very great man and a very intelligent man? Does

> not nature do a million times more than that every moment? Why not then fall down and worship nature? What avails it if you have power over the whole of the world, if you have mastered every atom of the universe? That will not make you happy unless you have the power of happiness in yourself, until you have conquered yourself. Man is bom to conquer nature, it is true; but the Occidental means by 'nature' only physical or external nature. It is true that external nature is majestic, with its mountains, and oceans, and rivers, and with its infinite powers and varieties. Yet there is a more majestic internal nature of man, higher than the sun, moon, and stars, higher than this earth of ours, higher than the physical universe, transcending these little lives of ours; and it affords another field of study. There the Orientals excel, just as the Occidentals excel in the other. Therefore it is fitting that, whenever there is a spiritual adjustment, it should come from the Orient.. . . It is also fitting that when the Oriental wants to learn about machine-making, he should sit at the feet of the Occidental and learn from him. When the Occident wants to learn about the spirit, about God, about the soul, about the meaning and mystery of this universe, he must sit at the feet of the Oriental to learn.
>
> I am going to present before you the life of one man who has put in motion such a wave in India.

Aldous Huxley calls the human products of the ancient civilisations 'wise fools,' and the modern civilisation 'intelligent fools,' and urges the need to produce *intelligent wise men and women.*

Vivekananda: 'A Harmony of All Human Energy'

The philosophy and vision represented by Vivekananda is meant to produce such fully integrated men and women. He himself was a remarkable synthesis of diverse values—ancient and modern. In the words of Jawaharlal Nehru *(Discovery of India,* p.400):

> Rooted in the past, and full of pride in India's heritage, Vivekananda was yet modern in his approach to life's problems, and was a kind of bridge between the past of India and her present

Swami Vivekananda and Modern India*

Vivekananda's Messages of Tyāga and Sevā

Vivekananda sought to combine two energy resources in our education: one is the energy of the Vedāntic vision of the spiritual nature of man and the possibility of its manifestation. The second is the energy of the scientific vision of clear thinking and practical efficiency—the capacity for penetrative thinking and the discovering of the truths hidden in nature. India must become a great nation of spiritual and scientific students and teachers. One is the ancient India and the other is the modern India. Combine these two energies and we will create a new India out of the process, unprecedented in our long history.

---

*Speech delivered at the 113th birth anniversary celebrations of Swami Vivekananda, held in Nagercoil (Tamiland) on 11 January 1976 in the S.L. Govt. High School hall under the auspices of the Vivekananda Kendra, Kanyakumari.

Here is Swami Vivekananda's central message; to implement it, we need a new approach, a new understanding. He exhorted us to develop two great values in our character: one is *tyāga*, renunciation, the other is *seva*, service. *Tyāga* is renunciation-renunciation, not of this woman or that man, not of this item of food or other objects, but renunciation of the flimsy little ego that is within us which distorts everything, which makes man selfish and exploitative. Manifest the divine that is within you, express the larger Self by knocking away the tiny ego. Grow beyond the ego into the true Self. That is renunciation, *tyāga*, the central teaching of the *Bhagavad Gītā*. When this *tyaga* comes, we shall express ourselves in natural and spontaneous *seva*, as a by-product of that *tyāga*. So Vivekananda said: (*The Complete Works, Vol.V, p. 228*):

> The national ideals of India are renunciation and service. Intensify her in those channels, and the rest will take care of itself.

Ours is a nation which has know only exploitation for several centuries—exploitation not only by foreigners, but also by our own people, exploitation of the weak by the strong—economic, social, political and intellectual. To that nation, Vivekananda gave this great message of *tyāga* and *sevā*. Rise to higher levels of thinking and action; manifest your own higher nature and express your energy in forms of service and dedication for the good of all. In several letters written from America, he has pointed out this weakness of our people, this motive of exploitation and its evil consequences. In one letter, he writers:

> So long as the millions live in hunger and in ignorance, I hold every man a traitor who, having been educated at their expense, pays not the least heed to them.

He wrote it about 1894; how true it is of the Indian scene even today! To educate a child today to be a doctor or an engineer, to be a M.Sc, the state has to spend between fifty thousand to a hundred thousand rupees. The student pays hardly three thousand or four thousand rupees as fees. How much the state does for us from out of the peopls's revenues? Yet we forget the nation, we forget the people, after getting such a costly education at the cost of the nation; we only run after our own profit and pleasure. This is called *treason* by Vivekananda. This sentence of his is an eye-opener to us today.

India: A Fascination to the Rest of the World

Even today, India's cultural and spiritual influence is great in all parts of the world. They have more faith in our nation and its ideals than many of us here in India have. Vivekananda exhorted us to have faith in our own culture, for though we have blundered, though we have committed mistakes, though we have failed to work out all the humanistic and social visions of our philosophy, the basic foundations of our culture are entirely sound, entirely human, entirely universal. It is for this that, as I have seen, India is respected by thinking people abroad, for her age-old culture, age-old spirituality. In university after university in the United States and European countries, I saw people listening with the utmost respect and reverence to the eternal message of India, the message of the Upaniṣads, of the *Gītā,* of Buddha, of Sri Ramakrishna. People sit for hours together to listen to the exposition of this great message. That is how India is viewed in the rest of the world. Love for Sanskrit is so pervasive in the Western world that after every lecture, there is express request to recite a few verses in Sanskrit, and, as they are being recited, the whole audience listens with the utmost attention and reverence. That is the love for Eternal India, for *Amar Bhārat,* for its culture, for its spirituality, and for the wonderful language which has transmitted it. That is the India that the world sees from the outside.

There is the other India, our own economically and socially weak India, that we see from within the country. We quarrel; we despise ourselves; we do all sorts of things that weaken our nation. That contemporary India also is there, coming to the attention of the outside world through newspapers, journals, and books. But that eternal India commands attention, commands respect, from thinking people all over the world. Can we change that contemporary India into the pattern of that eternal India? That, I feel, is the challenge that faces us today. All over the world, even in Communist countries, there is much respect for the ancient tradition and culture of our country; the philosophy of our Upaniṣads and the *Gītā* is respected everywhere; the teachings of Vivekananda and Ramakrishna are listened to with great respect in all parts of the world. We in India have to assimilate these so that we may capture the vision and the strength to create a really healthy, progressive, social order in our great country. Our problem is entirely physical; our problem is merely socio-political. Our national soul is strong, bright, and pure—it is immortal. But our body, our society, is weak. We are only to change our body-politic to fit in with the ever-healthy eternal soul of India. This cannot be said with regard to any other nation in the world.

In the Western countries, you find that they have a fine body-politic, a developed society, plenty of knowledge, wealth, and power, but they have lost their soul. They are in search of a soul; we are in search of a body. It is obvious that it is easier to find a body than to find a soul. Our work, therefore, is really easier. If only we are rooted in that eternal, pure, and dynamic soul of our nation, and work hard with the strength arising from that faith in our heritage, we can create, in two or three generations, a new healthy body-politic in our country, where men and women will breathe the air of freedom, dignity, and equality. That is the aim of that message of practical Vedānta that Swami Vivekananda conveyed to us.

Swami Vivekananda and Our Youths*

Total Integration of Personality

He combined in himself the ancient and the modern, the East and the West, the sacred and the secular. This is the appreciation of great thinkers who have written on Swami Vivekananda. Whether it is Tagore, or Jawaharlal Nehru, or Romain Rolland, all of them have said that in Swami Vivekananda you see the synthesis, the harmony, of all human energy. Such a great leader and teacher, full of love, full of human concern, full of patriotism, was with us, and is still with us in ideas and inspiration, yet finds no place in the thinking of many of our political and social leaders today; and they hope to solve the problems of India! It is impossible. Till now, we turned first to England, then to Europen countries, then to America, then to Russia, then to China, for inspiration. But

---

*Based on the address to the special meeting of the members and well-wishers of the Akhil Bharat Vivekananda Yuva Mahamandal, held at the Vivekananda Society Hall, Calcutta, on 11 June 1973.

now it is a healthy sign that our nation is slowly realising that those countries cannot guide us today. They are themselves in a mess. They are themselves faced with serious problems. We must turn to our own inheritance, to our own country's wisdom. This wholesome change is slowly coming on the horizon of India today. Within the next few years, I surely expect that the national mind will turn to this great national storehouse of inspiration, both ancient and modern, and, with that strength, gain the capacity to appreciate and assimilate the great storehouse of modern Western knowledge and experience as well. Then shall we gain true national greatness. This change will be a great change for India. Then we shall discover the unique greatness of our Vivekananda. *That change will come within the next decade or two.* Your Mahamandal is meant to be an agency to bring this awareness gently to the people of Calcutta, the people of Bengal, and later on, to the people of other states. That is the purpose of this Yuva Mahamandal. It bears Swami Vivekananda's name. What beautiful ideas are there in Swami Vivekananda—ideas which can transform human character, make man truly big in a big way! The teaching he gave us all is: Don't think we are small, don't think we are poor, we have the infinite Ātman as our real nature.

Youth and New India

Our creative energy is in our young people. Our old people will want to retain the present India. They have been accustomed to it. They may not want to change it. But we have to change our India, we have to create a healthy new India. Therefore, Swamiji put his faith in the young people; and his own teacher, Sri Ramakrishna, also put his faith in young people. He did not put his faith in the old, because he also wanted a new India to emerge which is truly spiritual, not just pious, not just religious; that can be done only by the young, the vigorous the vital. He saw such minds among our young people, the young who are not mere talkers, but who are devoted, sincere, energetic, and pure. This is the type of young people whom Swamiji repeatedly mentioned in his lectures in Calcutta, Madras, and elsewhere—young, vigorous, dedicated, full of hope. This kind of mind can change India. That is a great need in Calcutta, in Bengal, all over India. That is the genesis of this Vivekananda Yuva Mahamandal.

Organisation

He saw in America the power of organisation, the power of collective action. Swamiji wanted that power to be acquired by people in India That is why there is this Yuva Mahamandal here, and similar groups also here and elsewhere. Swamiji started the Ramakrishna Order also only with this object in view—how to organise our youths to serve God in man. Here is a holy man, there is a holy man, so many holy men or *mahātmas* we have, who teach religion and do good. But we want to have more energy, more power. For that, let us bring all these *mahātmas* together in a brotherhood and then let them work together; that will have a tremendous impact on society, he felt. That will do wonders. That is why he said in his Madras lecture *(The Complete Works,* Vol.III, pp.299-300):

> Why is it that organisations are so powerful? Do not say organisation is material . . . Therefore to make a great future India, the whole secret lies in organisation, accumulation of power, co-ordination of wills. . . . For mark you, the future India depends entirely upon that That is the secret—accumulation of will-power, co-ordination, bringing them all, as it were, into one focus.

Work together, put your wills together, put your little self behind, manifest your large self by putting the nation in front, its interests, its welfare. Then we can transform our politics and public life from ill-health to health. Surrender your little self, the little ego, for the cause of the good of millions before you. If the mounting problems of India are to be solved by us, it is only by our acquiring character and developing this power of organisation. It is the power of character that gives us the capacity for team—work. This capacity must come to us, all over India today. This suffering, this mass poverty, these dismal slums and dirty roads of Calcutta and Howrah—all these things—they are with us for years together. And the condition everywhere is getting only worse year by year. Why? We are so many people here, but this character-energy behind all efficient work has not been acquired by the nation. We have political and other organisations, but behind them we miss the presence of this character-energy and work-energy and the inspiration of this vision of human dignity. In the absence of these high motivations, organisations become ineffective everywhere. We see it every day. That is why, today, there is need for a re-education of our youths in the great ideas and ideals of Swami Vivekananda. If this Yuva Mahamandal can become that kind of a, small nucleus where these ideas are found expressed in life and work, we shall create a new force for gently and steadily working upon the national problems. This way would Swami Vivekananda ask us to live and to work. Active politics is not everybody's work. Only a few people should enter the active political field. Our misfortune in India today is that most of our people want to be politicians, including the teachers and students; whereas, before independence, all politicians are essentially educators and teachers!

'Be and Make'

Swamiji said: Be and make, that all be our motto. Be men yourselves and help others also to become men. That kind of educational work must come out of our politics, society, and education. That is why an organisation like this Yuva Mahamandal has a great responsibility, a great privilege, to assimilate the spirit of Swami Vivekananda and radiate it around. Without criticising, without abusing any other organisation, just try to live up to his ideas and be good and do good. Swamiji repeatedly said: Don't criticise. Everbody is doing some good. But give what little you can to improve the human condition around you. Don't curse darkness; but bring in a little light. That is the surest way to destroy darkness.

In this way, a constructive creative approach to national problems is to be adopted by an organisation like this Yuva mahamandal. We need politics to handle the political power of the nation; so political parties will be there. They will be struggling against each other in order to capture political power. But once they get the power, to make that power really useful to the people, we need a new attitude. That attitude will come to the nation from Swami Vivekananda today. But a much higher attitude is there, and also a greater power, which Swamiji and later, Mahatma Gandhi, presented to our nation and that is: when power is misused by the political parties or government, people must be able to correct it. Public opinion—awakened, enlightened, energetic, patriotic, public opinon—is the strength of democracy. Democracy is not strong because politicians or administrators or ministers have power in their hands. A democracy is strong because the people are educated, are conscious of their power that they are citizens, that all power is ultimately derived from them. This strengthening of people is the basic work in a democracy. An organisation like the Yuva Mahamandal is primarily to engage itself in educating the people about their democratic dignity as free citisens, about their democratic rights, and democratic responsibilities as well. Therefore, today, there is such a vast field of useful work but, unfortunately, the number of workers is very small.